# CRISIS INTERVENTION

## PROMOTING RESILIENCE AND RESOLUTION IN TROUBLED TIMES

LENNIS G. ECHTERLING
JACK PRESBURY
J. EDSON McKEE

James Madison University

PEARSON

Merrill
Prentice Hall

Upper Saddle River, New Jersey
Columbus, Ohio

Library of Congress Cataloging-in-Publication Data

Echterling, Lennis G.,
   Crisis intervention : promoting resilience and resolution in troubled times/Lennis G. Echterling, Jack Presbury,
J. Edson McKee.
     p. cm.
   Includes bibliographical references.
   ISBN 0-13-090897-5
  1. Crisis intervention (Mental health services) 2. Resilience (Personality trait) I. Presbury, Jack H.
II. McKee, J. Edson. III. Title.

RC480.6.E248 2005
616.89′14--dc22

2004014522

**Vice President and Executive Publisher:** Jeffery W. Johnston
**Publisher:** Kevin M. Davis
**Editorial Assistant:** Amanda King
**Production Editor:** Mary Harlan
**Production Coordinator:** Susan Free, *The GTS Companies*/York, PA Campus
**Design Coordinator:** Diane C. Lorenzo
**Text Design and Illustrations:** *The GTS Companies*/York, PA Campus
**Cover Design:** Ali Mohrman
**Cover Image:** Getty One
**Production Manager:** Laura Messerly
**Director of Marketing:** Ann Castel Davis
**Marketing Manager:** Autumn Purdy
**Marketing Coordinator:** Tyra Poole

This book was set in Berkeley by *The GTS Companies*/York, PA Campus. It was printed and bound by Phoenix Color
Book Group. The cover was printed by Phoenix Color Corp.

**Pearson Prentice Hall™** is a trademark of Pearson Education, Inc.
**Pearson®** is a registered trademark of Pearson plc
**Prentice Hall®** is a registered trademark of Pearson Education, Inc.
**Merrill®** is a registered trademark of Pearson Education, Inc.

Pearson Education Ltd.
Pearson Education Singapore Pte. Ltd.
Pearson Education Canada, Ltd.
Pearson Education—Japan

Pearson Education Australia Pty. Limited
Pearson Education North Asia Ltd.
Pearson Educación de Mexico, S.A. de C.V.
Pearson Education Malaysia Pte. Ltd.

10 9 8 7 6 5 4 3 2 1
ISBN: 0-13-090897-5

# PREFACE

## SURVIVING AND THRIVING

Whatever your background, whatever your current circumstances, and whatever your purpose is in reading this book, we can guarantee one thing: You are a survivor of crisis. You may be one of the fortunate people who has only faced and surmounted developmental crises that mark the transition points between major phases of your life. Perhaps you have dealt with a life-threatening illness or accident. It may be that you have been a victim of sexual assault or other form of violence. Possibly, you have been through the sadness and grief of losing someone close to you. Certainly, you experienced, either directly or vicariously, the shock, turmoil, and anguish stemming from the terrorist attacks of 9/11 and from the recent war in Iraq.

Not only have you survived crises, it is also likely that you have been able to thrive in many ways after coping with these challenges. You may be wiser now that you have gained some perspective about life's dangers and rewards. You may be more confident of your abilities to handle "the slings and arrows of outrageous fortune." Perhaps you have grown closer to other people as you realized their importance to you. You may have developed a deeper commitment to certain values, or gained greater insight into the meaning of life. Whatever crises you face in your life, when you resolve them successfully, you grow as a person and go on to live life more deeply.

These two assumptions, that everyone has survived crises and everyone has the potential to thrive after crises, are the foundation of successful crisis intervention. As a crisis intervener, you will be dealing with people as they confront situations that threaten their health, personal well-being, way of life, and even their lives. These situations pose both dangers and opportunities. Your goal is to help people survive the dangers and thrive on the opportunities.

This book is based on the growing literature documenting the resilience of people in dealing with crises. Research regarding a variety of traumas, catastrophes, and disasters has demonstrated that the vast majority of people in these situations successfully cope with these crises. More important, many studies have identified factors that promote a positive resolution. These findings have important implications for designing effective crisis intervention techniques. In the opening two chapters of this book, we introduce you to the principles of resilience and resolution. Throughout the remainder of the book, we return to these principles. Whether you're working with individuals, groups, or communities, it is vital that you believe in their resilience and that you focus your efforts on helping them achieve a successful resolution.

This book is also inspired by the recent and exciting theoretical perspectives of postmodern thought and positive psychology, including chaos and complexity theories, constructivism, narrative perspectives, teleonomy, and emotional intelligence. We discuss the implications of these concepts for crisis intervention and present specific techniques that are based on these perspectives.

## An Overview of the Book

Chapter 1, "Resilience and Transcendence: Surviving Crises, Thriving in Life," presents the background and history of the concepts of crisis and resilience. Crisis is an influential concept that is pervasive in the areas of art, literature, cultural myths, current events, and personal development. Although people suffer pain, confusion, and heartache as they undergo crises, most not only survive them, they also go on to thrive in their lives. *Merriam-Webster's New World Dictionary* defines the experience of thriving as: "to prosper or flourish; be successful; to grow vigorously." A fundamental attitude of successful crisis work is to recognize and value the essential resilience of people in crisis and that overcoming crisis instills a sense of resolve in survivors. In this opening chapter, you will also learn two basic techniques of crisis intervention. The first technique is offering the LUV Triangle of listening, understanding, and validating the person's crisis experience. The second technique involves using questions that presume resilience and "getting through" questions that help someone in crisis conjure up images of surviving and thriving.

Much of the literature on crisis has focused on the experience of traumatization rather than the process of resolution. Chapter 2, "Crisis Resolution: The Change Process," describes what takes place as people make their way through the process of successful resolution. Our goal as crisis interveners is not to rescue helpless victims, but to assist survivors by facilitating the natural process of resolving a crisis. You will practice three techniques that promote resolution: tracking resolution, transforming crisis metaphors, and asking "moving on" questions.

Recent studies in the areas of social support, meaning making, cognitive psychology, emotions, creativity, and positive psychology have revealed exciting implications for crisis intervention. In the subsequent four chapters, we present fundamental elements that contribute to successful crisis resolution. Chapter 3, "Making Contact: The Power of Connecting," summarizes the extensive evidence that states that social support is a powerful factor in helping survivors resolve crises. Relatives and friends often reach out to victims, offering practical assistance and emotional consolation. Our role as crisis interveners is to reconnect a survivor to these sources of support and to supplement this natural helping network. In this chapter, you will develop skills in "being with" a survivor, identifying resources, and offering an encouragement interlude.

Chapter 4, "Making Meaning: Transforming a Crisis Narrative into a Survival Story," explores the challenge of making sense of the often chaotic and confusing experience of crisis. We first draw upon the rich history of existential perspectives of survivors' search for meaning. We then go on to describe the recent research into the benefits of putting a crisis experience into words. You will practice crisis intervention techniques that are based on principles of narrative theory, such as serving as an audience to the crisis storyteller. Finally, we suggest how you may go about coconstructing survival stories that emphasize resilience and resolution from narratives that focus on the crisis experience.

Chapter 5, "Managing Emotional Arousal: Promoting Feelings of Resolve," presents a new view of emotions that has been emerging in the positive psychology literature. Until recently, many crisis intervention models encouraged survivors to reexperience the painful emotions of their crisis in order to promote catharsis. However, studies of these techniques suggest that they are, at best, ineffective and, in fact, possibly harmful. We offer a "kinder, gentler" approach that helps survivors reduce negative emotions of anxiety, depression, and aggression, while promoting such positive emotions of resolve as courage, hope, and compassion.

Most crisis intervention approaches focus on the traumatic events in the recent past and on the person's reactions in the present. We encourage you to invite someone in crisis to envision a future. In Chapter 6, "Envisioning Possibilities: Creative Coping," we describe how to facilitate resolution by helping survivors develop well-formed goals as they explore how to cope with the daunting challenges they face. Goals serve as beacons that can guide a survivor toward a positive resolution. The techniques you will practice in this chapter include using hypotheticals and scaling.

The final four chapters help you to "put it all together" in working with individuals, couples and families, groups, or entire communities. Chapter 7, "Crisis Intervention with Individuals: Working One on One," presents a model based on resilience that facilitates positive resolution of crises. Our goal as crisis interveners is to promote the natural change processes of reaching out to others, making meaning, taking heart, and moving on.

In Chapter 8, "Crisis Intervention with Couples and Families: Resolving with Relatives," we apply the concept of crisis to the most important human system: the family. We describe the challenges that families face at every phase of their life cycle. Truly, no crisis takes place outside of a family context. Family members may experience the emotional fallout of an individual's crisis, offer nurturance to someone reeling from some catastrophic event, or even instigate a crisis.

Chapter 9, "Crisis Intervention with Groups: Coming Together with Resolve," explores the unique challenges and opportunities of working with groups who are in crisis. The resolution-focused techniques include linking people in crisis, creating a collective survival story, promoting emotions of resolve, and facilitating the group's coping abilities.

Finally, in Chapter 10, "Crisis Intervention with Communities: Disasters, Catastrophes, and Terrorism," we discuss how natural disasters, large-scale accidents, and political violence can traumatize an entire community. Community crisis intervention techniques include public education, use of the media, and promoting systemic resilience.

Books on crisis intervention often are divided into chapters that cover separate situations, such as sexual assault, suicide, and violence. Such approaches highlight the specific issues and particular concerns involved in different crises. However, we have decided to organize our book in terms of the important factors that contribute to resilience and resolution in any crisis. The general principles and techniques that you learn in this book can be applied across all crisis events with individuals, families, groups, or communities.

Most crisis intervention books also begin with theory in the opening chapter and then go on in the remainder of the book to describe specific practices. Instead of following this traditional separation of the conceptual from the practical, we have integrated ideas and tools into every chapter to take full advantage of the synergistic qualities of theory and practice. Understanding theory helps you be a more successful crisis intervener, and practicing the techniques helps you to understand the concepts at a deeper and richer level.

## Chapter Organization

Every chapter includes the following important components:

- *Chapter Goals.* In each chapter, we begin by sharing with you the goals—what you can hope to achieve as the result of reading the chapter material, participating in the experiential learning activities, and practicing the techniques.
- *Overview.* We follow the goals with a broad overview that highlights the important concepts and techniques that will be covered in the chapter.
- *Crisis Story.* Every chapter offers a narrative based on our own experiences of working with people in crisis. To protect confidentiality, we have changed any identifying information. At times, we have combined situations, circumstances, and interventions of several cases into one crisis story.
- *Ideas.* A major portion of each chapter explores important concepts and principles that have important implications for crisis intervention. These principles apply to virtually all crisis situations and provide a theoretical foundation to the strategies that we describe.
- *Experiential Learning Activities.* The best way to truly know a concept is to experience it. Throughout each chapter, we regularly offer you an opportunity to actively engage with an idea by relating it to your own life and "trying it on to see how it fits." We invite you to take the time to focus on the exercise, immerse yourself in the process, and then reflect on what you discover.
- *Tools.* As you contemplate the possibility of working with someone in crisis, you may feel apprehensive that you will not perform adequately during a time when so much is at stake. You may think that it's imperative that you learn exactly what to say and precisely what to do under those circumstances. However, there are no "magic words" in crisis intervention. The techniques described in each chapter are based on the implications of the concepts that are presented. When you understand the rationale, you don't need to memorize lines. Instead, you are taking action that is based on understanding.
- *Listening In on Crisis Intervention.* These boxes give you the opportunity to see techniques demonstrated with the people involved in the crisis case studies. In these segments, you witness crisis intervention in action. However, keep in mind that one of the goals of this book is for you to find your own voice as a crisis intervener—not to parrot ours. As you read the sessions in this book, please regard the intervener's

statements as examples to illustrate, not scripts to memorize. Consider each of our suggestions in the spirit in which we offer it—as an example of what someone might say to a particular person in a particular crisis.

- *Practice Activities.* Once you have read about each tool and have seen it demonstrated, you will then have the opportunity to practice the technique in structured exercises. As you practice your crisis intervention skills, you will learn to trust yourself to give expression to these strategies. Successful crisis intervention requires authentic communication—not well-delivered quotes.

- *Crisis Resources.* One of your important working assumptions in crisis intervention is that you are not the only resource for a survivor. There are many resources that someone in crisis can use as he or she works to reach a resolution. These resources include organizations, Web sites, hotlines, readings, electronic mailing lists, volunteer programs, and advocacy groups. Each chapter offers a sampling of resources that address the particular crisis situation presented in the case study.

- *Segue.* At the end of each chapter, we offer a segue to the next. This activity is designed to prepare you for the concepts and techniques that you will be learning in the chapter that follows. Take some time to experience these segues. You can gain a sense of the interconnectedness of the ideas and tools presented throughout this book.

## A MESSAGE OF THANKS

Although they may struggle with feelings of alienation at first, people who successfully resolve crises soon discover that they are not islands unto themselves. The same is true for authors of crisis intervention books. Many people have supported and assisted us in completing this project. Our students read various drafts of the manuscript and gave us detailed feedback and thoughtful suggestions. Our colleagues generously offered both their professional expertise and personal encouragement. Our relatives, particularly Mary Lou Wylie, Lin Presbury, and Barbara McKee, were tireless in their support and forbearance.

We are grateful for the many constructive comments of the manuscript reviewers: Nicholas Mazza, Florida State University; Chris McCarthy, University of Texas–Austin; Thomas W. Rueth, University of Dayton; and Julie Schroeder, Louisiana State University. The final version is much better as a result of their thorough work, careful scrutiny, and insightful observations. We also thank Kevin Davis for his unstinting encouragement, valuable guidance, and tireless commitment to this project. Amanda King gave us diplomatic reminders, served as a steady liaison, and delivered information with good cheer. Melissa Messina has been wonderful as our copy editor. She corrected our errors, polished our writing, and checked our resources with meticulous care.

Finally, we would like to thank the survivors we have encountered in our crisis intervention work. They patiently overlooked our mistakes, taught us by example how to survive crises and thrive in life, touched our hearts, left us with unforgettable memories, and inspired us with their resilience. We are honored that they allowed us to share their life's journey through the most painful—and rewarding—passages.

# RESEARCH NAVIGATOR:
# RESEARCH MADE SIMPLE!

www.ResearchNavigator.com

Merrill Education is pleased to introduce Research Navigator—a one-stop research solution for students that simplifies and streamlines the entire research process. At www.researchnavigator.com, students will find extensive resources to enhance their understanding of the research process so they can effectively complete research assignments. In addition, Research Navigator has three exclusive databases of credible and reliable source content to help students focus their research efforts and begin the research process.

## HOW WILL RESEARCH NAVIGATOR ENHANCE YOUR COURSE?

- Extensive content helps students understand the research process, including writing, Internet research, and citing sources.
- Step-by-step tutorial guides students through the entire research process from selecting a topic to revising a rough draft.
- Research Writing in the Disciplines section details the differences in research across disciplines.
- Three exclusive databases—EBSCO's ContentSelect Academic Journal Database, *The New York Times* Search by Subject Archive, and "Best of the Web" Link Library—allow students to easily find journal articles and sources.

## WHAT'S THE COST?

A subscription to Research Navigator is $7.50 but is **free** when ordered in conjunction with this textbook. To obtain free passcodes for your students, simply contact your local Merrill/Prentice Hall sales representative, and your representative will send you the Evaluating Online Resource Guide, which contains the code to access Research Navigator as well as tips on how to use Research Navigator and how to evaluate research. To preview the value of this website to your students, please go to www.educatorlearningcenter.com and use the Login Name "Research" and the password "Demo."

# DISCOVER THE COMPANION WEBSITE ACCOMPANYING THIS BOOK

## THE PRENTICE HALL COMPANION WEBSITE: A VIRTUAL LEARNING ENVIRONMENT

Technology is a constantly growing and changing aspect of our field that is creating a need for content and resources. To address this emerging need, Prentice Hall has developed an online learning environment for students and professors alike—Companion Websites—to support our textbooks.

In creating a Companion Website, our goal is to build on and enhance what the textbook already offers. For this reason, the content for each user-friendly web site is organized by topic and provides the professor and student with a variety of meaningful resources. Common features of a Companion Website include:

## FOR THE PROFESSOR—

Every Companion Website integrates **Syllabus Manager™**, an online syllabus creation and management utility.

- **Syllabus Manager™** provides you, the instructor, with an easy, step-by-step process to create and revise syllabi, with direct links into Companion Website and other online content without having to learn HTML.
- Students may logon to your syllabus during any study session. All they need to know is the web address for the Companion Website and the password you've assigned to your syllabus.
- After you have created a syllabus using **Syllabus Manager™**, students may enter the syllabus for their course section from any point in the Companion Website.
- Clicking on a date, the student is shown the list of activities for the assignment. The activities for each assignment are linked directly to actual content, saving time for students.

- Adding assignments consists of clicking on the desired due date, then filling in the details of the assignment—name of the assignment, instructions, and whether it is a one-time or repeating assignment.
- In addition, links to other activities can be created easily. If the activity is online, a URL can be entered in the space provided, and it will be linked automatically in the final syllabus.
- Your completed syllabus is hosted on our servers, allowing convenient updates from any computer on the Internet. Changes you make to your syllabus are immediately available to your students at their next logon.

## FOR THE STUDENT—

- *Counseling Topics*—17 core counseling topics represent the diversity and scope of today's counseling field.
- *Annotated Bibliography*—includes seminal foundational works and key current works.
- *Web Destinations*—lists significant and up-to-date practitioner and client sites.
- *Professional Development*—provides helpful information regarding professional organizations and codes of ethics.
- *Electronic Bluebook*—send homework or essays directly to your instructor's email with this paperless form.
- *Message Board*—serves as a virtual bulletin board to post—or respond to— questions or comments to/from a national audience.
- *Chat*—real-time chat with anyone who is using the text anywhere in the country— ideal for discussion and study groups, class projects, etc.

To take advantage of these and other resources, please visit the *Crisis Intervention: Promoting Resilience and Resolution in Troubled Times* Companion Website at

**www.prenhall.com/echterling**

# BRIEF CONTENTS

# CONTENTS

# Resilience and Transcendence: Surviving Crises, Thriving in Life

"Every live thing is a survivor."
*Annie Dillard*

"Only through experience of trial and suffering can the soul be strengthened,
vision cleared, ambition inspired, and success achieved."
*Helen Keller*

## CHAPTER GOALS

After completing this chapter, you should be able to:

- Understand the concept of crisis as a turning point that involves both threats and opportunities
- Recognize the ability of victims to survive crises and to go on to thrive in their lives
- Know the six facets of the crisis experience—behavioral, affective, somatic, interpersonal, cognitive, and spiritual
- Listen to, understand, and validate a person's crisis experience
- Ask questions that help survivors conjure up possibilities for a positive crisis resolution

# Overview

We live in times of crisis. Glance at any newspaper and you are likely to find stories about an economic crisis in U.S. corporations, a political crisis in the White House, the crisis of another terrorist attack, an environmental crisis in South America, or a crisis of confidence in the news media. Turn on your local *Action News* television program, and you will see the stunned faces of people dealing with acts of violence, crimes, and catastrophes. Reflect on your own life and you can readily recall personal crises that have confronted you—the death of a loved one, a serious accident, a traumatic experience, or a major life transition. In fact, crisis is a fundamental part of the human condition—you don't go through life without experiencing at least the crisis of your own mortality.

Now more than ever, the world needs people who are willing to take on the daunting challenge of helping others in times of crisis. As a counselor, therapist, or other helping professional, you can expect to regularly deal with people in critical circumstances. Even if your school, community agency, mental health center, or private practice does not emphasize emergency services, you will find yourself consistently doing some form of crisis intervention.

There are several reasons that all helping professionals, no matter their area of specialization, will occasionally work with people in crisis. First, although children, adolescents, or adults may have been having serious personal, academic, or relationship problems for months, it is only when these difficulties reach a critical mass that many finally seek a professional helper. Therefore, your first contact with a person in need may be when he or she is in crisis. Second, clients in counseling are typically dealing with situations, such as troubled relationships, substance abuse, and depression, that make them a higher risk for crises. Difficulties that have been smoldering for months can suddenly burst into a full-blown catastrophe. Finally, the sometimes painful and disturbing personal discoveries involved in the counseling and therapy process itself can lead to crises.

A crisis is a turning point in our lives, a brief but crucial time in which there is the opportunity for dramatic growth and positive changes, as well as the danger of violence and devastation (Wethington, 2003). Looking back on their crisis experiences, survivors often describe them as "marking the end of one chapter and the beginning of another" (McAdams, 1988, p. 144). People often date other events in their lives as taking place either before or after one of these turning points. "Oh, yes," they may muse, "I remember now. That happened just a couple of months before the flood."

Whatever the outcome, people do not emerge from a crisis unchanged. If there is a negative resolution, the crisis can leave alienation, bitterness, devastated relationships, and even death in its wake. However, if the crisis is resolved successfully, a survivor can develop a deeper appreciation for life, a stronger sense of resolve, a more mature perspective, greater feelings of competence, and richer relationships. Such survivors achieve a level of transcendence in which they can become thrivers. With the lessons they have learned and the discoveries they have made from their crisis experience, thrivers can go on to engage more fully in life, savor it more deeply, and take advantage of its many opportunities.

In this beginning chapter, we introduce you to the concept of crisis and to the principle of resilience, which forms the foundation for any successful crisis intervention. We also present two important techniques that you can use in helping someone not only survive a crisis, but go on to thrive in life.

In the following section, you will encounter Marcos, who is facing the most painful crisis of his life. We have changed details to remove any identifying information, but the story is based on actual events. As you read, allow yourself to become emotionally involved in the experience, open your heart to the people you meet, and imagine what it would be like for you to offer crisis intervention in this situation. Later in the chapter, you will see how an intervener uses two fundamental techniques to help Marcos.

# CRISIS STORY

When he attended the birthing classes with his wife, Marcos could sense his growing excitement about the baby. Months earlier, when Juanita had first broken the news to him, he could tell that she was a little disappointed that he was not as thrilled as she was. But Marcos couldn't help it—he wasn't sure if he was ready to become a father, and because money was already tight, he was worried about their ability to support a child.

Then one morning Juanita cupped his hand on her swollen belly to feel the baby's surprisingly vigorous kicks. Marcos was intrigued, even mystified, by his own emotional stirrings deep inside. An hour later, with a wry, sheepish grin, Marcos told his buddies at the restaurant that he was going to be a father. He enjoyed their good-natured kidding over the next few weeks. Nevertheless, during the quiet moments in the middle of the preparations he and Juanita were making, he still had his misgivings.

All that changed when Marcos first saw his newborn daughter, Maria. It was love at first sight and all his reservations vanished. He felt his heart swell so much that it was like Juanita's belly just before the birth—stretched tight as a balloon and filled to the bursting point. His sense of awe in the presence of this new life, his feelings of pride in helping to bring a new person into the world, and his immense satisfaction in being a part of this mysterious process of creation made him certain that he would never forget this moment.

Maria's whimpering meow of a cry was so fragile and plaintive that Marcos wanted to hold her forever, banish all her frustrations, and satisfy her every whim. The tiny fingernails on the hand that grasped his own finger were so delicate, dainty, and fine that he marveled at the miraculous sight—and the strength of the baby's grip. And those eyes! Every time he looked into Maria's eyes, Marcos felt as if he was falling into those big, bright pools of shimmering light. At his next visit to the hospital, Marcos brought flowers for Juanita and a baseball glove for Maria that was nearly as big as she was.

Five months later, Marcos also knew that he would never forget the moment when he discovered his daughter lying so still and cold in her crib—he knew that she was dead. It was a case of sudden infant death syndrome (SIDS). Marcos had read about SIDS in a brochure he had picked up in the healthy baby clinic. He and Juanita had even taken the precaution of laying Maria on her back to reduce the risk of SIDS, but that safeguard now seemed so foolish. He realized that all their efforts to protect their baby—the child protective seat in the car, the covers on the electrical outlets long before Maria was old enough to crawl—had given him a false sense of security.

Shocked and dazed, Marcos and Juanita somehow muddled through all the arrangements for a funeral Mass, cemetery plot, and burial. In the casket, so obscenely tiny, they placed some parting gifts—a rattle given by Juanita's parents, a pacifier from Marcos' parents, a comforter knitted by Juanita, and the baseball glove.

Marcos bowed his head with the other members of the congregation, but he couldn't bring himself to pray along with them. There were no words, no thoughts, and certainly no prayers. There was only the searing pain—the incredible tightness in his chest. Marcos now realized just how true it was to say someone had a "broken heart." Later, when he overheard a neighbor reassure Juanita that Maria was now in a better place, it took everything he had to keep himself from throttling "that idiot."

Marcos noticed that his friends and relatives would avoid the subject of Maria. Even when he would begin to talk about her, the others seemed uncomfortable and ill at ease. Only Juanita would talk with Marcos about Maria, in spite of her tears. Everywhere he looked, there were reminders of Maria. At home, no room was safe—the kitchen had her high chair, the living room, her walker.

Away from home, Marcos found himself noticing babies, his eyes locking immediately on them, his breath catching, and his body reacting with a quick, wincing shudder. Even a weather forecast stirred up thoughts of Maria. When he heard a prediction for a hard freeze a few days after the funeral, Marcos' first reaction was to worry that the comforter would not be enough to keep Maria warm in her casket.

One night, Marcos had a dream in which he was tossing his daughter playfully in the air. As he held Maria before each toss, her body gleefully squirmed and her eyes widened with anticipation. As he flung her up, her squeals of delight cascaded around him like flowers. For a while it was just like old times, but then it happened. At the top of her ascent, the squeals suddenly stopped, her sparkling eyes became dull and glazed, her skin turned ashen, and then her body, limp and lifeless as a rag doll, fell into his waiting arms.

Marcos snapped awake, his arms clutching at the covers. Juanita, startled out of her own sleep, held him and asked what had happened. In the past, Marcos would have told her everything. He had discovered long ago that Juanita could sense when he was holding back. But now he hesitated to tell her about the horrific dream. Instead, he remembered that his priest had given him a card after the funeral. The card was for a grief hotline and included its telephone number. Marcos decided to call.

### Reflecting on This Crisis Story

1. What were your own reactions as this story unfolded?
2. How would it be for you to work with Marcos?
3. What could you offer Marcos as a crisis intervener?

## INTRODUCTION

### Working with People in Crisis

As you read this book, keep in mind that it is only natural for you to feel apprehensive about doing crisis intervention. The work is intense, the people are in anguish, the situations are explosive, and the stakes are high. In fact, it is likely that the first time you offer crisis intervention as a volunteer or professional, the survivor will not be the only one facing a crisis—you will be, too!

The first time you deal with a suicidal person, you may find yourself struggling with your fears of making a fatal mistake and fumbling to offer the perfect response to someone's anguished words. If you are caught up in these distracting issues, you can be neither yourself nor an effective intervener. The best way to deal with the crisis you face as a beginning intervener is to prepare. If you have prepared yourself well, you can engage quickly, genuinely, and successfully with someone in crisis.

How can you prepare to be a crisis intervener? Of course, reading about crises and practicing the techniques of crisis intervention are both essential. However, your most important preparation is to learn from your own life experiences with crises. Such seasoning helps you to gain an appreciation for the emotional turmoil of a crisis and to experience, at a basic level, the amazing capacity of humans to survive, recover, and thrive in the face of adversity. Successfully charting your way through your own crises can help you to recognize the resilience of us all.

## Your First Reaction

Like other species, humans are biologically wired to tune into and respond to the outcries of their fellow human beings (Eisenberg, 2002). We reflexively wince when we see another person harmed and cringe when we hear someone's cries of anguish. Instinctively, we rush to offer comfort and aid to someone who is in pain. Without thinking, we may even disregard our own safety to rescue a person in peril. When you read about Marcos' crisis experiences, you may have flinched when you encountered the nightmare of his baby's death. You may even have found yourself feeling overwhelmed and wondering what you could do to rescue him from all his pain and suffering.

In addition to your biological wiring, your training as a helping professional also tunes you into the distress of your clients. Counselors and therapists develop antennae that are particularly sensitive to emotional turmoil. This sensitivity can help you to be vigilant about the pain and suffering of someone in crisis. However, in your sympathetic response, you run the risk of ignoring the person's strengths and resilience (Fraser, 1998).

Focusing on only the victim can blind you to the survivor. From this narrow perspective, people in crisis are poor, pitiful victims in desperate need of rescue, instead of coping survivors who are doing their best to achieve some resolution. As a result, you may be more likely to believe that you must be the rescuer and take heroic measures to save these pitiful casualties of circumstances beyond their control. Or you may unconsciously take on too much responsibility for developing crisis resolution strategies. You may be tempted to offer simplistic reassurances, provide expert information about the crisis, or give trite suggestions on how to cope with the situation.

Unfortunately, your attempts to rescue, however well-intentioned, can sabotage someone's sense of personal efficacy. At the very least, you are ignoring people's innate potential to resolve crises in their own creative and personal ways.

# VICTIM

**FIGURE 1–1** Victim.

## *EXPERIENCING THIS IDEA*

Before you read this activity, glance quickly at Figure 1–1.

What did you see? The word *victim,* right? The letters forming the word are certainly large and clear for anyone who briefly scans the figure.

Go back and examine the figure more carefully. What smaller, fainter word is embedded in victim? Think back on the story of Marcos. What was more vivid and obvious to you—his ordeals and sufferings as a victim, or his personal strengths and capabilities as a survivor? Your challenge as a crisis intervener is to find the survivor, however faint and unformed, within the victim.

## Your Role as a Crisis Intervener

According to Fraser (1998), most practitioners who offer crisis intervention also have a negative tendency to focus on the troubling event and its impact, thereby losing sight of a survivor's coping abilities. Unfortunately, the people themselves who are in crisis have the same inclination. Less in touch with their personal resilience, people in crisis can feel overwhelmed not only by the circumstances, but also by their sense of hopelessness, powerlessness, and helplessness. These feelings can undermine their confidence, sap their motivation, and cloud their vision of a future resolution. Therefore, as you listen to people's stories of dealing with their crises, you must make a special effort to consciously seek out their strengths—to search for those clues that point to a resolution strategy—as you continue to be sensitive to their ordeals. In other words, look for the survivor in their stories, not just the victim.

When you encounter someone in a crisis, you may feel tempted to become the gallant knight in shining armor charging to the rescue. However, your fundamental role as a crisis intervener is far less heroic, but no less essential. Your job is like the carpenter's assistant—helping others to use their own tools in rebuilding their lives. Of course, people in crisis feel overwhelmed and distressed, but they also possess overlooked strengths and unmined capabilities.

As you engage in crisis intervention, you are working together with a person in crisis toward two important goals: to make it safely through this hazardous situation and to resolve the crisis positively. Simply put, you want to help a victim not only to survive the crisis, but also to go on to thrive in life. Someone who achieves a successful resolution may emerge from a crisis with some scars, but in deep and fundamental ways, he or she will no longer be the person who originally faced the challenge. Like a butterfly emerging from a cocoon, the person has become transformed.

In the next section, you will become familiar with the concept of crisis and how it has been used in a variety of ways for centuries.

## IDEAS

### The Concept of Crisis

**The Language of Crisis.** The etymology of the word *crisis* offers us some insight into the concept. The Greek word *krisis* refers to a decision or turning point. In Chinese, the symbol for crisis is also a combination of two other symbols—one that represents danger and another that stands for opportunity (see Figure 1–2). A crisis, in other words, paradoxically involves both risk and possibility.

The concept of crisis includes all of the following elements: confronting a momentous decision, encountering a pivotal moment in one's life, and facing both peril and promise. It is important to recognize the distinction between crisis and *trauma*. Trauma refers to a serious physical or psychological injury that has resulted from a threatening, terrifying, or horrifying experience. Not everyone in crisis is dealing with trauma. Someone, for example, facing the developmental crisis of leaving home is going through a major turning point in life that involves both dangers and opportunities. However, that person is not traumatized. On the other hand, people who experience some form of trauma, whether physical or psychological, are initially facing a crisis as well. At this brief but crucial point in their life, how they deal with this trauma will have far-reaching consequences—either positive or negative—for years to come.

**Myths and Crisis.** In every culture, the defining myths are, in fact, heroic stories of crises that are told and retold (Campbell, 1970). These *myths* portray individuals or groups at significant turning points in their personal lives or their culture's histories—developmental crises, crises of faith, situational crises, and identity crises. The common theme in these legends is that of struggle—against others, the gods, nature, the machine, and even oneself. It is the overcoming of these heroic struggles that forges human character and wins us our dignity.

For example, the *Odyssey* is Homer's epic story of Odysseus, a successful man who, after many years of waging war, yearned to return to his roots and sought to rekindle his relationship with his family. However, his search for intimacy and identity were plagued by monsters and demons who thwarted his efforts. Long before the phrase "midlife crisis"

Danger                    Opportunity

**FIGURE 1–2**  Chinese symbol for crisis.

became a cliché, the *Odyssey* gave voice to this universal struggle at one of life's turning points. One of the themes of this epic poem—that we are all survivors of crisis—is also one of the fundamental conditions of successful crisis intervention. Like Odysseus, you carry your own scars—symbols of your own past crises that you have resolved—that enable you to form empathic bridges with those who are struggling in the midst of a crisis.

The Choctaw Indians have a legend of how fire, which once lived in a distant land, was captured and brought to early humans, who then were able to use its power to flourish. The story has been passed down orally through countless generations and portrays fire, like crisis, as both a danger and an opportunity. According to the myth, animals that populated the Choctaw land tried to capture fire for humans. The first animal to make the journey was an opossum, who at that time had a large, bushy tail. When it discovered fire, the opossum attacked, using its tail to wrap around the flames. However, the beautiful fur was scorched away, leaving the tail raw and naked forever. When the opossum returned in failure to the land of the Choctaw, the powerful buzzard set out to bite fire with its large, sharp beak. However, the blaze burned the buzzard's head so badly that it remained bright red and blistered for all eternity. Finally, Grandmother Spider launched her quest for fire. Instead of attacking fire directly, she kept her distance while cunningly making a tiny clay container. Then Grandmother Spider tiptoed alongside of fire using her web and carefully placed a small flame in the container. When she returned with fire, Grandmother Spider taught humans how to use it safely to bring them warmth, protection, and light.

The Choctaw legend gives voice to another important principle. The best strategy in dealing with a crisis is often not the frontal assault or the use of brute force. Instead, you can join with the crisis to use its momentum and power in a positive direction. Obi-Wan Kenobi, in our society's mythic epic film *Star Wars,* advocated this approach by wishing, "May the force be with you."

**Crisis in the Popular Culture.** Just a glimpse at our recent Academy Award-winning movies reveals cinema's fascination with crises. The protagonists of *Chicago, A Beautiful Mind, Gladiator, American Beauty, Titanic,* and *Lord of the Rings* struggled with murders, psychiatric disorders, violence, rapes, family turmoil, catastrophes, wars, and suicide. In fact, it is difficult to think of any movie that does not involve at least one character facing a pivotal decision or turning point—in other words, a crisis. Even comedies deal with crises involving physical or psychological risks of some sort. Unlike dramas, lighter fare, such as *The Full Monty, As Good As It Gets*, and *My Big, Fat Greek Wedding* play economic, emotional, and family crises for laughs by emphasizing the absurdities of these predicaments and the ingenuity that people often display in trying to get out of these scrapes.

As pervasive as crises are in today's movies, they have also been favorite subjects of art, drama, and literature since antiquity. At the very heart of any satisfying story line is some form of crisis and its resolution, whether tragic or triumphant. Crises are where the action is, so it is no wonder that writers, artists, directors, and performers give creative expression to these memorable experiences. These portrayals of crises attract, intrigue, and captivate audiences because no one escapes life without a crisis. We turn to novels, plays, movies, and art to expand our own limited range of experiences, to see others grapple with circumstances that resonate with our own crises. These works are so popular because, at a basic level, they are actually about ourselves—our own adversities and ultimate resilience.

In the fields of psychology, psychiatry, social work, and counseling, the concept of crisis has been enormously helpful in stimulating exciting research and model programs in two areas: life span development and community mental health.

**Crisis Over the Life Span.** Erikson (1963) used the concept of crisis as the foundation of his stages of *human development*. His view of the span of life as a series of stages involving particular developmental crises has had an immense influence on how we conceptualize human growth across the life span. It has helped us to be sensitive to the different challenges that people face at each phase of life. More importantly, Erikson's perspective has alerted us to the implication that by successfully resolving each crisis, a person is able to move on to the next developmental stage. Life involves crises, but personal growth involves successfully resolving them.

The idea of developmental crises has had a tremendous impact on both research and practice. It has stirred developmental psychologists to expand their study from a focus on infants and children to adolescents and adults throughout the entire life span. Others have developed similar models to reflect the identity development of African Americans (Cross, Parham, & Helms, 1991) and women (Gilligan, 1983). The notion of developmental crises has inspired a gamut of prevention and intervention programs to help, for example, adolescents develop their sense of identity and the aging to address the issues of ego integrity (Aguilera, 1998).

**Crisis in Community Mental Health.** The idea of crisis served as a catalyst in the community mental health movement. In the classic study of the survivors who escaped Boston's Coconut Grove fire in 1942, Eric Lindemann (1944) recommended that community caretakers could be a resource for those experiencing such catastrophes.

In contrast to Erikson's broad strokes across the entire life span, Gerald Caplan, who was a colleague of Lindemann, applied the idea of crisis to time-limited, specific events that can overwhelm a person's usual problem-solving capabilities. This idea became the foundation for countless innovative programs and the rationale for crisis intervention as an essential community service.

According to Caplan (1964), people generally function at a certain prescribed level (see Figure 1–3). Some of us may be highly successful, whereas others may be just getting by. Whatever our typical level of functioning, when we face some challenging situation, we at first feel energized to give it our "best shot." Most of the time, especially if we are leading successful lives, we are effective in dealing with the problem at hand. Inevitably, however, a crisis occurs if we are unable to handle a disturbing event. When our efforts fail, we begin to feel overwhelmed, frightened, exhausted, and discouraged. As you can see in Figure 1–3, our level of functioning may deteriorate rapidly and we face two dangers. The first is that in this state of crisis, we are more likely to act in impulsive, self-defeating, or even violent ways. The second danger is that we may emerge from this temporary state of crisis at a lower level of long-term functioning—wounded, embittered, defensive—and perhaps even develop a psychological disorder, as in example C of Figure 1–3. From Caplan's perspective, in addition to these dangers, crises also present opportunities for growth. If, during our crises, we receive immediate help and practical support, or if we are able to deal with the problems in creative and original ways, then we can emerge from crises at a higher level of functioning—enlightened, matured, resilient— and less likely to develop a disorder, as in example A of Figure 1–3.

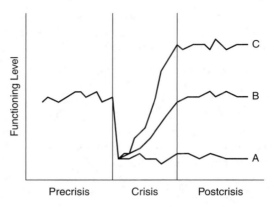

**FIGURE 1–3**   Caplan's concept of crisis.

Caplan's view of crisis as a time-limited period of intense distress, high risk, and potential for growth has important implications for how helping professionals should design and offer their services. According to Caplan, if we want to prevent problems and reduce suffering, then we need to focus our resources on crises by offering immediate, short-term, and easily accessible help. Our traditional psychotherapeutic services, with their waiting lists, limited hours of operation, and other barriers, are not designed to do effective crisis intervention.

The emphasis on the need for immediate services during times of crisis has led to the training of volunteers, paraprofessionals, law enforcement officers, bartenders, and hairdressers (Hendricks & McKean, 1995). Over the past 4 decades, there has been a tremendous growth in crisis telephone services, suicide hotlines, abuse shelters, rape crisis programs, teen hotlines, home-based crisis intervention programs, and outreach crisis services.

## Resilience in Crisis

Erikson (1963), Caplan (1964), and others have laid the conceptual groundwork for viewing crisis as an opportunity for successful development and growth. Unfortunately, in actual practice, most crisis interveners have concentrated on the dangers and negative consequences of crises (Fraser, 1998). They have focused on the deficits of people in crisis, instead of their strengths, and on the dangers in crisis situations, rather than the opportunities (see Figure 1–2). However, we now are discovering that people are extraordinarily resilient. New evidence about our *resilience* in times of crisis has exciting implications for using crisis intervention techniques that uncover strengths, identify coping abilities, and promote resolution.

Resilience is the ability to "bounce back" after significant adversity and risk. Instead of studying the dangers that crises pose, many researchers are exploring the opportunities that they offer. Positive psychology (Aspinwall & Staudinger, 2003; Keyes & Haidt, 2003; Seligman & Csikszentmihalyi, 2000; Snyder & Lopez, 2002) is a recent conceptual shift that is adding momentum to this movement. For decades, the focus in psychology has been on studying deficits and disorders, but now there is a new interest in exploring human strengths and positive experiences.

In the theory and practice of social work, Dennis Saleebey (1997) has also emphasized the strengths perspective, urging practitioners to "assail the victim mind-set; foreswear paternalism; trust people's intuitions . . . and believe in people's dreams" (p. 8). He has pointed out that the *Diagnostic and Statistical Manual of Mental Disorders* (*DSM-IV-TR*; American Psychiatric Association, 2000) is a best-selling and ever-expanding compilation of disorders and deficits. However, "there is no Diagnostic Strengths Manual" (Saleebey, 2001, p. 13). By building on strengths, social workers can demonstrate that successful empowerment strategies do not *give* power to people. Rather, such approaches enable people to discover, develop, and exercise their own strengths, talents, wisdom, and power.

Early researchers of resilience focused on children, discovering that many young people were surprisingly hardy, thriving under difficult conditions, including extreme poverty, family violence, institutional settings, and natural disasters (Masten & Coatsworth, 1998). After 4 decades, the research has consistently found that several factors promote resilience among children and youth. These protective factors include supportive caregivers, self-efficacy, meaning in life, good regulation of emotional arousal, and problem-solving abilities (Masten & Reed, 2002).

Recent studies have explored resilience among adults and have found that resilience is much more common than was once believed (Ryff & Singer, 2003b). Kessler, Davis, and Kendler (1997) documented that the majority of children who experience severe traumas, such as sexual assault or death of a parent, do not develop psychiatric disorders. Resilience, in fact, is the rule rather than the exception for people of any age who are facing traumatic events. To contrast with Seligman's (1974) concept of "learned helplessness," Antonovsky (1990) coined the phrase "learned resourcefulness" to characterize the successful strategies that most people develop to deal with catastrophes. Life history studies of psychological well-being by Ryff and Singer (2003a) and their colleagues provide compelling evidence for the resilience of most—not just a few—people, both young and old, in the face of adversity.

Marilyn Bowman (1997) argued convincingly that most trauma survivors show remarkable resilience. Studies on successfully overcoming adversity have been done in countries around the world, with people of all ages, and involving all types of crises (Glantz, Johnson, & Huffman, 1999). Researchers have investigated those who have directly confronted traumas, as well as those who are indirectly involved—witnesses, co-workers, friends, relatives, and rescuers (Kaniasty & Norris, 1999). Their findings have consistently demonstrated that the overwhelming majority of survivors overcome catastrophes and other adversities with no clinically significant consequences (McNally, Bryant, & Ehlers, 2003).

One epidemiological study (Norris, 1992), for example, found that 69% of a representative sample of 1,000 Americans had experienced at least one extremely traumatic event during their lives. However, the lifetime prevalence rate for posttraumatic stress disorder (PTSD) is only about 12% (Resnick, Kilpatrick, Dansky, Saunders, & Best, 1993). In another study, 76% of those encountering a severely traumatic event did not develop PTSD (Breslau, Davis, Andreski, & Peterson, 1991). Traumatic life experiences generally do not undermine long-term happiness or well-being (Myers, 1993). After Bowman's (1997) extensive review of the research on how people respond to combat, natural disasters, violence, sexual assault, and other traumatic events, she concluded, "While most people respond with some emotional distress . . . most do not develop clinically significant disorders, and most recover their pre-event emotional condition within a relatively short time" (p. 39).

In other words, humans are not merely products of their environment, even if the environment is horrific, threatening, and catastrophic. Instead, people show great resilience by relying on their personal strengths, ingenuity, and resourcefulness. As

Kaniasty and Norris (1999) have stated, "The obvious call for action, even during one's own time of crisis, propels many individuals into extremely high levels of coping. As long as they are physically capable, victims are doers" (p. 6).

## From Surviving to Thriving

As we mentioned earlier, resilience refers to the ability to bounce back after suffering a blow. A resilient person, therefore, is a survivor—someone who can recover from a trauma and return to his or her earlier state of well-being. However, many people do more than cope with catastrophes and survive them without developing a mental disorder. In resolving their crises, they accomplish more than merely bouncing back to their previous level of functioning. In fact, they achieve a positive transformation and transcendence involving a period of dramatic personal growth. It is not unusual to hear people later describe their crisis experience as "the best thing that ever happened to me" (Park, 1998). *Thriving* is more than resilience, as Carver (1998) pointed out, because the person achieves an even higher level of personal well-being than before the crisis. A survivor bounces back after a crisis, but a thriver reaches even greater heights.

Researchers are now exploring how people can flourish under stress. For example, Ryff and Singer (2003b) reviewed studies of people who were able to prevail in times of crisis to forge lifelong personal strengths and values. Tedeschi and Calhoun (1995) focused on the positive changes and personal growth many survivors of trauma can achieve. In their later work, Tedeschi, Park, and Calhoun (1998) offered an overview of how cultures throughout history have recognized that people can change in dramatically positive ways as a result of encountering devastating events. They proposed the term *posttraumatic growth (PTG)* to serve as a contrast to the field's heavy emphasis on PTSD as the consequence of trauma.

Their studies of PTG have found that survivors report profound changes in their perceptions of themselves, their relationships with others, and their philosophy of life. These benefits include feeling more confident, becoming more self-reliant, growing closer to others, disclosing more of oneself, feeling more compassion for humanity, appreciating life more deeply, reviewing their priorities, and experiencing a more profound sense of spirituality. Such PTG experiences have tremendous implications for a resolution-focused intervention.

---

## EXPERIENCING THIS IDEA

Everyone has been through crises—if not accidental crises, then certainly developmental ones, such as leaving home for college. We invite you to select a crisis from your past that you have successfully resolved. Once you have made your choice, take a few minutes to reflect on that experience by answering the following questions.

1. How did you manage to resolve the crisis?
2. In what ways are you a different person as a result of that experience?
3. How did your relationships with others change as a consequence?
4. What important lessons about life did you learn?

Keep your experiences of facing and resolving a crisis in mind as you continue reading the material in this chapter.

---

## The BASICS of the Crisis Experience

Most people successfully handle traumatic events and even achieve personal growth by dealing with these adversities. However, during the crisis itself, survivors experience turmoil and some are in danger of suffering long-term negative consequences (O'Brien, 1998). In this section, we describe the experience of crisis using the BASICS Model, based on Slaikeu's (1990) application of Lazarus' (1981) multimodal perspective. The acronym BASICS (see Figure 1–4) can be a useful mnemonic device to remember six significant facets of the crisis experience. As an intervener, it helps if you know the *BASICS*:

1. Behavioral—what people do
2. Affective—how people feel
3. Somatic—how people respond physically
4. Interpersonal—how people relate to others
5. Cognitive—how people think
6. Spiritual—what people believe and value

**Behavioral.** People in crisis often act in certain typical ways. On first impact of an event, they may be crying out in distress, fleeing, protecting others, or taking immediate action to confront the threat. Later, they may continue to feel that something—anything!—has to be done right now. They may be pacing, rocking, or fidgeting. At times, they may feel so discouraged that they do nothing and become nearly immobilized.

Even if they were not physically injured, people in crisis are generally unable to perform their typical duties at the same level as before. Work problems, such as absenteeism and inefficiency, may increase. A crisis usually disrupts the everyday living patterns of people. For months, they may find themselves crying unexpectedly.

Although they may not be functioning as effectively in their typical roles, many people display surprising creativity and adaptability in attempting to cope with the challenges of a crisis. Both adults and children may tell the story of their experiences many times, describing what they saw, heard, felt, and did during the incidents. Children who were witnesses to a violent incident may want to know many details, worry about what happened to friends or relatives, and ask numerous questions. Children are likely to

---

**B**ehavioral—what people do

**A**ffective—how people feel

**S**omatic—how people respond physically

**I**nterpersonal—how people relate to others

**C**ognitive—how people think

**S**piritual—what people believe and value

**FIGURE 1–4** The BASICS of a crisis experience.

reenact the experience in their play. It is common to see children acting out the events they have witnessed and drawing pictures of the scenes.

**Affective.** Crises are times of intense emotions, and survivors typically experience a range of powerful, negative feelings. Because these situations involve threatening circumstances, people commonly feel apprehensive, fearful, and anxious. They may also feel angry, resentful, and enraged if the crisis involves frustrations, adversity, physical threat, or personal violation. All crises involve some form of loss—one's health, a loved one, a way of life, or sense of meaning. Therefore, it is not unusual for people to feel depression, hopelessness, shame, or grief (Bifulco & Brown, 1996). It is only natural for them to go through a time of grieving for these losses. It is also not uncommon for someone to feel a powerful sense of shame about this victimization.

Crisis is certainly a time of heightened emotional arousal, but a common assumption is that people in crisis experience only negative feelings. Recent research has demonstrated that people going through times of loss and adversity actually experience positive as well as painful emotions (Larsen, Hemenover, Norris, & Cacioppo, 2003). These emotions of resolve include such feelings as courage, compassion, hope, relief, and joy. Acknowledging and giving voice to the gamut of emotions—both negative and positive—can help someone in crisis to achieve a successful resolution.

**Somatic.** In addition to any physical pain survivors may experience as a result of the crisis incidents, they are likely to have reactive physical sensations such as headaches and stomachaches, muscle tension, nausea, sleep problems, shortness of breath, and fatigue (O'Brien, 1998). People in crisis are at a higher risk for abusing substances (Ruzek, Polusny, & Abueg, 1998). Troubled by their physical and psychological distress, they may attempt to find relief by medicating or numbing themselves. Exposure to traumas, like other forms of stress, may also reduce the effectiveness of some people's immune systems. Consequently, they are much more vulnerable to illness after they have been confronted with psychological trauma.

In times of stress, survivors also typically show a physical hardiness and resilience that can energize them to carry out amazing feats of endurance and coping. You've heard of many stories, such as those of parents who were miraculously able to lift a car off a child, but were unable to repeat the feat later.

**Interpersonal.** At first, many people enjoy a "honeymoon" phase in their relationships after exposure to a catastrophic event. For example, following natural disasters, survivors typically report a surge in the sense of community, having just shared with others a dangerous, catastrophic experience and having lived through it. After an incident, individuals may be very talkative and want to tell their stories to others, including virtual strangers. Many friends and families grow closer as a result of the experience. Conversely, some survivors may develop problems with their friends, co-workers, neighbors, and partners (Bolger, Foster, Vinokur, & Ng, 1996). People in crisis may unexpectedly lash out at others or isolate themselves for long periods, leading to marital turmoil, separation, or divorce.

In addition to relatives and friends, others may reach out to people in crisis by offering assistance, support, and suggestions (Dunkel-Schetter, Folkman, & Lazarus, 1987). The heightened uncertainty of crisis events increases openness to social influence (Yates, Axsom, & Tiedeman, 1998). Crisis survivors turn to others for help in interpreting the chaotic situation. However, many survivors soon discover a tendency among some people to avoid, and sometimes even blame (Ryan, 1971), these hapless victims of a trauma.

**Cognitive.** People in crisis may at first be in a state of denial, in which they do not accept that this event has happened (Kalayjian, 1999). As Garrison Keillor once said, "Sometimes you have to look reality in the eye and deny it." At the point of impact, some people in crisis may be so disoriented, dazed, stunned, and bewildered that they are dissociating (Wagner & Linehan, 1998). Later, they may be able to acknowledge what happened to them, but they may be confused, not thinking clearly or completely about the current difficulties that they face. Just as with physical trauma when the body goes into shock, so it is with emotional trauma. It is nature's way of keeping us from having to deal with horrible events all at once.

At some point, many people in crisis may find themselves plagued with thoughts of self-blame. Those who have endured a trauma may be preoccupied with the incident to the point of obsession, wondering why this tragedy happened to them, trying to find meaning in this suffering, and attempting to gain some understanding of how to handle their present problems.

We are mistaken, however, if we portray the person's thinking as impaired throughout the crisis. In fact, resilient people in crisis may demonstrate chaotic thinking, which is neither random nor haphazard, but is often both creative and adaptive (Finke & Bettle, 1996). They also may act effectively without thinking about it.

As a result, survivors begin to *devictimize* themselves by a variety of creative strategies to portray their circumstances as positive. One way is to conclude that "it could have been worse" (Taylor, Wood, & Lichtman, 1983). They enhance themselves by downward social comparisons—they say to themselves that the loss was not as great, the experience was not as horrific, or the circumstances were not as terrible as those that others must endure.

Another approach is to take direct action by gathering information, developing personal coping skills, or promoting social change. In crisis, there are overwhelming forces that batter our sense of security, lash at our defenses, and leave devastation in their wake. However, when we are confronted with the inevitability of loss, injury, or even death, we still find ways to gain some sense of control as we face the uncontrollable. Those faced with terminal illness can orchestrate how they will deal with death. They can endure the terrible blows of fate without being defeated.

**Spiritual.** As they struggle with the problems of resolving the crisis, survivors often grapple with deeper and more profound issues (Ganzevoort, 1998). They confront the questions that have plagued theologians, philosophers, artists, and writers throughout the centuries. They wonder about the purpose of life, whether good deeds are, in fact, rewarded, and why bad things happen to good people. But people in crisis are not involved in ivory tower ruminations. They become practical theologians by asking how God could have allowed such tragedies to occur to them and their loved ones, and earthbound philosophers by questioning the meaning of life, when they know now how frail and ephemeral life can be. For some people in crisis, resolution involves a religious conversion experience (Saunders, 1995). Thrivers often say, "God would not give me a load too heavy for me to carry."

---

## EXPERIENCING THIS IDEA

Review both your own resolved crisis and the case study of Marcos. Use the BASICS Model to help you identify and compare the different facets of both experiences.

|               | **My Resolved Crisis** | **Marcos' Crisis** |
|---------------|------------------------|--------------------|
| Behavioral    |                        |                    |
| Affective     |                        |                    |
| Somatic       |                        |                    |
| Interpersonal |                        |                    |
| Cognitive     |                        |                    |
| Spiritual     |                        |                    |

---

In the following section, you will be learning the fundamental tools you will use whenever you intervene in a crisis. Before you turn your attention to these techniques, take a moment to review the key ideas (see Figure 1–5) that you encountered in the first half of this chapter. These ideas form the conceptual foundation for the tools of crisis intervention.

---

**Key Ideas**

- Crisis involves both danger and opportunity.
- Crisis is a basic theme in our mythic tales and popular culture.
- Human development involves successfully resolving crises.
- People can survive crises and go on to thrive in their lives.
- Look for the BASICS of a crisis.
    - ↳ Behavioral
    - ↳ Affective
    - ↳ Somatic
    - ↳ Interpersonal
    - ↳ Cognitive
    - ↳ Spiritual

---

**FIGURE 1–5**   Key ideas of Chapter 1.

# TOOLS

## The Fundamentals

Crisis intervention is any rapid, brief collaboration to assist someone in surviving a crisis, resolving it positively, and going on to thrive in life. As a counselor or therapist, you will regularly offer crisis intervention in a community agency, school, hospital emergency room, or private practice setting. However, you will also be providing it in nontraditional settings—at the scene of an accident, community recreation center, fire station, house of worship, or disaster assistance center. Most likely, you will be dealing face-to-face with people in crisis, but you may also connect with them over the telephone, through interactive television, or over the Internet. Whatever the setting or medium, your contact may only last a few minutes or it could extend to several hours. However, because it takes place at such a crucial turning point in someone's life, a seemingly small intervention can make a difference for years to come.

In this section, we will be describing two vitally important and essential techniques of crisis intervention. In fact, with many people in crisis, the two strategies you will be learning here may be all that you need to succeed in promoting a positive resolution. The first and most fundamental technique is offering the "*LUV Triangle*"—listen, understand, and validate (Presbury, Echterling, & McKee, 2002). The second technique is using *questions* that help survivors conjure up images of resilience and possibilities for resolution.

At first glance, you may think that these techniques are woefully inadequate and feeble compared with the intensity and severity of the situation. How can merely listening to someone make any possible difference in that person's struggle with seemingly overwhelming odds? What impact can questions have? Shouldn't the crisis intervener be providing answers instead?

The reason that these two techniques are so fundamental—and so powerful—is that they recognize and value the resilience of a person in crisis. As a crisis intervener, your role is neither the rescuer with all the power nor the expert with all the answers. By taking the attitude of "not rescuing" and "not knowing," you invite people in crisis to share their stories and to create their own positive resolutions.

## LUVing the Person in Crisis

If you have been counseling clients in other situations, you are aware that establishing a good working relationship can take time. Clients may first question you regarding your training and qualifications. They may test you in some way before they address the real issues that brought them to counseling. It is also typical for counseling clients to be tentative, hesitant, and reluctant to share at the beginning. In fact, most of your basic training in counseling and therapy is focused on developing a therapeutic relationship.

However, when people feel caught up in the turmoil of a crisis, they often frantically reach out to others and can bond quickly with someone, even if that person is a stranger. As sailors like to say, "In a storm, any port will do." Similarly, caught up in the turmoil of a crisis, people seem to have minimal, but fundamental, standards regarding potential helpers. They are less concerned about your diplomas and more likely to rely on their own intuitive hunch that you are someone to whom they can tell their story.

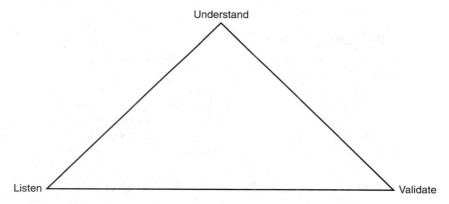

**FIGURE 1–6**   The LUV Triangle.

Even though people in crisis will engage with you quickly, you still need to nurture this relationship by listening, understanding, and validating—the LUV Triangle (see Figure 1–6). When you offer LUV, you are attending carefully to the crisis story, communicating that you comprehend, and bearing witness to the enormity of the crisis experience that this survivor has been enduring.

Keep in mind that you must successfully communicate these conditions to the person you are helping. It is one thing to intend to send a certain message, and quite another for the message to be received as you had hoped. There are specific techniques that you can use to transform your intentions into reality.

**Listening.** What can you do so that someone in crisis can see that you are truly *listening*? According to Egan (1994), you can demonstrate that you are listening in several particular ways.

- *Face the person with an engaged, inviting manner.* You are giving your undivided attention by setting aside any other tasks and focusing entirely on somebody who has come to you in crisis.
- *Assume an open, nonthreatening posture.* Your physical manner reinforces the idea that you are open to hearing whatever someone has to say, no matter how painful.
- *Lean toward the person with an expression of concern.* Showing a sense of dismay reflects that you are tuning into the distress signals that somebody is sending.
- *Maintain good eye contact.* People in crisis may be making less eye contact with you as they share their story. (You will learn more about this phenomenon, which is called "the transderivational search," in Chapter 7.) However, you should continue to look toward their faces because people will regularly glance to check that you are still connecting with them.
- *Keep a sense of poise.* In addition to showing your concern, you also want to keep your composure. Such a balance demonstrates you are committed to hearing out the person's crisis story, even if the account includes horrific and troubling de-

RESILIENCE AND TRANSCENDENCE: SURVIVING CRISES, THRIVING IN LIFE

tails. Assume a "therapeutic distance" between being too close, and thus overwhelmed, and being too distant, and not being affected at all by the story.

**Understanding.** The previous techniques can show that you are listening, but how does the person know that you really understand what is being said? There are a variety of strategies that you can use to successfully communicate your understanding.

- *Repeat or paraphrase* what the individual is saying. You are actively feeding back to the person the vital parts of the message that you are hearing.
- *Check your understanding* by stating what you think someone means and asking for a confirmation. You are inviting the person to verify, correct, or refine your comprehension of the message.
- *Nonverbally match the individual's mood* and talk in a way that mirrors the person's manner of speaking. Of course, your gestures, facial expressions, and speech will not have the same emotional intensity as the person in crisis. After all, you are responding with empathy—not *reacting* with emotional contagion—to the crisis.
- *Use words, phrases, and expressions that are similar to those of the person.* Be particularly alert for the metaphors that someone uses to describe the crisis experience. You will want to use them later when you invite the person to envision ways to respond to the crisis.

**Validating.** Once you have demonstrated that you are both listening and understanding, how can you convey validation? By validating, you are indicating, in every way you can, that you not only believe what someone is saying, but also *believe in* the person's abilities, strengths, and resilience. There are a number of simple behaviors you can use to communicate that you support and affirm the person.

- *Nod affirmatively* and slowly as the person speaks. This small gesture offers an ongoing, regular, and nonverbal refrain of affirmation of the individual and confirmation of the crisis experience. Even a slight nod of your head can be a wordless sign of acknowledgment, regard, and acceptance. Use it freely, but not continuously.
- *Smile warmly* and with understanding. A broad smile in which you flash your teeth is not appropriate with someone in emotional turmoil. As we mentioned earlier, by showing some concern, you are communicating that you are tuning in to the individual's distress. However, you want to balance your dismay for the situation with a warm expression of acceptance for the person.
- *Offer minimal encouragers* and interject rarely. These encouragers can take several forms, but they all have the advantage of not intruding into the flow of the person's story. For example, you can offer a few well-placed words, such as "I see," "Yes," or "Please, go on." Or give a well-timed paralinguistic utterance, such as "hmmm" or "ahhh."

  You can even communicate nonverbally to encourage the person to continue sharing. For example, when the person pauses in the story, you can lean slightly forward with a sense of anticipation. Or, at a particularly crucial point, you can tilt your head a few degrees to one side. Using this "Lassie Twist," you communicate that you are intrigued and absorbed in the person's experience. By bearing witness to the narrative, you honor, with your hushed attentiveness, someone's struggle for survival.

- *Communicate your faith in the individual* by expressing neither skepticism nor the desire to debate. When people are in crisis, they often doubt themselves, question their perceptions, and even wonder about their sanity. Your quiet and accepting manner can promote a sense of validation that the person is lacking during this time of crisis.
- *Convey your confidence in the person's resilience* by not dispensing glib advice. Advice giving carries with it the message that you do not trust the survivor to know the best course of action. Instead, by offering your unintrusive but supportive presence, you communicate your respect for the person's inner resources. Showing in such a manner your belief in someone's resourcefulness sends a powerful message of validation.

---

## PRACTICING THIS TECHNIQUE

Select two colleagues and form a group. One of you begins by sharing an experience involving a crisis that you have resolved successfully. Another member takes on the role of intervener by listening, understanding, and validating without offering any suggestions, advice, or expert information. The third person serves as the recorder who observes the activity and leads the feedback discussion. Once you have completed this process, rotate roles until each person has had an opportunity to practice this technique.

---

### Using Questions to Look for the Survivor

In addition to offering the LUV Triangle, as the crisis story is unfolding, you are constantly looking for the survivor. In fact, by your manner and questions, you are inviting the person in crisis to join you in this search. To help you look for the survivor, you will be using questions, which can be powerful crisis intervention tools. Questions gather information, of course, but more important, they communicate important messages. By asking about strengths and coping, you invite a person in turmoil to pause, reflect, and dig for material that can be used to piece together a response that holds promise for resolving the crisis.

You may feel tempted to use questions to gather details about the crisis. You may be curious about all who were involved, exactly what were the circumstances, and precisely how these events unfolded. However, such probing can be counterproductive because it focuses on the victimization, rather than the resilience of the survivor. Besides, people typically need little encouragement to talk about the sequence of events that make up their crisis experience. Therefore, your questions should explore strengths, resources, successes, and possibilities. These questions encourage the person in crisis to envision vivid and powerful images of surviving and thriving, rather than detailed portraits of victimization or despair. You continue to acknowledge "crisis-talk," but you also persist in seeking "survivor-talk."

**Presumptive Questioning for Resilience.** Ask open-ended questions, such as ones beginning with "What . . . ," "When . . . ," "How . . . ," "Where . . . ," and "Who . . . ," which presume strengths and resilience. Such questions are a part of an excellent strategy for finding the survivor. For example, if you were to ask tentatively, "Has there

## Listening In on Crisis Intervention

Review the narrative at the beginning of the chapter to refresh your memory regarding the crisis that Marcos is confronting. Following his nightmare, Marcos decides to contact a crisis counselor, who opens the session by introducing herself and asking simply, "What can we do together that would be most helpful to you?" An even briefer opening question would be, "How can I help you?"

Notice that the intervener doesn't ask, "*Can* I help you?", which suggests that the intervener is the expert and, furthermore, not really sure if she can help or not. Instead, the crisis intervener's question sets up expectations for resolution, promotes collaboration, and subtly underscores the survivor's resilience. We will discuss more presumptive questions later in this chapter, but we wanted to call your attention to the fact that your opening question implies resilience.

During the first 10 minutes of their session, Marcos pours out his story, including all the details in the narrative that you read. As we pick up their session, notice how the intervener communicates to Marcos that she is listening, understanding, and validating.

MARCOS:  At first, all I wanted to do was to make the pain go away. I wanted to drink myself into a stupor, the way I sometimes did before I married Juanita. (*He pauses and sneaks a glance at the intervener as if he were expecting some disapproval, but instead notices her expression of acceptance.*) Yeah, I was a pretty wild guy.

INTERVENER (*Nodding her head slightly and making eye contact*): Hmmm (*Leaning slightly forward to communicate that she is engaged and waiting to hear more*).

MARCOS:  I then remembered that dia de los Muertos (All Souls' Day) is gonna be celebrated in a few days. That's when Mexican families get together to honor their dead. Don't get me wrong, we're not crazy, but we do think that our departed loved ones communicate with us . . . in a lot of different ways. Maria was just a baby and couldn't talk, but she could really communicate with me—with her eyes, her crooked little grin, and her cooing. You know, like when mourning doves coo.

INTERVENER:  I can tell by the tender way that you talk about Maria that you love her dearly and you now miss her so much. I could almost hear those sad sounds of the mourning dove as you were describing their cooing.

MARCOS:  You're making me sound too sane, though. Hell, I've been having these really weird thoughts. As I was driving over here, this guy's name came popping into my head. He's an old drinkin' buddy from when I was hangin' around the docks. I never knew his first name, but everybody called him "Seagraves." I couldn't remember what his face looked like, either, but I suddenly pictured in my mind this coffin at the bottom of the sea. It sent a cold chill down my spine and I couldn't figure out what it meant. But then it came to me—"Seagraves" are graves at sea. You see, if I drowned, it would be just like Maria suffocating in her crib. (*He offers an ironic chuckle.*) I mean, I'm not really going to drown myself, but I wish I could get those weird thoughts out of my head.

## Reflecting on This Segment

1. In what ways has the counselor used the LUV Triangle?
2. How might you respond to Marcos' final statement?

ever been a time in your past when you have had to face a dangerous situation?", someone can easily respond with a simple "No." However, if you ask, "When you have had to face a dangerous situation in the past, how did you manage to handle your fear?", the person will likely feel more encouraged to come up with something. Use presumptive questioning any time that you want someone to explore strengths and discover resources.

**Presumptive Leads for Resilience.** A related technique invites a person to discuss strengths and resources but is not strictly a question. A presumptive lead could be a request, such as "Tell me about a time when you thought you did a pretty good job handling a tough situation." Or the lead could be a simple statement, such as "I imagine that you've been through some troubled times before." Implicit within these messages is the presumption that the person has had some successes in facing and dealing with crises. Such statements encourage the person to elaborate on survival experiences.

## Listening In on Crisis Intervention

Review the story at the beginning of the chapter and the previous segment. A little later in the session, the intervener uses the following questions with Marcos to invite him to explore his own strengths and resilience. Notice how the intervener uses both questions and the LUV Triangle in this segment.

INTERVENER: (*After listening and validating Marcos, the intervener uses the following question.*) How in the world did you get yourself to talk to me, a stranger, about all this?

MARCOS: Mmmm . . . Well, I'm not really sure how I did that. I guess that I just decided that I'd better talk with somebody fast because I was starting to sink into this deep, dark pit that I couldn't see any way out of.

INTERVENER (*Checking her understanding by offering a reflection*): So, as you felt yourself sinking into this pit, you decided that one way out of it might be to reach out to somebody else.

MARCOS: Yeah. I figured that it was worth a shot. My baby Maria loved life and I know that she wouldn't want me to waste the rest of mine.

INTERVENER (*Using the words of Marcos to frame an open-ended question*): What sort of things will you be doing when you're living your life more fully?

MARCOS: I don't know . . . (*Long pause as he reflects*) . . . I could . . . I mean, I guess that maybe I would be talking to Juanita like I used to.

## Reflecting on This Segment

1. In what ways has the counselor used questions productively?
2. How might you respond to Marcos' final comment?
3. Write two presumptive questions that you could ask Marcos.

## Listening In on Crisis Intervention

Let's return to the intervention with Marcos. Continuing with their interaction, the crisis intervener makes use of getting through questions. Again, note how the intervener continues to interweave questions and the LUV Triangle.

INTERVENER: You know, Marcos, as you've been sharing your story with me, with all the heartbreak you've been feeling, and the sadness you've been enduring, I've had a question that keeps popping up in my mind over and over again. How in the world have you been able to get yourself through all this?

MARCOS: (*Pausing, he sighs deeply, tilts his head, gazes off to the side, and brings his hands, clasped in a prayerful manner, to his lips.*) Mmmm . . . You know, I have no idea how I even got dressed for the funeral . . . It was like I was a zombie going through all the motions. Whenever I would feel that I just couldn't go a step further, that's when I just wanted to yell, "That's it! I've had it! I can't go on with this!" But somehow I'd wind up taking that next step.

INTERVENER: So even you aren't exactly sure yet how you were able to do everything that you wound up doing. I'm just wondering, where did you find the strength to somehow take that next step?

MARCOS: Well, it's kinda funny, but when I think back to those times, I would find myself reaching into my pocket and holding on to Maria's teething ring. I've been carrying it ever since I grabbed it to bring with her to the hospital. I thought then that she would be needing it, but I guess I'm the one who needs it now.

INTERVENER: Wow! By doing something as simple as holding onto Maria's teething ring, you were able to find the strength to go on.

MARCOS: Yeah, but we both know that it won't bring my baby back.

## Reflecting on This Segment

1. In what ways is the intervener using questions?
2. How does the intervener continue to use the LUV Triangle?
3. How might you respond to Marcos' final comment?
4. Write two more getting through questions that you could ask Marcos.

**"Getting-Through" Questions.** No matter how recently the crisis event has occurred, by the time that somebody has contacted you, he or she has already engaged in the active process of surviving. Somehow, some way, the individual has managed to chart a course through the chaos, turmoil, and dangers to connect with you. Asking about the ways that someone has been able to get through up to this point is a way of focusing your intervention on what is working, instead of what was broken. Such questions help crisis victims to begin seeing themselves as survivors. Remember—the fact that the person is alive is incontrovertible evidence of his or her ability to survive.

You are asking questions that underscore the fact that the person has surely done something right or you wouldn't be speaking together. The rape survivor was able to come up with some way to find refuge, the flood survivor did something to avoid being drowned, and even the person considering suicide has found a way to choose life long enough to connect with you. By the way, notice that obituaries always say the deceased is "survived by" those loved ones who remain alive.

Some common getting-through questions are:

- "How did you get yourself to do that?"
- "How did you manage to handle the crisis the way that you did?"
- "What did you draw from inside yourself to make it through that experience?"

With most crises, you can ask these questions with a sense of genuine astonishment. Imagining yourself in that situation, you must certainly wonder if you could have done as well.

## PRACTICING THIS TECHNIQUE

As you did in the previous exercise, select two colleagues and form a group. Again, one of you begins by sharing an experience involving a crisis that you have resolved successfully. Another member takes on the role of intervener by going beyond the LUV Triangle by using presumptive and getting-through questions and responses. The third person serves as the recorder who observes the activity and leads the feedback discussion. Once you have completed this process, rotate roles until each person has had an opportunity to practice these techniques.

## RESOURCES FOR DEATH AND DYING

In crisis intervention work, you are never the only resource. In addition to someone's relatives, friends, co-workers, and neighbors, there are community agencies, volunteer organizations, support groups, hotlines, and Web sites that can be important resources in times of crisis. The following are examples of possible resources for Marcos.

The Compassionate Friends
http://www.compassionatefriends.org

The Compassionate Friends is a nonprofit, self-help organization that offers support to bereaved parents, grandparents, and siblings who have experienced the death of a child. There are hundreds of chapters in the United States and this Web site provides a chapter locator for each state. It also offers links to chapter Web sites, grief resources, and newsletters.

Partnership for Caring
http://www.partnershipforcaring.org
1-800-989-9455

This organization is dedicated to promoting end-of-life care. This includes offering support for medical and psychological needs. This site provides information on decision making and obtaining proper health care, stories from people facing death, links to other sites and resources for planning, and chat rooms and discussion groups for those interested in talking to others who are coping with end-of-life issues. They also provide a toll-free hotline.

---

**Essential Tools**

- Rely on the LUV Triangle as your most basic intervention.
  - ↳ Listen.
  - ↳ Understand.
  - ↳ Validate.
- Use questions to find the survivor.
  - ↳ Ask open-ended questions that presume resilience.
  - ↳ Ask "getting through" questions.

---

**FIGURE 1–7**   Essential tools of Chapter 1.

# SUMMARY

In this chapter, we have emphasized that crisis is a turning point that involves dangers as well as opportunities. In an emergency, something new emerges, and you can intervene at this crucial time to invite the resilient survivor to arise, like a phoenix, from the victim. People in crisis behave in certain ways, experience intense feelings, have common physical reactions, relate to others in characteristic ways, have certain thoughts and images about the crisis, and struggle with the spiritual meaning of the event.

Crisis intervention has the goals of reducing the dangers of the crisis while facilitating a positive resolution. As you can see in Figure 1–7, the fundamental techniques of crisis intervention involve listening, understanding, validating, and asking questions that evoke images of resilience. In Chapter 2, we explore the process of crisis resolution in greater detail.

## Segue to Chapter 2

To help you in moving on to the concepts and techniques in the next chapter, find a newspaper or magazine photograph of someone who is confronted with a sudden, challenging, and unexpected incident. From what you see in this photograph, imagine what this person is experiencing internally. Jot down a few phrases or words that come to mind as you reflect on your experience.

# 2

# Crisis Resolution: The Change Process

"Great emergencies and crises show us how much greater our vital resources are than we had supposed."
*William James*

"One must still have chaos in oneself to be able to give birth to a dancing star."
*Friedrich Nietzsche*

## CHAPTER GOALS

After completing this chapter, you should be able to:

- Become acquainted with chaos and complexity theories, and their implications for understanding change
- Appreciate the dynamic change process
- Be aware of the factors that contribute to crisis resolution
- Discover how to "find the pony"
- Learn to "track" resolution
- Listen for the survivor's crisis metaphors and transform them into metaphors for resolution
- Ask "moving on" questions to promote a positive resolution

# OVERVIEW

In Chapter 1, you read a brief review of the research on how resilient most people are in dealing with traumatic events. Don't forget it! It is vital that you keep in mind that, as a crisis intervener, you need not expect to hear only tragic stories of wretched victims who are in desperate need of rescue. Although they may be dealing with painful issues, nearly all people in crisis come to consider themselves survivors and even thrivers—not hopeless victims. They would likely be offended by your displays of pity. Furthermore, by conveying pity to a person in crisis, you run the risk of embedding images of helplessness rather than the story of survival (Fraser, 1998a).

On the other hand, do not expect to hear simplistic, uplifting morality tales and heroic stories of people confidently overcoming incredible odds and achieving victories of mythic proportions. Crisis *resolution* is more complicated than either a simple tragedy or an inspirational story. As an intervener, your job is to offer immediate assistance to a multifaceted human being who is struggling with a complex situation and trying to achieve a meaningful resolution (Walker, 1994).

In this chapter, we describe the process of crisis resolution, which can go on for several weeks or months after the crisis event. Although the crisis event itself may have been disturbing, it is often just the beginning of a long series of cascading repercussions. Survivors may have to cope with chronic medical problems, physical pain, disabilities, discrimination, and economic hardships that can continue for years later. In spite of both the acute and chronic challenges, most people, particularly those with social support, a sense of meaning, good regulation of emotional arousal, and problem-solving abilities, are resilient in times of crisis (Masten & Reed, 2002).

Remember that many of the typical crisis responses that people display also have their adaptive uses. Denial, for example, offers a survivor at least a temporary reprieve from a painful reality. Remembering or dreaming about a crisis experience gives a survivor the chance to process and deal with the enormous implications of a life-changing event. As tragic as many traumatic events are, there is the very real potential for victims to emerge from them with positive psychological benefits. For example, some of the most effective crisis interveners are those people who have survived their own tragedies and have gone on to lead thriving lives. As part of their own resolution, former victims can contribute to the resolution process of others.

Fraser (1995) criticized most crisis interveners for placing too much emphasis on merely returning people to stability rather than facilitating positive change. He argued that such a stance may often escalate crises and not resolve them. Influenced by the Mental Research Institute's work, Fraser (1998b) proposed that crisis intervention should involve amplifying positive changes toward a better resolution. In this chapter, you will learn methods to promote positive resolution of crises.

# CRISIS STORY

Trey loved fighting fires. Her husband said that it was probably in her genetic makeup because both her father and grandfather had been firefighters. Trey, whose real name was Patricia, flourished in her occupational legacy. Many people around the firehouse were very leery when she first came on board, but it only took a few weeks for her to earn her first citation for merit. Now, after 5 years of dedicated service, Trey was one of the gang.

On that hot August day, the dispatcher's call sounded like a routine grass fire. Everyone was familiar with the drill. The firefighters would race to the scene, sirens screaming and horns blowing, assess the situation, warn onlookers to move back, and quickly douse the fire. Most of the time, it took the crew longer to get everything cleaned up and put away than it did to extinguish the flames.

The dispatcher had said that the grass fire began when a homeowner burned a pile of leaves, but it had gotten out of control on that dry, windy Friday. Even though the unofficial motto around the station was "Expect the unexpected," there was no way the crew members could have prepared themselves for the scene that lay ahead.

As they pulled off the state-maintained road and onto the gravel lane leading to the grass fire, they saw a man at the edge of the flames. Even though he was some distance away and surrounded by smoke, they could tell his clothes had engulfed him in flames. "Oh, my God," Trey thought, "this guy's nothing but a human torch." Despite the noise of the engine, they could also hear his screams. One of the firefighters quickly called the dispatcher and made an urgent appeal for the rescue squad.

To make matters worse, the terrain was uphill, rocky, and scarred by ditches that the truck had to negotiate. Once the firefighters cut through a locked gate, they still had to go around a sturdy barbed-wire fence. Finally, Trey and another firefighter jumped from the slow-moving truck and ran the last 30 yards to where the man had disappeared into the wall of smoke. When they finally spotted him, they could see that he was a frail, old man who was still on his feet, but now staggering blindly toward a grove of trees. No matter how loud the two firefighters shouted for him to drop and roll, he failed to do so.

When Trey and her friend reached the old man, they tackled him and frantically smothered the flames with their own bodies. The old man was now whimpering quietly and curling into a fetal position. His shoes lay nearby, still smoldering as if they were pieces of charcoal. Trey reached out to hold the man's left hand, just about the only place on his body that wasn't charred, and told him, "We're here to help you, sir. We're gonna do everything we can for you."

The old fellow stared at Trey. His eyes were pleading, trusting, and looking desperately to her for relief, comfort, and solace. Trey remembered a quotation from a literature class—something about a person's eyes being windows to the soul. She wanted to avoid his heartbreaking gaze, but her eyes seemed to be pulled magnetically back to his. She was mesmerized and could not turn away. She felt so ashamed—all her training and hard work didn't seem to make any difference at the one time in this old man's life when he needed it the most.

Three hours later, when Trey learned that the man had died in the intensive care unit of the hospital, she contacted the counselor who works with first responders after critical incidents.

## Reflecting on This Crisis Story

1. What were your own reactions to this story?
2. What would it be like to be the crisis intervener with Trey?
3. What strengths and resources does Trey have?

# IDEAS

## Crisis, Chaos, and Complexity

*Chaos theory* and *complexity theory* are recent scientific discoveries regarding change and order in the universe. These theories have important implications for crisis intervention because they portray human beings as living with a dialectical tension. On the one hand, we seek growth, change, and novelty. On the other hand, we desire certainty, stability, and order. Our minds are constantly attempting to adapt to new information, a process that initially throws our thoughts into chaos, until we can achieve a new order. When people come to you in crisis, they are in psychological chaos and are seeking some way to reorganize their lives and resolve the turmoil.

From the perspective of chaos theory and complexity theory, the nature of change has three principles that are important in crisis intervention. The first principle is that large changes can result from small perturbations (Gleick, 1987). The notion of the "Butterfly Effect" gives us a vivid and poetic image of a new cause-and-effect relationship in the universe. If a butterfly flaps its wings over Beijing today, the weather may, some time later, be altered over New York as a result. The implication for crisis work is that a small intervention may ultimately result in profound change.

The second principle is that change can begin suddenly and resolve rapidly. Therefore, the sooner you intervene in a crisis, the more likely you are to have an impact on the resolution process.

The third relevant principle of chaos and complexity theories is that change is a complete reordering—something unexpected and new will emerge, and nothing is ever the same afterward. If perturbed, people first experience mental confusion or chaos, but then they will accommodate and make sense of what has happened by restoring order at a new level. Wainrib and Bloch (1998) described this transcendence from crises as the "Phoenix Phenomenon" (p. 27), after the mythic bird that rose from its own ashes. Your job as a crisis intervener is to help a survivor achieve transcendence through a positive crisis resolution. In an emergency, you are promoting the emergence of something new.

## Sandpiles and Creativity

A crisis is an event in which someone's thoughts and emotions become destabilized. It is a period of chaos. Eventually, the person in crisis arrives at a place where the ground is more solid and the events are more predictable. But it is a new place. What was before will never be again—something new has been created.

Jacob Bronowski (in Fichter, Baedke, & Frangos, 2002) claimed that all complex systems evolve through a series of "stratified stability" (p. 10). This phrase means that systems in nature go along for a while in a state of relative stability until they are thrown into chaos by unexpected events. In the midst of their chaotic process, they struggle for a new stability—which eventually comes—and then they settle down again until the next crisis.

The physicist Per Bak likened this process to that of a sandpile (Lewin, 1999). He stated that all open systems tend to operate at the edge of chaos, a condition that he terms *self-organized criticality*. Imagine, for example, a thin stream of sand, flowing grain by grain, onto a round plate. With enough grains on the plate, the sand will begin to pile up in the shape of a cone—wide at the base and peaked at the top—as if reaching up for the source of the stream of sand.

When the limitations of the plate as a base, the downward pull of gravity, and the height of the sandpile reach a critical state, then one more grain of sand dropped onto the pile can cause an avalanche. Most often, the avalanche is small; a few grains of sand will go trickling down the incline of the pile. But every now and then, just one more grain of sand added to a pile that has reached the critical state will cause the entire sandpile to collapse as a result of the Butterfly Effect. In everyday parlance, it is called "the straw that broke the camel's back." However, after the collapse, if the stream of sand continues to be added, the pile will eventually regain its shape, but this time it will have a wider base and will be able to reach higher.

Per Bak (1996) presented the behavior of the sandpile as an analogy for humans: "A personality reaches the critical state; then the impact of each new experience reverberates throughout the whole person, both directly, and indirectly, by setting the stage for future change" (Fichter et al., 2002, p. 38).

Minor avalanches occur in our lives all the time. When we encounter information that is novel enough to force us to accommodate our thinking to it, we achieve what Piaget called *learning*. When the many small abrasive encounters in our day make us feel like we are being nibbled to death by ducks, we can easily handle these minor avalanches. We make adjustments to life events constantly, and this process is our everyday creativity at work. However, following a major collapse of our sandpile, in the midst of the chaos, for a time it remains unclear whether we will be able to build back and transcend the crisis.

Chessick (1999) suggested there are two possible paths we might take after such a major shake-up of our world. One track is "neurotic" and the other "creative." Exemplifying the danger and opportunity in Figure 1–2 of Chapter 1, either path is possible following a crisis. Both neurosis and *creativity* are attempts to solve the same problem, and in a crisis there will be a fluctuation between the neurotic and creative states. Both are ways the person will try to resolve the chaos and return to a stable state. The neurotic path is an attempt to put things back the way they were, whereas the creative path tries to make something new from the situation.

The neurotic path is everyone's default. When a crisis event changes our world so that we suffer the loss of stability, our loved ones, our prized possessions, and our belief in a just universe, then obviously we want to have our old world back. When you work with people in crisis, you must honor this universal tendency toward "repetition and freezing," as Chessick put it. Listening, understanding, and validating are powerful ways to give honor to the survivor's crisis story. But somehow you must also provide the support for the person to go on, to rebuild, and to have the courage to face an uncertain future.

There is potential for creativity in all of us. Otherwise, we would not be able to solve the smallest problems that come up in our lives. A major crisis, however, calls for the summoning of all the creative resources a person has to build a new sandpile with a broader base and a higher reach. Perhaps your most important job as a crisis worker is to help the person to get back in touch with his or her own creative power.

## How Change Really Happens

People often turn to counselors or therapists to help them change. In the case of a crisis, people are thrown into a chaotic cognitive and emotional spin that calls into question their basic assumptions about life, the world, and even themselves. They are changing so fast that they are often unable to accommodate to this process. As a crisis intervener, you help a survivor to channel this change in a productive direction. *Change*, for better or worse, is the "stock-in-trade" of crisis intervention. For you to be most effective in your work with people in crisis, you should understand the change process as thoroughly as possible.

What is the sequence through which a person or system travels as change is taking place? How can we understand this process and help to guide it in the desired direction? If change is a constant process in nature, how does nature do it? What makes for a helpful change? It seems our old notions of change are becoming inadequate to explain this process. The new sciences of chaos and complexity are beginning to inform us how change really happens. The idea of change is, well, changing.

We typically think of change as a smooth and gradual process (Casti, 1995). Common sense convinces us that the ideas of continuity and gradual change are inherent in all processes, even though some processes may be more rapid than others. For example, the weather changes more rapidly than, say, the height of the grass on our lawn. But our everyday experience of change is that one thing simply builds on another and that small changes need time to amount to big changes. Casti pointed out that a minor delay in a subway train's arrival normally results in someone being only a few minutes late for work, or that cooking a cake at slightly above the recommended temperature only results in a mildly over-brown cake—"gradual changes in causes give rise to small, gradual changes in effects" (p. 44).

However, if you have seen the movies *Sliding Doors* and *Run, Lola, Run*, or even the old Christmas standard *It's a Wonderful Life*, you have the idea of how small changes can result in major effects. The premise of each of these movies is that if the main character were to miss the subway by just a few seconds, or be delayed for a rendezvous only slightly, then these seemingly small lapses would end up being life changing. Change is not necessarily smooth and gradual, not always continuous and cumulative. In fact, it is often catastrophic.

## *EXPERIENCING THIS IDEA*

The *Butterfly Effect* expresses the idea that dramatically different outcomes can evolve from a seemingly insignificant event. Think of an event in your own life that seemed trivial at the time, but cascaded into something large. For example, what led you to choose to become a helping professional? What might have happened if that event had not taken place? Write a summary of what was and what might have been.

## Crisis Resolution Versus Crisis Solution

If you were to look up the words *resolution* or *resoluteness* in the thesaurus, you would find some of the following associated terms: confidence, courage, determination, purpose, tenacity, persistence, and effort. These are certainly the feelings and attitudes we hope for our clients to possess, especially as they cope with a crisis situation. When you look for the survivor within the victim, you are helping the person recover these attitudes. We refer to the approach as *resolution-focused crisis intervention*.

Although many of the techniques that we describe here are drawn from the various brief and solution-focused approaches to counseling and therapy, people's crises are not merely "problems" in search of "solutions." In a thesaurus, the words associated with *solve* are: figure out, decipher, unravel, explain, answer, and unlock. When people solve problems, they figure out how to fix something, explicate a mystery, or come up with an idea for how to put something to use. Solution usually refers to dealing with things *outside* oneself.

Resolution, on the other hand, is an *internal* event. It involves an alteration of mood, a shift in thinking, or a change of heart. It is a transformation in people's points of view about life, the world, and themselves. People who become resolute are no longer in a state of vulnerability, indecision, or uncertainty. They have changed their old way of viewing the world in favor of a new and more useful way of seeing things. Thus, they feel more confident, hopeful, and are more focused on future goals, rather than past and present concerns. They have become resolute, with their minds made up, hearts set, and vision clear.

The central notion of this approach to intervention is that your focus is on promoting this positive resolution—not on reliving the crisis. Your task involves searching for strengths and resources—not identifying weaknesses and deficits. And you strive to uncover future outcomes—not past histories.

## Beyond Restoring Equilibrium

According to Caplan (1964), a crisis is defined as psychological disequilibrium brought about by an event experienced as hazardous and which seems beyond one's familiar coping strategies. People usually live their lives with the expectation that they will achieve their goals. When they are in crisis, however, this sustaining feeling of hope is lost.

Your job as a crisis intervener is to help the person in crisis to find the way to these important life goals that temporarily appear to be blocked. People cannot remain indefinitely in psychological turmoil. They will immediately begin to seek a way out. You can capitalize on this innate tendency of humans to restore equilibrium and resolve their life crises.

There is an important difference between restoring *equilibrium* and crisis resolution. Disequilibrium is the chaotic state that is characterized by confusing emotions, somatic complaints, and erratic behavior. Survivors feel strongly compelled to relieve their distress and reduce the disequilibrium. Most people can achieve this balance, with or without crisis intervention, within a few weeks or months.

However, restoring their former homeostasis is only the first step in the resolution process. Equilibrium is not resolution. People in equilibrium may be able to carry on with their lives, despite nagging feelings of vulnerability, rage, guilt, and shame. They may even be able to make some sense of the crisis event, despite their loss of hope that things will ever be better.

Viney (1976) suggested that crisis resolution is both the restoration of equilibrium and a sense of mastery of the situation, along with the development of new coping methods. Similarly, Fairchild (1986) stated that crisis resolution was an adaptive consequence of the crisis in which a person grows from the crisis experience by discovering new coping skills and resources to employ in the future. This is the result we hope for when we are doing crisis intervention.

## The Process of Crisis Resolution

The resolution of a crisis is not an endpoint, but a path. Horowitz (1986) offered a description of the entire process from the moment of impact. A person's first reaction may be an outcry of shock, a reflexive emotional response that often serves as a signal for help from others (Witztum & Malkinson, 1999). Or, psychologically recoiling from the experience, some may immediately turn to a period of denial, during which they do not accept the reality of the event and feel emotionally numb.

However, sooner or later, many people in crisis go through a period of frequent intrusions, during which there is a flooding of images and feelings about the event. Distracting and unwanted thoughts about the experience may disturb the survivor. There is a danger in considering the process as simple sequential steps that progressively and inevitably lead to a resolution. In reality, there is much ebb and flow to resolution. People in crisis may go for some time without thinking about the event and be unprepared when the images and thoughts once again intrude.

The longest period in the process of resolution is that of working through the crisis. Working through takes place at several levels. See Figure 2–1 for an overview of crisis resolution.

**Making Contact with Others.** Most victims of crisis develop into survivors without any formal counseling, but no one ever reaches resolution alone. From the very moment of impact, most people seek help from others and attempt to gain asylum from any physical or psychological threats. When they link with others for support, survivors usually turn to their relatives, neighbors, friends, or religious leaders, who form a natural helping network that can promote crisis resolution (McCarroll, Ursano, Wright, & Fullerton, 1993).

Because individuals in crisis often feel separated and cut off from others, it is essential for them to experience that they are not alone—that there are others who care about them and are available to help them (Benezra, 1996). *Social support* serves as an important buffer for those who are confronted with traumatic events (Sarason, Sarason, & Pierce, 1990).

In Chapter 3, you will examine in more detail the research documenting the importance of social support in helping someone to successfully resolve a crisis. You also will learn specific techniques to enhance your relationship with someone in crisis and to reconnect a survivor to these sources of support.

**Making Positive Meaning of the Crisis.** People in crisis may at first be in a state of denial, in which they do not accept that this event has happened (Kalayjian, 1999). At the point of impact, some people in crisis may be disoriented, dazed, stunned, and bewildered (Wagner & Linehan, 1998). Later, they may be able to acknowledge what happened to them, but they may be confused, not thinking clearly or completely about the current difficulties that they face. Just as with physical injury when the body may go into shock, with emotional turmoil, people seem to go into psychological shock. It is nature's way of keeping us from having to deal with horrible events all at once.

At some point, many people in crisis may find themselves plagued with thoughts of self-blame, in which they believe that they are responsible for failing to prevent the violence or the tragic consequences (Joseph, Brewin, Yule, & Williams, 1993). This self-blame is especially true for children who are in a stage of magical thinking in their

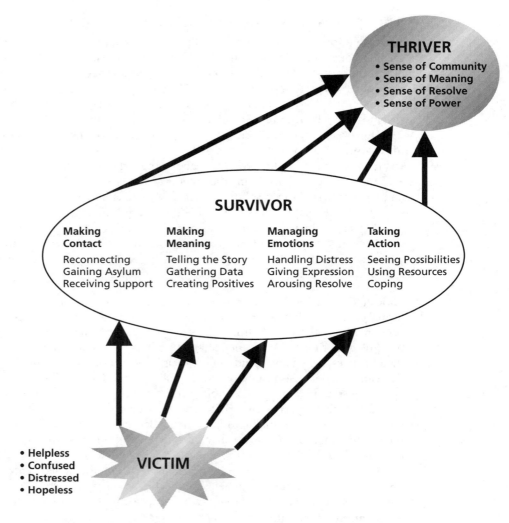

**FIGURE 2–1**  Crisis resolution process.

development. They believe that events are caused by their own wishes, fantasies, and behavior. Although many would consider self-blame to be maladaptive, research is emerging that such rumination may help survivors in reestablishing a sense of personal agency (Janoff-Bulman, 1992).

Those who are enduring a crisis may be preoccupied with the precipitating incident to the point of obsession, wondering how this tragedy could have happened to them, trying to find meaning in this suffering, and attempting to gain some understanding of how to handle their present problems. Their thoughts may be marred by constant worries, they may find themselves being easily distracted, and they may have problems remembering important facts.

Like a video cassette recorder, our mind is sometimes able to picture and replay mental images. This capacity to visually recall images from the past can be particularly upsetting for those who have faced catastrophic incidents. Months and even years later, certain sights or smells may still trigger in some survivors vivid and upsetting memories, or "flashbacks," of the events (Horowitz, 1986). Many individuals can close their eyes and picture in their minds a detailed scene of the incident. However, as psychologists have shown, memory is constructive and troubling experiences can be reconstructed in many ways. This is good news. You can help people reconstruct memories of the events in ways that also include the creative and determined ways they went about surviving.

For survivors of earlier crises, a more recent episode may be particularly disturbing because it stirs up frightening images, powerful emotions, and painful memories from the past. Still other survivors may not remember anything at all about the trauma. It is not unusual for people to have amnesia for part or all of such a terrible experience. At night, they may have disturbing nightmares that play out the events of the crisis. Children may have night terrors, which are especially vivid dreams that reenact traumas.

After the initial impact of the crisis event, survivors begin to recognize more completely the enormity of what has happened and its consequences. They start to collect any information needed to assess the impact and understand their situation. And, most important, those who successfully resolve crises begin to find some positive meaning in the event that has taken place.

The crisis shatters basic assumptions survivors have made about themselves, the world, and the meaning of life (Janoff-Bulman, 1992). In Chapter 4, you will read more about Janoff-Bulman's ideas, which provide an essential component of resolution-focused crisis intervention. What you can appreciate now is her point that by developing a new set of fundamental beliefs—ones that are richer and more complex—people can successfully resolve their crises.

Many survivors use stories, rituals, philosophical reflections, and theological contemplations to find *meaning* in times of crisis. Thompson (1985) found that survivors who identified some positive meaning in the experience were able to cope better. In another study, those people who were able to find meaning in the death of a loved one reported less intense grief reactions (Schwartzberg & Janoff-Bulman, 1991). Likewise, parents who were more involved in religion had a greater sense of meaning and less distress after losing an infant (McIntosh, Cohen, & Wortman, 1993). Studying survivors of three separate catastrophes, McMillen, Smith, and Fisher (1997) interviewed them about a month after the incident and 3 years later. The researchers found that those survivors who, during the first interview, were able to identify some perceived benefit, such as greater closeness with others or personal growth, were significantly better adjusted at follow-up.

In Chapter 4, you will examine more closely the process of making meaning of the chaotic and confusing experience of a crisis. You will practice specific techniques for coconstructing survivor stories from crisis narratives.

**Managing Emotions.** People in crisis often struggle with the intense emotional distress they are experiencing. In that struggle, they may acknowledge certain painful feelings they are having. They may have some difficulty in accepting these feelings in themselves. And, finally, people in crisis may grapple with the problems of expressing the feelings they are having.

Although we may speak of these powerful *emotions* as being separate from thoughts, at a fundamental level they are interconnected. In his autobiography, Carl Jung (1965) described his encounter with a Native American, Ochwiay Biano, who was chief of the Taos Pueblos. Ochwiay Biano told Jung that Whites were all mad because they said that they thought with their heads. Surprised, Jung replied, "'Why of course. What do you think with?'. . . 'We think here,' he said, indicating his heart" (p. 248).

We now know that it is with both head and heart that people think and that both must work in concert to make cognitions productive (Damasio, 1994). When people are in crisis, they think with profound emotion and they feel ideas deeply. Many survivors attain rich levels of emotional expression by articulating their experiences through writing poetry, drawing pictures, or playing music. We have all heard the cliché that an artist must suffer, but it is also true that those who are suffering often turn to art to give some creative form to their emotions.

Chapter 5 will discuss the recent and exciting conceptualizations of emotions. You will also learn how to help someone in crisis to reduce negative emotions of anxiety, depression, and aggression, while promoting such positive feelings of resolve as courage, hope, and compassion.

**Taking Action.** People resolve crises by beginning to take actions that address their dramatically changed circumstances. As described in Chapter 1, survivors often demonstrate an amazing resilience in coping by creatively drawing on the physical, emotional, financial, social, and political *resources* they have at hand (Bowman, 1997). For example, soldiers who have greater coping resources are less likely to have PTSD symptoms after being exposed to combat (Macklin, Metzger, Litz, & McNally, 1998). Survivors of sexual assault immediately begin to use active *coping* strategies following the incident (Frazier & Burnett, 1994).

In Chapter 6, you will learn how to facilitate resolution by helping survivors cope with the daunting challenges they face. The techniques you will practice in that chapter include reframing, using hypotheticals, and scaling.

**Transcendence.** The final period in the process of resolution is that of *transcendence*. Yogi Berra recommended, "When you come to a fork in the road, take it." It appears that many survivors of crisis have followed Yogi's seemingly impossible advice. The crisis was a major fork in their lives and many took both paths. They may carry to this day some scars, but they also carry that transcending sense of resolution as thrivers. By this time, thrivers have integrated the crisis experience into a new identity and have built a new life.

In a real sense, thrivers never truly reach a point where a crisis is forgotten or "behind" them. Instead, they incorporate that central experience within themselves by reauthoring or reshaping it. As one survivor of a natural disaster observed, "The flood is etched in our memories." But because the disaster is now seen from the standpoint of a thriver, rather than that of a victim or survivor, the etching is a different picture. This is the essence of "reframing," a technique that we will discuss in Chapter 4.

People who have resolved a crisis see both the turmoil and the resilience. As a result of this resolution, they have learned some important lessons about life and about themselves. They are different persons because of the resolution and they carry those memories, discoveries, and lessons with them as they continue on to thrive in their lives.

As Elizabeth Kubler-Ross (1997) said, "Should you shield the canyons from the windstorms, you would never see the beauty of their carvings" (p. 285).

---

## EXPERIENCING THIS IDEA

Return again to your resolved crisis and the story of Trey. Use the Resolution Model to help you gain a sense of the strategies that you used successfully and of the possibilities for crisis resolution in the narrative.

|                     | **My Resolved Crisis** | **Trey's Crisis** |
|---------------------|------------------------|-------------------|
| **Making Contact**  |                        |                   |
| **Making Meaning**  |                        |                   |
| **Managing Emotions** |                      |                   |
| **Taking Action**   |                        |                   |

---

Review the key ideas (see Figure 2–2) that you have learned in this section. The tools that you will be using in the second half of this chapter are based on the implications of these concepts. By understanding their rationale, you will then be doing much more than merely reciting catchphrases or spouting lines from a script—you will be applying principles to practice.

---

**Key Ideas**

- Chaos and complexity theories help us to conceptualize the change process.
- The Butterfly Effect reflects the cascading of consequences in which a seemingly minor event can lead to dramatic changes.
- Crisis resolution is a process that includes four important facets:
  - ✎ Making contact
  - ✎ Making meaning
  - ✎ Managing emotions
  - ✎ Taking action
- By resolving a crisis, people can achieve transcendence.

**FIGURE 2–2** Key ideas of Chapter 2.

# TOOLS

## "Finding the Pony"

*"Finding the pony"* (Presbury, Echterling, & McKee, 2002) is an approach that is helpful not only for someone in crisis, but also for you as the intervener. Finding the pony refers to a joke in which parents attempt to change their incredibly optimistic son. They hire a highly unconventional therapist who offers a treatment that requires the optimistic child to work all day shoveling out a huge room full of manure. The purpose of this procedure is to teach the boy that life is often harsh and unfair.

When the parents and therapist return to the child at the end of the day, they find the boy whistling cheerfully as he shovels scoop after scoop of manure. Perplexed, the therapist asks the incurable optimist what he's so happy about. The boy gleefully replies, "With all this horse crap in here, there's gotta be a pony somewhere!"

The point of the story for crisis intervention is that in every situation, no matter how awful, there is a beginning resolution that is hidden in the midst of all the adversity. Keep reminding yourself that the person in crisis is a survivor and avoid being sucked into any portrayal that suggests that he or she is a completely helpless and passive victim. Focusing on the survivor in the crisis story can help you restrain your impulse to rescue someone. Instead of "saving" people in crisis, your task is helping them find their pony—the strengths and resources that help them to persevere—under all the manure of a crisis.

In Chapter 1, you learned the fundamental crisis intervention technique of the LUV Triangle—listening, understanding, and validating. You also learned how to use both presumptive and getting through questions to look for the survivor in the crisis story. Both of these techniques, which are based on the resilience of the survivor, tend to emphasize the past. In this chapter, you will build on this foundation by adding three techniques that invite the person in crisis to build on the resolution that is unfolding in the present. These tools are tracking resolution, transforming crisis metaphors, and asking "moving on" questions.

## Tracking Resolution

Much like a miner who goes through the uncomfortable, tedious, and filthy process of sifting through sludge to find gold, your job as the intervener is to help the survivor find nuggets of resolution amid the muck and mire of the crisis experience. In the midst of their turmoil, survivors may wonder if they are going crazy; they may feel ashamed about the thoughts and emotions they are having, and they may be concerned that their reactions may be abnormal. Your attitude in these situations, communicated by your manner, is that many of the survivor's responses are not only normal and natural, but also adaptive and resilient. They are the very real beginnings of a successful process of resolution.

You walk a tightrope when you normalize the survivor's crisis experience. If you offer gratuitous comments like, "It's not your fault," "You couldn't help it," "Everyone feels like that," or "You're not crazy," you present yourself as the authority on *their* situation, rather than communicating that the survivor is the true expert of his or her own crisis. Your task is not to negate their feelings of guilt, debate them out of their shame, or convince them that they are not crazy. Instead of disconfirming their pain and anguish, your task is to help people recognize how they are already embarking on a process of resolving their crisis.

One technique you can use to achieve this goal is *tracking resolution*. As we described in the first half of this chapter, people confronted by catastrophic events begin immediately to try resolving the crisis using four common strategies. They reach out to others for support, grapple to make meaning of the experience, work to manage their emotions, and come up with coping strategies. From the point of impact, survivors are beginning their resolution process, to a greater or lesser degree, on all four of these fronts. However, people in crisis are more aware of their sense of alienation, confusion, distress, and failure.

Tracking is a basic counseling technique that communicates that you are following the client's words or actions. In play therapy, you are using the technique of tracking when you describe the actions of the child engaging in play (Landreth, 1991). Tracking, in the purest sense, is acknowledging, paraphrasing, or describing whatever the person is saying or doing. The technique is a fundamental part of the LUV Triangle because following someone's words and actions can communicate that you are listening, understanding, and validating. However, tracking resolution is a subtle and gentle intervention that does more than merely follow the words. In fact, you are beginning to coconstruct a story of resolve from the person's crisis narrative.

Tracking resolution involves two simple maneuvers:

- When you acknowledge someone's initial crisis experience, you take care to *refer to it in the past tense and place it within a particular situation*. With this technique, you are underscoring that the incident occurred in a certain time and place. Using the past tense and emphasizing the specific circumstances are subtle ways of framing the crisis experience in a temporal and situational context. You are suggesting that the crisis experience took place back there and then, while change is taking place here and now. It is typical for the crisis incident to dominate the survivor's attention and to take on proportions that seem to dwarf a person's abilities and resources to deal with it. Tracking resolution offers the survivor some beginning sense of distance from the turmoil and an appreciation for his or her own strengths. At times, people sometimes seem to fall under the dramatic power of their crisis stories and tell them in the present tense as if the events were unfolding in the moment. For example, a survivor might describe her sexual assault by saying, "I'm walking toward my car when this guy comes out of nowhere and grabs me." By placing this experience in a particular time and place in the past, your tracking response to this statement could be, "It sounds like you *had* absolutely no idea at all that you *were* in any danger when that guy *assaulted* you."
- When you note the strengths that the person is displaying, you *describe the resolution in the present tense*. By this technique, you are drawing attention to the dynamic process of resolution that the survivor is currently undertaking. Be particularly alert to the ways that the person is connecting to others, exploring issues of meaning, managing emotional arousal, and coping with the crisis. Remember that the one obvious act of resolve that you can always turn to is the fact that the person is talking to you.

Examples of tracking resolve using the present tense include:

"Now *you're getting* together with the people who can give you a lot of emotional support during this tough time."

"You're *finding* out everything you can about this particular form of cancer."

"It sounds like you're *taking care to handle* all the feelings that this has stirred up."

"From what you're saying, it seems like *you're exploring* lots of ways to deal with this situation."

You can also combine these two maneuvers into a single intervention that places the crisis incident and initial reactions in the past tense and uses the present tense to describe the beginning process of resolution. However, in your attempt to alert people to the emerging resolution, take care not to negate or diminish the pain and suffering that the crisis incident has caused.

For example, the person might say, "I just can't keep anything straight. I'm walking around in a daze most of the time, and I just keep going back to that moment. You know, I must be going crazy." Your response could be something like, "It sounds like since this happened, *you've felt* really confused and dazed. Sometimes *you've even wondered* about your own sanity. Now, I see you *sorting* through all these reactions to get back to where you're feeling more like yourself again." Notice how the intervener gently placed her distress in the past tense and subtly put the resolving process in the present tense.

## Listening In on Crisis Intervention

Before listening in on the following crisis intervention, go back and review Trey's story at the beginning of the chapter to familiarize yourself with her crisis. In the first 15 minutes of their time together, Trey describes the incident while the intervener offers active listening, empathic understanding, and respectful validation. At times, he also asks getting through questions about how Trey was able to handle the incident.

In the following segment, the intervener tracks the resolution he sees Trey demonstrating. Notice how Trey refers to the crisis event by using the present tense. Pay attention to how the intervener then subtly places the crisis in the past and tracks Trey's resolve using the present tense. Finally, note that the intervener also regularly returns to the LUV Triangle.

The segment begins as Trey focuses on a particular aspect of the incident.

TREY: The part that really gets to me is when I'm holding this guy's hand. (*As Trey says these words, she reaches out as if she is gently grasping an imaginary hand.*) He's staring at me with these big, stunned eyes, just quietly whimpering like a poor puppy dog who's been hit by a car. This man, who's old enough to be my grandpa, is putting his total faith in me to save him . . . (*She turns her head to gaze out the office window. Then, as if she is witnessing the scene being reenacted outside on the lawn, she brings her hand to her mouth, and begins to cry. She speaks haltingly, trying to choke back a sob or two that breaks out.*) But there's really nothing there for me to work with. There's *nothing* that I can do.

INTERVENER: Back there, when that man was looking up into your eyes, you sensed that he was putting his trust in you to do whatever could be done. And now you're trying to figure out how you can come to terms with the fact that everything you could do then was not enough to save his life.

TREY: You know, when I'm working with someone who's been injured, I'm always saying encouraging things like, "Hang in there," or "You're gonna be OK," or "Everything's gonna be fine." But with this old man, I just couldn't bring myself to say those things. When I was holding his hand and looking into his eyes, I didn't want the last words he heard in his life to be lies. All I could do was say things like, "This shot will help reduce the pain," and "We're gonna do everything we can for you, sir." I was feeling so helpless knowing that there's nothing I could do for him.

INTERVENER: Besides giving this dying man the best medical care that you possibly could, it sounds like you made a commitment to honor his final moments with your compassion and personal honesty.

TREY: You know, I feel badly for admitting this to you, but I was relieved when I heard that he had died. My first reaction was to say a prayer of thanksgiving for God sparing him any more pain.

INTERVENER: As I hear you talk about this, one thing that goes through my mind is that you're making the same commitment here in talking with me that you made with that man—to be honest and real.

### Reflecting on This Segment

1. In what ways does the intervener track Trey's resolution process?
2. How does the intervener continue to use the LUV Triangle?
3. What are some of Trey's strengths that are emerging?

## *PRACTICING THIS TECHNIQUE*

Form a practice group with two colleagues. One of you begins by describing a crisis that you have resolved successfully. Another member takes on the role of intervener by tracking the resolution. The third person observes the interaction and facilitates the sharing of feedback. When you have concluded, switch roles until each of you has practiced this technique.

### Transforming Crisis Metaphors

As they tell their stories, many survivors automatically turn to metaphoric language to give voice to the intensity of their crisis experiences. Like a poet, they strive to express themselves in more figurative ways than merely stating the facts in detached, concrete, or objective terms. For example, in their account of the events, they may describe themselves as "being caught in a trap," "feeling lost," or "carrying a heavy burden."

Pay careful attention to the metaphors that the person is using. Sometime later in your intervention, you can transform these metaphors of crisis into ones of resolution. This technique accomplishes two important objectives. First, by using the language of the person, you are communicating that you are listening carefully and engaging in a dynamic process of building on his or her ideas. Second, by revising the metaphor to express resolution, you are inviting a survivor to contemplate future coping strategies.

When people use the common crisis metaphors mentioned previously, you can transform the metaphors in the following ways to encourage people to explore a future resolution:

- "And when you begin to make your escape from this trap, what will be the first thing you'll be doing?"
- "As you start to find your way again, what's one of the ways that you may be handling this situation?"
- "When you decide to share some of this heavy burden, who will you be turning to for help with this load?"

## Listening In on Crisis Intervention

As he continues his work with Trey, the crisis intervener transforms some of the crisis metaphors into ones of beginning resolution. Notice, however, that the intervener also regularly uses the LUV Triangle and tracks resolution.

TREY: You know, this whole thing is like a horrible nightmare. When I first see that man covered in flames, I'm thinking to myself, "This is just too bizarre to be true. It can't be really happening."

INTERVENER: Wow, that incident was so awful and unreal that it felt like a bad dream for you. I'm wondering, as you're beginning to wake up from this nightmare, what are you starting to do to reassure yourself that you're back to a safe reality?

TREY: I don't know for sure that I'm ever going to wake up . . . (*She pauses, sighs, and continues in a soft and carefully enunciated voice, her head tilted as if she is trying to hear a barely audible, distant sound.*) I remember having nightmares as a kid where a monster was chasing me. I'd try to get away, but I was running in slow motion. That's how I felt today when I was trying to get to that guy. It seemed like it took me *forever* to reach him.

INTERVENER: It was almost as if that nightmare you had as a kid had morphed into that real nightmare you went through today when you were trying so hard to move as fast as you could.

TREY: When I *finally* got to him, I had to jump on him, knock him down, and roll with him around on the ground to put out the flames. I got burnt, too, but that wasn't the worst part. What was really awful was that I could smell this sickening, sweet smell of scorched flesh . . .

INTERVENER (*He leans forward, engaging her further, and says with more intensity*): Trey, I *can't* imagine what it must have been like for you to have gone through all that and then to come in here and talk about it with me.

TREY: (*Now she looks directly at the intervener and she draws her face in a contorted, painful expression.*) You know how the smell of cigarette smoke can seep into your clothes? I feel like the smell of that charred man has seeped into me. All I can smell and even taste is that death that I couldn't stop.

INTERVENER: And this smell of death is sure a lot deeper and harder to get rid of than any cigarette smoke. I'm wondering what you're going to be doing to begin cleansing that smell of death from deep down inside you.

## Reflecting on This Segment

1. In what ways is the intervener using Trey's metaphors of crisis to invite talking about resolution?
2. How does the intervener continue to use the LUV Triangle and to track resolution?
3. How might you respond to Trey if she continues to dwell on her nightmare?

---

## *PRACTICING THIS TECHNIQUE*

Form a practice group with two colleagues. One of you begins by describing a crisis that you have resolved successfully. Another member takes on the role of intervener by listening for crisis metaphors and transforming them to metaphors of resolve. The third person observes the interaction and facilitates the sharing of feedback. When you have concluded, switch roles until each of you has practiced this technique.

---

### Using "Moving On" Questions

Most traditional crisis intervention approaches have focused on the *past*—the precipitating event and the survivor's reaction to it. Certainly, survivors have a need to tell their crisis stories, but you want to listen carefully for some kind of sign or evidence of an emerging resolution. At this point, you can ask questions that invite the survivor to begin thinking about the *future*.

In Chapter 1, you learned about getting through questions, which explore the strengths of the person, instead of his or her experience of victimization. These questions looked to the past to find nuggets of resilience, but you can use another kind of question to mine the future for clues of possible resolution strategies.

No matter what your favorite kind of music—country, hip-hop, rap, blues, or folk—you've heard many songs that deal with the theme of crisis. However, the most compelling songs go beyond merely giving expression to the pain, anguish, and heartbreak of a tragic situation. They also give voice to the possibility of a resolution. Songwriters have used a variety of metaphors for resolving a crisis, such as the dawning of a new day, the ending of a rainfall, or the lifting of a burden. However, one of the most common metaphors for the resolution process in songs is that of "moving on." For example, a highlight of the Academy Award-winning movie *Chicago* was the song, "Movin' On." In fact, in poetry, novels, movies, and other media, "moving on" is a phrase that you regularly encounter that symbolizes embarking on the resolution process.

Therefore, *moving on questions* are *open-ended, future-oriented,* and *presume an inevitable resolution*. These queries are excellent tools for inviting the survivor to envision a resolution. Instead of using the form of a question, you may offer a moving on lead, such as the request, "Now that you've begun rebuilding your life, tell me about the next step that you'll take." The lead also could be a simple statement, such as "I'm wondering what are some of the things that you'll be doing as you embark on this new chapter in your life."

Implicit within these messages is the presumption that the person *will* be resolving the crisis in some way. You're merely expressing curiosity about how this particular person will be achieving this resolution. Such statements encourage the person to explore the future as he or she embarks on the resolution journey.

Some common moving on questions are:

- "As you begin to resolve this painful time in your life, how will your life be different?"
- "When you leave here, what do you see yourself doing right away?"
- "As you embark on your journey of resolving this crisis, what will be your next step?"

## Listening In on Crisis Intervention

Let's return to the intervention with Trey. Continuing with their interaction, the crisis intervener has been listening, understanding, and validating Trey's story, which includes an emerging resolution process. Note how the crisis intervener makes use of moving on questions, but interweaves these questions with offering the LUV Triangle.

TREY (*Bringing her head up to face the intervener with an expression that seems both pained and curious*): You remember that movie, *Dead Man Walking*? Well, that's what that old man was—a dead man who was still walking. From my training, I knew that the kind of burns he had all over his body had turned his skin into something like dry, brittle leather. He couldn't last more than a few hours and then he was going to die a painful death. Now, that guy Sean Penn played in the movie was a cold-hearted murderer who deserved to be electrocuted, but I keep asking myself, "What in the *world* did this sweet old man ever do to deserve this kind of death?"

INTERVENER (*Leaning forward, looking into Trey's eyes, and tilting his head to one side*): So the thought that you've been pondering is, "How horribly unfair it is that an innocent, harmless old fellow like that would have to suffer such an awful death."

TREY: Yeah, I can't think of any reason at all. It just doesn't make any sense. Nobody should have to die like that!

INTERVENER: And as you continue to go on with your life without any easy answers coming to mind, I imagine that must be really disheartening for you. What's one of the things that you're going to do to help yourself begin to feel better about life again?

TREY: I don't know for sure . . . (*She glances down, slowly waving her hand in front of her face, almost as if she's clearing away the cobwebs.*) I just want my husband to hold me. Right now, I feel really beat up, but also kinda numb. It's like when I've gotten a shot of Novocaine at the dentist, only this time I got the shot in my heart. When the Novocaine starts wearing off, it's still gonna hurt and so I'll want to start taking it easier on myself.

### Reflecting on This Segment

1. In what ways is the intervener using questions?
2. How does the intervener continue to use the LUV Triangle and to track resolutions?
3. How might you respond to Trey's final comment?
4. Write two more moving on questions that you could ask Trey.

## *PRACTICING THIS TECHNIQUE*

As you did in the previous exercise, select two colleagues and form a group. Again, one of you begins by sharing an experience involving a crisis that you have resolved successfully. Another member takes on the role of intervener by going beyond the LUV Triangle by using moving on questions and responses. The third person serves as the recorder who observes the activity and leads the feedback discussion. Once you have completed this process, rotate roles until each person has had an opportunity to practice this technique.

## RESOURCES FOR FIRST RESPONDERS

Law enforcement officers, firefighters, and emergency medical technicians are some of the first responders to dangerous and tragic events. Just because they are trained professionals does not mean that they do not have personal responses to these life-threatening and painful circumstances. In addition to someone's relatives, friends, co-workers, and neighbors, there are community agencies, volunteer organizations, support groups, hotlines, and Web sites that can be important resources in times of crisis. The following are examples of possible resources for Trey.

National Volunteer Fire Council
http://www.nvfc.org/index.html

The National Volunteer Fire Council (NVFC) is a nonprofit membership association representing the interests of the volunteer fire, EMS, and rescue services. The NVFC serves as the information source regarding legislation, standards, and regulatory issues.

*The Firefighter's Guide to Managing Stress*

This practical book by Wayne D. Ford was published by Management Advantage in 1998 and includes an audiotape of stress management exercises.

---

**Essential Tools**

- "Find the pony" by discovering the beginnings of resolution.
- Track resolution.
  - ⮡ Refer to crisis in the past tense and place it in a particular situation.
  - ⮡ Describe the survivor's resolution in the present tense.
- Transform crisis metaphors into ones of resolution.
- Ask moving-on questions that presume future resolution.

---

**FIGURE 2–3**  Essential tools of Chapter 2.

## SUMMARY

In this chapter, we described how crisis resolution involves connecting with others, making positive meaning of the experience, making use of distress, and taking action. As you can see in Figure 2–3, you also learned techniques, such as tracking the resolution, using the survivor's metaphors, and asking moving-on questions, that encourage the person to continue resolving the crisis. In the next chapter, we turn to the practical challenges and opportunities of providing support to individuals in crisis.

### Segue to Chapter 3

At the end of Chapter 1, we asked you to browse through a newspaper or magazine to find a photograph of someone in crisis. To prepare you for the ideas and tools in the next chapter, look for a photograph that also includes at least one other person relating to the survivor. Reflect on that interpersonal encounter. What does the other person offer?

# 3

# Making Contact: The Power of Connecting

*"By ourselves we suffer serious limitations. Together we can be something wonderful."*
*Max DePree*

## CHAPTER GOALS

After completing this chapter, you should be able to:

- Appreciate how social support provides a powerful buffer in times of crisis
- Understand the central roles of altruism, attachment, empathy, and rapport for humans in distress
- Value the relationship as a fundamental tool of intervention
- Use the telephone, the Internet, and outreach services to make contact with people in crisis
- Use "reaching out" questions to identify resources
- Offer an encouragement interlude to a crisis survivor

# OVERVIEW

People do not resolve crises alone. Some of our greatest sources of strength in troubled times are other human beings. From birth to death, our lives are interwoven in an intricate tapestry of relationships that nurture, protect, enliven, and enrich us. However, when people are in crisis, they are even more likely to turn to others for support, comfort, and assistance (Berscheid, 2003).

As we discussed in Chapter 2, making contact with others helps to promote a positive crisis resolution. One of the major contributing factors to resilience is social support. In American society, with its strong value of rugged individualism, we typically do not appreciate just how embedded we are in a complex web of interdependence throughout our lives (Berscheid, 2003). At a fundamental level, successful crisis intervention can take place whenever a person in crisis comes into contact with someone who is not in crisis—but who happens to care. The sooner a survivor makes this contact, the better.

Traditional approaches to counseling and therapy typically involve conditions that limit someone's immediate access to help and set up unnecessary barriers. For example, most community agencies and private practices offer services that take place only in their offices and only with clients who have made appointments, participated in screening procedures, and arranged for payment of fees. As a result of these hurdles, only those people who meet certain conditions actually engage in formal counseling. Clients of counseling services are more likely to have adequate financial resources, time available during work hours, easy access to transportation, and a cultural perspective that values formal counseling.

In contrast to clients of traditional counseling and therapy, people who are experiencing crisis may feel stigmatized talking to a helping professional or momentarily caught in the belief that there is no assistance available. Therefore, it is essential that your crisis intervention efforts include outreach: going to the site of the crisis or to a natural setting, such as the school, home, or workplace. When it comes to crisis intervention, passively waiting in our offices is a strategy that offers too little, too late.

In this chapter, you will explore how the bonds that tie us to one another as human beings—altruism, attachment, empathy, and rapport—are also the heart and soul of any successful crisis intervention. You will become acquainted with the special opportunities and challenges of making contact with survivors by telephone, Internet, and outreach services. Finally, you will also practice specific techniques, such as "being with" someone in crisis, exploring resources, and engaging in an encouragement interlude.

# CRISIS STORY

Still dressed in his fast-food uniform, Ralph had rushed to the hospital when he heard the news about his son, Brad. Now, sitting in the waiting room, Ralph thumbed through old magazines, unable to concentrate on anything for more than a minute or two. He found himself feeling the same way he had over 17 years ago as an expectant father waiting in the maternity ward—hopeful, yet also full of dread. His wife's pregnancy had been difficult from the start, and on more than one occasion, they feared that she had miscarried. The birth turned out to be both complicated and tragic because Brad had been a breech baby and Nancy died. All these years later, Ralph was waiting again—this time to see what his meeting with the emergency mental health people would bring.

Brad had been a charming, playful child who went through a transformation when he became an adolescent. Now, he was a brilliant, complicated, and artistic teenager. Until recently, Ralph had assumed that his son's mood swings were fairly typical for somebody his age. However, the emotional roller-coaster ride of adolescence had been much wilder for Brad. The highs were higher, the lows were lower, and both the ascents and descents were much steeper. When Brad was feeling dejected, his sense of melancholy was funereal. But when he had some new idea for a sculpture, the inspiration struck him like a bolt of lightning. Brad would scramble to find a piece of scrap paper, furiously scrawl a rough sketch in broad, sweeping lines, and then frantically begin to sculpt. Ralph could almost see the sparks flying around his son.

The scene reminded Ralph of the old black-and-white Frankenstein movies when the scientist threw the switch, the arc of electric current flashed, and new life was created. At first, Ralph was delighted with his son's exuberance because it evoked such enchanting memories of Brad's mother, who had also been an artist with frequent periods of inspired and intense creativity. But now, Ralph thought, life had become, like in the old movies, a monster. During the past few months, Brad's episodes had grown more frenzied but less creative, more pressured but less joyful, and more reckless but less productive.

Over the weekend, Brad didn't sleep at all as he immersed himself in a marathon sculpting session. He was finishing a work for a local youth art exhibit. Ralph grew increasingly concerned when Brad remained in the basement and refused to stop working, even to eat a meal.

Whenever Brad had one of his "lightning bolts," as he called them, Ralph found that his own behavior changed, too. Worried and distracted, he would only nibble at the food—his son's favorite dishes—that he had prepared to entice Brad into eating. At night, he stayed restless and awake, listening for the sounds of his son finally coming to bed. Every so often, Ralph would open the basement door and call out his son's name in a tentative, questioning manner, as if he were uncertain who the person downstairs really was.

Brad's response was typically a forced and breezy message of "Yeah, Dad, don't worry! I'm fine!" But Ralph could tell that Brad's reply was tinged with annoyance for yet another interruption. He would try to reassure himself by thinking, "I have a teenage son who's staying at home, working on a big project, and not doing drugs. I should just let him be," but he remained apprehensive.

When Ralph awakened from an uneasy sleep Monday morning, he found a long and rambling note on the kitchen table. Brad's "divinely inspired creation" was finally completed and he was taking it to the local community center for the exhibit. Concerned about his son's state of mind, Ralph tried telephoning the center, but it was not open. After all, it was only 7:00 in the morning. He decided to go to his morning job and call from there during his break.

Later, when he was able to piece together the sequence of events, Ralph calculated that he was probably sitting quietly at the bus stop when "all hell broke loose" at the center. Brad had arrived long before the center was scheduled to open. He had run around the building, trying every door to see if it was unlocked, and was pacing at the front entrance when one of the maintenance workers arrived. The worker grudgingly helped carry in and set up the sculpture but noticed that Brad was glaring at the other artwork, muttering that they were "unfit to share the same space as my beautiful gift to the world."

Brad's words became even more agitated and rapid. "These aren't art—they're crap! I feel degraded just looking at them!" He then launched into a frenetic diatribe against the other works, deploring their superficiality, their lack of any depth or authenticity. At times, the maintenance worker would try to soothe the teenager, but Brad brushed aside the comments and continued his harangue, barking every word in a rush of protest.

"There's only one truly artistic statement I can make to communicate my complete abhorrence and total disgust with this crass pandering to popular culture! Life may be ephemeral, but true art is forever. Here's my final sculpture!" Brad took out a knife that he used on wood sculptures and began to carve away a piece of skin from his arm.

Horrified, the startled maintenance worker gasped, held up his hands as if to offer a benediction, and pleaded, "Son, please stop hurting yourself and put that knife down!"

With a dazed look of confusion, Brad silently held the severed hunk of flesh on the side of his knife. He examined it in a detached manner, as if he had merely sliced some gristle from a rare steak. Frozen in that position, like a child playing the game of statue, Brad remained until the ambulance and the mobile mental health crisis unit arrived on the scene. By the time Ralph called the community center, Brad had been taken to the emergency room of the local hospital.

### Reflecting on This Crisis Story

1. Certainly, Brad is in need of emergency mental health services, but what could you also offer Ralph at this time of crisis for him?
2. What are some of Ralph's strengths that emerged in this narrative?
3. What are some possible interpersonal resources that may help Ralph deal with this crisis?

## IDEAS

### Social Support

Connecting to other people is not only necessary for a fulfilling and meaningful life, it is also a fundamental need of human existence. Social support improves physical and mental health, promotes recovery from illness, and is particularly crucial to people who are going through periods of high stress (Holahan, Moos, Holahan, & Brennan, 1996). In fact, having few close relationships in one's life is a major risk factor for premature death—higher even than the well-known risks of smoking and obesity (Atkins, Kaplan, & Toshima, 1991). Smoking kills, but alienation from one's fellow human beings is even more deadly.

Like most other species, humans appear to be hardwired to turn to others in times of threat (Berscheid, 2003). In particular, people in crisis have a profound need to quickly share their stories with others. Rimé (1995) found that people share a vast majority of their emotional experiences—over 95%—within a few hours. When survivors confide their crisis stories with others, they typically experience immediate and positive physiological changes, including reduced blood pressure and muscle relax-ation (Niederhoffer & Pennebaker, 2002). Research on social support has consistently found that relationships offer many vitally important resources, such as affection, advice, affirmation of worthiness, useful information, practical assistance, and nurtur-ance (Reis, Collins, & Berscheid, 2000).

Pennebaker and his colleagues (Pennebaker, Francis, & Booth, 2001) have made some fascinating discoveries about how our interpersonal world can be a resource in times of crisis. By studying how people refer to themselves and others in their narratives, these researchers found that our use of language is a vivid reflection of our sense of con-nection to others. For example, the poems of poets who commit suicide do not differ in content or emotional tone from those by other poets. However, poets who take their own lives use more first person singular forms, such as "I" and "me," and mention other peo-ple less often in their poems. In subtle ways, their words give expression to their sense of isolation and alienation from others. In another study, Pennebaker and Graybeal (2001) found that people's sense of social identity expands dramatically in times of crisis. During the week following a highly publicized traumatic incident, people more than doubled their use of "we" and "us" (by 135%) and reduced their use of "I" and "me" by 12%.

---

## *EXPERIENCING THIS IDEA*

Think about a time in your life when you made important discoveries. These discoveries may have been how you thought about yourself, your attitudes about life, or your place in the world. Now pick one per-son who influenced you the most as you went through this experience—someone who was there for you during this time of dramatic change. Recall your experiences with this person.

1. How did this person influence you?
2. What was it about this person's manner, apart from specific words or actions, that you found par-ticularly helpful?

---

### Why Do We Help?

In light of Darwin's notion that traits favoring survival tend to be passed on to subse-quent generations of a species, the question is, "What is the survival value of helping?" After all, for one individual of a species to help another, to display altruism, would ap-pear to have no survival value for the helper. So, why do we do it?

Often, the explanation given is that we humans have risen above our nature and have developed a moral code that includes altruism. Frans de Waal (1996) objected to this portrayal and argued that it is actually in our nature to help others. In fact, altru-ism, which has its origins in nurturance and attachment, is present in many varieties of mammals. One example is the prairie vole, a small furry rodent. This variety of vole is monogamous, and the female is particularly nurturing with her offspring. In contrast to some other types of voles, the prairie vole has a large number of receptor sites in its brain for oxytocin, a chemical that is sometimes referred to as the "cuddle chemical." Voles that lack these receptors are indifferent to their offspring and are sexually promiscuous. Oxytocin is associated with social attachment and love in animals and humans (Carter, 1998). Just before giving birth, females show a marked increase in oxytocin levels, which increases the availability of breast milk and seems also to stimulate maternal nurturing.

De Waal (1996) suggested that succorance has its origins in nurturance and made the following distinction between the two: "Succorant behavior [is] defined as helping, caregiving, or providing relief to distressed or endangered individuals other than progeny. Thus, a dog staying protectively close to a crying child shows succorance" (p. 41). If this same dog, according to de Waal, were to display helping behavior in response to the distressed yelps of her puppies, then this would be nurturance. He goes on to suggest that once we have been nurtured, we may go on to display succorant helping behaviors to others.

> Once tender exchanges between parent and offspring had evolved—with the one asking for and the other providing care—they could be extended to all sorts of other relationships, including those among unrelated adults. (p. 43)

So, being nurtured leads to attachment to the caregiver, which then extends to attachment to others, which then brings about helping behaviors. This benign cycle seems to be nature's plan to help us survive crises and go on to thrive in our lives as interdependent beings.

## How We Attach to Others

Our propensity for attachment, like many "wired-in" instinctual behaviors, comes as original equipment in the newborn. A baby seeks contact and attention from a parent by expressing discomfort, distress, or alarm. Ideally, this "primary attachment person" responds by caring for the child, ensuring the child's safety, and serving as a guide. From this relational base, the child will learn to control emotions, soothe himself, and form close attachments with others throughout life. Failing this, the child will grow up lacking what Goleman (1995) called "emotional intelligence."

The work of John Bowlby (1969/1982, 1973, 1980), perhaps more than the writing of anyone else, has influenced current thinking on the phenomenon of "attachment." The notion that a human infant requires certain responses from a primary caregiver to fully develop psychologically is now generally accepted and "solidly embedded in developmental psychology" (West & Sheldon-Keller, 1997, p. 1). Moreover, attachment is a lifelong process. As Bowlby (1977) put it, "Whilst especially evident during early childhood, attachment behavior is held to characterize human beings from the cradle to the grave" (p. 129). Well-nurtured infants become well-attached adults who help each other in times of crisis.

## How We Develop Empathy

Researchers have distinguished between affective empathy, which is the ability to understand another's emotions, and cognitive perspective taking, which is the ability to understand another's way of thinking (Flavell, 1992). Piaget (1926) performed famous and influential experiments on the failure of young children in perspective taking. His notion of "egocentrism" suggested that, before a certain age, children cannot escape their own experience and imagine what others might see from their different perspectives.

According to Piaget, before children would reach the next developmental stage, they would remain "clueless." However, recently researchers have found that even very young children can tune into others. According to Eisenberg, Murphy, and Shepard (1997), infants can discriminate among facial expressions of emotion in others. In fact, infants under 12 months of age can read adult expressions to monitor and guide their own behavior. Later, they learn to recognize and label the emotions of adults.

It appears that empathic understanding is present long before a child can even express it in words. According to Buck and Ginsburg (1997), our empathic ability is a wired-in social ability that has evolved over the eons and is suited to the condition of our being social animals. De Waal (1996) described touching cases of animals behaving "empathically" with one another in the wild. Species of animals, including the human animal, seem to care about their fellows, can understand their mental states, and will often help them in times of distress.

## Rapport

The term *rapport* is derived from the French verb *rapporter*, which means to bring back or refer. *Merriam-Webster's Collegiate Dictionary* defines the English meaning as "a relation of harmony, conformity, accord, or affinity." Your attitude is the crucial element in establishing rapport with another person. If you do not believe, deep down, that people are natural survivors who can resolve their own difficulties, then you cannot achieve full rapport with others. You will be suspicious of any signs of strength and resilience, and you will be on the lookout for evidence of pathology or denial. You may view their recovery as a "flight into health" and think that they are failing to appreciate the seriousness of their situation. In such a frame of mind, you would betray your misgivings by the tone of your voice, the reactions on your face, and the comments you make. So, the first step in the establishment of rapport in crisis intervention is to affirm your belief in the natural resilience of the person you are trying to help.

Walter and Peller (1992) discussed the *rapport* that is established between two people as being like dancing. In a dance, two people move together in rhythm, and it appears that one is leading and the other following. "However, on closer examination, one can see that the movements of both dancers are closely matched, calibrated, and mutually influenced. The dancing is a collaborative process, a nonverbal conversation" (p. 44). Rapport, like couples dancing, is not something you can do alone. It is something you both do. You can initiate the relationship, but rapport does not happen until the other person "buys in" and you establish a mutual rhythm. Furthermore, although you must continue to maintain your part of the relationship, you will find that you both lead and follow, making sure that you adjust your movement to changes in the movement of the other.

It may appear that you are the active member, while your helpee is passive. However, real rapport requires that both members be active. In typical ballroom dancing, the man appears to lead while the woman follows. But someone has pointed out that Ginger Rogers did everything Fred Astaire did when they were dancing—only she did it backwards and on high heels.

## Common Factors

All approaches to counseling and psychotherapy are nearly equal in their success rates, provided that certain *common factors* are present (Wampold, 2001). These factors appear to account for 9 times more of the variance in outcome studies than do the specific techniques designed for certain disorders. The most important common factor of successful interventions is the relationship, or alliance, that is established between the helper and helpee.

Frank and Frank (1991) identified three important conditions for successful counseling:

1. An emotionally charged, confiding relationship with a person who is offering help.
2. A belief that the counselor can be trusted and is able to provide help.
3. A mutually agreed upon perspective that explains the client's concerns, and a process for resolving these concerns.

Let's apply these conditions to crisis intervention. When you meet people in crisis and develop rapport with them, you can count on the relationship being emotionally charged. In fact, you may find that the person is so emotionally aroused as to not be in a position to carry on a productive interaction with you. In such cases, you must ask what practical help this person needs from you. For example, if you were to encounter someone who, after a flood, was frantically digging in the muck of her former residence for a photo album of her children, you probably should dig, too. Whenever people are too emotionally aroused, your job is to do something that will help soothe them, even if it is not a traditional counseling technique.

On the other hand, you may find people in crisis who appear rather stunned or emotionally numb. Instead of trying to get them to emote, you must realize that they are in psychological, and possibly physiological, shock. The time will come when they are more amenable to dealing with their emotions, but the moment has not yet arrived for them to talk about their feelings. You would do better to ask for their story, even if their narrative is not emotionally charged. Often people who initially appear emotionally flat and unresponsive will break through to their feelings in the telling. The important thing is for you to create a safe and undemanding relationship with them and be guided by what they need for you to do at the moment.

As for the second common factor, you must realize that when you arrive at a crisis scene, you may not be immediately trusted and accepted as a resource. It will be your actions, and not your words, that will convince people of your trustworthiness and helpfulness.

When you do *outreach* work, you may feel as though you are arriving dressed only in your underwear—all your protective armor is missing. You don't have your diploma attesting to your expertise, you are in unfamiliar surroundings, and you may wonder how helpful you can be in the current situation. This experience relates to the third set of common factors. You do not have the mythology that would exist if the person were coming to an agency or school office, being greeted by a secretary, and sitting in a consulting room with all the trappings that speak to your legitimacy as a counselor. You must rely solely on your ability to connect with someone and to convey your willingness to help.

Depending on the setting in which you meet people in crisis, you may have to start from scratch. If you are fortunate to have an intermediary, such as a school principal, a supervisor, or an influential friend who introduces you, then you have a "leg up," so to speak. This introduction will increase the chances that survivors will accept you. But the

```
┌─────────────────────────────────────────────────────────────────┐
│                          Key Ideas                                │
│  •  Connecting to others is a fundamental human need.             │
│                                                                   │
│  •  Social support is particularly important in times of crisis.  │
│                                                                   │
│  •  Human beings are hardwired to help one another.               │
│                                                                   │
│  •  Infants who are nurtured form healthy attachments and grow    │
│     into altruistic adults.                                       │
│                                                                   │
│  •  Humans develop empathic abilities before they even learn to   │
│     talk.                                                          │
│                                                                   │
│  •  Having rapport with someone requires that you believe in that │
│     person.                                                       │
│                                                                   │
│  •  Forming a helping relationship is in itself a powerful        │
│     intervention.                                                 │
└─────────────────────────────────────────────────────────────────┘
```

**FIGURE 3–1**    Key ideas of Chapter 3.

quality of the relationship you establish provides your entree and increases your chances of success.

As you review the key ideas of this chapter (see Figure 3–1), keep in mind that the most important aspect of successful crisis intervention is the relationship. Therefore, you must communicate to the survivor that you care, demonstrate that the person can trust you, and show that you will do your best to help. Without this foundation, your techniques will fail. In the following section, we describe how you can make contact with survivors, enhance your relationship with them, connect survivors to others who can assist them, and use your encounter to offer encouragement.

# TOOLS

## Linking

Most of the descriptions of crisis intervention techniques start with the encounter between the helper and the person in crisis. However, your work of crisis intervention begins long before that meeting. In this section, we describe how you can set the stage for successfully linking with people in crisis.

Your most fundamental task is to make yourself known as someone who can help in a crisis. You may be a school counselor who is wonderfully prepared to deal with children's crises, but if the teachers, parents, and children do not know you are such a resource, then it is unlikely that they will seek you out at those times. Or, your community agency may have developed an innovative program for suicide prevention, but if the people at risk do not know about your services, then you are merely a hidden resource. Whether it is done in person, in writing, over the telephone, or through the Internet, making contact with the person in crisis is an essential step in crisis intervention. Therefore, you need to do a great deal of planning and ground-work to have a service that is well-known, immediately available, and easily accessible.

No matter what particular form your crisis intervention service may take, you should develop an ongoing public relations campaign. Pursuing three strategies can help to ensure a successful campaign:

- First, identify not only those who comprise your *target population*, but also those community "*gatekeepers*" who may refer people in crisis to you. Are you focusing on one particular form of crisis—sexual assault, for example? Are you working with a particular age group, such as adolescents? What are your referral sources? Parents, school officials, social service workers, law enforcement officers, or court officials?
- Second, *develop your image* with these groups. You want to present your crisis intervention service as a trustworthy, reliable, and ultimately helpful resource.
- Finally, use informal networks and the media to *advertise* your service. Get your message "out there" through word-of-mouth, in-service training, program newsletters, public service announcements, brochures, newspaper articles, and community education programs.

Because crises are not limited to regular business hours, intervention services should be available 24 hours a day, 7 days a week. The more convenient a service is, the more likely people will turn to it in times of crisis. Telephone hotlines, interactive Web sites, and outreach services are just a few of the strategies for increasing accessibility. In the following sections, we describe each of these approaches, discuss their opportunities and challenges, and offer several guidelines for using them.

## Linking by Telephone

For North Americans and Europeans, crisis intervention has been, for several decades now, as close as the nearest telephone. However, now that wireless phones are ubiquitous, the telephone has become an even more important tool of crisis intervention by reducing response time and increasing accessibility (Ackerman, 1997).

Since their emergence in the late 1960s, *hotlines* and other telephone crisis services not only have increased in number, but also have gained acceptance by both the helping professions and the public. Many regional and national hotlines have 800 numbers so that people can call long distance free of charge. Even 10 years ago, an estimated 5 million telephone calls were made to hotlines in the United States (Roberts & Comasso, 1994). The advantages of these crisis telephone services are that they can provide free, anonymous, and immediate help. Their services include offering information, emotional support, and referrals.

In addition to hotlines, schools, social services, counseling agencies, and community mental health centers also rely heavily on the telephone for responding quickly to crises. Many community agencies offering emergency services have staff on call 24 hours a day, 7 days a week. From the initial notification to the follow-up contact, crisis counselors perform much of their work over the telephone (Kleespies & Blackburn, 1998).

The telephone also has become an integral part of traditional counseling. Most counselors and therapists offer telephone crisis intervention as an important adjunct to their face-to-face work with clients. However, few professionals have any training in using the medium.

**Power and Boundary Issues.** The telephone line is the "slender thread" that provides the only connection between you and the person in crisis. The survivor is in complete control of the duration of this conversation. At any point, the interaction can be terminated by merely hanging up the telephone—as anyone knows who has received a telephone solicitation. Although the telephone can be a valuable rapid response tool, many therapists find counseling over the telephone to be challenging and stressful (Kleespies & Blackburn, 1998). You have, however, many resources at your disposal for "hooking" the person on the other end of the line. Offering the LUV Triangle is a powerful way to reach out to the caller and to maintain contact.

**Dynamics of Intervening by Telephone.** Because the telephone medium is limited to the transmission of sound communication, the interaction between the caller and helper is affected in subtle, but potentially dramatic, ways (Echterling & Hartsough, 1989). To be an effective telephone crisis intervener, you need to consider the medium within which you are working (Waters & Finn, 1995). Here are a few suggestions to help you use the telephone productively in your crisis intervention work.

- *Track more. Tracking* is the term for "uh-huh's" and other paralinguistic utterances that let the speaker know that you are following the flow of the message. In face-to-face counseling, the client knows you are listening, even when you are silent, because you are able to communicate your attention and understanding with your eyes, face, gestures, and posture. However, on the telephone, the sounds you make are the only evidence you can offer that you are actually listening and understanding.

  If you are a beginning counselor, you may recall initially feeling uncomfortable with silences, but eventually you learned to tolerate, and even value, the significant pauses and lulls in face-to-face counseling. Silences can be powerful opportunities for personal reflection and inner exploration. "The silence around a thought," said Ackerman (1997), "can free it from distraction, give it perspective and dignity" (p. 248).

  However, even though times of silence can be beneficial, you are likely to find yourself offering a few more "uh-huh's" and other tracking comments just to let the caller know you are still there on the other end of the line. You will make up for the lack of visual cues by providing additional auditory signals that you are listening, understanding, and validating the caller.

- *Tune into nonverbal cues.* Verbal communication, the information transmitted by the words alone, is only a small part of what is communicated over the telephone. For example, the identical words, "Oh, yeah," could be said differently to communicate a defiant challenge, a grateful acknowledgment of a helpful reminder, or an enthusiastic endorsement. It is how the words are said that expresses the emotional tone, intensity, shading, and subtle nuances of a message.

  In face-to-face counseling, you can rely on the visual forms of nonverbal communication to gain a deeper understanding of the words. On a crisis call, however, you are restricted to only what you can hear. Without the luxury of visual cues, you need to be especially sensitive to how the words are spoken.

- *Appreciate the intimacy of telephone communication.* The telephone may be limited to audio transmission, but it is also a medium that can have a confidential and intimate quality that promotes disclosure. Over the telephone line, callers are able to make contact with another human being, speak privately into the listener's ear, and yet remain anonymous, pouring their "hearts out into the small confessionals of telephones" (Ackerman, 1997, p. 177).

- *Use your body as you talk.* Even though the person in crisis cannot see you, it is still a good idea to express yourself as you normally would by your gestures, facial expressions, and body posture. Your physical involvement will help your attentive and engaged concern to come across clearly and naturally through your voice.

- *Take notes.* Because you don't have to make eye contact, you are free to focus on writing notes, drawing diagrams to connect information, jotting a reminder to check on a detail, or scribbling the outline of a strategy to pursue. Taking notes will help you organize your thoughts and remember salient aspects of the conversation. Be prepared—keep a pad and pen handy by the telephone.

- *Have vital resource information near your telephone.* In addition to writing materials, it is crucial to have relevant information, such as a reference book on drugs and a directory of local referral resources, at your fingertips. In a crisis, seconds count. Keep your resource information current and accurate. Programs and services are in constant flux in a community, so it is an ongoing task to stay current.

- *Maintain contact.* It is essential that you keep in continuous contact with someone in crisis until you both agree to end the call. Of course, no one likes to be put on hold. However, a person in crisis, who may already feel alienated, can easily feel abandoned, isolated, and rejected if you take another telephone call or put the call on hold. Never hang up until you are confident that the survivor is out of imminent danger and is ready to take the next step toward a positive crisis resolution.

---

## USING THIS TOOL

Form a group with two colleagues. One of you volunteers to share a concern while another volunteers to be the intervener. To simulate communicating over the telephone, sit with your backs to one another during the interaction. You can use Figure 3–2 as a guide for offering telephone crisis intervention. The third person volunteers to serve as observer and offers feedback after you have completed the helping session. In your group discussion, be sure to explore how the experience differs from face-to-face interaction. Take turns until everyone has had an opportunity to practice intervening over the telephone.

---

### Using the Internet to Link

An astounding number of Web sites have been developed to assist people in crisis. For example, a recent Google search using the word *suicide* had more than 4 million hits. Many of the sites provide helpful information about suicide, give opportunities for

---

**Successful Telephone Crisis Intervention Involves . . .**

- Tracking more.

- Tuning into nonverbal cues.

- Appreciating the intimacy of telephone communication.

- Using your body as you talk.

- Taking notes.

- Having resource information nearby.

- Maintaining contact.

---

**FIGURE 3–2** Telephone crisis intervention techniques.

people to share their stories, enable individuals who may be in crisis to electronically contact a volunteer, and provide referral information regarding local community resources. However, the quality and accuracy of the resources vary tremendously. In fact, one of the top 10 matches for suicide was a pornographic site. Like the Chinese symbol for crisis, the Internet offers both opportunities and dangers.

**Intervening in the Cyberworld.** Why go virtual? Seeking help by computer has a number of advantages. In the comfort and privacy of their own homes, people can connect with any resource that is on the Internet. With over 164 million computers in the United States alone, more and more people have easy access to online resources. In fact, help is as close as the nearest computer. Typically, no appointment is necessary to contact any of the crisis-related Web sites. People can take whatever time they may need to compose their messages before they actually contact a particular online resource.

Michael Feeny (2001) asserted that an immense number of online counseling and therapy sessions will be taking place every day in the not-too-distant future. At the time of his article, Feeny stated that estimates of online contacts between counselors and clients already ranged between 5,000 and 25,000 per day. As people become more sophisticated in the use of the Internet and as computing technology continues to become even more affordable, more and more people will turn to their computer when they are confronted with a crisis.

**Dynamics of Cyberintervention.** To do successful *online crisis intervention*, you have to recognize the dynamics of this medium. Like telephone hotlines, e-mail does not involve visual cues, but according to Feeny (2001), this apparent limitation may actually be an advantage. Because the person is not seen, he or she may feel a sense of anonymity and, as a result, be less inhibited and more candid. Here are a few suggestions for enhancing your effectiveness as a cyberintervener.

- *Use emoticons.* It is likely to be some time before computers will make it possible for you to do virtual face-to-face intervention. In the meantime, your cyberinterventions will remain text based. In person, you may be skilled in communicating warmth and acceptance, but you may have some problem doing so online. Bloom (2001) stated that new cybercounseling techniques must be developed to use the existing technology effectively. For example, Bill Lubart (in Feeny, 2001), who has a Web site called here2listen.com, uses certain ASCII icons to communicate nonjudgmental and caring messages. For example, he employs emoticons, such as the now typical :-) to communicate a smile, the :- ( for a frown, and ;-) for a wink. Other emoticons include :'( for shedding a tear, :-O for expressing surprise, and :-& for feeling tongue-tied. Such icons are quick and easy ways to communicate facial expressions that the reader cannot see.

- *Use acronyms.* Another online phenomenon is the common use of acronyms for the sake of brevity. If you are new to cyberspeak, you probably are not familiar with the dozens of acronyms that pop up in e-mail messages, electronic mailing lists, and chat rooms. The following are a sampling of acronyms that may be relevant to crisis intervention:

    > AFAIK = As Far As I Know.
    > AISI = As I See It.
    > ASIG = And So It Goes.
    > FWIW = For What It's Worth.
    > HIT = Hang In There.
    > HTH = Hope This Helps!
    > IMHO = In My Humble Opinion.
    > OTOH = On The Other Hand.
    > OTTOMH = Off The Top Of My Head.
    > POV = Point Of View.

- *Use emotional bracketing.* Developed by Murphy and Mitchell (1998) for online counseling, emotional bracketing involves inserting words and phrases that disclose the counselor's emotions that are behind the written text. In face-to-face interaction, these emotions can often come across easily through nonverbal communication. However, using a text-only medium, a counselor could quickly communicate emotions by writing, "It has been several weeks since I heard from you, John [concern, worry] and I would very much appreciate it if you could at least acknowledge this e-mail [feeling pushy, demanding]" (Bloom, 2001, p. 200).

- *Offer descriptive immediacy.* Another online self-disclosure technique is descriptive immediacy (Murphy & Mitchell, 1998), in which the counselor describes his or her own facial expressions, gestures, and body posture at the moment of reading or responding to the client's text message. Of course, these details would be easily available to a client in face-to-face counseling. By offering descriptive immediacy, a counselor can enrich the encounter with vivid texture. For example, the counselor might write the following text:

    > I was deeply moved by reading your account of how your young son is dealing with the events of 9/11. Even now, as I type this e-mail, I find myself stopping at times, lifting my hands from the keyboard in a prayerful gesture, closing my eyes, and imagining the scenes that you described.

The tone of this passage is reminiscent of White and Epston's (1990) narrative therapy, in which letter writing is employed to add power to brief therapy. One advantage of a written communication is that the person can read it over as many times as he or she desires and reflect in ways not possible in the moment-to-moment exchanges of the actual counseling session. On the other hand, by analogy, would you rather have a love letter from your sweetheart, or real live contact with her or him? A virtual, versus an actual, relationship may have its advantages, but it must also have its drawbacks.

- *Be aware of ethical concerns and legal issues.* It is easy to imagine the ethical difficulties you could encounter if you rely heavily on cyberintervention. The National Board for Certified Counselors (NBCC) recently developed guidelines for cybercounselors (http://www.nbcc.org). These policies include standards regarding the integrity of the counselor-client relationship, confidentiality, informed consent, client safety, quality of the hardware and software in use, attention to cultural issues, and appropriate local backup measures in case of emergencies. Helping professionals will need to pay more attention to the issues that emerge as online counseling becomes more prevalent, but at least this is a start. Clearly, more research is needed to determine the relative efficacy of online crisis intervention. Although it does involve some perils, computer technology's potential as a crisis intervention tool is astounding.

## *USING THIS TOOL*

Meet with two colleagues at a computer lab that offers secure online access. To simulate online crisis intervention, sit at different computers and communicate with one another by text only. One of you volunteers to share a concern while another volunteers to be the intervener. You can refer to Figure 3–3 as you respond by e-mail. The third person serves as observer and gives feedback after the interaction. Continue until everyone has practiced.

---

**Successful Internet Crisis Intervention Involves . . .**

- Using emoticons.
- Relying on acronyms.
- Using emotional bracketing.
- Offering descriptive immediacy.
- Being aware of ethical and legal issues.

**FIGURE 3–3**  Internet crisis intervention techniques.

## Using Outreach Services

In recent years, some emergency mental health agencies, family preservation programs, disaster response teams, and other crisis organizations have offered outreach services to people at the site of the crisis, at a place of refuge, or in the person's home. Mobile crisis units, operating 24 hours a day, 7 days a week, are in place in many jurisdictions across the country. These programs offer free or low-cost emergency intervention throughout the community, providing a combination of telephone hotline and on-the-scene services.

The idea is simple: Instead of sitting back in your office and requiring people in crisis to come to you for help, you go to them. This approach has its dangers and special challenges, but actively reaching out as rapidly as possible can set the stage for successful crisis intervention.

## "Being With" the Person in Crisis

However you are making contact with someone in crisis, by telephone, online, or face-to-face, it is vital that you connect authentically. Therefore, one of the best techniques for helping people in resolving a crisis is to "be with" them. In fact, survivors later report that the most helpful aspect of their crisis intervention experience was the helper's genuine commitment to stand by them through a difficult time. By connecting with empathy, warmth, and regard, your relationship provides a safe haven for someone in emotional turmoil.

Keep in mind that, in and of itself, making contact with a survivor is a powerful intervention technique. Just by genuinely encountering the survivor—human to human—you can influence the person's sense of hope. With this in mind, you must always do the best you can to "be with" a person in crisis by establishing and maintaining a respectful, caring, and genuine alliance. If there is any power in crisis intervention, it is in the relationship that you develop with a survivor. Without this fundamental connection, any techniques you use are mere gimmicks and games.

## Listening In on Crisis Intervention

Review the story at the beginning of the chapter. The emergency mental health counselor began the meeting with Ralph by reviewing Brad's medical history, current status, and treatment options. A little later in the session, the intervener listens intently as Ralph shares some of his own reactions and concerns.

RALPH:  I just can't *believe* that my son might be dangerous to himself. When he was a kid, he was always reminding me to put on my seatbelt and warning me about the junk food I liked to eat. For the past couple of years, Brad's been a health and fitness nut.

INTERVENER:  The way you just described the healthy Brad, it must have been quite a shock for you to find out that he had hurt himself.

RALPH:  (*He pauses, shakes his head slowly, and exhales.*) Well, not a shock really . . . I guess. I always knew something wasn't quite right with Brad. Looking back, I can see that he was too . . . what do you call it . . . tense and excited at the same time about his art stuff. But, hell, I don't understand, I mean . . . Was there something I should have done? I'm no shrink! (*Ralph glances sheepishly at the intervener, wondering if he may have offended the intervener.*)

INTERVENER: (*He leans forward slightly and replies in a softer voice.*) Ralph, when you just said that you didn't know what you could have done, I want you to know that I don't know anyone—shrinks included . . . (*He smiles slightly.*) . . . who could have predicted that Brad would have cut himself. I'm guessing that you might be feeling pretty exasperated about everything the shrinks and other people on the staff have asked you.

RALPH: (*Shoulders slumping forward, he pulls a handkerchief out of his back pocket and wipes his tearful eyes and blows his nose before continuing. He laughs and mutters.*) I must be getting a cold.

INTERVENER (*Decides not to pick up on the social rescue cue and, instead, waits respectfully for Ralph to continue*): Mmhmm.

RALPH: (*His voice is anguished and he contorts his face with a pained expression that suggests both anger and shame.*) All their questions! I feel like I'm the one who sliced a hunk out of Brad!

## Reflecting on This Segment

1. In what ways has the intervener contributed to a relationship of "being with" the person in crisis?
2. How might you respond to Ralph's final comment in a way that expresses "being with" him?

## Using "Reaching Out" Questions to Look for Resources

In Chapter 1, you learned about how you can use questions to look for the survivor. The specific techniques included asking questions and offering leads that presume personal resilience. No person is an island. Therefore, it is safe to presume that an individual in crisis not only has some personal strengths, but also can reach out to others who can contribute to a successful resolution. In this section, we describe how you can encourage someone in crisis to identify others who may offer informational, emotional, practical, and professional assistance.

**Looking Beyond Oneself.** Because they are so narrowly focused on their crisis experience, survivors may not spontaneously think of the people, programs, and community resources that could assist them. As a result, their crisis story may be devoid of any obvious possibilities for help, relief, or support. Your job is to invite the person to take a broader perspective—to use a wide-angle lens, if you will—that offers a better view for identifying resource possibilities. When you ask someone about past experiences of receiving assistance and support, you invite the person to take a moment to look beyond herself.

**Presumptive Questions and Leads.** You can ask open-ended *"reaching-out"* questions that presume resources. You might say something like, "What people have made a difference for you in the past when you've had to deal with crises?" Of course, you continue to acknowledge any feelings of alienation and isolation, but you also presume that there is someone, somewhere, who can contribute in some important way to the resolution process. Although such a question can be valuable, you need to take care with your timing. Questioning about resources can come across as trying to rush or abandon someone before the person has felt heard. Whenever a survivor returns to sharing the crisis story, that's your signal to return to offering the LUV Triangle.

A related technique is to offer a lead—a request or statement that invites someone to discuss resources. One example would be, "Tell me about a time in your life when someone really came through to help you deal with a tough experience." Another example is, "It's my hunch that there have been some people who have been there for you in some way when you've faced troubled times." The implication of these messages is that there have been some resources that have assisted someone in dealing with crises.

## Listening In on Crisis Intervention

Review the story at the beginning of the chapter and the previous segment. A little later in the session, the intervener uses the following reaching-out questions and leads to invite Ralph to explore resources. Again, take note of how the intervener uses both questions and the LUV Triangle in this segment.

INTERVENER: Raising a child without your wife must have been quite a job. What other people were there to help you out?

RALPH: Well, it was sure tough when Nancy died, but then I didn't have much time to feel sorry for myself 'cause I had a baby who needed me. In a lot of ways, though, Brad helped me more than I helped him. You see, he was the last thing that Nancy gave me. Through thick and thin, we've stuck together. But I'm afraid that it's all gonna fall apart if these spells of his keep getting worse.

Intervener: You and Brad have been through a lot right from the time he was born, but what happened this morning really scared you.

RALPH: I know that I'm in over my head, but I have never asked for charity and it's really hard to even think about doing that right now. My dad always told us two things: never air our dirty laundry and never take nothin' from nobody.

INTERVENER: As you think about getting some help now, it sounds like you're beginning to realize just how far back that idea goes. I'm wondering how you got yourself to come in here in the first place and violate that old family rule right from the start.

RALPH: Well, rules are made to be broken, especially where Brad's concerned.

INTERVENER: Yeah, OK then. Earlier, you said how you and Brad have stuck together. And I imagine there were other family members—like a grandmother, uncle, or cousin—or maybe even friends—who helped you through the tough times you two must have faced as he was growing up.

> RALPH: (*He pauses, reflects, and gets a smile on his face.*) Yeah, family is OK to ask once in a while, but with friends, I always feel like I owe them something.
>
> ## Reflecting on This Segment
> 1. In what ways has the intervener used reaching-out questions productively?
> 2. How might you respond to the final comment?
> 3. Write two presumptive questions that you could ask.

## The Encouragement Interlude

In the two opening chapters, you learned techniques, such as asking getting-through questions and tracking resolution, that can help you find the survivor in a crisis. In other words, you were looking for someone's personal strengths, resilience, and potential for achieving a successful resolution. Now that you have found the survivor and have observed someone demonstrate resilience and resolve, you have the opportunity to share that new information, from your perspective, with the person. This "news of difference" (Bateson, 1972) can inspire people to expand their views, consider new ideas, and soften up their rigid and limiting ways of thinking about themselves.

When you are involved in crisis intervention, at some point near the end of your encounter, take a few moments for an *encouragement interlude*. During this brief time, you can highlight the survivor, the person's resilience, resources, and resolve, in the crisis. By offering your impressions, you can discuss the positive qualities that you have noticed and give your hunches about how the person will be resolving this situation. Of course, you acknowledge the pain and hardships, but you also track resolution, emphasize strengths and resources, use the client's metaphors, and work to coconstruct a survival story.

**Encouragement Versus Praise.** Every person in a crisis is dealing with at least two serious concerns. The first, and more obvious, challenge is how to cope with the dangers, losses, suffering, and turmoil of the crisis itself. The second issue, which is an insidious one, is the risk of becoming discouraged and demoralized. In times of crisis, people feel overwhelmed, have a sense of hopelessness, and doubt their abilities. Such deep discouragement can damage their self-esteem, drain them of any motivation, and deplete their sense of personal agency. Therefore, one of your fundamental jobs as a crisis intervener is to offer encouragement to people in crisis.

Encouraging statements are different from praise, gratuitous compliments, or pep talks. When you offer encouragement, you are reflecting an internal positive state already existing within the survivor. In contrast, praise is used to reinforce a specific behavior. Encouragement is designed to increase someone's sense of personal power, whereas praise is a form of external control. Witmer (1986) pointed out that encouragement can inspire, hearten, and instill confidence.

For example, when a child does well, you might offer praise, such as, "Super job!" or "I'm really proud of you!" On the other hand, an encouragement would be, "I noticed how you were really hanging in there to finish that project, and you did it!" or "With all that determination, I wonder just how far you'll be going in your life." In the latter two responses, you offer an observation and a wonderment. In both cases of encouragement, the sense of personal agency and evaluation remains with the child.

There is certainly nothing wrong with praising or cheering when someone does well. It is just that these behaviors are not powerful in promoting a survivor's sense of autonomy, internal locus of evaluation, and personal agency. And, of course, there's always the danger that you would foster dependency by becoming someone's primary source of reinforcement, rescue, and reassurance.

In crisis, people are more likely to doubt their abilities, judgment, and resilience. At such a time, a person is in particular need of encouragement. Remember, even if you have just met someone, the special circumstances make it likely that you have become a significant other, at least for the present, to that person. The way in which you respond will affect how the survivor sees himself. If you want to improve the person's self-concept, then offer encouragement and avoid praise.

**Guidelines for a Successful Encouragement Interlude.** You can increase the power of this interlude by following a few simple guidelines (Friedman, 1997).

- *Set the stage.* Up to this point, the survivor has been doing most of the talking. Your job has been to bear witness to the crisis experience while inviting the person to talk about his or her strengths, resources, and resilience. Now, you are setting the stage for a brief interlude during which you will be presenting encouraging feedback.

  You can begin with an introduction and then offer a dramatic pause to hook the person. For example, you might say:

  "I have something that I wanted to say . . ."
  "Let me just collect my thoughts because there are some important points I want to share with you . . ."

- *Acknowledge the crisis experience.* Someone is more likely to hear news of difference when you first demonstrate that you have listened, understood, and validated the person's pain, turmoil, and concerns. The person must see that you recognize the magnitude of the trauma and have an empathic feel for the distress he or she is experiencing. For example, you might say, "I guess that the first thing I want to say is how overwhelming it must be to be hit with such enormous adversities. First your mother died, and then you got the diagnosis of your breast cancer . . . both in the same week!"

- *Be positive with your observations.* To heighten your impact, be sure to point out the person's strengths, resources, and successes. Avoid "hollow compliments" and hackneyed generalizations. Instead, comment genuinely on the person's specific actions that you have observed and the particular information that the survivor has shared with you.

- *Be tentative* rather than authoritative. Make your remarks concerning the survivor in a manner that emphasizes that these observations are your impressions, which are neither definite nor irrefutable. For example, as you speak, you can assume a posture that is inviting, make gestures that are nonthreatening, and use a tone of voice that is comforting. Avoid asserting decisive and conclusive claims regarding the person's character traits, motivations, or intentions (Friedman, 1997). Instead, begin your remarks with such tentative phrases as "I'm wondering if . . . ," or "It's possible that . . . ," or "Perhaps. . . ."

- *Highlight the survivor in the crisis.* You can increase your effectiveness by emphasizing the ways the person has succeeded, either completely or partially, in coping with the crisis. When you do acknowledge the person's concerns, you can add follow-up statements of "finding the pony." For example, you might ask, "Given that you still have serious questions about your safety, I'm wondering how you were able to get past your fears and make your way here."

  Or you might say, "With all that has happened, and as vulnerable as you say you have felt, I'm amazed that you were able to summon the courage to be here, with me, working on this issue! How did you get yourself to do that?!"

  In crisis situations, you can also offer a more helpful variant on the old "things could be worse" idiom: "With so many catastrophic things happening, how have you been able to keep the situation from becoming much worse than it is?!"

  You may have noticed that some of these prototype responses end with an exclamation point. This punctuation is to indicate that you should freely express your sense of amazement and wonderment over the heroism, determination, and creativity of the survivor. Displaying your own excitement can also heighten the person's emotional resolve.

- *Use metaphors, images, fantasies, and wonderments.* Whenever possible, expand on the metaphors that the survivor already has used during your encounter. If they were crisis metaphors, you can transform them into metaphors of resolution by conjecturing about positive outcomes or unexpected twists. Use terms, images, themes, or cues that have personal meaning for the survivor.

  For example, you might say to the person, "Earlier, you said how you felt that you were trapped in a deep, dark hole. I'm remembering how you also talked about all the decisions that you had to make when that tornado hit. And now I have this image of you on a rope, actually pulling yourself up from the bottom of that deep, dark hole . . . like you did right after the tornado. I'm wondering what you're going to be doing next to keep on climbing up that rope."

- *Speak from the heart.* Finally, you are most productive when you express yourself naturally. Rather than attempting to speak as an expert or objective observer, you can speak genuinely from the heart, drawing on your personal experience of "being with" someone during this encounter.

- *Invite the person to talk about the experience.* It's not unusual for people to have some strong emotions as they go through the encouragement interlude. Therefore, you end the interlude by giving the survivor an opportunity to process the experience. For example, you might invite the person by saying, "I'm wondering what it was like for you to hear this," or "What are some of your thoughts and feelings about what I've been saying?" As the person discusses this experience, you may find yourself returning often to the LUV Triangle as you collaborate on processing reactions.

### Listening In on Crisis Intervention

Review the story at the beginning of the chapter. In the following segment, the crisis intervener interjects an encouragement interlude while continuing to engage in active listening, empathic understanding, and consistent validating.

CRISIS INTERVENER: Ralph, I'd like to take a couple of minutes to share with you some things that have struck me since we first started talking . . . First, I really appreciate your willingness to share so much with me, somebody who's a stranger to you. You know, the fact that you are here in a new and scary situation is evidence that you care deeply about Brad.

A couple of things just struck me and I'd like to share them with you. This may take a little while.

The first thought about you that's knocking around in my head is, "How did he manage to handle all the challenges of raising a child by himself? And where does this guy get the energy and determination to work two different jobs to support his family and to cope with Brad's illness?"

As you were talking about your memories of waiting for your son to be born, it was almost like you were saying that this could be the start of a new life for both of you right now. While you sound apprehensive, you also seem hopeful about the new directions that you two can take.

### Reflecting on This Segment

1. What crisis metaphor did the intervener use here?
2. What strengths did the intervener point out to Ralph?
3. What other comments could you add to this encouragement interlude?

When you offer the encouragement interlude, you perform several vital functions. By pointing out strengths and resources, you are offering people a more productive view of themselves and others. By creating alternative stories, you are opening space for fresh perspectives. By speaking metaphorically, you generate images that can intrigue and alter their understanding of the crisis. And by highlighting the changes you've already observed, you are authenticating the resolution process.

## USING THIS TOOL

Meet with a colleague to experience the impact of an encouragement interlude. One of you shares a crisis experience that you have successfully resolved. The other actively listens to the story. After about 10 minutes, the listener then shares impressions of the survivor's resilience by following the guidelines presented in Figure 3–4. Afterward, discuss your reactions to this process from your perspectives as survivor and intervener. Switch roles and repeat the entire sequence.

---

**A Successful Encouragement Interlude Involves . . .**

- Setting the stage.
- Acknowledging the crisis.
- Giving positive observations.
- Being tentative.
- Highlighting the survivor in the crisis.
- Using metaphors, images, fantasies, and wonderments.
- Speaking from the heart.
- Inviting the survivor to talk about this experience.

---

**FIGURE 3–4** Guidelines for an encouragement interlude.

## RESOURCES FOR MENTAL HEALTH

Although the rate of bipolar disorder is the same among African Americans as it is among other Americans, African Americans are less likely to receive a diagnosis and, therefore, treatment. About 25% of African Americans do not have health insurance.

National Mental Health Association
http://www.nmha.org
800-969-NMHA

For decades, the NMHA has been an excellent source of reliable information and committed advocacy for people with serious psychiatric disorders.

National Alliance for the Mentally Ill
http://www.nami.org
800-950-NAMI (6264)

NAMI offers information, referrals, advocacy, and support for anyone who is affected, directly or indirectly, by serious mental illness.

## SUMMARY

We do not resolve crises on our own. As interdependent beings, we gain sustenance from others during times of pain and turmoil. "Being with" a person in crisis is the essence of successful intervention. As you can see in Figure 3–5, you learned about making contact with survivors by telephone, Internet, and outreach services. You also

---

**Essential Tools**

- Linking with the person is the heart of crisis intervention.
- Use the telephone.
- Use the Internet.
- Reach out to where the people are.
- "Be with" the person in crisis.
- Ask reaching-out questions.
- Offer an encouragement interlude.

---

**FIGURE 3–5**   Essential tools of Chapter 3.

practiced techniques that involve making contact, including "being with" someone in crisis, asking reaching-out questions to identify resources, and offering an encouragement interlude.

## Segue to Chapter 4

To prime you for the concepts and techniques in Chapter 4, think about a time when you were dealing with a riddle or puzzle that was perplexing at first, but at some point, something clicked and you were able to make sense of it. How did your energy level change? What was the effect on your mood?

# 4

# Making Meaning: Transforming a Crisis Narrative into a Survival Story

"Meaning, not raw facts, is what humanity seeks."
*Alvin Kernan*

## CHAPTER GOALS

After completing this chapter, you should be able to:

- Understand how crises can shatter people's basic assumptions about the world, the meaning of life, and their self-worth
- Recognize that creating meaning is one of our fundamental characteristics as human beings
- Appreciate the value of a narrative perspective in understanding how people make meaning out of their crisis experiences
- Enter into a crisis story
- Coconstruct with someone a survival story from a crisis narrative

## OVERVIEW

In this chapter, you will learn how crises can destroy people's basic assumptions about their world, undermine the sense of meaning in their lives, and sabotage their feelings of self-worth. You will also learn specific techniques that you can use to help people make meaning of the chaos, pain, and turmoil of a crisis.

When people are in crisis, they are also experiencing a crisis of meaning. Although we all exist in the physical world, we also live in a world of meaning. In fact, it is more important to be thriving meaningfully than physically. Meaning is not encoded in facts or data, nor is it expressed in logic. Instead, we organize meaning by creating our life stories.

Telling one's crisis story offers the survivor an opportunity to face, acknowledge, accept, and express powerful emotions. The narrative process helps a person to begin recognizing the enormity of what has happened and its consequences. The act itself of telling the story helps someone organize the information needed to assess the practical impact of a crisis, and think more clearly and completely about the current circumstances. Perhaps most important, the process of telling one's story helps that person find some meaning in the catastrophic event that has taken place.

We not only tell stories, our stories tell us. In other words, the life narratives that we create do more than organize our experiences. They influence us to take on certain roles, behave according to particular values, play out our expectations, and choose some options over others. By transforming our crisis narratives into survival stories, we are able to reach a successful resolution and go on to thrive in our lives.

## CRISIS STORY

Salmaan's parents had immigrated to the United States from Pakistan when he was a small child. His parents were both professionals and they had a comfortable, if somewhat disconnected, life in suburbia. The disconnection was due to ongoing clashes between the old and the new. The Kahn parents wanted to preserve as many of the cultural, religious, and family traditions as possible. Yet, they also yearned for their offspring to become fully accepted and successful members of their adopted country. It was Salmaan's idea to go to military school. What better way to prove that he belonged? His parents were reluctant, but finally gave their permission because their youngest son was so resolute about his decision.

When the commandant interrupted classes to announce the terrible news on September 11, 2001, Salmaan felt his classmates' eyes on him. He could think of nothing to say or do that would reassure people that he was one of them—an American. Classes were suspended and most of the students gathered in the auditorium to view the tragedy play itself out again and again on television, with its countless compulsive replays of the trauma. As he watched, Salmaan found himself flashing back to the previous year, his first at the school.

Hazing was officially forbidden at every military school in the country, but somehow first-year students were still subjected to protracted and sustained harassment. At times, the lack of sleep, long marches, and tedious close-order drill sessions were almost too much to bear. Factor in the mindless hectoring and incessant threats that anyone who was a little "different" had to endure, and an outsider would only have a hint of how painful his first year had been.

During that time, Salmaan had hidden his misery from his parents by filling his weekly letters with imaginary tales of what he thought they might like to hear. However, he was the only Muslim in school and was forced to conduct his five daily prayers in front of formations standing at attention, marching squads, and singing groups. He was even accused of being a "lazy rag head" who used his prayers as an excuse to avoid work.

Ramadan, the 9th month of the Muslim calendar, had been the worst. It is at this time that Muslims fast during the daylight hours for the entire month. At the holiest and most sacred time of worship and contemplation, Salmaan suffered the humiliation of being tempted by upperclassmen holding plates of pungent fried foods under his nose. Others tried to break his concentration by setting fire to his prayer rug, yelling commands, and taunting him with ugly names, such as "sand nigger," while he was praying or contemplating.

It was difficult for Salmaan to ignore his persecutors, but he succeeded. He even gained a measure of respect from them, or so a friendly classmate told him. But where would he stand with them now after the terrorist attacks? What about his family? What would happen to his brothers who were in the Middle East visiting relatives? What did all this mean? As Salmaan watched the Twin Towers collapse, he couldn't help but wonder if his own way of life was also falling into ruins.

## Reflecting on This Crisis Story

1. What are some of your impressions of Salmaan?
2. In what ways is this a story of victimization? In what ways is it a story of survival?
3. What would it be like to work with Salmaan in crisis intervention?
4. If you were to offer Salmaan an encouragement interlude, what would you say?

# IDEAS

## Crisis and the Assumptive World

People find themselves in a crisis when their view of the world is suddenly assaulted and challenged. Of course, the world is always changing and, as a result, we are constantly revising our views to accommodate to these changes. However, this change is usually gradual—a layering of new experiences on top of the old. Rather than experiencing new situations as decidedly different from former ones, as we can see in the stratifications of the earth's crust, people easily integrate their new experiences into their *assumptive world*. Slow change gives people the opportunity to adjust and adapt their story, and because change in our day-to-day existence usually takes place so leisurely, it is often imperceptible. That is why things that change gradually may appear as if they stay the same. And it is because a person experiences change in this familiar way that he or she can feel at home and safe in the world.

Janoff-Bulman (1992) used the phrase "assumptive world" to describe people's slowly changing representational system. Humans are able to maintain relatively stable assumptions about life and about how things are likely to turn out. Most of the time, life experiences confirm the beliefs of our assumptive world. Perhaps life is as we assume it to be, or maybe we selectively attend to those events that confirm our beliefs. The reality is probably a combination of both.

But what happens when tumultuous changes shatter our assumptions? A loved one suddenly dies, a serious injury handicaps us, we are sexually assaulted, or our home is destroyed by a tornado. We then experience a crisis that threatens our assumptive world and has the potential to create radically new assumptions. We cannot make sense of what is happening, because we have no representational schema in which to fit our radically new experience. We are lost in a place that once was familiar, but now seems strange and menacing. Our old map for negotiating the territory appears hopelessly out-of-date. Without an assumptive world that can accommodate to the events of the outer world, we wander aimlessly and in fear. This state of alienation is the very definition of crisis.

**Three Basic Assumptions.** Janoff-Bulman (1992) proposed that at the core of most people's preferred assumptive world are three basic beliefs:

1. The world is benevolent.
2. The world is meaningful.
3. The self is worthy. (p. 6)

With these beliefs as the basis of our assumptive world, we can proceed with relative confidence that the world can provide what we need, that we will find our efforts fulfilling and meaningful, and that we deserve whatever success or happiness comes to us. When bad things happen to us, these are unusual events and we are undeserving of them. Janoff-Bulman suggested that the biblical story of Job, in which God visits countless troubles on a good and righteous man, is the prototype for undeserved human suffering: "The attention this biblical story has received reflects the deeply disturbing nature of seemingly unwarranted human suffering . . . [and] our unwitting acceptance of the three fundamental assumptions" (p. 6).

If it is true that these three assumptions are the foundation of people's attitudes toward the world and their place in it, then the assumptions certainly seem to be a useful heuristic for living happily and for coping with changing events. But when these assumptions are shattered by a catastrophic event, the victim may reinterpret each of these assumptions as its opposite:

1. The world is unkind and hostile.
2. Nothing makes any sense.
3. I deserve all the pain and suffering that has been visited upon me.

With such a set of assumptions, people in crisis no longer see the world as a hospitable place, they are constantly confused, and they see themselves as unworthy of happiness. The long-term danger is that a victim will accept these negative assumptions as her new life story. Given such an assumptive world, a person in crisis can lose hope and see the meaning of life as nothing but suffering. However, the good news is that, given the right conditions, a survivor can recover her original assumptive world and carry on with a revised map. Life will, once again, be worth living.

Your job is to help people in crisis regain their hopeful assumptive world. In this situation, you have the on-the-spot opportunity to interrupt the process of committing to the negative assumptions mentioned earlier. Besides assisting with immediate basic needs, helping people to rebuild their shattered positive assumptions may be the most valuable psychological contribution you can make in crisis intervention.

---

## *EXPERIENCING THIS IDEA*

Think about a time in your own life when your basic assumptions about yourself, life, and the world were challenged in some troubling way. What was it like to experience that challenge? How did you make your way to a wiser, richer view of yourself, life, and the world?

---

### Crisis and Meaning

Our sense of identity, our storied selves, rests on our ability to tell a coherent narrative of our past experiences, current circumstances, and future dreams (McAdams, 1996). However, in a crisis, the narrative fabric of our lives is torn. The pieces no longer fit and they do not make any sense. The process of crisis resolution, on the other hand, involves reweaving our shredded lives once again into a meaningful and integrated whole (Emmons, 1999). Like a message written in code, the meaning of a crisis is not readily apparent to us. However, we are compelled to make sense of our traumatic experience (Neimeyer, 2000), discover its point or purpose, tie together the loose ends, and make connections that previously escaped us.

Building on his pioneering work on Holocaust survivors, Viktor Frankl (1969) promoted the achievement of meaning as the central task of resolution. In crisis, there are overwhelming forces that batter our sense of security, lash at our defenses, and leave devastation in their wake. However, when we are confronted with the inevitability of loss, injury, or even death, we still find ways to gain some sense of meaning. When we have meaning, we can endure the terrible blows of fate without being defeated.

In his research on loss and grieving, Christopher Davis (2002) identified two fundamental and different processes that are involved in meaning making. These two dynamics are *making sense* of the crisis—determining the "how"—and *finding benefits* that emerge from the crisis experience—discovering the "why." In research on the importance of meaning, Davis and his colleagues studied caregivers who had lost a loved one. In follow-up interviews 6, 13, and 18 months after the death, they found that those who had made some sense of the death and had found some benefits were more emotionally adjusted to the loss.

Making sense of a crisis often happens at different levels. One level of understanding concerns the sequence of events, the causes and effects, and the underlying dynamics. Putting together these pieces of the puzzle can help someone gain a cognitive mastery by understanding the physical, social, environmental, economic, psychological, or historical forces that created the crisis. For example, a survivor typically gathers extensive information regarding a medical condition that has precipitated a health crisis. People also attempt to integrate traumatic experiences into a consistent worldview and spiritual framework.

All crises are victimizing experiences in one way or another. However, once people begin the resolution process, most quickly shed the role of victim. Few individuals want to see themselves as poor, pathetic victims. In Chapter 1, we described some of the ways that people devictimize themselves. In addition to comparing their own circumstances with the actual situations of others, survivors often favorably contrast the reality, however bad, with hypothetical possibilities that would have been much worse.

When you do crisis intervention, you will regularly hear someone describe a painful incident and its consequences with the amendment "but it could have been worse." Many people will conclude their accounts by exclaiming how lucky they are, compared with what might have been. If their home has been destroyed in a flood, they will point out that, if the circumstances had been slightly different, they could have been killed. If they have been struck with a serious disease, they will declare that they could have been afflicted with an even worse disease.

In a study that documents this devictimizing strategy, Milo (2002) found that mothers grieving over the death of their disabled child typically did not portray themselves as victims of a doubly cruel fate of having a child with serious disabilities and then losing this child to an early death. Instead, they mourned the deaths with deep sadness but took comfort in their children's good fortune of not suffering an even worse fate. By dying young, their children would not outlive the essential support and exhaustive care that these mothers would not have been able to provide in the future.

Successful survivors are able to identify benefits or gains that they have made from the crisis experience. In fact, most survivors feel more self-confidence, deeper appreciation for life, closer relationships, and greater wisdom (Echterling & Wylie, 1999). Looking back on their crisis experience, many see themselves as having been on a mission and having served a higher purpose. As one survivor stated, "I just don't believe that all this stuff happened for no point and for no reason" (Milo, 2002, p. 127). People who achieve resolution are able to identify how their lives are richer, deeper, and more meaningful by dealing with the challenges of a crisis. They may describe the crisis as "a blessing in disguise" that has transformed their lives.

No matter what the specific adversity, most survivors report that, as a result of dealing with this event, they have grown in character, have improved their perspective on life, and have deepened their relationships with others (Davis, 2002). They may have discovered some things about themselves that they found upsetting at first, but they go on to learn important lessons from the experience (Wethington, 2003). Some survivors give meaning to their tragedies by advocating for political change and promoting public awareness of the problem (Milo, 2002).

## Vivid Memories

Our *memory* is not a passive recording device that merely reproduces past experiences. Instead, it is an active process in which we construct and transform the past in ways that give our lives meaning, form, and purpose. Pillemer (1998) argued that vivid memories, even if they are of crisis incidents, can serve important functions. First, such memories can promote personal growth. Remembering the crisis events, however horrific and painful they may be, and recounting them to others are essential components of a successful resolution. Judith Herman (1992) observed that telling the story "actually transforms the traumatic memory, so that it can be integrated into the survivor's life story" (p. 175).

Another function of vivid memories is to offer direction. Our memories of momentous events can direct our future lives by goading us to revisit these crisis experiences and recommit ourselves to the important lessons that we learned at those times. Crises are turning points in our lives. Looking back on these episodes, survivors see them as "marking the end of one chapter and the beginning of another" (McAdams, 1988, p. 144).

Vivid memories also motivate us to communicate with others. People who have experienced momentous events feel compelled to make contact with others to tell them all about the incidents. However, perhaps the most important function of vivid memories is that they play an important role in creating our personal identities. As Bruner (1987) noted, we become our "autobiographical narratives" (p. 15). The crisis is no longer alien, strange, or intrusive. Instead, through the process of making meaning, the crisis event has become part of our self—an important artifact stored in our personal archives.

**Reconstructing Memories.** Our memories about incidents are also influenced by the context in which we try to recollect them. For example, Elizabeth Loftus and her associates are well-known for their work in establishing the inadequacy of eyewitness testimony in court.

In a typical experiment on the accuracy of memory, Loftus and Palmer (1974) showed participants a film of a car accident, followed by a question asking them to estimate the speed of the cars. The question was identical for everyone, except for the word used to describe the accident. For example, for some participants, the question was phrased that the cars *smashed* into each other, whereas for other participants the cars *hit* or *contacted* one another. Even though they had seen the same film, those who responded to the verb *smashed* gave an average estimate of 40.8 miles per hour, whereas the participants who were given the verb *contacted* gave an average speed of 31.8 miles per hour. The study also provided striking evidence that people can develop false memories. The accident had not involved any broken glass, but when asked if they had noticed it, 32% of the *smashed* group remembered seeing broken glass, whereas only 14% of the *hit* group recalled it. Not only can events be misremembered as to their details, but certain aspects of an event can be totally constructed.

So when people tell you their stories of crisis experiences, keep in mind that the words you use will color the way the story is told, because the way an event is remembered will depend on the way you ask about it. Certain aspects of the memory can be strengthened with the right questions and other aspects can be "overwritten." Knowing this, you can set out to phrase your questions in such a way as to bring out details that will help the storyteller to construct a tale of hope and competency rather than one of despair and failure.

**Evolving Recollections.** Brown and Kulik (1977) coined the term *flashbulb memory* to describe the vivid mental pictures of tragic events that many survivors can evoke. Researchers have studied people's recollections of public tragedies, such as an assassination (Christianson, 1989) or natural disaster (Neisser et al., 1996). At first, such a shock is recorded primarily at the sensory level—the visual, auditory, olfactory, tactile, and kinesthetic experiences of the event. Later, as the survivor returns to reflect on the experience through many retellings, the memories also become archived in a narrative form.

The evolving crisis story, like a poem that combines narrative and imagery, interweaves chronological events and sensory experiences. Such a combination can evoke powerful emotions in both the listener and the narrator. The crisis survivor, as Pillemer

(1998) pointed out, "does not simply present a narrative account of what was seen, heard, or felt; he or she can 'see' the situation, 'hear' what was said, and 'feel' the accompanying emotions" (p. 54).

## Sharing One's Crisis Story

Most survivors feel a compelling need to tell their stories. However motivated they are to give voice to their suffering, they face the challenge of transforming the raw materials of a chaotic and confusing experience into a coherent story. Survivors enhance the power of their crisis stories by including particular details, sensory impressions, and a range of thoughts and emotions. For example, one survivor of a serious auto accident described the experience of being flung from his careening car:

> All of a sudden, I was thrown out the window like I was nothing but some piece of litter. The wind was beating me all over my body while I was spinning and twisting in the air. My arms were flailing around and blood was spraying from my hands like from a water sprinkler. When I hit the ground, there's this rattling, gurgling sound that comes out of me. It's sort of a screeching noise, kinda like grinding gears, only much deeper, and it's being yanked from the deepest part of my lungs.

Note the variety of details and metaphors that are in this brief account. Did you notice that the verb tense shifted from the past to the present in this brief account? As we discussed in Chapter 2, this shift is common as a survivor becomes so engaged in the narrative that he or she is describing the incident as if it were happening in the here and now.

All stories take place in a relationship between those who tell the stories and those who hear them. Even if we are talking to ourselves or writing in a private journal, we are affected by hearing and seeing the words we use. Smyth and Pennebaker (1999) argued that "when people put their emotional upheavals into words their physical and mental health seems to improve markedly" (p. 70). In the following paragraphs, we summarize the findings of Pennebaker's extensive research on the benefits of sharing one's crisis stories.

Pennebaker (2002) found that writing about traumatic experiences is a powerful tool for resolving these crises. In a series of studies, each participant was asked to write about the most traumatic experience of his life. They wrote about their deepest thoughts and emotions concerning such crises as sexual assault, suicide, and family violence for about 15 minutes a day over 4 consecutive days.

Compared with control groups who addressed everyday and nonemotional topics, people who wrote about their crises improved their physical health and emotional well-being. In numerous studies (Lepore & Smyth, 2002), expressive writing reduced blood pressure, improved quality of life for cancer survivors, enhanced academic and employment functioning, reduced visits to health care providers, improved immunological outcomes, and elevated mood level.

Over the course of several days of writing, participants were able to return to their crisis experience and, in retelling their story, add coherence and depth to their accounts. Remarkably, those participants whose daily writings changed the most in the use of singular and plural personal pronouns also improved the most dramatically on follow-up measures. Writing a personal account of a crisis, as reflected in the many "I" statements, can be an opportunity to explore oneself and seek personal meaning. A retelling that includes many more "We" statements can reflect the sense of cohesion and social support that many discover in times of crisis. Both perspectives, the personal and the social, are important components of a multifaceted narrative that promotes positive resolution.

## Human Meaning

Humans are the only meaning-making species (Emmons, 2003), but psychology has practically ignored the subject of human meaning. Polkinghorne (1988) pointed out that the attempt to study meaning was fraught with difficulty. Because meaning exists in a different form than natural objects, it cannot be picked up and held or measured by an impersonal instrument. Meaning is an experience, not a thing, and it does not necessarily manifest itself as behavior. Because of this, human meaning violates two rather important criteria for the methods of science. Meaning cannot be observed in the way that objects can, nor can it be precisely replicated at another time. Instead, meaning is like an image reflected in a mirror: "It presents itself in our consciousness as a fleeting trace or indication; it appears as a wisp . . . continuously being reconstituted as the rudimentary perceptions of consciousness change" (p. 7). We have direct access only to one meaning system—our own. Therefore, we can only experience meaning by shifting our focus inward through reflection, introspection, meditation, or prayer.

**Making Life Meaningful.** In spite of the challenges in researching meaning, there recently has been a resurgence of studies exploring the process of making meaning and the benefits of a meaningful life (Emmons, 2003). Researchers have found that meaningfulness and purpose in life predict positive functioning (French & Joseph, 1999). People who have a strong sense of meaning are more likely to be happy and satisfied in life (Wong & Fry, 1998). Even when they are confronted with crises, survivors whose lives remain meaningful have greater life satisfaction, positive affect, and vitality (Emmons, 2003). A sense of meaning has been found to result from being vitally engaged in absorbing, satisfying, and challenging activities (Nakamura & Csikszentmihalyi, 2003).

**Meaning and Language.** Human beings express themselves in language, not data or numbers. Korzybski (1933) said that words themselves do not have meanings; people have meanings. Because of this, a linguistic analysis of a transcript cannot reveal the true meaning of any verbal utterance. Language exists in context, and that context gives clues as to what a person had in mind when he or she said something.

In addition, within any statement, there is a second level—an accompaniment—that tells a listener how the utterance is to be taken. For example, if I were say, "Hey!" Am I joking? Am I serious? Am I angry? Am I crazy? All of these possibilities can be accompaniment to the same statement, but if it is only the statement itself that becomes data, its meaning is lost in the translation.

In Chapter 3, we pointed out that emoticons are one attempt to provide some accompaniment to online text messages. Of course, because of the complexity of language, it may never be possible to know precisely what a speaker means. The translation of an experience into a word is always a reduction, and words are never the same as the experience itself. Much of life is ineffable—no matter how hard we try, we cannot capture it completely in words. For example, just what exactly is the taste of chocolate or the feeling of satin? You *know*, but you can't fully say.

Meaning is only possible within the experience of a single individual. When you truly *listen* to someone's story, you are not focusing on finding out if the story matches the facts of reality. Neither are you trying to identify logical flaws. Instead, you are searching for the *meaning* the story holds for the storyteller and trying to communicate your understanding in return.

## Making Sense of a Narrative

The broadest definition of a *narrative* would include such literary examples as poetry, fictional mythology, and allegory (Payne, 2000). These forms of narrative are designed to illuminate the human condition in general and to capture some universal truth about life. However, we are not concerned here with people in general, but rather with the life circumstances of the individual we are attempting to help in a time of crisis. For the purposes of this book, we shall define narrative as an account or story about events that have actually taken place in someone's life.

McLeod (1998) suggested several ways in which narratives can be analyzed. You may find his discussion of narrative analysis useful as you attempt to make sense of a crisis story you are being told. McLeod proposed that there are three distinct lines of approach to understanding narrative: the psychodynamic, the constructivist, and the social constructionist approaches.

**Psychodynamic View.**  In the psychodynamic view, you are to look for the core conflictual relationship theme (Luborsky & Crits-Christolph, 1990). As troubled people tell their life stories of distress and woe, a common theme will often surface in their relationships, whether the association is with parents, employers, friends, or other significant others. The theme may be fear of rejection, mistrust of intimacy, or hostility toward authority. You may find that keeping a psychodynamic perspective in mind will help you in making sense of transference issues that can sometimes emerge in crisis intervention work. Someone with a lifetime of troubled relationships will expect from you what they feel they have received from everyone else.

**Constructivist View.**  The constructivist view of narrative focuses on the way a person makes meaning. As the person retells the story of an event, the multiple drafts of the narrative will occasionally conflict with each other in some way. For example, a tale of victimization differs from one of successful coping. Piaget discovered that when someone is dealing with different accounts of a situation, the person feels compelled to resolve these competing schemas. Therefore, you can help someone to reach a higher level of understanding by resolving the differences in that person's retellings.

**Social Constructionist View.**  The social constructionist approach to narrative therapy expands the constructivist view by suggesting that personal experience and meaning are not simply created by the individual, but are embedded in, and shaped by, the culture in which the person lives (McLeod, 1998). "We are born into a world of stories. A culture is structured around myths, legends, family tales and other stories" (p. 153). By embedding ourselves in some of these stories and rejecting others, we create our personal identity.

We tend to accept as real the stories of our culture, often without question, and we interpret any experience through the filter of our culture. For example, ask yourself,

"What does it mean to be a man?" or "What does it mean to be a woman?" Some definite images and attributes of gender roles will probably come to your mind. Then ask, "Where did I get these ideas?" You will realize that because you were born in a particular place, in a particular family, and had certain experiences, your ideas about gender have formed. Had all these contextual and cultural experiences been different, your ideas about who you are, and how you should act, would be different.

Our lives are lived within the dominant narratives of our families and culture. Sometimes our actual experiences do not match the cultural myths. When something bad happens to a person, the meaning of the event will already exist within the myths of the culture. The dominant narrative can restrict or impoverish our lives.

## The Agony of Sisyphus

All stories can be taken in more than one way. Literature is full of stories in which someone who seemed to be a victim turned out to be a hero. One such parable that illustrates this point is the story of Sisyphus.

According to Greek myth, there were two locations in which human souls could spend eternity. First, there was Elysium, an area of dim light in which existence was perhaps a little dull, but not so bad. Then there was Tartarus, the equivalent to our notion of hell (Guerber, 1960). In Tartarus, people who were to be punished for misdeeds in life acted out their punishments in ways that are metaphors for the earthly struggles we all share. The Danaides, for example, were compelled to toil forever attempting to fill a water cask with a hole in its bottom. Tantalus was sentenced to stand in a pool of water up to his neck without being able to satisfy his burning thirst. This is the origin of our word *tantalize* (Guerber, 1960).

Finally, there was Sisyphus, who had defied the gods and was therefore condemned to roll a huge stone up a mountain. Each time he nearly reached the top, the stone would roll back down to the bottom and Sisyphus would have to begin again. Each time, and for eternity, Sisyphus would lose his grip on the stone just as it seemed he was about to triumph, and he would have to start once more.

If you were listening to Sisyphus tell his story, you might find yourself feeling overwhelmed by the futility and the agony of his plight. This might seem to you to be a story of defeat. But Camus (1955) wrote that Sisyphus was at his noblest at that moment when, realizing the stone-rolling pursuit was a lost cause, he nevertheless started back down the mountain to repeat the process. There can be nothing noble in the behavior of the rock because it simply conforms to the laws of motion and gravity. But Sisyphus, who understands his place in the scheme of things, courageously perseveres. He chooses to carry on in the throes of angst, rather than dwell in the dim and dull existence of Elysium. He chooses to live vividly, and to suffer vividly, rather than opt for half a life. Camus (quoted in Kaufmann, 1975) stated, "At each of these moments when he leaves the heights and gradually sinks toward the lairs of the gods, he is superior to his fate. He is stronger than his rock" (pp. 313–314).

The story of Sisyphus seems, on the face of it, to be a story of despair. If you hear it that way, you will miss the nobility and heroism of the man who perseveres despite seemingly overwhelming forces. If you wish to hear of the nobility that is inherent in the story of someone who has survived a crisis, you must listen with great care and deep intention. Listen for the survivor in the crisis story, the hero in the tragedy.

+--------------------------------------------------------------------+
|                            **Key Ideas**                           |
|                                                                    |
|   •  In crisis, people's basic assumptions about the world, life, and |
|      their self-worth are shattered.                               |
|                                                                    |
|   •  Successfully resolving a crisis requires making meaning of the ex- |
|      perience.                                                     |
|                                                                    |
|   •  Many survivors have benefitted from their crisis.             |
|                                                                    |
|   •  People have vivid memories of crisis events.                  |
|                                                                    |
|   •  Survivors have a need to share their crisis story.            |
|                                                                    |
|   •  Listen for the survivor in the crisis story, the hero in the tragedy. |
+--------------------------------------------------------------------+

**FIGURE 4–1**   Key ideas of Chapter 4.

Before you embark on the next section, take a few moments to reflect on the key ideas summarized in Figure 4–1.

## TOOLS

### Entering the Person's Crisis Story

Every crisis survivor has a story to tell, and your immediate task as a helper is to bear witness as the survivor gives voice to the experience. Telling one's crisis story is more than merely recounting the events. Translating the experience into words is a complex, multifaceted, and transcending process that promotes successful resolution (Lepore & Smyth, 2002). It should not be discounted as unnecessary or minor, even in the middle of the dangerous, chaotic, and demanding circumstances of a crisis.

**Telling One's Crisis Story.** Using language to transform the raw experience of a crisis into a story is like catching a single powerful ray of the sun, redirecting it through a prism, and creating a spectrum of colors. Describing the ordeal can take many retellings to capture the wide range of its facets, complexity, and various meanings. No important story is told only once. Retelling a crisis story is not only common, it is a vital part of the resolution process as a survivor returns to expand on important themes, dig more deeply for new discoveries, and give voice to unexpressed emotions.

In Chapter 1, you learned about offering the LUV Triangle of active listening, empathic understanding, and respectful validation as the foundation of any successful intervention. Then, in Chapter 3, we offered the related technique of "being with" the survivor by developing a relationship that is characterized by authenticity, warmth, and regard. When you enter into the crisis story, you rely on both of these basic tools, but you also allow yourself to be carried along with the narrative, to listen to it from the inside out.

---

**How to Enter the Person's Crisis Story**

- Focus your concentration.
- Be a responsive audience.
- Mirror the person's emotions.
- Use paralinguistic utterances.
- Convey your engagement.
- Show your gratitude and admiration.

---

**FIGURE 4-2**   Entering the person's crisis story.

Although you may continually strive to learn everything you can about crises, you will never become *the* expert on another person's crisis. In fact, your job is to help survivors recognize that the real expertise always remains within themselves. Instead of adopting the position of an expert with people in crisis, you must instead adopt a position of ignorance—of not knowing. Taking an "I'm not from around here" attitude is an excellent way to remind yourself that the survivor is the true authority of this particular crisis story. By adopting this stance, you can enter into the crisis story.

In addition to assuming the position of not knowing, you must also be willing to enter the person's story to share vicariously—although less intensely than the survivor—in the crisis experience. Therefore, open yourself up to the risk of seeing, hearing, feeling, sensing, and experiencing the person's crisis as you engage in the story. By entering into the narrative, you honor, with your hushed attentiveness and emotional responsivity, someone's struggle for survival.

As you can see in Figure 4–2, there are several behaviors you can use to communicate that you are entering into the crisis story:

- *Focus your concentration.* Nod expectantly and give your full and complete attention to the story. Even if the account is painful, your job is to honor the survivor by bearing witness to the experience.
- *Be a responsive audience.* Allow yourself to communicate nonverbally with a wince, grimace, smile, or tear when you feel startled, shocked, amazed, touched, or hopeful. The crisis story will evoke feelings in you, so give yourself permission to let the storyteller know how you have been affected.
- *Mirror the storyteller's emotions*, but in a subdued and unintrusive way. Like an echo answering someone's cry, your manner can parallel the person's distress, but in a softer, muted way. In Chapter 5, you will learn how you can use this technique to help people manage their emotional arousal.
- *Use paralinguistic utterances*, such as "Oh!" or "Wow!" to communicate concern, surprise, or awe.
- *Convey your engagement* in the person's story by neither interrupting nor offering intrusive commentary.

- *Show your gratitude or admiration* for the person taking the risk of sharing this crisis story.

The crisis event may have been a solitary experience, but by telling the story to someone willing to bear witness, a survivor makes contact with a fellow human being. Because sharing one's story necessarily involves another person to hear it, the process helps to reconnect the survivor, who often feels alone and alienated, to someone who can offer concern and support. "Attention must be paid!" vowed Willy Loman's wife in Arthur Miller's *Death of a Salesman*. By giving attention to a crisis story, you offer a powerful affirmation of the survivor.

The first story you are likely to hear from a survivor is a "troubled, hurt, angry story . . . of calamitous events that conspire against a sense of well-being, self-satisfaction, or efficacy" (Gergen, 1997, p. 237). However, do not dispute the story. Instead, accept the fundamental accuracy—but incompleteness—of the storyteller's rendition.

**Retelling a Crisis Story.**  In Chapter 1, we compared flashbacks with hitting the replay button on a video cassette recorder, but retelling a crisis story is much more than a replay. Instead of merely repeating the story identically like a recording device, crisis survivors create new narratives that differ conspicuously from earlier accounts.

As we mentioned earlier in this chapter, immediately following an incident, crisis stories tend to be impressionistic, chaotic, and intensely agitated. With retellings, the stories gain coherence, achieve meaning, acquire more elaborate details, and change their emotional tone. Survivors retell their stories to work through the different facets of a crisis experience and "process the meaning of an event" (Ferrara, 1994, p. 53). Over time, most crisis stories take on more of the classic components of narratives, such as an introduction, a chronological account of the events, character descriptions, conflict, and resolution (Labov, 1982). If a victim tells a nearly identical crisis story over and over again, then that person is somehow stuck at a particular point in the resolution process.

One of the functions of retelling a crisis narrative is that it can serve as a reenactment of the incident. Just as rehearsal improves an actor's performance, so does rehearsal improve the survivor's mastery of the circumstances. In the retelling, the narrator may unintentionally use classic storytelling techniques to intensify the portrayal. The survivor may set the scene, imitate different voices, use dramatic pauses, mimic actions through gestures, vary the pace and volume of speech, and use facial expressions to depict emotions. Throughout this performance, the storyteller may make little eye contact with the listener. In fact, the storyteller's eyes may be defocused. Instead of being in the "here and now," the storyteller is in the "there and then" of the crisis event.

Many successful survivors, those who have positively resolved the crisis, have been able to create stories that give voice to their ordeal and offer coherence to what had been chaos. They sometimes use words so simple and pure that they have the sharp clarity of poetry. For example, years after a horrific flood nearly destroyed a man's home, he shared a story that had helped him come to a positive resolution:

> We had an empty canning jar with a lid on it way back behind our basement stairs. When we were cleaning up after the flood, we found that jar unbroken and it still had its lid on it. But what was so amazing was that canning jar was now half full of flood water. We've left it there way back in the basement all these years. We decided we'd leave it for the next owners.

The story poignantly expressed the survivor's acceptance of the crisis experience, together with an acknowledgment of the power of resilience. The storyteller cleaned up and rebuilt his home and his life, but he also kept a souvenir, a reminder that, deep down inside, the flood was still a part of his life. The power of this story lies in its ultimate acceptance of both the enormity of the crisis event and the storyteller's own resilience. The jar served as a wonderful metaphor for surviving a disaster—it contained some flood water, but it also remained unbroken. You should convey your sense of awe at such moments in the telling of the crisis story.

## Listening In on Crisis Intervention

Review the story at the beginning of the chapter. Salmaan calls a telephone hotline that has been established to help people cope with the terrorist attacks of 9/11. The intervener quickly establishes a relationship with Salmaan by active listening, empathic understanding, and validation. Pay attention to how she enters Salmaan's crisis story during this segment of the call.

SALMAAN: I promised my girlfriend that I'd talk to someone before I dropped out of school and since I can't trust anybody there, I guess you're it. I go to a military school and I'm the only Muslim there. If things weren't bad before, since 9/11, my life's been hell . . . (*His voice is strained and he sounds as if he's close to tears.*) I've been more or less avoiding everybody all week. I can see the hate on their faces . . . People I don't even know have actually threatened to kill me.

INTERVENER: I can tell from the sound of your voice that things have been really painful and scary. Just now I was trying to imagine what it would be like and I . . .

SALMAAN (INTERRUPTS): Did you ever see the movie, *Lords of Discipline*?

INTERVENER: Yeah, I think so, but it was quite a while ago. What I remember vividly was a lot of hazing that was pretty brutal.

SALMAAN: The thing is, the movie didn't even come close to what it's like for somebody like me. In addition to the regular harassment that everybody gets, I get even more since the terrorist attacks . . . because I'm Pakistani and Muslim . . . (*He sighs.*) I've just really had it. (*His voice becomes louder and angry.*) Dammit, I'm just as much an American as any of them. I was born in this country. I actually served in the military for 2 years—and in a combat zone, too! These guys are just playing soldier here and I'm sick of their crap!

INTERVENER: I can't imagine putting up with that kind of humiliation and abuse day after day—and it especially angers you when these toy soldiers question your patriotism when you're the one who's served your country. Man, you must have incredible patience and tolerance.

## Reflecting on This Segment

1. How did the intervener enter into Salmaan's story?
2. What did Salmaan's question about the movie represent?

---

## Using This Tool

Form a group with two colleagues. One of you volunteers to share a crisis story and another takes on the task of entering the crisis story. You can use Figure 4–2 as a guide for being an engaged and involved audience. The third person serves as an observer and facilitator. After each of you has practiced this technique, give one another feedback and discuss the experience.

---

### Coconstructing a Survival Story

How people portray themselves in times of crisis can either help or undermine their attempts to achieve a successful resolution. For example, Seligman (1974) found that attributing personality characteristics as the reason for bad events is related to developing clinical depression. Therefore, you need to pay careful attention to how survivors depict both the crisis and themselves in their stories. After people have experienced a crisis in their lives, their stories will be fragmented, emotionally laden, and selective. Furthermore, because of the negative emotions associated with the telling, the person is likely to focus on the worst aspects of the narrative.

People in crisis may hint that they somehow deserve the pain, blame themselves for being victimized, or assert that it will be impossible for them to ever recover. These are notions you want to address as you coconstruct a survival story from the crisis narrative. Coconstruction is a subtle and collaborative process based on the story the survivor tells you. When you are coconstructing, you are not debating or disputing. Instead, you are merely offering another view of the crisis story that also fits the "facts" of the telling. Steve de Shazer (1985) called this the "binocular view" of the story—as the crisis intervener, you supply a second lens to view the circumstances from a different perspective.

Throughout this book, we have emphasized that your most important job as a crisis intervener is to *listen* to the survivor's story. But you are doing much more than merely passively hearing the account. In a state of crisis, the person is telling a story that is still in draft form, still open to revision. As hard as a survivor may try to fully capture a crisis experience in a story, the account is never truly complete. Therefore, you have the opportunity to collaborate on this work in progress to coconstruct the most useful final version possible.

Sociolinguistic studies have demonstrated that "people often construct their discourse out of bits and pieces of others' talk, that is, they speak interactively, jointly building discourse" (Ferrara, 1994, p. 108). In crisis intervention, the person is likely to interweave your comments with his or her own words to revise the story.

When you coconstruct a survival story, you are forming a resolution duet with the storyteller to transcend the original tale of pain and terror (Gergen, 1997). You are beginning to subtly emphasize certain aspects of the story to highlight the strengths and resources that are latent in the crisis narrative. By "reauthoring" (White & Epston, 1990), you and the person in crisis find heroic themes that were overlooked, accomplishments that were disregarded, metaphors of hope that had gone unnoticed, and new options that were undiscovered.

Your work can only be successful if you avoid the temptation to offer the glib consolation or the "magic words" to give instant solace. Offering aphorisms, such as "When the going gets tough, the tough get going" or "When life deals you lemons, make lemonade," does not inspire someone in crisis. Instead, such empty slogans merely communicate that you do not appreciate the anguish and pain that the person is experiencing.

In addition, as Wainrib and Bloch (1998) cautioned, never gloss over the survivor's distress with such empty reassurances as, "Don't worry—everything's going to be OK." For example, never rush to comfort a grieving parent with the consolation that "You may have lost this baby, but you can try to have another one soon." Such trivializing comments not only are offensive, they also reflect your own unwillingness to encounter someone authentically who's struggling with a painful tragedy.

Instead of offering such verbal "chicken soup" maxims, you can enter into the story that is being told and open yourself up to witnessing the ordeal that the survivor has been enduring. As you honor the crisis story, you also will be looking for opportunities to coconstruct a story that includes the possibility of a successful resolution. As Korzybski (1933) put it, "The map is never the territory." This disparity between the event and the story offers you an opportunity to help shape the final version of the narrative.

Like a photographer in a darkroom, you are engaging in a process of developing the image of a survivor that at first is barely visible in the photograph—like the one you saw in Figure 1–1. However, with patience and careful attention, you can help an image of resolution to develop into one of vividness, clarity, and power. The two primary techniques of coconstructing a survival story are asking "making meaning" questions and reframing.

**Asking "Making Meaning" Questions.** As a crisis intervener, you may feel the need to provide answers, but your most potent tool is to ask questions that encourage survivors to find their own answers. Through reflection and reevaluation, survivors often experience small epiphanies—moments of discovery and illumination—that offer insight, discovery, comfort, and revelation.

Making meaning questions that you might ask a survivor include:

- "What have you discovered in this experience?"
- "What have you found out about yourself?"
- "What keeps you going through this painful time?"
- "What lessons about life have you been learning?"
- "What have you relied on to carry you along as you make your way?"
- "What do you see as the purpose of this experience?"
- "What sense do you make of this?"

By asking such questions, you are inviting the person to reflect on the meaning of this experience. Because you are coming from a position of "not knowing," you treat the survivor as an important resource who has valuable lessons to teach you. You consider the survivor to be an explorer who has successfully returned from uncharted territory with important discoveries to share with you and others. Therefore, you'll also be asking such questions as:

- "What beliefs are sustaining you during this time?"
- "What values have been affirmed by this experience?"
- "If you knew somebody who was facing this crisis, what advice would you give that person?"

When you get an answer, be curious about the particulars. Ask follow-up questions to gain more details about the lessons they have learned, the benefits they have gained, and the beliefs that they have reaffirmed. Look for aspects of the telling that may be left out or de-emphasized. Capitalize on "sparkling moments" and become a more excited listener as these moments present themselves.

**Reframing.** Another technique of coconstructing is reframing. To see a demonstration of reframing, glance at the top sequence in Figure 4–3. You probably interpreted the middle figure, which is framed by the letters *A* and *C,* as the letter *B.* Now, take a look at the bottom sequence. You likely perceived the middle figure, framed by the numbers *12* and *14,* as the number *13.* In fact, of course, the middle figure is identical in both sequences. However, depending on how you frame it, you can entirely transform its meaning.

Similarly, when you look carefully at a picture hanging on a wall, you notice that the different colors of the frame can pick up, bring out, and highlight different hues and shades of the picture. By changing the context of a painting, you can change how it is perceived.

When you apply the concept of reframing to a crisis situation, if the context draws you to focus on the turmoil, anguish, and pain of victimization, you can vividly see a scene of utter tragedy. However, when you view the crisis experience in a context that highlights the courage, compassion, and coping of a survivor, the story becomes one of potential triumph.

In earlier chapters, you already learned some specific techniques that can offer a possible reframe. These tools include asking getting-through questions, "finding the pony," tracking resolution, asking moving-on questions, and offering an encouragement interlude. You can offer many variations on the theme of finding the survivor in the crisis story. For example, "After all that's happened to you, how did you find the

**FIGURE 4–3**  The effect of framing.

---

**Techniques for Reframing the Crisis Story**

- Place the story in a *situational* context.

- Place the story in a *temporal* context.

- *Normalize* any pathological and negative self-labeling.

---

**FIGURE 4–4**   Reframing techniques.

strength to . . ." is an excellent beginning to giving voice to the evidence of the person's ability to survive.

As you can see in Figure 4–4, there are several specific techniques that you can use to help a survivor reframe the crisis experience.

- Placing the crisis in a *situational* context. While sharing their crisis story, survivors sometimes make a negative *global* pronouncement that could sabotage the potential for a successful resolution. People in crisis may characterize themselves as absolute failures, portray the world as completely senseless, or describe their life as totally hopeless. Such characterizations can sabotage someone's potential for successfully resolving a crisis. For example, a person may declare, "I've made a horrible mess of things! What a fool I am! There's no way that I can ever go on after this." When people depict themselves in such pathetic ways, they are likely to then feel demoralized and discouraged.

  When you hear such a dismal global pronouncement, you can subtly offer a reframe by placing the person's statement in the situational *context* of a specific incident. You can then interpret the person's statement as giving voice to a specific and temporary reaction that happened during that time and under those circumstances. In other words, instead of arguing that all of life is not a hopeless "mess," you are merely validating that the survivor was feeling hopeless in the immediate wake of the crisis. And you are not debating the assertion that someone is a helpless "fool." Instead, you are pointing out that he or she simply could not decide on a course of action at that particular time.

  In the previous example, the survivor portrayed the crisis events as proof that he or she is a loser who is doomed to remain a complete failure. However, your interpretation is not about the *person*, but about the *situation*. You might say, "So, *when* that happened, you felt overwhelmed and confused."

  Contrary to the person's self-portrayal, you are assuming that this individual is resilient and has had some successes in the past in resolving crises. Therefore, you can use the tracking resolution technique from Chapter 2. As you recall, you place the negative reaction in the context of the crisis incident and describe the actions that the person is taking to cope. For example, you can say to the person, "You were feeling so overwhelmed and confused at that time that you even wondered if you were going to make it. How are you managing to be so persistent and determined in spite of those feelings?"

- Placing the crisis in a specific *temporal* context. When a survivor recounts past crisis events in the present tense, he or she may be saying, for example, ". . . and so now I'm so fed up with my life, there's no choice but to kill myself."

  Your coconstructing strategy here is to refer to the crisis in the past tense and offer the current conclusion as only one of a number of menu options. Responding to the client statement, you might empathically engage in the deconstruction process by saying, "So far, you've felt like nothing has worked and as you sorted out your options, the one that came up first as a possibility was suicide."

- *Normalizing.* At times, people in crisis will use pathologizing labels to depict themselves. They may use diagnostic terms to describe themselves. For example, they might say, "I'm really getting paranoid about things," or "I think I'm going psychotic with all this stress," or "The way I've been acting lately, I must be manic."

  Your task is to destigmatize such characterizations. For example, if someone is inappropriately labeling oneself as being "clinically depressed," you can acknowledge the feelings without confirming the diagnosis by saying, "You've been feeling down and really lousy."

  Working to reframe a negative portrayal involves responding to the pejoratives in a neutral manner, normalizing them, and separating the behaviors from the labels. For example, you might say to someone, "So, it sounds like you have been seeing yourself as being 'paranoid' because you've been particularly careful ever since the attack."

  Keep in mind one final point about normalizing. As the crisis story in Chapter 3 demonstrated, people who have such disorders as schizophrenia or bipolar disorder can also have crises. In fact, they are more likely to experience such serious incidents in their lives. In these cases, you can still portray such people as survivors who are doing their best to cope with a current troubling situation while also handling a long-term psychiatric disorder.

There will be times when people portray themselves in their crisis stories as completely passive victims of circumstances that are totally out of their control. You may be tempted, but don't offer an inspirational speech to convince them of their capabilities. Instead, you can pursue a coconstructive strategy by asking getting-through or moving-on questions that help people discover their own strengths, appreciate what they have been able to accomplish, and enhance their sense of personal power.

You need to acknowledge those feelings of victimization while finding other elements of the story that reveal the survivor. However—and this is crucial—you do not approach the narrative as an expert who is trying to "swap" one story for another. Neither should you be trying to help the storyteller gain more "realistic" insights. Both these "modernist" approaches are "outside-in" attempts to force your perspective on another person. It is not your role to convince people to bring their meanings into compliance with reality. Their meanings *are* reality.

One way to coconstruct a survival story is to look for sparkling moments in the crisis narrative—"times when they have escaped the clutches of the dominant narrative" (White & Epston, 1990, p. 153). As the intervener, you maintain a not-knowing attitude regarding their crisis story, realizing that the survivor is the expert on how to tell the story.

## Listening In on Crisis Intervention

Review the story at the beginning of the chapter and the earlier segment of the crisis hotline call. After bearing witness to Salmaan's crisis experiences, the intervener begins to focus on coconstructing a survival story.

SALMAAN (*With a sad and soft voice*): No one wants me to be here. I mean, my friends at home and my family think I'm nuts. I guess they're right. What's wrong with me? Why can't I go to a regular college and study computers or some other boring crap? I'm like this martyr or something.

INTERVENER: You said that sometimes you've felt like a martyr . . . almost like you've been carrying a huge weight on your shoulders and no one has helped you and no one has appreciated what you've been going through.

SALMAAN: Right! Like that guy in mythology who was sentenced to carry that huge rock up the mountain all by himself. I know how he must have felt.

INTERVENER: Yeah, it sounds like it. Even the "all by himself part."

SALMAAN: I do have a couple of Black guys in the barracks that I'm buddies with. But they can't do anything and I'm pretty sure they're sick of hearing me complain . . . (*He pauses for a second or two.*) . . . especially Edward!

INTERVENER: You said, "especially Edward." How so?

SALMAAN: This morning, he was looking for me and he asked a couple of guys from our company if they had seen me. They gave him some crap and made a big scene about him being friends with a "camel jockey." There was some pushing and shoving and a platoon leader broke it up and put all of them on report.

I saw Edward right after that and he was still mad. He blamed me and told me to quit feeling sorry for myself and that he was tired of having to stick up for me. The last thing he said really got me, though . . . (*He pauses, and when he starts speaking again, his words are barely audible.*) He said that I ought to try being an African American for awhile!

INTERVENER: Wow, that must have felt like getting the wind knocked out of you! Your friend sticks up for you and ends up getting in trouble. He must really value your friendship to stand up for you knowing that there might be consequences. You know what, though, from what you've told me I'll bet you are wondering what Edward was really saying in that last part, like what kind of message was he hoping to hear from you, maybe? What do you think he was trying to say?

## Reflecting on This Segment

1. How did the intervener try to get Salmaan to find meaning in his experience?
2. What did the intervener do to get Salmaan to open up to her?
3. What do you think Edward was trying to say?

## USING THIS TOOL

Regroup with your two colleagues who collaborated with you in the previous practice. Return to your crisis stories, but this time practice coconstructing survival stories using Figure 4–4 as a reminder. Once each of you has practiced this technique, share your observations and feedback.

## RESOURCES FOR SURVIVORS OF PREJUDICE, RACISM, AND OPPRESSION

In Chapter 10, you will find resources for dealing with terrorism and other community-wide catastrophes. The following are examples of possible resources for Salmaan and others who are confronted with crises resulting from racism and prejudice.

"Stop the Hate!" Campus Hate Crime Prevention Program
http://www.stophate.org/stophate

This program, developed by the Association of College Unions International (ACUI), is dedicated to combating hate and promoting a sense of community on campuses. Victims of hate can report incidents and learn about their rights and options by contacting this Web site.

Council on American Islamic Relations (CAIR)
http://www.cair-net.org

CAIR is a nonprofit, grassroots membership organization that was established to promote a positive image of Islam and Muslims in America.

## SUMMARY

How people represent their crisis experiences, and how those representations may help or sabotage successful resolutions, is the focus of the constructivist approach to crisis intervention. The ways in which a survivor assigns meaning to a crisis is your crucial consideration. As you can see in Figure 4–5, you enter the crisis story and begin coconstructing a story with possibilities for resolution.

---

**Essential Tools**

- Enter the person's crisis story.
- Help coconstruct a survival story.
  - ✎ Ask making-meaning questions.
  - ✎ Reframe the crisis.

---

**FIGURE 4–5**   Essential tools of Chapter 4.

## Segue to Chapter 5

Watch about 10 minutes of any television news program. During that time, you will observe at least one person who is going through a crisis. As you watch, notice the facial expressions, body posture, and gestures of the person. As you listen, pay particular attention to the person's tone of voice. What emotions is this person experiencing? What emotions does this encounter stir up in you?

# Managing Emotional Arousal: Promoting Feelings of Resolve

"There are times when we must sink to the bottom of our misery to understand truth,
just as we must descend to the bottom of a well to see the stars in broad daylight."
*Vaclav Havel*

"To the question whether I am a pessimist or an optimist, I answer that my knowledge
is pessimistic, but my willing and hoping are optimistic."
*Albert Schweitzer*

## CHAPTER GOALS

After completing this chapter, you should be able to:

- Understand that people in crisis experience not only emotions of distress—fear, rage, and grief—but also positive emotions of resolve—courage, compassion, and hope
- Understand that emotional arousal has no valence until someone assigns meaning to it
- Discover how emotions and thoughts are intertwined
- Recognize the distinction between emotional catharsis and expression
- Help a survivor to manage the intensity of emotional arousal to resolve a crisis successfully

## OVERVIEW

In this chapter, we explore the crucial place of emotions in crisis intervention by discussing several common misconceptions. One of the typical myths is that people experience only negative emotions in times of crisis. Although they are confronted with intense feelings of distress, survivors actually have the entire range of emotions—both positive and negative. Think about the times that you have gathered with relatives and friends to grieve over the death of a loved one. In addition to shedding tears together, you probably also laughed together as you recalled joyful times, offered expressions of love to one another, and perhaps savored the small but wondrous consolations of life. Therefore, when you do crisis intervention, you can expect people to express both positive and negative emotions.

Another common myth is that emotions interfere with effective problem solving and successful coping. The typical view, particularly in Western societies, is that we must first "let out" our emotions or "put our feelings aside" to resolve a crisis rationally. However, new discoveries in neuroscience are revealing that emotions are actually essential to productive thinking.

All *emotions*, particularly in times of crisis, are impulses to take action. The origin of the word emotion is *motere*, the Latin verb "to move." When you encounter someone in crisis, he or she is typically moving *away* from a threatening and dangerous situation. However, as an intervener, your job is to help the person move *toward* a successful resolution. In both cases, emotions play a vital part in producing this necessary movement.

This chapter offers an exploration of innovative ideas taken from recent research into how emotions work and how they contribute to crisis resolution. You will learn techniques to help survivors manage their emotions. As a crisis intervener, you will be soothing negative emotions and promoting positive feelings of resolve.

## CRISIS STORY

Nelda Ann was frantic. She was running late because she had to stay after her shift to help Weldon, the store manager, total up the day's receipts. Nelda Ann knew that he was nervous about making a mistake and that she would be his excuse if anything went wrong. It wasn't a situation that she was happy about, but she really needed the job and, after all, she had gotten overtime for staying late.

Still, if she didn't have Jimmy's dinner on the table at 6:00 sharp, there would be hell to pay. The speedometer needle inched toward 50 and the old truck sprayed gravel as she careened around the tight turns on route 754. Clouds of gray-brown dust followed her arrival as Nelda Ann rushed down the lane to the trailer of her mother-in-law, who was babysitting.

"Nelda Ann, look what you've gone and done! My wash is ruined 'cause you're late again. Dammit girl, what am I gonna do with you?"

Her mother-in-law's loud, shrill, nasal voice resounded in the heat and dust. Nelda Ann's headache was even worse. The baby started wailing, adding to the cacophony of sound, which washed over the three of them like a tsunami.

"I'm sorry, Marie, but it couldn't be helped. I'll come over later and do your wash over, but right now, I've gotta get before Jimmy gets home. You know how he . . ."

Her voice trailed away as she remembered where her mother-in-law's loyalties lay and absently fingered a scar under her left cheek made by her husband's wedding band. She had bought him that ring with her high school graduation money and now wished she could cram it down his beer-swilling throat. After the last time, he had begged for her forgiveness and had promised never to do it again. However, even after his dramatic, tearful performance featuring miles of regrets and a litany of promises, she was sure that the beatings would continue.

"Jimmy is like a dark sky at noon, it's just a matter of time before something bad is almost sure to happen," she thought to herself.

Swallowing hard, Nelda Ann's face paled and her legs began to tremble as her mind raced back to the last beating. They had been increasing in frequency since the baby was born and, 3 weeks ago, she had to drive herself to the emergency room to have stitches in her lip and cheek.

She didn't dare leave the baby with him—there was no telling what he'd do if her crying upset him. Nelda Ann's eyes filled with tears, and hopelessness began to engulf her like a dense fog. She had no family to speak of—an older sister she couldn't stand and a great-aunt somewhere out West who was close to 80 by now and no help.

"That bastard will not hurt me or you again, baby girl." Nelda Ann realized that the words she had just heard had come from her own lips, and she began to feel stronger. She pulled over to the side of the road, adjusted the baby's blanket, and gently leaned over and rested her head on the child's rosy cheek. She wasn't sure how long she sat there with the motor running, but it must have been a while because the baby had fallen fast asleep.

Slowly, the unmistakable image of a handgun began to form in her mind's eye. And it wasn't just a fantasy TV or movie weapon, either. It was real. Some time back, she had been looking for a paper clip in one of the manager's bottom desk drawers when she saw the pistol. She quickly shut the drawer and moved away from the desk, feeling strangely ashamed, almost like a child who had discovered a forbidden secret.

Nelda Ann shook off that feeling and brought herself back to the present. She had the keys to the store in her purse and, at that moment, she realized that she could put an end to her problems once and for all. She drove back to the store, went through a side entrance, and gently put the baby into the makeshift crib she kept in an office closet.

Nelda Ann opened the drawer, picked up the gun, and looked at it for a minute. Finally, she laid it down on the desk, unsure of what to do next. She turned away to look at her baby and accidentally brushed against the telephone book, knocking it to the floor. She reached down to pick it up and noticed that it was open to the yellow pages, and her eyes went to a large, prominent box in bold type that read, "24-Hour Assault Hotline." Her eyes moved to the telephone, then to the gun on the desk, and finally she found her gaze turning toward her 13-month-old daughter, beautiful and innocent in sleep.

## Reflecting on This Crisis Story

1. What were your own emotional reactions to the events in this story?
2. What negative emotions did Nelda Ann experience?
3. What positive emotions did she have?

# IDEAS

### Catharsis and Crisis

Aristotle believed that viewing theatrical dramas aroused emotions to the point that audience members experienced a purging effect that would rid them of negative feelings (Hothersall, 1990). His idea was that if people experienced a tragic event and had a "good cry" or even unleashed a "primal scream," then they would feel a lot better. *Catharsis*, in other words, is like an ethereal laxative that discharges pent-up emotions.

Freud made this idea of the cathartic emotional experience the centerpiece of his psychoanalytic theory. It fit well with the dominant technology of his time—the steam engine. Such an engine must have a release valve to keep its internal pressure from building up to a dangerous level. Even today, people often speak of "blowing off steam" and believe that "letting out" pent-up feelings is preferable to "keeping it all inside."

Since the pioneering work by Lindemann (1944) on the survivors of the Coconut Grove disaster, the literature on crisis intervention has similarly emphasized that emotional catharsis is necessary for resolution to take place (Kanel, 2003). Crisis interveners and trauma therapists have stressed that an abreaction, a reexperiencing of negative emotions, is essential to working through the feelings (O'Brien, 1998). This view is based on the assumption that unvented emotions will fester and build until the person eventually explodes. For example, Puryear (1979) urged that "for healthy adjustment to a traumatic event or loss, the feelings need to be experienced and expressed" (p. 38). Television, movies, music, and other media of popular culture have unquestionably embraced the therapeutic value of catharsis. As Bowman (1997) observed, "It seems there is now a general belief that a vivid emotional display is the expected expression of inner experiences in crisis situations" (pp. 80–81).

The emphasis in traditional crisis intervention on catharsis suggests that survivors must let out all their feelings so that such feelings do not become repressed and lead to problems in the future. Furthermore, if people have repressed their emotions in an earlier crisis, then they must recover and reexperience these feelings before they can feel purged.

The idea of the therapeutic release of emotions has become so ingrained in our culture, it seems to be just common sense that if you feel tense or angry, you should vent it. However, according to Williams and Williams (1998), this venting is not only nontherapeutic, but a steady diet of emotional catharsis can actually kill you. In their book *Anger Kills,* they cite many physiological complications, including death, resulting from the chronic ventilation of aroused emotions. Other social scientists are now suggesting that, contrary to Aristotle and Freud, witnessing violence in movies or on television is not cathartic, but may increase one's level of hostility and aggression (Hothersall, 1990). So the commonsense idea of blowing off steam may not be as productive as was once thought.

### Expressing, Managing, and Making Meaning of Emotions

Recent evidence also casts doubt on the usefulness of emotional catharsis in portraying the complex and rich process of dealing with feelings during a crisis. In contrast to strategies that give voice to a range of emotions, such as talking or writing about traumatic experiences, merely venting negative emotions by screaming and yelling has no health benefits (Niederhoffer & Pennebaker, 2002).

Besides expressing their feelings in more productive ways, people can also use strategies to manage their emotions when they are confronted with crisis incidents (Gross & Munoz, 1995). These strategies include redirecting their attention, reframing the events, or taking the perspective of others. For example, a pilot trying to avoid an accident may focus entirely on carrying out the immediate tasks at hand, postponing any emotional expression until perhaps later. In addition to distracting oneself, a person can also reframe the crisis in such a way that the feelings are not so overwhelming. After 9/11, rescue workers managed their emotions while picking up body parts scattered around the Twin Towers by reframing their grim task as an act of respect and honor for these final remains. Gross and Munoz (1995) viewed emotional regulation as a necessary skill in dealing with the challenges of such horrific situations.

In Chapter 4, we discussed how making meaning was a vital component of a successful resolution of a crisis. However, we not only make sense out of *external* events, we also construe our *internal* experiences by interpreting our inner physiological states. Oatley and Jenkins (1996) suggested that emotions are protean, unfinished products that are given form through expression. This means that emotions are open to change. "They tell us something is happening to which we should pay attention. Often, they demand a creative response" (p. 370). A crisis challenges us to form our inchoate emotions into useful and positive forms of expression. By giving form to our emotions, we are making them more manageable and assigning meaning to them.

One of the common myths that many crisis interveners have about negative emotions is that people can decide how to express feelings, but once they have a feeling, they are stuck with it until they let it out in some way. However, a constructivist view of emotions is that people engage in a creative process of molding different emotions, such as excitement, fear, or hope, from the raw material of the physiological state of arousal that they are experiencing.

Bowman (1997) has summarized the results of social psychology experiments demonstrating that others can influence how a person interprets emotional states. Many of these studies involved the injection of adrenaline into the bloodstream, which increased physiological arousal (Bruner, 1986). When the experimental circumstances promoted negative expectations, participants experienced such feelings as anxiety, anger, or sadness. However, when the situation suggested positive expectations, the participants, who received the same dosage of adrenaline, interpreted their arousal as elation and other positive emotions. When we are stressed, we become emotionally aroused. This stress is the result of stimulus overload, which we interpret as either distress or excitement, depending on how we view the situation in which we find ourselves.

One important implication of these findings is that if human beings can interpret their own physiological world, they are not helpless victims of their emotions. Many people lead troubled lives because they believe that they are on emotional leashes—jerked into abusive relationships, yanked into self-defeating lifestyles, and restrained from reaching their full potential. "Yes, he beats me, but I love him, so I can't leave" and "I can't help feeling so angry all the time" are examples of the ways that people can portray themselves as powerless victims of their feelings. However, we do have the power to be the masters of our own fate—instead of the passive victims of our environment—because we ultimately author the interpretation of events in our lives. Even if we have lost everything else, Frankl (1969) affirmed that we can still focus on "the last of human freedoms—the ability to choose one's attitude in a given set of circumstances" (p. 73). At a fundamental level, making such an existential decision can affect how we feel in times of crisis. It is the meaning we assign to events that makes the difference. Frankl went on to assert that a person who has a "why" to live can bear almost any "how."

## Thinking and Feeling

There are a couple of major misconceptions regarding thoughts and *feelings*. The first is that emotions only interfere with thinking. The assumption is that, in order for people to be effective problem solvers, they must reason dispassionately. You may not have studied much philosophy, but you're probably familiar with Rene Descartes and his famous line, "Cogito ergo sum" ("I think, therefore I am."). With this statement, Descartes placed thought at the peak of human existence. Since Descartes, most people in Western society have accepted the notion that cognition ranks above emotion in importance. However, Damasio (1994) argued that Descartes' omission of emotions in the enterprise of good thinking was an error. From his neurological research, Damasio concluded that there is an intuitive-emotional side to knowledge, which, if missing, can hinder the reasoning process. In other words, we make the best decisions when our thoughts and emotions are integrated.

Another common myth is that feelings come from the heart or gut, whereas cognitions arise from the brain. After all, people in crisis will talk about experiencing a "broken heart" or having a "gut reaction." However, neuroscientific findings have cast some doubt on the general assumption that we feel with our heart. In his book *Emotional Intelligence*, Daniel Goleman (1995) cited Joseph LeDoux's work on the function of the amygdala in the human brain. The amygdala is an almond-shaped cluster of neuronal structures located just above the brain stem, deep within the temporal lobes, in an area sometimes called the "nose brain." It is so called because the olfactory sense sends messages to this area, and it is from this location that the more recent brain sections, such as the neocortex, evolved. The hippocampus and the amygdala are the key structures of the nose brain.

The hippocampus seems to be the area that encodes and consolidates cognitive memory. The amygdala, on the other hand, appears to be an older and more efficient processing location for helping human beings to respond to emotionally "hot" situations. When thought and emotion are working harmoniously, through both the hippocampus and the amygdala, human information processing is complete.

Typically, our senses transmit signals through the thalamus to the cortex, and then the brain assigns meaning to the sensed objects. For example, if the sensed object is a poisonous snake, the cortex assigns the meaning of danger, sends a message to the limbic area that activates the emotional centers, and initiates action—in the form of running away. However, LeDoux (1996) identified a "smaller and shorter pathway—something like a neural back alley" (p. 17) of neurons that makes it possible for the amygdala to receive threatening data directly from the senses and to trigger an immediate emotional reaction before the cortex itself is activated.

Goleman (1995) suggested that the *amygdala* emotionally "hijacks" the stimulus before we can even make cognitive and conscious sense of what it is (see Figure 5–1).

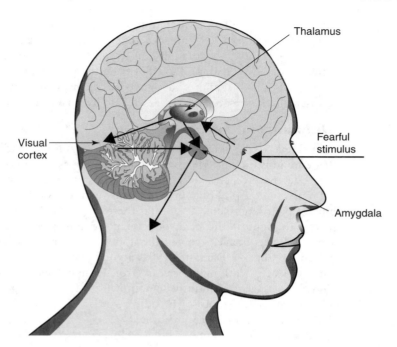

**FIGURE 5–1**   Amygdala "hijacking" a fearful stimulus.

He offered a fine example to demonstrate how emotions can have a sudden and powerful impact on how people think and act. Imagine, for example, that you are hiking alone in an isolated area of Yellowstone Park when you are suddenly confronted face-to-face with a ferocious grizzly bear. At that precise moment, you are not composing a grocery list, balancing your checking account, or reflecting on the problems of grizzlies as an endangered species—you are only concentrating on this particular bear, scanning quickly for avenues of escape in this specific situation, and focusing all your thoughts on surviving. Strong emotions bring certain thoughts to the foreground of our attention and cause all other thoughts to recede into the background. Our emotional system is older and operates more rapidly than our thinking system. As a result, when intense emotions arise, our ability to exercise cortical control over them is not equal to the task.

## Emotional Arousal and the Yerkes-Dodson Law

Two extreme emotional reactions are possible in crisis situations. The most obvious reaction is the feeling of being overwhelmed by intense distress. The person may be sobbing, screaming, crying for help, running in panic, or striking out in a blind rage. The other extreme is a kind of "emotional shock" in which the person doesn't appear to have any feelings or reactions.

As you can see in Figure 5–2, there exists a curvilinear (inverted-*U*) relationship between the level of *emotional arousal* and efficiency of performance (Martindale, 1981). The *Yerkes-Dodson Law*, first articulated in 1908, reflects this relationship. Simply put, the quality of your performance on any task, whether physical or mental, is related to your

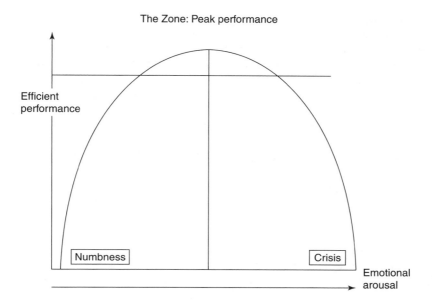

**FIGURE 5–2**   Yerkes-Dodson Law—"the zone."

level of emotional arousal. If you're feeling either very low or extremely high levels of emotional arousal, then your performance is likely to be impaired. You are likely to do your best when your emotional level is sufficient to motivate you, but not so high as to sabotage your abilities. Our counseling students have dubbed this optimal area "*the zone.*"

Remember that emotions are motivating—having emotions means that a person is poised to act. The distress serves an adaptive purpose in crisis resolution by spurring a survivor to take immediate and extraordinary action. However, too much distress can hinder the person's ability to perform the essential tasks involved in resolving a crisis. As a crisis worker, your job is to help people to find their zone, their ideal state of arousal. At this optimal midpoint of the Yerkes-Dodson curve, the different brain structures are working together successfully.

---

## *EXPERIENCING THIS IDEA*

Think about a time in your life when you experienced being in the zone as you successfully dealt with a particular challenge. What strategies did you use to "psych" yourself up to perform your best? What strategies did you use to handle the anxiety when it threatened to interfere with your performance?

---

### **Negative Emotions of Crisis**

For the sake of simplicity, we can divide the *negative emotions* by colors—yellow, red, and black. *Yellow emotions*, like the traffic light that signals caution, are characterized by anxiety, fear, and panic. Many crisis experiences are dramatic reminders of our vulnerability and mortality. It is only natural that people would be fearful at these times because dangers, both physical and psychological, are inherent in crisis. Apprehension and anxiety can be highly adaptive, even essential, in threatening circumstances.

Some survivors continue to be hypervigilant (O'Brien, 1998), constantly on guard, and, in the words of one survivor, "as tight as a coiled spring" long after a catastrophic event. Feeling apprehensive that another calamity could threaten them around every corner, survivors may be easily startled by unexpected sights and sounds. Some people find it difficult to relax and be at ease. Instead, they may often feel on edge. Survivors may also be extremely fearful, even when there is nothing threatening nearby (Kalayjian, 1999).

*Red emotions* are anger, resentment, and hostility. Certainly, anger can be a very appropriate and valuable emotional response to adversity, physical threat, and personal violation. Outrage and fury can energize people to protect themselves and others, persevere in overcoming obstacles, and mobilize their resources. At times, however, the anger can be maladaptive. For example, the survivor may be easily irritated by petty annoyances or inexplicably burst into a violent rage. Survivors may feel resentful, embittered, and mad at the world (Novaco & Chemtob, 1998).

One particular red emotion that you are likely to have in crises involving victimization is that of vengeance. Often, we tend to consider the emotion of vengeance to be an unsavory and undesirable way for people to feel. We may feel the impulse to talk a person out of such feelings. But you will find that those who have been injured by others, or who believe that another person has caused the crisis event, will sometimes entertain strong fantasies of "getting even." They will become obsessed with justice or parity in which the other person gets what he or she has coming. You will recall that when bad things happen to good people, their assumptions regarding a "just world" are shattered. They consider that although they have lived a good life and treated others with respect, the "bread they have cast upon the waters" has not returned. The world has been thrown out of balance.

In such cases as sexual assault, arson, burglary, or the murder of a loved one, the person may feel helpless and at the mercy of the vagaries of life. One way that a survivor can temporarily restore a sense of control, and balance the scales, is to imagine getting even with a perpetrator. For a time, the survivor may be consumed with such thoughts and may desire to do something to the perpetrator that is totally out of character with the survivor's normal behavior or even against his or her own values.

You must recognize that this desire for vengeance is simply another way that some survivors use to begin to restore their world to a more hospitable and predictable place. Vengeance is a sort of prosthetic device that can help survivors get through until they feel more confident and in control. At such time, they may turn the former desire for vengeance into socially constructive behavior, as in the case of John Walsh turning the kidnap and murder of his son Adam into a nationwide campaign against crime, or the parents of a murdered little girl establishing the "Amber Alert."

Don't ignore or attempt to minimize someone's talk of vengeance because of your belief that it is not an emotion good people should feel. Although it states in the Bible that God said, "Vengeance is mine," it seems He is willing to lend it to survivors of crimes until such time as they no longer need it.

*Black emotions* are the depression, hopelessness, shame, and grief that many people in crisis experience (Bifulco & Brown, 1996). The victims may have lost their health, a loved one, or their way of life. It is only natural for them to go through a time of grieving for these losses. It is also not uncommon for someone to feel a powerful sense of shame about this victimization. In extreme cases, some survivors have turned to suicide.

In the case of police officers, firefighters, rescue workers, soldiers, and others in hazardous occupations, the crisis incidents may happen frequently. But human beings are not wired to handle such violent and dangerous episodes on a regular basis. Eventually, such situations can take their toll, even on brave and well-trained professionals who face them routinely. To make matters more challenging for helpers, some survivors may have the "John Wayne Syndrome"—a reluctance to admit any physical or emotional pain. Successfully managing these emotions involves experiencing and working through these feelings rather than suppressing them (Gross, 1998).

## Positive Emotions

The study of human emotions, for the most part, has been a study of negative feelings. If you type "anxiety" as your subject heading in PsycINFO (http://www.apa.org/psycinfo/), you will find thousands and thousands of studies. Change the topic to "anger," and again you will have an overwhelming number of hits. Try "depression" and you will have similarly impressive results. However, if you submit "courage," "compassion," or "joy," you will find only a handful of studies. Even comprehensive models of the basic affective states have far more negative than *positive emotions* (Fernandez-Ballesteros, 2003). For example, Levenson and colleagues (1992) posited four negative and only one positive emotion.

Recently, both researchers and practitioners in counseling, social work, and psychology have turned their attention to positive emotions (see, for example, Frederickson, 2002; Larsen, Hemenover, Norris, & Cacioppo, 2003; Watson, 2002). They see positive emotions as a frontier of uncharted territory that holds vast potential for improving lives (Haidt, 2003). Recent studies have examined a wide range of positive feelings that have rarely been mentioned in the psychological literature. For example, Frederickson (1998) focused on four positive emotions, including joy (elation or happiness), interest (curiosity or excitement), contentment (tranquility or serenity), and love (compassion or affection). Others have explored such feelings as gratitude (McCullough, Kilpatrick, Emmons, & Larson, 2001), inspiration or elevation (Haidt, 2003), and awe (Keltner & Haidt, in press).

Crisis is a time of heightened emotional arousal, but a common assumption is that people in crisis have only negative feelings. Recent research has demonstrated that people going through times of loss and adversity actually experience positive as well as painful emotions (Larsen et al., 2003). These *"rainbow" emotions* of resolve include such feelings as courage, compassion, hope, inspiration, and joy.

In fact, acknowledging and giving voice to the gamut of emotions, both negative and positive, can promote a positive crisis resolution. For example, in one study, caregivers told their stories shortly after the deaths of their partners by AIDS (Stein, Folkman, Trabasso, & Richards, 1997). Although their narratives were intensely emotional, surprisingly, nearly a third of the emotional words that caregivers used in their accounts were positive. At follow-up 12 months later, the survivors whose stories expressed more positive feelings showed better health and well-being. They were more likely to have developed long-term plans and goals in life.

In other research, Emmons, Colby, and Kaiser (1998) explored how some survivors were eventually able to transform their losses into gains. They found that even during the crisis experience itself, such thrivers were able to take some degree of pleasure in savoring the few desirable events that took place, appreciating discoveries that they had made, and celebrating small victories. Successful coping in crisis situations seems to involve both positive and negative emotions (Folkman & Moskowitz, 2000).

Another example of the expression of a positive emotion is laughter. Over the years, many counselors and therapists have dismissed the use of humor in times of crisis as merely a defense mechanism. They saw it as a cheap attempt to find comic relief and to avoid dealing with painful emotions. However, Milo (2001) identified using humor as one of the important coping strategies used by mothers grieving for the death of their child. Humor is a positive emotion that embraces the enigma, paradoxes, and mysteries of a crisis.

## Emotions of Resolve

What are these emotions of resolve—the "rainbow" emotions? There are many feelings that people experience as they go through the process of resolution. For example, three emotions that reflect flourishing under stress are courage, compassion, and hope. *Courage* is the emotion of resolve that survivors draw on to face the threat and deal with the danger, while all along managing the anxiety. *Compassion* for one's fellow creatures is the emotion of resolve that tempers the rage, serves as an empathic bridge with other survivors, and strengthens the emotional ties that make up a sense of community. These "ties that bind" hold people together in networks of social support through troubled times.

Although courage and compassion are important feelings of resolve, we will be focusing our discussion on another rainbow emotion that has been documented to be vital in the process of crisis resolution—hope. *Hope* is the optimistic feeling that a resolution is possible in spite of the overwhelming odds, painful losses, and grief that a survivor may be experiencing. People with high levels of hope are better adjusted, enjoy more social support, and have more meaning in their lives (Snyder, 2002).

Hope is an emotion with an eye to the future. For this reason, when you are attempting to help someone by instilling hope, any probing of the past that you do is likely to be counterproductive. Instead, actively listen to the person talk about these past events, acknowledge the feelings and meanings the person has regarding them, but do not probe for more details. You are intervening with someone because of a crisis event that has taken place in the past. But hope, although it is experienced in the present, can only be about the future.

At first, survivors feel compelled to talk about the past crisis experience, but as they tell their story, you can explore facets that suggest future possibilities. Techniques such as tracking resolution and moving-on questions can help a survivor get in touch with a sense of optimism. Remember that this process of coconstructing a survival story does not involve disputing the person's portrayal of the "facts" of the crisis. Neither is it an attempt on your part to reassure someone that everything is going to be okay. Bringing emotions of resolve to a survivor story requires looking for openings that are about positive emotions. The survivor who is telling the story is the one who provides these glimpses of hope—your job is to call attention to these sightings.

Snyder, Michael, and Cheavens (1999) conceptualized hope as how people think about their goals, and as an emotion that involves two basic elements. The first component of hope is a person's feelings of confidence about creating or discovering a route to a goal; the second ingredient is someone's belief that he or she can actually navigate the journey toward the goal. In other words, the first component is called "pathways thinking" and the second is known as "agency thinking" (p. 181).

When people are in despair and feeling discouraged, it is because they are either unable to see the pathway out of the crisis, or they believe that the desired goal lies beyond their ability to reach it. Worse yet, a tragic incident may sabotage both elements of hope. Someone in crisis may believe that there is no path available and, even if one were found, that he or she does not have the ability to reach the goal. The person is likely to feel what Lazarus (1991) called "goal-incongruent emotions"—anger, anxiety, guilt, sadness, and shame.

---

## EXPERIENCING THESE IDEAS

Pick one of your own successful experiences of dealing with a challenging situation. What emotions of distress—anxiety, sadness, or rage—did you experience? What role did these feelings play in meeting this challenge? What emotions of resolve—courage, hope, or compassion—did you experience? How did these emotions help you?

---

### Broaden-and-Build Theory

Frederickson (2002) offered substantial support for a *broaden-and-build theory* of positive emotions. Negative emotions narrow our options to those few actions that are usually adaptive in a threatening situation. When we are frightened, for example, we have an immediate urge to escape. Our thoughts quickly focus on finding the safest route to safety. We may chance upon a clever scheme for fleeing a danger, but the fear propels us to take immediate and decisive action without wasting much time on reflection, consideration, and exploration.

In contrast, positive emotions can actually broaden our ways of thinking and acting. When people experience such feelings as love or joy, they are more likely to think creatively, to surprise themselves by what they are able to accomplish, and to explore new possibilities. Over time, people use these broadening experiences to build enduring personal resources that enhance their capabilities of dealing with future crises. Reflecting on the implications of her broaden-and-build theory, Frederickson (2002) concluded, "So, through experiences of positive emotions, people transform themselves, becoming more creative, knowledgeable, resilient, socially integrated, and healthy individuals" (p. 123). In other words, cultivating positive feelings can help survivors to become thrivers.

There is more scientific evidence that adds support to Frederickson's ideas. PET scans of the brain reveal that when people are experiencing positive emotions, there is more activation in their left frontal lobes, whereas negative emotions are accompanied by more activation in the right frontal area (Davidson, 1993). Furthermore, positive emotional states have been found to inhibit the amygdala (Kosslyn & Koenig, 1995). When you are successfully intervening with someone who is distressed, you are reducing the activation of the right frontal lobe, inhibiting the amygdala, and decreasing the chance that the person's emotions will be hijacked. By focusing on stories of survival, you are also activating the left frontal lobes and encouraging positive emotions. You facilitate these changes in brain functioning by expressing more emotion yourself when clients speak of survival, thereby entraining their emotions in a "reverse empathy."

## Reverse Empathy

Perhaps no one did more to legitimize the place of empathy in the counseling process than Carl Rogers. Empathy comes from the Greek *empatheia*, which means "to perceive the subjective experience of another." Early on in his career, Rogers insisted on what he called the "necessary and sufficient" conditions for a therapeutic relationship. Included in these conditions was the notion that the counselor must experience "an empathic understanding of the client's frame of reference and . . . communicate this experience to the client" (in Corey, 1991, p. 212). This "accurate empathic understanding" takes place when the counselor senses clients' feelings as if they were his or her own without becoming lost in those feelings. By moving freely in the world as experienced by clients, the counselor "can not only communicate to them an understanding of what is already known to them but can also voice meanings of experience of which they are only dimly aware" (p. 214).

Although we agree with Rogers, we believe his idea to be an incomplete understanding of empathy. In his model, Rogers focused only on the counselor's empathic ability. However, accurate empathy, in which the counselor attempts to understand and communicate this understanding to the client, is only one side of the story—clients have empathy, too. Appreciating the empathy that survivors bring to crisis intervention offers you another opportunity. By creating an empathic resonance in the person, you can elevate emotional arousal and set the stage for a reframe or a shift in focus. Before considering the techniques involved, let's take a final look at empathy.

*Empathy*, then, is the ability to become emotionally aroused and resonate with the person you are encountering. Goleman called it "emotional contagion" (p. 114), in which people transmit and catch moods from each other. Furthermore, it seems that when two people are in contact, it is the more expressive person who sets the emotional tone of the encounter. "The person who has the more forceful expressivity—or the most power—is typically the one whose emotions entrain the other" (p. 117). As a crisis intervener, you can stimulate a survivor's empathy by being emotionally expressive. In doing so, you may be able to change the focus of the discussion from problem-saturated talk to resolution talk.

Before you turn your attention to learning crisis intervention techniques in the following section, take a moment or two to reflect on the key ideas that you have encountered

---

**Key Ideas**

- Crisis survivors experience the entire range of emotions—positive and negative.

- Merely venting negative emotions has limited therapeutic value.

- Emotions play a crucial role in dealing successfully with crises.

- Our performance is curvilinearly related to our emotional arousal.

- Crisis events can "highjack" the amygdala.

- Positive emotions can broaden our ways of thinking and acting.

---

**FIGURE 5–3**  Key ideas of Chapter 5.

here. As you can see in Figure 5–3, some of these ideas run counter to the popular views of emotions. Keep these ideas in mind because they form the conceptual foundation for the tools you will be learning to use.

# TOOLS

## Managing Emotions in Times of Crisis

Television news programs often show live footage of people confronted with violence, disasters, and other catastrophes. In the midst of the turmoil, these riveting scenes show survivors in obvious and extreme distress. People are likely to be shrieking in terror, sobbing hysterically, screaming in rage, or pleading for help.

Inevitably, once the danger has passed, interviewers shove a microphone into the faces of survivors and intrusively ask, "What was it like for you to go through that?" By then, you can easily tell that the survivors' level of emotional distress has reduced dramatically. They may appear haggard, drained, determined, or dazed, but they definitely have shifted emotional gears. If you pay close attention, you may also notice a subtle difference in the way they now talk about their emotional reactions. "Well," many survivors respond, "when something terrible like that happens, *you* feel. . . ."

When people are first facing a threat, they *are* their emotional distress. They embody the fear, rage, or grief that consumes and drives them to cope with the onslaught. However, once the threat has passed, they begin using a number of strategies to manage their emotional distress. For example, in a variety of creative ways, they devictimize themselves, as you read in Chapter 4. Or, as in the previous interview example, they speak in terms of "you" as they discuss their own emotions. When people use "you" when they mean "I," they are defending themselves from the full impact of the incident. In a subtle way, they are adding a layer of insulation between the ordeal and themselves so that the experience is not as devastating.

Although Gestalt therapists often direct clients to give "I messages" to take full responsibility for their feelings, we encourage you to allow people to use whatever strategy they may need to gain some emotional distance from the pain of a crisis. Survivors need to proceed at their own pace and to deal with their feelings in a way that's manageable. Little by little, they will be able to accommodate to the event, and will begin to say, "When that happened to me, *I* felt . . ."

The primary tools you have for helping survivors manage their emotions in times of crisis are to help lower emotions of distress, raise emotions of resolve, and help survivors stay in the zone.

## Lowering Emotions of Distress

In spite of their efforts, for some people, the emotional distress can last beyond the point where it is needed. One of the reasons for this dilemma is that the connections in the brain that run from the frontal cortex to the amygdala are much weaker than those running from the amygdala to the cortex. Because our neurological dice are loaded in this way, emotions can often take over our thinking, and our thoughts have trouble inhibiting our feelings (Hampden-Turner, 1981; LeDoux, 1996).

This portion of the human brain is evolutionarily quite old and has served our species well. When you are confronted by Goleman's bear, it is better to let your emotional brain immediately get you moving. If you allow your analytical cortex to ponder the situation, you are not likely to escape. However, as Yerkes and Dodson found years ago, a little stress is a good thing, but too much shatters one's ability to think clearly and respond effectively.

As you intervene with someone in crisis, tune into the person's current emotional level to determine whether he or she is too aroused to be in the zone. If a survivor is still in a state of intense distress, you can use the following techniques to reduce the heightened emotional arousal:

- *Address basic needs.* When someone is deeply distressed, you must respond quickly to address basic needs. Ensure the person's safety from threat and take steps to offer physical comfort, shelter, food, important information, and opportunities to contact loved ones. Offer assurances such as, "You're in a safe place here" or "It's good that you contacted us" or "Let's see what we can work out together to deal with this situation."
- *Rely on the LUV Triangle.* You learned this fundamental crisis intervention tool in Chapter 1. However, when someone is feeling overwhelmed with distress, you may find yourself forgetting the power of this technique. Remember that one of the purposes of emotional expression is to send a signal of distress to others—to sound the alarm. Once survivors feel heard and see that others are rallying to their call for help, they feel less distressed and more hopeful. In fact, they will often later report, "I feel as if a weight has been lifted off my shoulders."
- *Acknowledge feelings of distress.* The most important response you can offer to someone who is in distress is to recognize these feelings with openness and concern. The best way to acknowledge feelings of distress is to reflect them.

Offering a reflection is an essential helping skill in which you serve as an emotional mirror to someone. Other mirrors merely show people their outer appearance, but as a crisis intervener, you can reflect back their specific inner feelings. The following are possible reflections that you could offer someone in extreme distress:

> "It sounds like you're still feeling shocked and scared."
> "Those tears tell me that you have a powerful sense of sadness about your loss."
> "You're feeling outraged that someone has treated you so terribly."

Although you are reflecting the survivor's distress, do not force the person to reexperience the crisis by probing for details about the suffering. Remember, your role is not to compel someone to endure a painful ventilation of emotions. Instead, you are offering the comfort of an empathic ear.

Breggin (1997) wrote convincingly of the therapeutic power of empathically responding to someone in crisis. Reflecting the person's feelings is a powerful way to help normalize the intense distress that people typically experience during times of crisis. Putting these emotions into words and communicating them back to the person in a nonjudgmental, respectful, and accepting manner is suggesting—not instructing—that these feelings are normal, typical, and natural. On the other hand, if you were to say, "It's normal for you to feel this way in these circumstances," you would be placing yourself in the exalted position of the expert on these feelings.

- *Speak in a concerned, but soothing tone of voice.* Your manner and voice should communicate that you recognize that the person has been through a terrible experience, but now he or she is safe and the future holds promise for a successful resolution. Your empathic responses offer an echo of the survivor's intense feelings, but at a quieter and more muted level.

  It is important that you offer your reflections in a way that communicates the intensity of the emotions as well as your admiration for how the person has been dealing with these powerful reactions. Tracking resolution, which was described in Chapter 2, can involve acknowledging the crisis event. However, you take care to place it in the past and also give recognition to the survivor who is now dealing with this experience. For example, you may say, "At that moment, you were—as you said—'scared out of your wits,' and 'certain that you were going to die.'" As you speak, you may be slightly shaking and tilting your head, expressing your sense of awe and wonder over how this person has come through the experience.

- *Keep in close and comfortable contact with the survivor.* Decide how physically close you should be to the person to offer comfort. Some people want you to be quite near to them, whereas others will "need more space." Many feel soothed by a comforting touch, a shoulder to cry on, or a sympathetic hug. There is no formula for determining how close to be or when it is OK to touch someone. You can read the person's body language and use your own instinct. If you're wrong, you can always offer a genuine, short apology.

- *Maintain appropriate eye contact.* Some people may want intense eye contact to confirm that you are paying close attention. Others may prefer less eye contact because they believe that they "look a mess" or that you will easily detect their sense of shame or guilt.

## Listening In on Crisis Intervention

Review the crisis story at the beginning of the chapter. A crisis intervener might help Nelda Ann manage her distress in the following way:

NELDA ANN:  The other evening I saw a TV show about battered wives syndrome. They showed some women that got fed up and got a gun and shot the son-of-a-bitch. They got themselves a good lawyer and they got off—they're free! They didn't have to go to jail, and now they're free from all the fear and the beatings. (*As she warms to the subject, her voice grows shrill, her normally pleasant face contorts in rage, her hands clench into fists, and her crossed leg bounces spasmodically.*) I could do it! I really could! I know how to shoot, too! My daddy taught us kids how to shoot all kinds of guns—pistols, rifles, shotguns—you name it, he had one.

INTERVENER:  (*While the survivor has been talking, the intervener has been looking her in the eyes, leaning forward, slowly nodding her head, and reacting with empathic grimaces to Nelda Ann's accounts of the violent episodes that she has endured. The intervener speaks and gestures with some energy and expressiveness, but slower and softer than Nelda Ann.*) As you think about that program, you sound like it brings back some terrible memories. You remember getting beaten and you start to feel the rage build again, almost like a wave sweeping you out to sea.

NELDA ANN:  (*She looks at the intervener for the first time since she started talking about the television show.*) Yeah, that's right and that wave feels good—uh—justified. That's it, justified.

INTERVENER:  It looks like you just figured something out. You sounded courageous and defiant, too, when you . . .

NELDA ANN:  (*She interrupts.*) If that means I'm tired of this shit and I'm not going to take it anymore, then that's it. (*She looks indignant and still aggravated.*) See, you don't know what it's like. Nobody does unless you've been through it.

INTERVENER:  (*She leans forward, speaks deliberately and softly.*) Nelda Ann, you're right, I'm really in the dark about the hellish things you've been through. Please, fill me in, make me smarter about what it was like for you.

NELDA ANN:  (*She sits up straighter in her chair, smooths the wrinkles of her sweat pants, and looks off in the distance. Her voice is softer but still intense.*) You lay there at night in that hot trailer, listening for him to come roaring in from one of his drinking, drugging, and whorin' sprees and when you hear his truck pull into the gravel drive, you really start to sweat and shake. I hold my breath and pray that he's not pissed off about something. (*She pauses, tilts her head to the side, and gazes off in a thoughtful manner.*) Funny, the waiting part is harder than the beating part. I don't cry and shake while he's beating me up.

**Reflecting on This Segment**

1. What was it like for you to hear Nelda Ann's story? How did you sense the emotions in your body?
2. If you were the intervener, what would you say to her next?
3. How did the intervener move Nelda Ann back into the zone?
4. Did you notice Nelda Ann change from using second person to first person pronouns while describing the wait?

## USING THIS TOOL

Form a small group with two colleagues. One of you volunteers to role-play, with emotional intensity, a character dealing with a crisis. Another volunteers to use the techniques listed in Figure 5–4 to lower emotional arousal. Keep in mind that although your words are important here, your body language and tone of voice are essential influencing factors. Finally, the third person serves as the recorder who observes the activity and leads the feedback discussion.

## Enhancing Emotions of Resolve

In contrast to the impression that you may gain from reading much of the crisis literature, positive emotions play a vital role in the resolution process. Your approach is dramatically different from the traditional crisis intervention techniques. Instead of encouraging survivors to have an emotional catharsis about being a victim, you help them experience positive emotions connected with being a survivor. When people begin talking about their longings, their hopes, and their successes, they feel more resolved, emotionally involved, and inspired.

In terms of Goleman's example earlier, once someone has escaped from a bear, you don't force him or her to dwell on the immediate feelings of terror and panic back then.

---

**Lower Emotional Distress by . . .**

- Addressing basic needs.
- Relying on the LUV Triangle.
- Acknowledging feelings of distress.
- Speaking in a concerned, but soothing tone of voice.
- Keeping in close and comfortable contact.
- Maintaining eye contact.

---

**FIGURE 5–4**  Techniques for lowering emotional distress.

Those emotions already have served a purpose in stirring the person to react quickly. In crisis intervention, your job is to help survivors turn their attention to how they now can orchestrate their resolution.

In essence, you are attempting to transfer their emotional arousal from negative images of painful experiences in the past to positive ones of possibilities in the future. If you ask distressed people to dwell on images and memories of threats, then you may escalate their fear and vulnerability. On the other hand, if you invite survivors to describe how they successfully escaped, they are more likely to begin feeling a sense of satisfaction, relief, confidence, and pride.

When you look for the survivor, you are not simply trying to make the distress disappear by replacing it with emotions of resolve. Instead, you are helping the person to experience the positive feelings along with the negative ones. This is not the "look on the bright side," Pollyanna-style attitude in which one looks reality in the face and denies it.

Instead, the resolution focus is like the Necker Cube in Figure 5–5. As you look carefully at the figure, at times it appears that the nearest face of the cube is up and to the left. At other times, the image shifts so that the nearest face appears to be down and to

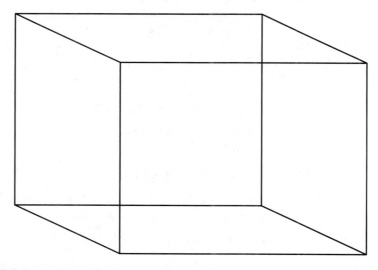

**FIGURE 5–5**   Necker Cube.

the right. If you only glance long enough to see one image or the other, then you have a restricted view of the possibilities that are there. However, when you take the time to fully experience this figure, you discover that there are rich and complex possibilities here. Even though you cannot see both at the same instant, you always know that the other image is there. With a balanced perspective, you do not get stuck with an impoverished, one-sided view.

In times of crisis, people often feel demoralized, discouraged, and overwhelmed by the "black," "red," and "yellow" emotions. In your training to become a helping professional, you have learned to detect and uncover such negative feelings as grief, rage, and fear. However, as a crisis intervener, you need to develop antennae that are also sensitive to people's positive emotions. Your job is not only to reduce distress, but also to help survivors recover their rainbow emotions. When people recognize and enhance their feelings of courage, compassion, and hope, they regain their sense of resolve.

Feelings of resolve create a positive momentum for a survivor. Just as you cannot truly "empower" another person, neither can you give someone a sense of resolve. Like meaning in life, people must discover and nurture resolve for themselves. Obviously, you must convey your own compassion and hopefulness, but this process is not like giving blood—you cannot transfuse resolve from yourself to another person. Instead, your job is to "mine" the debris of someone's tale of agony for the small gems of courage, compassion, and hope that will shine through in spite of the chaos and confusion that may be hiding them from the survivor.

The following are specific techniques that you can use to promote a survivor's feelings of resolve:

- *Look for exceptions to the distress.* Mixed in with the distress-saturated talk will be comments indicating relief, resilience, and perseverance. For example, survivors might say any of the following:

  "Without even thinking about it, I suddenly was in the water, pulling him to the shore."
  "I can't believe I was able to find my way out, with all that smoke!"
  "I don't know how I came up with that idea, but it seemed to work."

  You can "spotlight" these statements by checking your understanding with the person and highlighting them. For example, you might say, "Let me make sure I've got this right. You're saying that you dived into the water and rescued him from drowning?" Such comments can call the person's attention to acts of bravery, kindness, and resourcefulness.
- *Be presumptive about resolve.* As you learned in earlier chapters, you can safely presume that a person in crisis has some feelings of resolve, even though he or she may not be aware of them. As you deal with emotions, you can also presume that, somehow and someway, this individual has experienced a glimmer of hope, a hint of compassion, and a trace of courage. You can phrase all your questions and statements in ways that suggest that the person has had some feelings of resolve, however briefly and however faintly. For

example, you would not be asking, "*If* the situation changed for the better, how would you be feeling?" Instead, you would phrase the question presumptively, "*When* the situation changes for the better, how will you be feeling?"

- *Reflect emotions of resolve.* Whenever you are picking up on positive emotions that someone is experiencing, then reflect them back to the person. As we mentioned earlier, offering a reflection is a basic technique of counseling, but we have been much more likely to use it with negative emotions. However, reflecting feelings of resolve can be a powerful way of helping a survivor become aware of such emotions. Although they are often keenly in touch with their shock, rage, and pain, survivors may not be conscious of their feelings of determination, fortitude, and inspiration.

  Some examples of reflecting emotions of resolve are:

  "It sounds like you truly love your daughter with all your heart and would do anything in your power to keep her safe."
  "You seemed to have been determined to do whatever you could to make a positive difference in the middle of that chaos."
  "I get the sense that you had a glimmer of hope at that moment and realized that maybe you could prevent something worse from happening."

- *Ask "taking-heart" questions.* "Taking heart" is a phrase that captures the essence of the feelings of resolve. When someone takes heart, the person feels hopeful, determined, inspired, and encouraged—in spite of the pain and suffering. No matter how much distress people endure, they turn to positive emotions to buoy them through these tough times, stir them to cope somehow, and comfort them in their grief. In crisis, survivors take heart.

  Whenever you notice any signs of positive emotion, such as humor, love, joy, elevation, or gratitude, ask *taking-heart questions*. Invite the person to give detailed elaborations of the circumstances, nuances, sensations, and images associated with these emotions. For example, you might ask,

  "How did you find the courage to put yourself at risk to rescue your friend?"
  "What was it like for you to tell your daughter how much you love her?"
  "How did that feel to finally believe that there might be a way out of this mess?"
  "How in the world were you able to joke when things seemed to look so bleak?"

Fundamentally, your job as a crisis intervener is to acknowledge people's distress *and* to be curious about their feelings of resolve. By inviting survivors to explore and give expression to their positive emotions, you are bringing survivors into a more productive zone of arousal. After you reflect someone's distress, you can follow through, with an amazed tone, with the question, "So, how did you overcome those feelings and take action to get yourself out of there?" As you ask such questions, be sure to communicate your own positive emotions, such as astonishment, interest, and confidence in their resilience.

## Staying in "the Zone" of Resolution

According to Goleman (1995), a mildly elated, or energized, state is optimal for creative breakthroughs. When people are in a good mood, they can think more flexibly, are more capable of solving complex problems, and generally perceive the world more positively.

As a crisis intervener, if you can help survivors experience positive emotional arousal, you are actually helping them toward resolution. Many of the techniques you have already been practicing, such as looking for the survivor and conjuring up images of success, have the added benefit of helping people feel better. You can serve as a catalyst for a benign cycle, rather than a vicious one, by encouraging survivors to focus on resolution, which in turn helps them experience positive emotional arousal, which then leads to better coping.

Managing emotional arousal in survivors is very important to your eventual success with them. One useful technique is to imagine that you are viewing a survivor through a screen on which the Yerkes-Dodson curve is superimposed. Then picture the needle indicating where the person is functioning emotionally from moment to moment. Assessing someone's emotional arousal is, of course, more art than science. But there is good science to indicate that when you are helping to manage the emotional arousal of a survivor, you actually are changing brain functioning (Vaughan, 1997) and promoting positive resolution.

### Listening In on Crisis Intervention

Review the crisis story at the beginning of the chapter. In this segment of crisis intervention, the helper works to increase Nelda Ann's positive emotional arousal in the following way.

NELDA ANN: (*She stares out the window at the cloudless blue sky and begins talking in a distracted monotone.*) It's going to rain, I can smell it . . . Oh, look at me, I'm a mess. I never wear makeup anymore or dress up much . . . not ever, really. I just slop around in a tee-shirt and sweats. (*Her shoulders are slumped forward and her voice becomes barely audible as she continues.*) At first I thought it was my fault that he was beating me, so I was embarrassed to have people see me. I wore a lot of makeup and long sleeves to hide the cuts and bruises. I guess I don't care anymore. (*While she had been talking, the sky darkened and now raindrops begin hitting softly on the glass.*) Reminds me of that blues song, "The sky is cryin'."

INTERVENER: (*She starts to speak, but Nelda Ann seems to be headed somewhere, caught up in her own story, so the intervener continues to attend, keeps silent, and nods her head slowly*).

NELDA ANN: (*Her speaking slows to a crawl, sounding tired, resigned, and defeated. She takes long pauses between her sentences.*) I don't go out much . . . just to the store or to rent a video . . . You should see some of the looks I get from people

*(Continued)*

I know . . . I swear I can see it on their faces. It's like they think it's my fault . . . Some of them do feel sorry for me though, I can tell. (*She looks out the window and sighs again.*)

INTERVENER: (*She leans forward and begins to speak almost as slowly and softly as Nelda Ann.*) That's quite a gift you have. When you said earlier that it was going to rain, *I had to bite my tongue!* (*She smiles and shakes her head in awe. Her voice is somewhat louder now and her rate of speaking is faster. She employs almost theatrical emphasis to some words.*) You're like the weather reporter on TV—*except you got it right!* It's almost like you've developed a sixth sense. You seem to be able to read people, too. I guess that's how you were able to keep your daughter from getting hurt. From what you've told me, *in spite of all that happened,* she's turned out to be a very well-adjusted little girl.

NELDA ANN: (*Her face brightens considerably as she reaches into her purse for a picture of her daughter.*) You are right about that. If it weren't for her, I might be one of those women on that TV show.

## Reflecting on This Segment

1. How did the intervener help Nelda Ann to move toward a more productive emotional state?
2. How did allowing Nelda Ann to talk about her appearance relate to emotional arousal?

---

## USING THIS TOOL

Regroup with your two colleagues who collaborated with you in the previous practice. Return to your crisis stories, but this time practice enhancing emotions of resolve. If you like, you can use Figure 5–6 as a reminder. Once you all have practiced this technique, share your observations and feedback.

---

> **Enhance Emotions of Resolve by . . .**
>
> - Looking for exceptions to the distress.
> - Being presumptive about resolve.
> - Reflecting emotions of resolve.
> - Asking taking-heart questions.

**FIGURE 5–6**  Techniques for enhancing emotions of resolve.

## RESOURCES FOR DOMESTIC VIOLENCE

There are a number of national organizations that are committed to providing information, resources, and support for those confronted with domestic violence. The following are examples that offer advocacy and crisis intervention services.

National Domestic Violence Hotline
http://www.ndvh.org
Hotline:1-800-799-SAFE (7233) or 1-800-787-3224 (TTY)

The purpose of this national hotline is to provide service to all areas in the United States. The hotline is staffed 24 hours a day by trained counselors who can provide crisis assistance and shelter information.

Feminist Majority Foundation
http://www.feminist.org/911/crisis.html

This site is dedicated to providing a major resource directory of state coalitions and national organizations for women in domestic violence situations. Individual coalitions and organizations are listed, along with their addresses, phone numbers, e-mail addresses, and links to their sites. This site is a major resource of counseling centers across the nation.

## SUMMARY

In this chapter, you explored a new view of emotions that has been emerging in the positive psychology literature. Until recently, many crisis intervention models have encouraged survivors to reexperience the painful emotions of their crisis to promote catharsis. However, studies of these techniques suggest that they are, at best, ineffective and, in fact, possibly harmful. As you can see in Figure 5–7, you learned a "kinder, gentler" approach

---

**Essential Tools**

- Lower the emotions of distress.
  - ↳ Anxiety
  - ↳ Anger
  - ↳ Depression
- Enhance emotions of resolve.
  - ↳ Courage
  - ↳ Compassion
  - ↳ Hope
- Stay in "the zone" of resolution.

---

**FIGURE 5–7** Essential tools of Chapter 5.

that uses techniques that help reduce negative emotions of anxiety, depression, and aggression, while promoting such positive emotions of resolve as courage, hope, and compassion.

## Segue to Chapter 6

We all know people who tend to look on the bright side of things—they are called *optimists*. And if they are too optimistic, no matter what, they may be called "Pollyannaish." On the other hand, a person who is too much of a pessimist may be described as a cynic or even a "wet blanket." Max Lerner, the noted author and columnist, said he would rather be a "possibilist." Think of a time after a personal crisis when you were neither optimistic nor pessimistic, but instead thought of some possibilities.

# CHAPTER

# 6

# Envisioning Possibilities: Creative Coping

"Nothing contributes so much to tranquilizing the mind as a steady purpose—a point on which the soul may fix its intellectual eye."

*Mary Wollstonecraft Shelley*

## CHAPTER GOALS

After completing this chapter, you should be able to:

- Help survivors to envision a resolution to their crisis
- Offer hints about future possibilities
- Ask "what if" questions
- Use scaling techniques to help survivors envision possible resolutions with greater detail and vividness
- Make effective suggestions and referrals
- Write follow-up notes to survivors

# OVERVIEW

When you work with people in crisis, you will find that they initially may be in a frame of mind that makes it impossible for them to envision any possible resolution. If you ask them for a goal, their first reaction simply may be to say that they wish the crisis would "go away," or better yet, it would never have happened.

You will also find that, if survivors do articulate a goal, it likely will be an immediate one: to feel safe, to know where they are going to sleep tonight, to get some clothes, or to connect with people they know. Depending on the situation, their immediate goals are likely to be at the foundation of Maslow's hierarchy—the basic survival needs. Beyond these basic needs, survivors usually wish for their lives to quickly resume as close as possible to the way they were before the crisis. However, as you hear their crisis narratives and begin to coconstruct a survival story, their goals will begin to emerge. You then can invite people to turn their focus from the crisis experience in the past to the resolution possibilities in the future.

In the field of counseling and therapy, one of the predominant paradigms has been the medical model. The medical model assumes that a psychological crisis is similar to a physical trauma. Therefore, according to this perspective, the counselor or therapist is considered to be a health professional whose specialty area is mental illness. The counselor follows the medical model by looking for symptoms, making a diagnosis, and then prescribing a treatment program. One of the assumptions of the medical model is that knowing the etiology, or cause, of a person's current symptoms is necessary to find a cure. Because etiology always exists prior to symptoms, taking a client's history has been the traditional beginning of the counseling and therapy process.

However, as a crisis intervener, you often will invite survivors to look to the future to resolve their present concerns. How can something that has not yet happened actually change someone's current condition? In fact, hope and a sense of purpose, which are both essential parts of any successful resolution, are rooted in the future. When people act now to realize an anticipated possibility, their future is *causing* their present. This idea, which Aristotle first articulated, is known as teleology, or final cause. Our envisioned future gives us both motivation and direction, pulling us forward by the power of our hopes, dreams, and aspirations.

Your crisis intervention philosophy follows an old and anonymous admonition:

> As through this life you wander,
> As through this life you roll,
> Keep your eye upon the doughnut,
> And not upon the hole.

You want the survivor to gaze across the crisis space of the hole, scanning for a possible resolution—the doughnut. Once you've helped the person spot promising possibilities, then you help concretize—make explicit—the desired resolution.

Crises rob people of their envisioned futures. As a crisis intervener, you help survivors to revise their futures by creating new goals. Once articulated, goals serve as beacons that light the way for the resolution journey. In this chapter, we discuss how you can help people in crisis to envision their goals, to cope successfully, and to connect with other resources by a referral.

# CRISIS STORY

John had been looking at the wonderful old oak tree outside his office for most of the afternoon. This particular tree never seemed to lose all of its leaves, even after its neighbors became barren skeletons against the gray light of January. Brown withered clumps of leaves still clung tenaciously to the branches and refused to fall, even though they had lost their color and any visible traces of life.

"Why in hell don't they just give up?" he muttered to himself. "It's easier all the way around." The personal metaphor struck him hard and he felt an icy chill that had nothing to do with the room temperature.

John was at a crossroads. Every time he misplaced his keys, had difficulty finding his car in a parking lot, or fumbled embarrassingly for the name of a colleague or former student, he felt that same sickening sensation. He was sure that he was in the early stages of Alzheimer's, the insidious brain disorder that had begun to muddle his father's thinking 15 years before.

At that time, John's mother had repeatedly warned him and his sisters about how bad their dad's memory was becoming. However, none of them realized—or chose to acknowledge—how much he had changed in the few short months since they had celebrated Christmas together. John decided to see firsthand just how much his mother was exaggerating. As it turned out, she had downplayed, rather than embellished, his condition.

John leaned back in his creaking swivel chair and remembered back to the day of that trip. After an uneventful flight, he parked the rental car in an empty space in front of his parents' apartment and prepared himself for their traditional greetings. His mother would hug and kiss him repeatedly. His father, on the other hand, would slap John on the back and tease him about his thinning hairline.

Instead something unexpected and very unsettling happened—like a scene straight out of a suspense movie. His dad greeted John with a friendly, but formal greeting, a welcoming smile, and a firm handshake that a host might offer a visitor to whom he had not been introduced.

John's father made cheerful conversation, as if to make this stranger feel at home. "Marie is still getting ready, so I'll just show you around our home. Say, do you want a drink? You aren't the preacher, are you?" John's father laughed heartily at his little joke, took his son by the arm, and began telling him about each of the family pictures that adorned the mantel above the fireplace.

"This is a picture of my dad. He's been dead for a long time now, and this . . .," said John's father, pointing to one prominent photograph, ". . . is my son, John. He teaches psychology at a college in Virginia. My oldest daughter lives . . ."

John put his hand on his father's shoulder to interrupt this monologue. He peered deeply into his father's eyes, and in a quavering voice that was apprehensive, questioning, and unbelieving, asked, "Pop, don't you know who I am?"

Pop's smile seemed to be a combination of embarrassment and amusement. "Well, I have to admit that you do look familiar, but I'm sorry . . . I can't recall your name."

John pointed to his own picture on the mantel taken 5 years earlier and rasped, "That's me, Pop! I'm your son." Tears welled in his eyes as John realized that he had lost his father—without being able to say goodbye. On the outside, his father looked the same, but on the inside, he was becoming as hollow as that old oak outside John's office.

The rest of the story was a familiar one. John's father grew worse and worse until his mother finally surrendered, admitting that she was no longer able to care for him. His behavior deteriorated and he began to act like a troubled child. He ran away several times, shoplifted at the grocery store, and refused to eat anything but dessert. When the people at a local adult day care program could no longer handle him, he was sent to various care facilities, finally ending up on the Alzheimer's unit in a community hospital close to his youngest daughter.

John's father remained in the unit for almost 5 years. He was not allowed to wear either his hearing aid or his glasses because he kept throwing them away or flushing them down the toilet. All of his teeth had to be pulled because he forgot how to brush them and he refused to let anyone help. John's father had first-rate care, regular visits from his family, and the best medication available, but nothing seemed to help. He died not knowing where or who he was. At the funeral, John swore a silent oath that he would never allow himself to end up the way his father had.

Now, even though he had found some refuge by watching the oak tree, John was not having his best day. He had just finished a telephone call with his son, who had recently moved to another state, where his new laptop computer had been stolen. His son had no insurance, and so John was still seething about this lack of responsibility. Worse yet, John discovered that his wife had already sent their son a check to replace the stolen computer.

John left the office to walk across campus, head down, grinding his teeth in frustration, when he met his dean. They chatted for a few minutes under one of the old shade trees on campus. John did his best to put on a brave front, but it was very difficult to be social. The dean happened to mention that he had seen John's name on a list of professors who were eligible for early retirement. At first, John thought the dean was just teasing him because they were old friends, but then that fateful visit with his father flashed through his mind.

After he and the dean parted, John suddenly felt a tightness in his chest, as if an invisible hand were squeezing his heart, and he had trouble breathing. Slowly and deliberately, as if he were carrying some fragile and valuable object, John walked over to the hospital emergency room, which was nearby. As he passed the old oak tree outside his office, he wondered if he would ever see it again.

## Reflecting on This Crisis Story

1. What do you see as the primary issue that John faces?
2. If you were a crisis intervener, how would you help John to address this primary issue?

# IDEAS

## Optimism and Envisioning Possibilities

It has become a hackneyed question, but asking whether a glass is half-empty or half-full still conveys an important idea: that the answer to the question depends on your outlook. If you are feeling discouraged, you are likely to see a glass as half-empty. If you are feeling hopeful, you see it as half-full. This metaphor illustrates that humans tend to adopt a single perception of a situation, while ignoring an alternative possibility. The water level either represents a deficient condition or it indicates potential completion. The actual level of the water in the glass does not change—the fact is the fact. But how we view the facts of the present depends on our personal vision of the future.

In his 1991 book, *Learned Optimism*, Martin Seligman stated the following:

> Life inflicts the same setbacks and tragedies on the optimist as on the pessimist, but the optimist weathers them better. . . . Even when things go well . . . the pessimist . . . is haunted by forebodings of catastrophe. (p. 207)

In a way, you could say that both the optimistic and pessimistic outlooks are delusional, because nobody can truly predict what the future will bring. Stuff, both good and bad, will happen. But it is better to maintain the delusional style of the "cockeyed optimist," who is generally happier, more able to cope with crises, and capable of envisioning a positive future.

## Etiology and Teleology in Crisis

If people in crisis are asked to explain the reason they are acting so distressed, they naturally point back to the past as the cause. They explain that a personal tribulation, family tragedy, or catastrophic event has taken place. In other words, they present a past event as causing their current behaviors. Knowing the *etiology* is useful for understanding a survivor's distress reactions. However, relying only on etiology, which is a deterministic notion based on traditional scientific thought, does not help us to understand resilience and resolution. We need a theoretical framework that acknowledges *teleology*, which conceptualizes the future as a cause of the present.

But is it possible that behaviors in the present could be caused by the future? At first glance, this idea sounds a bit preposterous, doesn't it? Nevertheless, recognizing how our envisioned future can influence us *now* offers a valuable perspective for a crisis intervener. Taking this point of view, your job is to help survivors construct a future image that will change their current ways of thinking, feeling, and acting. People are in crisis at the precise moment when their present is intolerable and their future seems grim. It is your challenge to help them imagine a future in which they could achieve a positive resolution to their crisis. With such a possibility, survivors are more hopeful, motivated, and creative in their coping.

Aristotle, who said that everything is on its way to realizing its potential (Palmer, 1994), originated the idea that our present actions are attempts to achieve a future goal. In fact, according to Aristotle, the prime motivator in our lives is our striving for a more perfect future, which is the final cause or teleology. *Telos* is Greek for end, goal, or purpose. In the teleological view of crisis intervention, it matters little how someone got into the present crisis. What matters most is where the survivor hopes to go from here.

Teleology—not etiology—is, therefore, the thrust of crisis intervention. Your job is to assist someone in formulating a goal that is the presence, rather than the absence, of something, and to help the person in feeling hopeful about achieving this goal. In this way, crisis intervention becomes the teleological pursuit of a hopeful future, and the survivor's cognitive map begins to develop paths that are leading somewhere.

## EXPERIENCING THIS IDEA

For this exercise, join with two colleagues to form a small group. One of you volunteers to share your story of a current dilemma that is confronting you. Another volunteers to serve as the intervener. The intervener's task is to focus only on the future, helping the storyteller to picture in detail exactly how things will be different when this dilemma is resolved. The third person serves as an observer who leads the feedback discussion. Switch roles and engage in the same process until everyone has had a turn in each role.

### Reflecting on This Experience

1. How was the experience of envisioning a time when this dilemma is resolved?
2. What effect did this focus on the future have on the speaker's present mood?
3. What possibilities for achieving a successful resolution emerged?

### A Teleological Theory

Rychlak (1980) considered teleology to be the essence of our free will. He pointed out that humans possess the ability of "telesponding" to events as well as responding to them. To put it more succinctly, what we do now is based in part on how we think things will turn out. Some more ordinary words for telesponding are "anticipating," "planning," and "preparing."

To the extent that we telespond, we are self-determined beings. Moreover, because the future has not yet happened, it can still be changed. We cannot go back in time to change a crisis incident. However, we can seize our future—it is only the next moment, hour, or day that can really be changed. Ironically, though, changing our future can result in changing our past. What's done is done, of course, but the meaning we have assigned to our past can be dramatically altered. "It's never too late to have a happy childhood" (Furman & Ahola, 1992, p. 18) is a statement that may seem a bit extravagant. Nevertheless, it is possible to let go of old injustices, grudges, desires for vengeance, notions about our histories as our destinies, and preoccupations with past events that obscure any view we may have of a brighter future.

At a fundamental level, every person is a prophet—we proceed by predicting how events will turn out. Therefore, we are not so much impelled by our instincts or our history as we are compelled by our goals in life and our predictions of the future. It is our mythic quest.

### Tipping the Balance Toward Resolution

In Chapter 1, you read that the Chinese symbol for crisis is a combination of danger and opportunity. In every crisis, there is the potential for a future resolution that could be tragic or transcendent. Your intervention can "tip the balance" toward a positive and growthful outcome. However, you must "be with" the survivor and enter the person's crisis story before a clear path toward resolution begins to emerge. Keep in mind that no matter how well you think that you are empathically "walking in someone's shoes," you have never actually been over that person's crisis terrain.

Ultimately, therefore, survivors—and not you—determine the *goals* of crisis intervention. To be truly helpful, you must journey with the survivor, offering compassion and comfort, respecting the person's need to rest, and assuring safety and asylum. It is at these times that your humanity is much more important than your techniques. Although you take your cues from the survivor as to how to proceed moment-to-moment,

---

**Key Ideas**

- Optimism helps survivors resolve their crises.

- Teleology affirms that we are compelled by the future goals we envision.

- Survivors determine the goals of crisis intervention.

- Crisis resolution is a journey, not a destination.

---

**FIGURE 6–1**   Key ideas and tools of Chapter 6.

you must at the same time remain strategic, deliberate, and mindful of the need for the person to establish a goal.

Successful resolution is an ongoing process in which goals evolve and change over time. In other words, crisis resolution is a journey, not a destination. Effective survivors may or may not accomplish particular goals, but they continue to move forward in a hopeful manner. Coming to believe that they can get to a better place helps restore their feeling of hope and resolve (see Figure 6–1).

# TOOLS

## Emerging from Emergencies

As we have emphasized throughout this book, humans are resilient beings. We are much more likely to recover from "the slings and arrows of outrageous fortune," as Shakespeare put it, than we are to fall apart and be left devastated by crisis events. Something new will emerge when we find ourselves faced with seemingly impossible situations. This emergent property, as it is sometimes called, is the curative factor. As we have mentioned before, there is no emergence without an emergency. First comes chaos, then comes resolution—either positive or negative. As a crisis intervener, your task is to facilitate the movement of the survivor toward a *positive* resolution.

After people have been jarred by a crisis, they initially are thrown into a psychological emergency. Nevertheless, the creative process that is the human struggle for surviving and thriving is always at work. When you intervene in a crisis situation, you must always remain humble with regard to your limited ability to direct the resolution process. At the same time, you must always be in awe of the power of the human spirit to mysteriously recover from life's insults. Although you do not have the ultimate control over a survivor's resolution, you can certainly encourage that person to begin seeing a hopeful future.

As the intervener, you are much more curious about the strengths, resources, and resilience of survivors than you are about their foibles, vulnerabilities, and victimizations. Remember the Necker Cube in Chapter 5? You were able to discover another view of the situation by gaining a different perspective. People in crisis are coming to you able to see, in discouraging clarity and detail, their frustrations, distress, and mistakes. However, they don't see the alternate image because they fail to notice their personal skills, talents, and resources—the clues for resolutions. By asking questions regarding their successes and competencies, you help survivors become aware of these experiences and characteristics. Your job, then, is to capitalize on this opportunity by pursuing a description, at great length, of their successful survival strategies.

## EXPERIENCING THIS IDEA

To gain an appreciation for the power of envisioning, look at Figure 6–2. At first glance, what does this figure look like to you? Perhaps you see it as a meaningless assortment of block-like shapes of different sizes. Or maybe the figure seems like a maze without any particular beginning or end.

To envision something more meaningful than blocks or a maze, you don't really need to force it to happen. Instead, just relax and focus your eyes on one specific point in the figure. It doesn't matter where, just as long as you stay focused. At first, you may experience the same sense of doubt and frustration that you have when you look at one of those "Magic 3-D" pictures and can't see any hidden figures. But by keeping your attention on that one spot for 20 or 30 seconds, something meaningful seems to pop out of the chaos—everything comes together into a unified vision.

If you didn't have much luck with that strategy, keep your eyes about 12 inches away from the figure and stare fixedly at the center point for about 30 seconds. Then, look at a white surface somewhere—a wall or a blank sheet of paper, for example. What word appears?

Of course, when you are doing crisis intervention, you are using a variety of techniques to encourage people to focus on particular spots in the midst of the chaos that can help them envision a positive resolution. For example, asking getting through questions, transforming crisis metaphors into ones of resolution, and offering an encouragement interlude are only a sampling of the tools that prime a survivor for seeing a promising future. In addition to those, another useful technique for instilling hope is to hint at possibilities.

### Hinting at Possibilities

Dropping some hints of a possible resolution to someone's crisis story is an excellent way of planting the seeds of change. When the survivor describes some painful or difficult facet of the crisis experience, you can acknowledge the statement. However, you can also

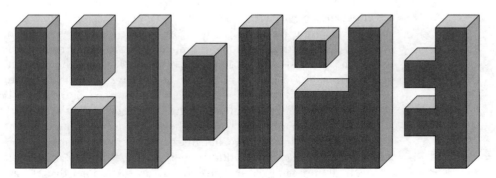

**FIGURE 6–2**  What can you envision with this figure?

add a comment that suggests the possibility of a successful resolution. For example, you might say:

- "You haven't *yet* been able to reach your goal of resolving this matter."
- "You haven't *quite* settled on a plan of action here."
- "You're not sure how you're going to do it, but you *still* really want to make the most of this painful situation."

Notice that all these statements validate the person's past experiences of frustration, confusion, and uncertainty. You merely add a word or two that also hints that the future may be different.

In addition, you can rephrase someone's assertions about the crisis situation into more tentative terms. Instead of colluding with someone's negative pronouncements, you can interpret the person's declaration as a point of view or "one way to look at it." For example, you can preface your acknowledgments with such phrases as, "So, in your opinion . . . ," or "The way you see it . . . ," or "It seems to you that. . . ." Each of these statements suggests that it is the person's perception, rather than reality itself, that is being considered here.

## Helping Survivors to Envision Goals

You can begin your goal-setting work with survivors by simply asking them, in one form or another, what they hope to achieve by working with you. You are seeking a well-formed goal that is likely to advance someone toward a positive resolution of the crisis.

Once a survivor has started to envision the future, you then will be helping to crystallize this initially amorphous goal statement. Your job is to help someone craft a well-formed goal: one that is explicit, specific, realistic, and valued by the person (De Jong & Berg, 1998). In fact, developing a well-formed goal helps survivors create a vivid and powerful vision of their future. By setting such a goal, survivors gain a sense of direction and hope, become more motivated, and increase their momentum toward resolution. By practicing a few simple principles described in the following segment, you can help people in crisis to develop well-formed resolution goals.

- *Help create positive goals.* The first, and most fundamental, principle is to help the survivors state their goals in the positive, describing what they will be doing or thinking rather than what they will not. Studies have found that people who strive for positive goals have higher levels of well-being than those who try to avoid negative goals (Emmons, 1999).

  Sometimes, people in crisis just want the pain to go away or for the event to not have happened. When you spot these absences, you can encourage survivors to formulate better goals that involve the presence of some positive behavior or attitude. You can ask about how they will be feeling when the pain becomes manageable or when they have accepted that the event took place. Helping survivors fill in the blanks of their goals can help them develop a powerful vision of the possibilities in their future. As you learned in Chapter 1, looking for the survivor is a valuable technique when you are listening to the crisis story, but it is also useful in helping someone to envision positive goals. Successfully surviving is one achievement that the person has already accomplished, however temporarily. Therefore, when you call attention to these dramatic moments, a survivor can discover unknown strengths, appreciate unrecognized resources, and achieve a sense of hope. These survival successes are Bateson's (1972) "news of difference," the lubrication that "unsticks" the crisis story.

If someone gives a negative goal, you can invite the person to begin developing a well-formed positive goal by using a variety of questions. For example, you can ask what someone will be doing when the negative condition is no longer present. A survivor may say, "My goal is that I'd like to stop feeling so scared." In response to this statement, you could ask either of the following:

"How will you be feeling when you're not so scared anymore?"
"What will you be doing when you are no longer having these fearful feelings?"

Another strategy for redirecting a negative goal into a positive one is to use terms that encourage survivors to see possible alternatives and choices. Beginning your questions with phrases such as, "instead of," "when you are no longer," "in place of," and "rather than," invites someone to begin thinking outside the box of a negative goal statement (Sklare, 1997). For example, the opening of the sentence "When you're no longer overwhelmed with grief, what will you be doing with your life?" suggests a positive future, and the ending question encourages the client to fill the void with a positive goal.

- *Help survivors create their own goals.* The second principle for developing successful goals is to ensure that people "own" their intervention goals. No matter how well-formulated goals may be, if they are to be successful, people must embrace these goals as belonging to *them.*

Working with survivors whose initial goal statements seem harmful can be particularly challenging. The first thing you must realize is that such goal statements represent a yearning for thwarted, but unstated, positive goals. For example, the urge to commit suicide may reflect a desire for peace and tranquility. The desire to injure someone else is often the survivor's attempt to seek justice.

Your job in these situations is not only to dig for the positive goal beneath the surface of a harmful goal statement, but also to acknowledge the person's sense of discouragement. People do not move from a discouraged position to a hopeful one without first feeling that someone has understood their pain. You can acknowledge the person's sufferings and frustrations without amplifying them. At the same time, you can also slip in a possibility statement. This is where tracking resolution comes in handy. You can say, for example, "Wow! It sounds like you tried everything you could think of back when this happened, and you succeeded in part or you wouldn't be talking to me. Now you're trying to figure out some other ways to get further out of this mess."

Finding the goal that exists beneath a harmful goal statement is always difficult. This is where your skill as an intervener comes into play. In this book, we can offer suggestions, but they are only guidelines that point out what you must do—find out what the person ultimately wants and have him or her state it in positive and workable terms. Sometimes, to accomplish this task, you must rely heavily on your skills of looking carefully for the survivor and asking moving-on questions. Keep in mind this rule: If the person does not respond to your invitation to talk about goals, then you probably have not acknowledged the crisis story enough.

Some survivors may be so discouraged that they cannot seem to muster the energy necessary to become involved in the goal-setting process. In this case, you are well advised to proceed slowly. As the old adage goes, "You can lead a horse to water, but you can't make it drink." Your challenge is to see if you can discover their tastes well enough to get them to "swallow" the notion of working with you toward a resolution of their situation.

- *Help create action goals.* The third principle for forming goals is that you are more likely to develop an effective goal if you use action words ending in "ing." If, for example, a survivor says, "My goal is a happy life," you might ask, "What will you be doing differently when you are feeling happy?"

  When you ask for a goal statement, the person may answer simply, "I don't know." At these times, you can nudge someone toward a goal statement by inviting him or her simply to guess. For example, Sklare (1997) offered such counselor responses as, "If you did know . . . ," "If you did have an idea . . . ," "If you could figure it out . . . ," "If it weren't beyond you . . ." (p. 27) as possible leads that might set aside the person's reluctance and arrive at a hypothetical. By asking the hypothetical "if," you relieve someone of any obligation for knowing the answer. Instead, you offer an invitation to speculate on a possibility.

- *Be presumptive as you help survivors envision change.* The fourth principle of effective goal setting is to be presumptive. You are already familiar with presumptive questions. In Chapters 1, 2, and 3, we discussed using questions that presume resilience, resolution, and resources as the crisis story is unfolding. Now that you are inviting a survivor to envision goals, you can continue being presumptive. Word all your statements and questions in ways that suggest that a positive resolution is not only possible, but inevitable. For example, you would *not* be asking, "*If* the situation changed for the better, how would you be feeling?" Instead, you would phrase the question, "*When* the situation changes for the better, how will you be feeling?"

- *Help keep the goal simple.* Finally, a person in crisis is much more likely to develop an achievable goal if you help in keeping the goal simple. Make sure the survivor's aspirations are concrete, focused, and doable. One common complication in crisis intervention is that a person gives a goal that is out of reach—at least for the near future. With such an unattainable goal, you can explore what here-and-now, "on track" goal would be a successive approximation. For example, you can ask, "So, if you were already on track to, as you said, 'leading a rich, productive and satisfying life,' what would you be doing differently now that would get you there?" The goal should either be behavioral, a change in doing, or it should be meaningful, a change in *viewing* (O'Hanlon & Beadle, 1994). A workable goal cannot be "pie in the sky."

  Even positive goals can be stated in such a way as to not be well formed. For example, the person may say, "I want to be happier" or "I want to be a

---

**Helping Survivors to Make Well-Formed Goals**

- Help develop a goal that involves the presence of something positive.

- If the person gives a goal of making something "go away," ask what would be present to replace it.

- Make sure that survivor "owns" the goal.

- Help the goal to be action oriented.

- Be presumptive that the person will resolve the crisis.

- Help keep the goal simple.

---

**FIGURE 6–3**   Principles for helping survivors make well-formed goals.

success." These goals are too vague to be useful for crisis intervention. If, for example, the person wishes to "be happier," you might help him or her get closer to a well-formed goal by asking, "Tell me about a time since your accident that you were able to feel some sense, no matter how small, of joy or happiness. What was going on then? How were you different?" Returning to the crisis story to look for the survivor can lead to a more concrete description of what it means to the person to be happy, which then might be converted into a goal.

Before you listen in on the following crisis intervention, review in Figure 6–3 the principles for helping a survivor create a well-formed goal.

## Listening In on Crisis Intervention

Let's continue with this chapter's story. After a thorough examination, nothing physical showed up and John was referred to a crisis worker at the hospital who was able to see him immediately.

**INTERVENER:** I've looked over your file, but it doesn't tell me much. Sounds like you had a pretty rough morning.

**JOHN** (*Proceeds to tell the intervener everything that happened that morning and adds the following*): When the dean brought up retirement out of the blue, I was shocked. I wanted to ask him, Who had betrayed me. Who told him that I was over the hill? It hit me all of a sudden that this might be it. Hell, I can't afford to retire, I just bought a $3,200 computer! (*He sighs audibly.*) What will I do if I can't teach? All my friends are here, my books, all my memories . . . I was devastated.

**INTERVENER:** Wow, that seems like a lot of stress to endure all at once. And what a time to be visited by the memory of your father developing Alzheimer's.

JOHN: That's about right, that scene with my pop is like a rerun of a bad movie that's always on channel 4. And today was like seeing the previews of an even worse movie. In that one, I'll be the one who's demented and I'll be put out to pasture.

INTERVENER: So talk of retirement brings up memories of your dad's condition and those thoughts of your dad's condition lead to these devastating thoughts about your retirement. *So far*, at least, you haven't come up with a way of getting off that channel.

JOHN: Yeah, I really want to change the damn channel, but it's like the remote doesn't work. (*He seems noticeably perturbed.*) Now why in the hell did that happen? Let me think about that a minute. (*He seems to be in deep thought, his eyes move back and forth and his brow wrinkles as he concentrates. The intervener decides to wait him out.*)

I was already upset with my son and my wife, then the dean caught me by surprise and all of a sudden before I know it, I'm watching channel 4. Yeah, I think that's what happened. In the past, I was always able to switch off that scene or at least change the channel. Too damn many things happening to me all at once, I guess.

INTERVENER: How have you managed to do that in the past?

JOHN: You do know that I teach psychology, I'm not a counselor or therapist.

INTERVENER: Oh, right, I remember that from your folder. So what are some of the techniques that have worked for you before?

JOHN: Well that depends, sometimes I concentrated on my breathing, other times I visualized a pleasant scene, while other times I've had to employ a behavioral technique like thought stoppage.

INTERVENER: Wow, being a psych professor has given you a lot of techniques to get yourself back on the track you want to be on. Tell me about a time when you used one of those techniques. I'd really like to hear the details.

JOHN (*Sighs again, his voice flat, almost without energy*): It's kind of sad really, here I am almost a senior citizen and I still have to resort to psychological tricks in order to function properly. This morning I think I was beyond help from any of those techniques—I was lucky they didn't commit me.

INTERVENER: As you were talking just now about your actions of this morning, I confess that I am having a completely different reaction.

JOHN: (*He seems to brighten a bit, his interest piqued.*) What do you mean?

INTERVENER: Earlier, I remember being struck by how much composure you showed when you walked over to the emergency room as soon as you felt the tightness in your chest and the other scary symptoms. And I still am very impressed by the way you took control of the situation. I mean, it's one thing for someone to calmly and capably help another person in an emergency, but *you* were the emergency! How in the world did you know to do what you did?

## Reflecting on This Segment

1. What technique did the intervener use to get John to see another side to himself?
2. Did the intervener disagree with John? What other positive aspects about John could the intervener have picked up on?

## USING THIS TOOL

Join with two colleagues to form a small group. One of you volunteers to share some goal that is initially ill formed. Another person volunteers to help develop it into a well-formed goal according to the principles listed earlier. Finally, the third person serves as the recorder who observes the activity and leads the feedback discussion. Take turns until everyone has performed each role.

## Asking What-If Questions

When a person in crisis seems to be overwhelmed by the weight of circumstances to the point that he or she has difficulty offering a goal, you can invite someone to set aside the painful realities to explore a hypothetical future. For example, Erickson (1954) asked his clients to imagine looking into a crystal ball and seeing a future in which their problems had been eliminated. Then, he would have them peer back to the present from their place in the future and identify how they had been able to accomplish this change. A similar technique is the "miracle question" developed by de Shazer (1985) and his associates. The client is asked to imagine that while he or she is asleep, a miracle happens that resolves the client's issues. The counselor then asks for a detailed description of what the client would notice that is different upon awakening.

   Neither of these techniques may be appropriate for people in intense crisis circumstances because of their mystical and enchanting premises. Such portrayals can tap into someone's desperate search for a miracle or magic wand that will make the crisis disappear. Instead, we prefer a more mundane and less dramatic approach of asking *"what-if"* questions. One example would be:

> What if you woke up tomorrow morning and, without even realizing it, you were one step closer to living the kind of life you want to live again. How would you know? What would be different?

   Once the person responds, you can help make the image as clear and concrete as possible. Whatever the survivor says about the difference, it can serve as a road sign on the path to a well-formed goal statement and, ultimately, toward resolution of his or her current difficulties.

## Listening In on Crisis Intervention

Review the story at the beginning of the chapter and the previous segment. A little later in the session, the intervener uses a what-if question with John in the following way.

INTERVENER: (*He leans forward.*) Let me ask you something, John. What if you went home after this session, spent a typical evening of maybe having something to eat, reading for awhile, and then going to bed. Suppose that, while you were sound asleep in bed, something happened that gave you a little nudge toward finding the answers that you seek. However, since you were sound asleep, you didn't even know that this change had taken place. What would be the first thing that you would notice when you woke up in the morning that would show you that something had happened?

## Reflecting on This Segment

1. Based on your impression of John, how might he respond to this what-if question?
2. What alternative what-if question can you offer?

---

# USING THIS TOOL

Divide into groups of three. One of you volunteers to share some aspect of your life that you would like to change. Another volunteers to listen, understand, validate, and, when appropriate, pose the what-if question. Finally, the third person serves as the recorder who observes the activity and leads the feedback discussion.

---

## Scaling

Resolving a crisis is not an end point, but an ongoing process that the survivor begins immediately after the disturbing event. However, in the midst of the confusion and turmoil, a person in crisis may not be aware of the steps that he or she has already taken along the resolution journey. One useful strategy to help people become more aware of their progress toward resolution is to invite them to participate in a scaling exercise (Walter & Peller, 1992).

*Scaling* techniques can be helpful in three important ways. First, participating in scaling can encourage survivors to recognize that resolution is not an all-or-nothing proposition. They have not resolved the crisis yet, but they have been creatively, even courageously, involved in getting through the dangers and threats they have endured to get to where they are now. Second, the activity can help them to envision their goals with greater detail and vividness. Scaling is a task that invites a survivor to compare the past with the present to enter into an imagined future. Finally, scaling can help people recognize the progress they have made in dealing with the challenges of the crisis. The very fact that they have survived to connect with you suggests that they are making headway toward a resolution. Scaling can help you convey to survivors that being on track toward resolving a crisis is success.

The scaling technique involves five simple steps:

1. Begin by asking the survivor to imagine a scale that ranges from 1 to 10, with 1 representing the crisis at its worst and 10 representing the best possible resolution.
2. Invite the person to assess the current situation by giving it a rating according to the scale.
3. When the survivor has rated the present circumstances, you then ask, "As you make your way to [the next higher number], what would be happening that is different from now?" You can also ask the person, "What have you been doing to get yourself to that number?" Out of either question can emerge the beginnings of a goal for your work with the survivor.

4. Explore for details to bring this goal to greater clarity, detail, and vividness.
5. Ask what number the person would have to reach to know that he or she was in control and on the way to resolution.

Anything can be placed on a scale if the number has meaning for the survivor. You don't need to ask someone to explain the reason a particular number has been chosen, nor do you have to be concerned about its "accuracy." The number simply gives you a starting point in your search for a higher number that would symbolize progress toward crisis resolution.

This scaling technique can be used for almost any issue related to the crisis. For example, you can use scaling questions to assess the person's "self-esteem, self-confidence, investment in change, willingness to work hard . . . perception of hopefulness, evaluation of progress" (Berg, 1991, p. 88).

Walter and Peller (1992) pointed out that younger children sometimes have trouble keeping the scale in mind. In such situations, you can use more concrete devices. For example, you might ask:

"If one crayon shows how scared you felt when the accident happened, and this whole box of crayons stands for when you are feeling safe, how many crayons do you have in your box right now?"

With another child, you might say:

"Draw a circle on the board to show me how you're sleeping. A small circle would show that you're not sleeping well at all, and a big one would show that you're sleeping the way you'd like to."

## Listening In on Crisis Intervention

In this segment, see how the intervener uses scaling as an intervention tool in his work with John.

**INTERVENER:** So this one time, two sensitive issues—three, really—ganged up on you and caught you by surprise. It would help if we could get some idea of what things might be like when you're better able to handle these issues. Let's say that a 1 represents being completely at the mercy of those three issues. And let's say that a 10 represents the kind of confidence you'd like to have to deal with those issues. Where would you put yourself right now on that scale?

**JOHN:** Oh I don't know, maybe a 3. Remember, I did freak out earlier, so it can't be any higher.

**INTERVENER:** Wow! Tell me what you have done to get yourself to a 3 already!

**JOHN:** Well, I'm not sure exactly. (*John pauses and reflects a moment.*) Maybe it started when I was walking over to the emergency room. I first thought that I was having a heart attack and I was feeling like my body was a brittle stick ready to break. I was shuffling along holding myself as if I were going to fall apart. I noticed this old oak tree and I wondered if I would ever see it again. This sounds hokey, but I kinda identified with that tree and—now this part is going to sound strange—I began thinking about my own roots and ways that I have contributed to life . . . and I felt a sense of peace.

INTERVENER: Wow, John, that was so vivid I almost felt like I was there with you. What was it that helped you feel more at peace?

## Reflecting on This Segment

1. How do you think John will answer the intervener's last question?
2. Using your own words, how would you have phrased the scaling question for John?
3. What metaphor from John stands out for you in the session? How else might the intervener have used it in the session?

## USING THIS TOOL

Divide into groups of three. One of you volunteers to share some aspect of your life that you would like to change, but you feel stuck. Portray your concern in a simplistic, self-defeating way by characterizing it as "all or nothing" and a "right or wrong" proposition. Another volunteers to listen, understand, validate, and, when appropriate, use the 1–10 scaling technique. You can use Figure 6–4 as a guide. Finally, the third person serves as the recorder who observes the activity and leads the feedback discussion.

---

**Scaling**

1. Set up the piece.

   ↳ Imagine a scale of 1 to 10.

   ↳ Anchored points are at each end.

   ↳ 1 is the worst point of crisis.

   ↳ 10 is the best possible resolution.

2. Invite the person to rate the current situation.

3. Ask what the person would be doing to be progressing to the next higher number.

4. Explore for details to encourage the survivor to envision possibilities.

5. Ask what number someone would have to reach to know that the person was in control and on the way to resolution.

**FIGURE 6–4** The five steps of scaling.

## Offering Suggestions and Making Referrals

Crisis survivors rarely achieve resolution during your interventions with them. At best, crisis intervention offers an opportunity for people to connect with a caring human being, make some meaning of their crisis, enhance their emotions of resolve, and come up with a promising strategy or two for coping. In the vast majority of cases, people will leave their encounter with you with their crisis unresolved, but with a positive momentum to continue along their path of resolution. Therefore, it is vital that you send them along their way with some suggestion for building on the progress that they have already made. Typically, your suggestions will include a referral to an agency, organization, or some other local resource that can assist them.

**Offering a Suggestion.** As you approach the end of your meeting with someone in crisis, you will want to decide what *suggestions* to offer. As you can see in Figure 6–5, the process of making suggestions follows a sequence of simple steps:

- *Reacknowledge the person's crisis.* Use the survivor's own words and crisis metaphors in summarizing the circumstances. At this point, you are speaking in a sympathetic, but not energetic, tone of voice.
- *Highlight the survivor in the crisis.* If you offered an encouragement interlude earlier, you can mention some of the strengths and resources the survivor is using to get through the crisis. Make sure that you include some of the strategies that the person has tried, even if they were unsuccessful. Quickly summarize the resolution you have been tracking, and the survival story you have been coconstructing. Now you are speaking enthusiastically to entrain the person's emotional arousal of resolve.
- *Determine whether the person is in a "yes set."* The *yes set* is a concept that originated in the writings of Milton Erickson (Erickson & Rossi, 1979). Yes set refers to the experience of agreeing, accepting, and affirming in an encounter with another person. If your statements of acknowledgment and survival have been close to what someone has told you, then the person will likely be in a yes set. According to Erickson and Rossi, "Rapport is the means by which the therapist and patient secure each other's attention. Both develop a yes set or acceptance of each other" (p. 2). Dolan (1985) characterizes the yes set as the agreement and deep acceptance between the counselor and client that is a "strikingly beautiful experience of the 'I/thou' nature" (p. 44).

    Usually, at this point in the crisis intervention, the survivor is nodding affirmatively to your acknowledgments and compliments. If someone does not appear to be affirming your statements, you may wish to be immediate to create a yes set. For example, you could say, "As I am saying these things, I notice that you are looking down, shaking your head, and frowning. I guess that there's something I've said that doesn't ring quite true to you." If the person answers in the affirmative, then you have started developing the yes set.

    In this situation, you also can use scaling by saying, "I guess you think I'm a little more optimistic right now than you are. On a scale of 1 to 10, with 1 being that you believe that there's no way things will ever get better, and 10 being that you are absolutely convinced that they will improve, where are you now?"

- *Offer a bridge.* Restate the goal that the person has formed and connect it to your suggestion. For example, you might say, "And because you said that what you would like to be able to do is live your life again feeling better about yourself, I wonder if you could. . . ."
- *Present the suggestion.* Keep in mind that your suggestions should fall into one of the four categories of a successful resolution process: making contact with others, making meaning, managing emotions, and taking action.

  All good suggestions either begin or end up as the survivor's idea. Your suggestions can take several forms—speculations, wonderments, and direct advice (Lankton & Lankton, 1986). Whatever form they may take, make sure that you know what the person in crisis has already tried.

  You can offer suggestions in a gentle, supportive, and encouraging tone of voice, emphasizing the parts that you wish to punctuate. Be sure that your suggestions are tentative, nonauthoritarian, and fit the crisis story that the survivor has shared with you. Take care not to come across as "the expert" on this person's experience or to sound dogmatic or pedantic. Resist the temptation to give a lecture showing off your expertise or to argue your case for a particular response.
- *Invite the survivor to collaborate.* Ask for the survivor's ideas about this suggestion. What could make it more workable? What might be some of the challenges in carrying it out? What information would be helpful for the person to better understand the suggestion?
- *Ask for a follow-up.* When you have coconstructed a plan of action, ask the person to let you know how it goes. The survivor can pass along an e-mail message, call back with an update, or stop by to discuss face-to-face the progress he or she is making. If someone has encountered some unexpected difficulties in following through on your suggestions, then you have another opportunity to address these issues together.

  Obviously, this protocol for offering suggestions is more a process than a script. Because you can never anticipate exactly how someone will respond, you should regard this protocol as only a guide.

---

**Offering Suggestions**

↳ Reacknowledge the crisis.

↳ Highlight the survivor.

↳ Determine if the person is in a "yes set."

↳ Offer a "bridge."

↳ Present a suggestion.

↳ Invite collaboration.

↳ Ask for a follow-up.

---

**FIGURE 6–5** The steps for offering suggestions.

**Making a Referral.** Finally, we want to mention a few important points about making a particular kind of suggestion—the *referral*. As a crisis intervener, you must remember that you are not the only resource available to someone in crisis. In fact, your primary role may be to act as a conduit, connecting the person in crisis to the needed resource. That resource may be a special friend, relative, faith leader, mental health counselor, therapist, psychiatrist, volunteer organization, or community agency.

Because you often serve as the bridge between the person in crisis and community resources, you need to gain a working knowledge of the available resources. The following are the basic strategies you should pursue to be successful in making referrals.

- *Know what resources are available to people in crisis.* Learn about the individuals, volunteer organizations, Web sites, toll-free numbers, professionals, and agencies that can be resources to people in crisis. In particular, investigate closely any possible local referral sources. Learn their hours of operation, addresses, telephone numbers, policies, transportation, languages, and procedures.
- *Compile referral information in a way that you can use easily in times of crisis.* Many communities have developed directories of services that include information regarding eligibility, fees, locations, contact information, procedures, and programs. The local United Way or Mental Health Association may have listings. Even if you have directories available, you will need to compile the information in a way that is useful, readable, simple to use, easily accessible, and relevant to the needs of the people in crisis that you typically serve.
- *Develop working alliances with emergency resources.* Contact the local hospital emergency care units, the mental health emergency services teams, social services agencies, and faith-based organizations that serve people in crisis. Develop collaborative relationships with them so that you can work together successfully.
- *Understand how the system works.* Become familiar with the referral process in your community. Develop a working knowledge of the "nuts and bolts" of linking someone in crisis with the services needed.
- *Keep your referral information current.* Check addresses, telephone numbers, Web site URLs, and other contact information. Update your directory on the basis of the experiences of your referrals.
- *Have your information handy.* All the information in the world is useless if you do not have easy access to it.
- *Be specific when you offer the referral.* Fill the person in with the "who, what, when, where, and how" of any referral. The more that someone knows what to expect, the easier it will be to take that big step of getting help.
- *Give options.* Whenever possible, discuss several possible referrals. People prefer to have a sense of choice about such an important matter.
- *Follow through on the referral.* The most common mistake in making referrals is the failure of the intervener to follow through on the referral. Ask the person to let you know what happens, even if the person is a stranger on the telephone. Whenever possible, check back if you have not heard from the person. Checking gives you another chance to relink if the person has any difficulties with the referral, and it also serves as an additional motivator. An ambivalent person may just go ahead and keep the appointment because he or she knows you will be asking about it.

## Put It in Writing: Offering a Follow-Up Note

For a person in crisis, just being able to talk to a caring and empathic listener is a rare and wonderful gift. How often do people get this opportunity? But even beyond oral communication, there is another powerful medium for crisis intervention—the written word. In Chapter 2, we discussed using the Internet as a means of connecting with someone in crisis. Here, we are focusing on a particular form of written communication that you can use to enhance crisis intervention—the *follow-up note.*

A follow-up note can be an important tool to support a survivor's discoveries, decisions, and changes. Of course, people enjoy receiving correspondence—both old-fashioned and electronic versions. "You've got mail!" is the favorite greeting our computer can offer us. Words in written form, even if on the computer screen, offer us a tangible record of someone's thoughts, observations, and reflections. However, people in crisis especially appreciate receiving a follow-up note because they are going through times of both tremendous distress and dramatic change. As they face new struggles or make progress toward resolution, they can return to your written words whenever necessary.

The follow-up note may be as simple as an encouraging comment that you write on the back of your business card or on a referral note. When you are doing face-to-face crisis intervention, you often will be giving the person a note that includes basic referral information. You can make this a much more powerful message by simply adding a few personal words.

For example, Gloria, a waitress, noticed a brochure on suicide that a crisis intervener had brought to his breakfast. She asked if she could have a copy because she had a friend who was worried that her granddaughter might take her own life. The intervener invited her to share her story. It turns out that the waitress was particularly sensitive to this issue because her own daughter had tried to kill herself years ago. The woman had found her unconscious daughter, rushed her to the hospital, and actively supported her daughter's involvement in a successful treatment program for bipolar disorder.

Now Gloria was a resource for others with loved ones who were contemplating suicide. The intervener gave her a copy of the brochure and discussed with her some referral possibilities in the local community. When the intervener finished his breakfast, he left behind the following note:

Dear Gloria,

I felt honored that you shared with me, a complete stranger, your worries about your friend who attempted suicide. I hope that our talk was helpful and that you find this handout material useful. You've been a real support for your friend and a true lifesaver for your daughter. I wish you the best!

Sincerely,
Lennie Echterling

Your follow-up note could take the form of a more elaborate message that you send to someone by e-mail or postal service.

A study conducted by Nyland and Thomas (1994) indicated that the impact of a letter written to a counseling client was equivalent to more than three face-to-face sessions.

In fact, many of those surveyed responded that the letter alone was responsible for their major gains in therapy.

Especially now that e-mail has resurrected written correspondence as a popular form of communication, writing to survivors is a crisis intervention strategy that should be part of your tool kit. When you write a follow-up message, you can follow the protocol for offering suggestions described in Figure 6–5. In this case, you can also ask for an update on how the person is doing.

---

## Listening In on Crisis Intervention

In this segment, see how the intervener uses a follow-up note with John.

Dear John,

It's been a couple of days since our talk and I wanted to share a few words with you. First, I appreciated your candor in sharing your concerns with me and I admired your creativity in describing your feelings so metaphorically. When I watched channel 4 on my TV last night, I thought of you! More importantly, I was moved by the struggle that you are facing—the one that we all must confront if we're honest with ourselves. That struggle, as you powerfully expressed it, involves our mortality.

Like that favorite oak tree that you mentioned, you also have deep roots that can help you weather the storms of life. I was moved by your account of your encounter with your father when he no longer remembered you. Just as moving was your commitment to support and care for someone who, by that time, thought you were a stranger.

I wish you well as you pursue the stress management techniques that we discussed. And please let me know how the referral is working out for you. I'm sure that you're continuing to lead the busy and productive lifestyle that you thrive on. I'm also wondering what creative ideas you've come up with to take better care of yourself and to bring even more meaning and richness to what you called "the twilight" of your professional career.

Take care,
Harry

---

## USING THIS TOOL

Gather a small group of your colleagues to participate in this activity. Each of you anonymously composes a note to every other member of the group. Start your note with "The thing I like best about you is . . ." and complete the phrase. Then tell about a particular time when this person showed this trait. Exchange the notes with one another. Each person then reads his or her notes aloud and then shares reactions.

## RESOURCES FOR ALZHEIMER'S PATIENTS AND FAMILIES

The following are excellent resources for information and help for individuals dealing with the effects of Alzheimer's disease.

Alzheimer's Association
http://www.alz.org

This national organization provides education and support for people diagnosed with the condition, their families, and caregivers.

American Health Assistance Foundation (AHAF)
http://www.ahaf.org

AHAF is a nonprofit charitable organization that is dedicated to supporting research on age-related and degenerative diseases, educating the public about these diseases, and providing emergency financial assistance to Alzheimer's disease patients and their caregivers.

## SUMMARY

In this chapter, we described how envisioning possibilities can encourage someone in crisis to embark on the resolution process. You also learned techniques that invite the person to continue resolving the crisis (see Figure 6–6). In Chapter 7, we turn to the practical challenges of integrating the ideas and tools you have learned in working with individuals in crisis.

### Segue to Chapter 7

To help you get into the mind-set for the next chapter, think about some complex skill that you have mastered. It may have been driving a car, speaking a foreign language, or learning to dance. Whatever the skill, you began with learning the basic components of the skill before you integrated them into a coordinated and graceful whole. Reflect on your thoughts and reactions as you found yourself putting it all together.

---

**Essential Tools**

- Hint at possibilities of resolution.
- Help survivors to make well-formed goals.
- Ask what-if questions about a resolution in the future.
- Involve the survivor in scaling.
- Offer suggestions and make referrals.
- Whenever possible, write a follow-up note.

---

**FIGURE 6–6**   Essential tools of Chapter 6.

# Crisis Intervention with Individuals: Working One on One

*"We don't get offered crises, they arrive."*
*Elizabeth Janeway*

*"I have fantasies of killing myself and thus being the powerful one, not the powerless one."*
*Anne Sexton*

## CHAPTER GOALS

After completing this chapter, you should be able to:

- Integrate the specific crisis intervention techniques that you have been learning
- Understand the issues involved in preventing suicide
- Follow the steps of resolution-focused crisis intervention with an individual by
  - linking with the person in crisis
  - cocreating a survivor story
  - helping the person manage emotions
  - inviting someone to envision possibilities
- Be an effective intervener with people who pose a risk for suicide

## OVERVIEW

In the previous chapters, we described important ideas and tools of successful crisis resolution. In this chapter, you will be integrating these concepts and techniques to engage in successful crisis intervention with individuals. You will be applying the concepts of resilience by focusing on strengths and resources. You will be using crisis intervention tools to facilitate the resolution process—helping a victim become a survivor who goes on to thrive. As you can see in the overview provided in Figure 7–1, the techniques that you have been learning are designed to enhance the factors of resilience: relying on social support, meaning making, managing emotions, and coping. Finally, you will be putting together such tools as offering the LUV Triangle, asking moving-on questions, offering an encouragement interlude, and scaling into a protocol for working with a person in crisis.

No matter what the precipitating event may be, when you are working with someone in crisis, you often must address the possibility of suicide. In this chapter, you will learn how to check for risks of suicide while also exploring the strengths and resources that can help someone survive a crisis.

## CRISIS STORY

Throughout her childhood, Jasmine had the energy, bounce, and vitality of a healthy, intelligent, and involved girl. She had passionate interests that included dancing, drawing, and writing. She loved to create plays with her cousins who lived on nearby farms. They would ride their bicycles to a meadow where a decrepit wagon served as a makeshift stage.

Jasmine's life changed dramatically when she entered adolescence and began to wonder about her sexual identity. She became aware of her growing feelings of attraction to other girls. As her fascination with the physical appearance of some of her girlfriends intensified, Jasmine began to feel anxious and concerned about not fitting in. Once an independent thinker who had serious interests in the environment and injustice, she became self-conscious and worried about being accepted. She dropped out of dance lessons because she became so embarrassed performing in front of others, and she became even more involved in her solitary activities of drawing and writing. At school, she was moody and reluctant to voice any opinion that would identify her as different. Her grades, which used to be outstanding, were now mediocre at best. Her parents were concerned and wondered what had happened to the happy, engaging girl they once knew.

Jasmine discovered that she did enjoy being with Derrick, a shy boy who, although his appearance was in stark contrast to hers, shared her interests in art and literature. He was short, stocky, and always dressed neatly in colorful clothes, whereas she was tall, waif-like slender, and wore black exclusively. When he invited her to a dance, Jasmine happily accepted—she was glad to have a friend and was excited about dancing along with everyone else. They continued to go out together and talked to one another on the phone every day. Jasmine was tickled by Derrick's wry sense of humor, flattered by his praise of her drawings, and relieved that he was satisfied with affectionate kisses and hugs. Jasmine's parents also felt reassured because she was less moody and isolated.

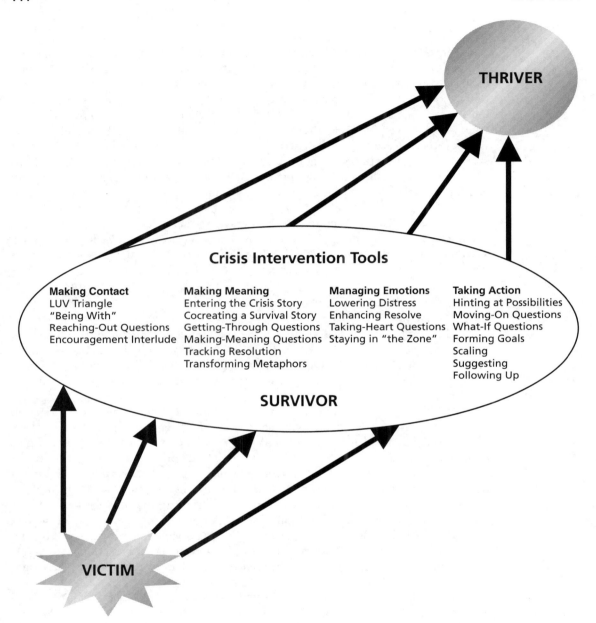

**FIGURE 7–1**    Putting it all together to promote resolution.

One summer evening, Jasmine took Derrick to the meadow and shared with him stories of her childhood theatrical days. Suddenly, with uncharacteristic dramatic flair, Derrick jumped up on the old wagon, gestured broadly like a master of ceremonies to an imaginary crowd, and said, "Ladies and gentlemen, I have an important announcement to make!"

Derrick stood there in silence, his grandiose manner disappeared, and he turned his gaze to Jasmine with tears in his eyes. "Please forgive me," he said. "I've been stringing you along. I'm gay." Jasmine quietly stepped up to the stage, hugged him, and shared her own secret that, before then, she had only entrusted to her diary. Three weeks later, they went together to a Lambda chapter meeting held on the local college campus.

That fall, when Jasmine and Derrick returned to school, the harassment began. Neither of them could believe just how quickly the word spread, but both, especially Derrick, bore the brunt of cruel jokes, taunts, and threats. "Hey, fag!" and "Hi, queer!" became such common greetings in the halls that Derrick joked to Jasmine that he couldn't remember his real name anymore.

It was on one of their regular evening walks in Jasmine's meadow that they were attacked. Six older high school boys ran out of the surrounding woods and pounced on them, screaming that it was time for their "fag therapy." Pinning the couple to the ground, they repeatedly kicked Derrick in the stomach, head, and genitals, while gang-raping Jasmine. When the attackers left, Jasmine realized that Derrick was unconscious and may have suffered a concussion. She called 911 on her cell phone and kept him awake until medical emergency services arrived.

When Jasmine told her parents at the hospital emergency room about the circumstances of the assault, they urged her not to file charges because of the publicity. Instead, they arranged for her to live with her grandparents 200 miles away and forbade her to have any contact with Derrick. At her grandparents' home, Jasmine spent her time drawing the fragmented images of the attack that she dreamed about every night. She wrote long letters to Derrick, often blaming herself for taking him to such an isolated place. Her diary entries recorded her growing sense of guilt, her feelings of alienation, and her despair for the future. Jasmine began to write poems about suffering, anguish, death, and suicide.

### Reflecting on This Crisis Story

1. What were your own reactions to this story?
2. What are Jasmine's strengths?
3. At what points could others have offered helpful intervention?
4. How can others be of help in Jasmine's crisis?

# IDEAS

## Pathologizing Versus Normalizing

In the previous story, as well as those in other chapters, you may have noticed that we did not mention posttraumatic stress disorder (PTSD). The recent interest in PTSD has been useful because it has drawn attention to both the tremendous challenges of individuals dealing with the consequences of trauma and the limitations of traditional counseling in addressing these needs. However, one of the unintended consequences of this focus on PTSD has been the tendency of counseling professionals to see vivid memories of the trauma, emotional distress, and avoidance of similar situations *only* as symptoms of pathology (McNally, Bryant, & Ehlers, 2003).

Conversely, we can also positively reframe such "symptoms" into potentially adaptive responses to adversity. Instead of intrusion, arousal, and avoidance, we can speak of attending to important lessons that trauma memories offer, using distress to mobilize resources, and taking precautions to reduce dangers. As you read in Chapter 1, most people show surprising resilience when dealing with traumatic events and do not develop PTSD. In fact, as Tedeschi, Park, and Calhoun (1998) pointed out, many survivors experience posttraumatic growth (PTG).

Of course, being aware of psychopathology and having diagnostic skills can be useful tools for you. But you need to take care. Just as everything looks like a nail to the child with a hammer, your training may goad you to notice symptoms you can diagnose, rather than a natural process you can facilitate (Maslow, 1966).

## Preventing Suicide and Promoting Resilience

Working with someone who is considering *suicide* is one of the most stressful situations that a counselor can face. However, if you are planning to offer crisis intervention services, then you can expect to work regularly with people who are seriously contemplating the possibility of killing themselves. Because crises are times of anguish and pain, many people begin to see death as "a way out of this mess," "an end to this unbearable suffering," and as "the only possible solution." When you are working with people who pose a risk of suicide, there are several important points for you to keep in mind.

First, remember that the risk of suicide is not an either/or condition. Instead, the probability that someone may take his or her own life is on a continuum, ranging from low, through moderate, to high levels of risk (Shneidman, 1999). In fact, Menninger (1973) once declared, "There is a little . . . suicide dwelling in everybody's heart" (p. 142). However, the self-preservation instinct is profoundly deep and abiding. The fact that you are helping people in crisis realize their resilience and resourcefulness means that you are assisting them to overcome discouragement and get in touch with their will to live. Even when the situation is so serious that suicide seems imminent, it never has to be "inevitable." As long as someone is talking to you, he or she feels some ambivalence about taking this drastic, final, and permanent step.

Second, when you are addressing the issue of suicide with someone, remember that suicide is not the crisis—suicide is only an attempt, however impulsive it may be, to resolve a crisis that seems to be overwhelming. Therefore, although you may be taking some time to check for the risk of suicide, your goals of crisis intervention remain fundamentally the same: to help the person survive the crisis and resolve it positively. The primary difference is that, in the case of possible suicide, the immediate stakes are literally a life-or-death matter. Remember, when you facilitate a positive resolution to the crisis, you are also successfully preventing a suicide.

Third, when someone is considering suicide, it may be tempting for you to engage in a debate to talk the person out of this option. If you have such an inclination, then keep reminding yourself that arguing, no matter how sincerely and articulately, against suicide is ultimately counterproductive. Saying, "But you don't realize just how fortunate you are" or "You have so much to live for" does not change someone's mind about suicide. Such words only serve to validate the person's profound sense of alienation, thus sabotaging your working alliance (DeJong & Berg, 2002). When you find yourself feeling the temptation to argue with someone, we recommend that you return to the LUV Triangle to strengthen your relationship and to look for the survivor in the crisis story.

It is also important to remind yourself that bringing this issue out in the open does not drive someone to suicide. Instead, discussing the topic in a concerned but direct manner can be a relief to individuals who believe that such suicidal thoughts prove how abnormal, crazy, and disturbed they truly are. If they are not suicidal, then they will dismiss this topic as irrelevant and return to other matters. If you suspect that someone may be thinking about suicide, then you need to address this issue with the person. Ignoring your suspicions and avoiding the issue can be disastrous. When in doubt, ask.

Finally, and most importantly, the possibility of suicide is no reason to abandon the principle of resilience, forsake the power of the relationship, and forget your crisis intervention skills. In fact, clients who successfully overcame their suicidal thoughts and behaviors reported that the most important contribution from counseling was the relationship itself (Paulson & Worth, 2002). They particularly valued the commitment of their counselor to stand by them through their crisis. They did not recall any particular technique that was especially crucial to the success of counseling. Instead, these former clients pointed to the experience of being listened to, understood, validated, and supported as an essential component.

Of course, it is vital that you immediately address the issue of suicide, but instead of focusing on the problem by only checking for suicide risk, you can also explore strengths and resources that promote the person's capacity for survival. Two factors that mitigate the possibility of a suicide attempt are support and resolve. As the crisis intervener, you are providing the support and are working to help a person strengthen the resolve to persevere.

Keep in mind that the vast majority of people struggling with the possibility of suicide are nevertheless resilient enough to choose life. Resilience and the will to survive are evident even among those people who actually make a suicide attempt. In the general population, the ratio of attempted to completed suicides is at least 10 to 1 (Hendin, 1995). In other words, even when people make a serious suicide attempt, the majority of them survive.

Thinking in terms of both risk and resilience is more than a mental gimmick of looking on the bright side of a potentially tragic situation. While never ignoring any signs of possible suicide, you can also use resolution-focused strategies to help someone survive a crisis. In fact, techniques such as looking for exceptions and building on strengths can go a long way toward preventing suicide and facilitating positive resolution. We will discuss these and other intervention tools later in the chapter.

## EXPERIENCING THIS IDEA

Imagine that you encounter someone who is suicidal and is seeking your help. Vividly picture the person's appearance—the look in the eyes, the posture, the clothes, and the gestures. Now add sounds to your imaginary portrait—the words that the person is saying to you and the tone of voice. Take a few minutes to explore your own reactions.

1. What is going through your mind?
2. What feelings are you experiencing?
3. What is more obvious to you—the risk of suicide or the person's resilience?
4. How can you gain a deeper, richer understanding of the entire person?

## Demographics: The Broad Overview of Suicide Risk

About 30,000 people kill themselves each year in the United States, making suicide the 11th leading cause of death. Because population size varies from year to year and from place to place, suicidologists use a standard rate to measure the incidence of suicide. The rate is calculated as the number of suicides per 100,000 people per year. Currently, the overall suicide rate in the United States is about 10.8, but this rate has varied tremendously from year to year, as you can see in Figure 7–2.

Figure 7–2 depicts a "century of suicide" in the United States. It is hard to imagine a more poignant graph because its few simple lines represent over a million lives cut tragically short, leaving behind countless grief-stricken relatives and friends. As you look over the chart, certain trends may strike you. First, let's contrast the dramatic differences in the suicide rates of men and women. As you can easily see, the rate for males was higher every single year of the century. In general, men are 3 to 5 times more likely to commit suicide, although females report making more attempts. Another gender difference is that the men's rates have much more variance from year to year, whereas the rates for women have remained consistently flat. In other words, women are less likely to react to major historic events and economic forces.

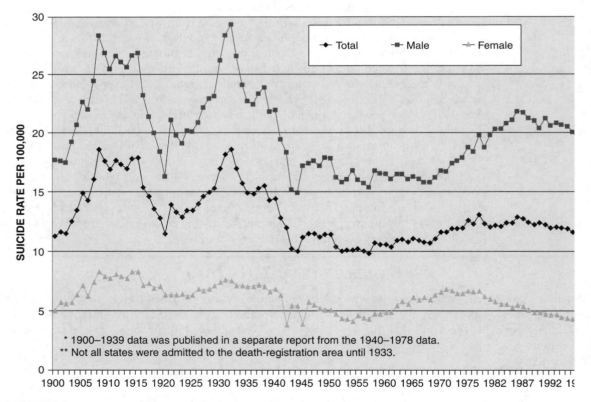

**FIGURE 7–2**   A century of suicide in the United States, 1900–1999.

*Source:* From *United States Suicide Rates: 1900–1999.* American Foundation for Suicide Prevention, 2004. Available from http://www.afsp.org/statistics/USA.htm

Notice where the sharp peaks in suicide rates, especially for men, take place during the past century. The highest was in the early 1930s, when the impact of the Great Depression was at its height. The second highest rate was in 1908, during another time of great economic turmoil in the United States. As the traditional "breadwinners," males suffered a tremendous loss of self-esteem when they were unable to find employment and could not support their families.

Now turn your attention to the two steepest drops in the rate of suicide, again particularly for men. Both of these dramatic reductions in suicide came during the times that the United States felt most threatened—during World War I and World War II. During those perilous times, there was a widespread attitude that every American citizen was a valuable resource in achieving the shared mission of defeating a common enemy.

Finally, take note (and take heart!) of the encouraging recent trend during the last decade and a half of the twentieth century. There was a small reduction in the suicide rate over these years for both males and females. Suicidologists have speculated regarding the possible explanations for this drop. It may be due to the consistently strong economy during much of that time, to more effective treatment of depression, or to stricter gun control laws. Whatever the reason, contrary to the popular myth, the overall suicide rate is lower now than it had been throughout most of the twentieth century. In fact, although the U.S. population has been increasing, the actual number of suicides has remained roughly the same in the last decade.

For an overview of the changes in suicide rates across the life span, look at Figure 7–3. Because there are both race and gender differences in rates, the chart presents four areas

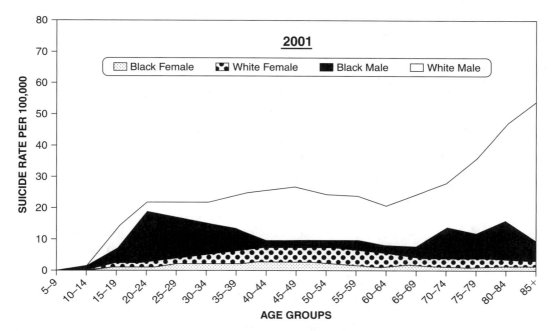

**FIGURE 7–3**    Suicide rates by age and gender, 2001.

*Source:* From *U.S. Suicide Rates by Age, Gender, and Racial Group.* National Institute of Mental Health, 2004, Bethesda, MD: National Institutes of Health, U.S. Department of Health and Human Services. Available from: http://www.nimh.nih.gov/SuicideResearch/suichart.cfm

reflecting black female, white female, black male, and white male trends. You may be surprised by what you discover in this chart. The common perception is that adolescents and young adults have the highest rates—after all, there has been tremendous publicity regarding teen suicide. Although the suicide rate among youth has tripled over the last three decades, older people are still much more likely to commit suicide. Those who pose the highest risk are white males 65 years and older. In contrast, women's rate of suicide does not vary dramatically as they grow older.

Epidemiological research has consistently identified certain demographic characteristics, such as gender and age, to be associated with risk of suicide. In addition, White Americans are more likely to commit suicide than African Americans, whose rates are higher than Hispanic/Latino Americans. People with a family history of suicides are more likely to kill themselves. However, the most powerful demographic predictor is mental health. In particular, people with mood disorders, substance abuse problems, or schizophrenia are much more likely to commit suicide. In fact, nearly 90% of those who have committed suicide had a diagnosable psychiatric disorder.

There are two cautionary notes we must make about the demographics of suicide. First, all these trends can be useful in providing general rules, but beware of being lulled into complacence when an individual does not match the demographics of higher risk. As consistent as these tendencies are, there are exceptions to all of these guidelines. Although women are less likely to commit suicide, they in fact do kill themselves. And adolescents, even children, also take their own lives. To be safe, you should *never* rule out the possibility of suicide simply because the demographics do not suggest it.

Our second cautionary note is that it is also possible to overreact by assuming that someone is going to commit suicide merely because of demographic factors. In the end, you can never rely on statistics to determine if a person will either choose or reject life. In other words, you should never concentrate on the demographic "forest" and lose sight of the individual "tree."

Only after authentically encountering the person and carefully listening to someone's unique crisis story can you develop any real hunches about what he or she may decide. One source of consolation—but not complacency—is that, despite their age, gender, race, psychopathology, or family history, the overwhelming majority of human beings can, and do, choose to live.

## Situational Factors

A state of crisis, precipitated by a tragic loss or traumatic event, is the most powerful situational factor in suicide. For young people, the precipitating event is more likely to be an interpersonal conflict or rejection. Economic hardships, such as the loss of a job or financial strain, are more common stressors in midlife suicides. And for older adults who commit suicide, the predominant stressor is medical illness (Rich, Warstadt, Nemiroff, Fowler, & Young, 1991). At any age, the sudden loss of self-esteem in a scandal, arrest, or failure can lead to suicide. Many suicidal crises, however, are not the result of a single incident. Instead, they involve a complex assortment of stressors involving relational, economic, health, and self-esteem losses.

Two other important situational factors relate to the means of committing suicide. The risk for suicide is higher if the person has the means, such as a firearm, readily available (Kaplan, Adamek, & Johnson, 1994). And the risk increases sharply if the available

---

**Key Ideas**

- Many responses to trauma may be adaptive coping, rather than symptoms of pathology.

- Suicide risk is on a continuum, rather than an either/or condition.

- Suicide is an attempt to resolve a crisis.

- When working with suicide, keep faith in people's resilience, use the power of the relationship, and rely on your crisis intervention skills.

- Psychiatric disorders, historic events, economic conditions, gender, age, and race are related to suicide.

---

**FIGURE 7–4**    Key ideas of Chapter 7.

means is highly lethal. For example, a firearm is generally more lethal, that is, more likely to result in death, than pills. In one study, 92% of attempts by firearms were successful (although using "successful" to describe such a tragedy somehow seems inappropriate), compared with only 4% of attempts by cutting (Card, 1974). About 60% of all completed suicides are committed by means of firearms (Moscicki, 1999).

As you can see in Figure 7–4, the key ideas regarding suicide can serve as a useful backdrop for using the tools that you will be learning in the following section.

# TOOLS

## Checking for Suicide Risk and Exploring Strengths

Later in this chapter, you will be putting together all your crisis intervention skills into an entire helping encounter, but first you will be learning specific techniques to work with someone who poses a risk for suicide. Why begin with suicide? We are addressing this issue now for a couple of reasons.

First, as you saw in Figure 1–2, crisis includes both danger and opportunity. On the opportunity side, you have been learning a variety of techniques to promote resilience and build on strengths. On the danger side, you now are adding suicide prevention tools to your crisis intervention tool kit. When you integrate all these techniques later in the chapter, you'll be able to reduce the dangers and enhance the opportunities of crises.

The second reason is that, in times of crisis, people turn to the basics and, to borrow from Shakespeare, reflect on one of life's most fundamental questions: "to be or not to be." Even if someone is not contemplating suicide, a crisis survivor is at a turning point in which one path involves living life more fully and more deeply, whereas another path is less vital, alive, and fulfilling. As a crisis intervener, you promote resilience by helping a victim become a survivor. Suicide prevention is helping someone to literally survive.

Finally, most likely your greatest fear in crisis work is dealing with suicide. In Chapter 1, you read that the first time you offer crisis intervention to someone, you'll also be having a crisis. Well, no matter how experienced you are with crisis work in general, you will be challenged and stressed whenever a life is on the line. In that situation, you may forget your training and regress to old habits. You might abandon your intervention skills and begin offering unhelpful reassurances and suggestions.

For these reasons, you begin with the basics of life-or-death issues in crisis intervention. When you are working with someone in crisis, a useful rule to follow when you have any concerns about the risk of suicide is to cover the BASICS, a model that we introduced to you in Chapter 1 to represent the different facets of the crisis experience.

Most traditional models for crisis intervention include specific guidelines and procedures for assessing *suicidality* (Rogers, Lewis, & Subich, 2002). Although checking for the risk of suicide is certainly necessary in many cases, these practices have several limitations. First, they focus only on the person's dangers, weaknesses, failures, and vulnerabilities. When people feel caught up in a crisis, they are already less in touch with their strengths and resources. Unfortunately, if the crisis intervention centers on people's losses, failures, and limitations, it can reinforce their sense of hopelessness and powerlessness. As a crisis intervener, you can offer a more complete picture that includes both risks and strengths. By following the dual strategy of checking for risk and exploring for strengths, you can reduce the danger of suicide and enhance the potential for a positive resolution.

Another limitation is that most protocols for assessing *suicide risk* fail to emphasize the power of the relationship. When the context of an authentic and caring encounter is missing, the questions take on a tone that departs dramatically from the sense of genuineness and collaboration that you want to foster. The inquiries feel like a detective's interrogation instead of a helper's concerned exploration of a vitally important issue. Whenever the question of suicide risk emerges, rather than abandoning your relationship, you want to emphasize it even more. For example, you might say, "You know, as we've been talking about your situation, you've mentioned a couple of things that worry me about your personal safety. I appreciate that you have been so open about the fact that you've been thinking about killing yourself. Your trust in me means a lot to me and I want you to know that. I also would like us to talk more about this issue of suicide. . . ."

In the following section, you will learn to check for risk and explore strengths by covering the BASICS. As you can see in Figure 7–5, you will identify the behavioral, affective, somatic, interpersonal, cognitive, and spiritual factors that relate to suicide risk. At the same time, you will also promote the person's resilience by, for example, asking reaching-out, getting-through, taking-heart, and moving-on questions.

Notice that the risk questions and strengths questions you will use in crisis intervention differ from one another in their form. First, in contrast to resilience questions, the questions about suicide risk do not involve presumptive language. For example, you presume that someone has successfully coped, at least in part, with crises in the past. Otherwise, the person would not be alive now. Therefore, you ask questions such as, "When you've faced tough times in the past, how have you gotten through them?" However, you do *not* suggest that you fully expect someone to have attempted suicide in the past. Instead, you say, "Just now, you mentioned that you were thinking of suicide. I'm worried about your safety and I'm wondering *if* you had ever tried to kill yourself before." You presume resilience, but you check on risk.

**Covering the BASICS**

Behavioral

    Previous Attempts - - - - - - Previous Coping

    Current Preparations - - - - Current Coping

Affective

    Depression - - - - - - - - - - Hope

    Anxiety - - - - - - - - - - - - - Courage

    Bitterness - - - - - - - - - - - Compassion

Somatic

    Illness - - - - - - - - - - - - - Health

    Pain - - - - - - - - - - - - - - - Physical Comfort

Interpersonal

    Alienation - - - - - - - - - - - Support Network

Cognitive

    No Alternative - - - - - - - Possibilities

    Suicidal Ideation - - - - - - Ideas for Coping

    Suicide Plan - - - - - - - - - - Survival Plan

Spiritual/Meaning

    Meaningless - - - - - - - - - - A Sense of Meaning

    No Future - - - - - - - - - - - A Sense of Future

**FIGURE 7–5**    Checking for risks and exploring strengths: Covering the BASICS.

Another difference is that the risk questions are typically closed-ended and specific. For example, you might ask someone, "Are you thinking of killing yourself?" As you can see, such questions narrow in on the particular concern of suicide. In contrast, the strengths questions are usually open-ended and broad. You could ask, "How did you get yourself to talk about these painful experiences with me?" You are casting a wide net in search of someone's resourcefulness, determination, and talents that he or she can use to survive this crisis.

- *Behavioral.* What is the person *doing* that presents a risk for suicide or affirms a commitment to life? Instead of exploring options to resolve the crisis positively, someone may be openly threatening suicide or merely hinting at the possibility. If something about the person's words or manner gives you the slightest suggestion that the person poses a risk for suicide, you must address this serious matter.

If the person openly *threatens* suicide by telling you, for example, "I'm thinking about killing myself," you can respond not only to the words, but also to someone's actions of honestly sharing this intention with you. In other words, you intervene by validating the obvious pain and anguish beneath those words, while also affirming the survivor who is taking positive steps. You might say, "It takes a lot of courage to come in here and talk about this."

Instead of a threat, the person may bring up the issue of suicide by merely giving a vague *hint*. For example, after describing his or her difficulties and concerns, someone may say, "Oh well, at least I won't have to worry about these things much longer." In this case, your response can be to ask simply, "You know, when you said that you 'won't have to worry about these things much longer,' I had this gut reaction that I need to check out with you. What did you mean by those words?"

Whether it is a threat or hint, when someone discusses the possibility of suicide, you need to explore how the person has handled crises in the past. People who have made *previous suicide attempts* pose a greater risk of committing suicide. Again, you should be direct by simply asking, "You said earlier that you are thinking about suicide. Right now, I'm feeling concerned about your safety and want to ask you some questions about this issue. Have you ever tried to kill yourself in the past?"

Keeping a resolution focus helps you to appreciate that the person has survived these suicide attempts. Like the majority of people who attempt suicide, the person may have selected methods, such as poisons or sleeping pills, that are slow acting or less effective. As a result, he or she had more opportunities for second thoughts or rescues. Although others may dismiss them as merely attempts to gain attention, you can think of such suicide attempts as reflecting some form of survival instinct.

Once you have information that somebody has attempted suicide, however, you can then explore the many exceptions when someone *chose life* in spite of a crisis situation. For example, you might say, "What did you tell yourself then to talk yourself out of suicide?" or "How were you able to get through that terrible time without trying to kill yourself?"

In addition to discussing past behaviors, you want to explore how the person is behaving in the present. For example, making *preparations* to commit suicide, such as purchasing a gun, indicates serious risk. Once again, you can ask directly, "Are you doing anything right now to carry out your idea of killing yourself?" As you gather information regarding any preparations, you want to be specific about exactly what the person is doing. The more preparations, the higher the risk is for suicide.

Even if someone is taking some actions in preparation of committing suicide, the person is also engaged in some *coping* activities that indicate resilience. After all, the survivor is still alive and has contacted you for crisis intervention. Therefore, you also explore the person's success experiences, however small, in dealing with the crisis. You can ask something like, "With all your suffering and personal turmoil, how did you manage to make this decision to meet with me?"

- *Affective.* Intense feelings of fear, rage, and especially depression can provoke someone to commit suicide. In particular, mood disorders are one of the factors that are most highly related to suicide risk. People with mood disorders have been found to be 8 times more likely to commit suicide—an incidence rate of about 90 per 100,000 each year (Jacobs, Brewer, & Klein-Benheim, 1999). The person who is feeling overwhelmed by *depression*, overcome by *hopelessness*, or burdened by a powerful sense of *guilt* is a high risk for suicide.

If you are sensing such bleak affective themes in the person's crisis story, then you should check for the risk of suicide. You could say, for example, "When people are feeling as hopeless as you are now, thoughts of suicide sometimes pass through their minds. What about you?" Another way to check for risk is to begin by offering a reflection such as, "It sounds like you're still feeling enraged with your girlfriend and bitter about the break-up. Listen, I'm concerned about something that I want to check with you because things seem so awful for you. Are you thinking about hurting yourself or somebody else?"

Never discuss these emotions of crisis without looking for such *feelings of resolve* as hope, courage, and compassion. Ask taking-heart questions, such as "Where did you find it in your heart to reach out like that?" Be alert to the small courageous step that someone may have taken. Once you notice it, you can call it to the person's attention by commenting, "That must have taken a lot of guts to go through that situation." One way to explore for hope is to simply invite the person to talk about goals by saying, "Tell me about what you'd like to see happen in your life."

A more elaborate method to explore feelings of resolve is scaling, a technique you learned in Chapter 6. You can say something like, "On a scale of 1 to 10, with 1 being the least hopeful you've ever felt and 10 being the most hopeful, where are you now?" If, for example, the person responds with a "4," you can respond with, "Wow! So you aren't at a 1! What have you been able to do to get yourself to a 4?" Once you have discussed the coping strategies the person has been using up to the present, you can turn to the future. You might follow up with, "What would be different in your life that would let you know that you are on your way to a 5?"

- *Somatic.* Someone who recently has been struck by a seriously debilitating condition or life-threatening illness can pose a higher suicide risk. If the crisis event involves such an illness or condition, then be alert to any signs that the person may be considering the possibility of taking his or her own life. If you find yourself having vague concerns, share your worries with the person by saying, for example, "As you've been sharing with me the struggles you've faced, the pain you've endured, and the poor prognosis you've been given about your chances for survival, I've had this question that's been running through my mind. Are you thinking about ending your life?"

Whenever someone comes to you in crisis because of such serious somatic concerns, then be sure to explore resilience in addition to checking risk. For example, you might say, "Now that you're dealing with this illness that threatens to end your life, how are you finding the will to continue on?"

Intoxication during a crisis is a significant risk factor for suicide, particularly among young people (Fowler, Rich, & Young, 1986). Individuals who are intoxicated have impaired judgment and lowered impulse control. Combining these two conditions with suicidal thoughts can have deadly results.

You can check your impressions with the person by saying, in a nonjudgmental tone of voice, "I'm having some trouble understanding what you're saying because your words seem to be slurred. Have you been drinking or taking anything?"

- *Interpersonal.* The fewer significant people—lovers, relatives, or friends—in the person's life, the higher the suicide potential (Jacobs et al., 1999). And if the person's support network has been recently struck by serious conflict or tragic loss, there is a greater potential.

  You can assess this factor by asking, "Who are the important people in your life?" Or you may inquire, "How are the important people in your life involved in this situation?"

  Although suicide clusters, the dramatic increase of suicides in a community, are rare in the United States, the experience of encountering, either directly or through the media, the suicide of a friend, peer, relative, or public figure increases the suicide risk of vulnerable young people (Moscicki, 1999).

  One approach you can use to intervene is circular questioning, which involves asking what others will be noticing or saying about someone as the person makes his or her way toward a positive resolution of the crisis. Such questions explore the interpersonal dimension to the survivor's view of the world and help the survivor to take a broader perspective of the situation. An example of a circular question is, "When you have handled this crisis in a way that others will notice, how will you be different? What will they say they have observed about you that allows them to feel better about your commitment to living?"

- *Cognitive.* To check for risk of suicide in someone's thinking, you might directly say, "I'm wondering if you're thinking of killing yourself." If the idea of suicide has only momentarily crossed someone's mind, then the risk for suicide is relatively low. An occasional, vague, and fleeting episode of *suicidal ideation* is not unusual during a time of crisis. Nevertheless, it is essential that you check for risk whenever someone mentions thinking, no matter how briefly, about suicide.

  If a person is having thoughts about suicide, then immediately follow up to determine if the person has a *suicide plan* by asking, "You said that you might kill yourself. Do you have an idea how you would kill yourself?" If the person has a definite plan of when, where, and how to commit suicide, along with a highly lethal method, the risk for suicide rises dramatically.

  An individual who thinks that there are alternatives to suicide for resolving a crisis has greater potential for surviving. In contrast, someone who poses a higher risk of suicide seems to be wearing cognitive blinders that allow him or her to see only the options of continuing to live in an unchangeable, unendurable situation—or to escape it through suicide.

  Besides checking for suicide ideation, you can use this opportunity to explore the coping ideas and insights the person has discovered in the process of dealing with this crisis. For example, you can ask, "What advice would you give somebody in this situation?" In addition to determining if the person has a suicide plan, you should also explore for a survival plan. If you hear the survivor mention a possible option or two for coping with the crisis, you might say something like, "It sounds like you've got some ideas about what you might do. Tell me more about those possibilities."

- *Spiritual.* It is a particularly troubling sign of high risk for suicide if someone is expressing the belief that life no longer has any meaning, that the person or situation is irredeemable, or that life is not worth living. Someone who is feeling a profound sense of spiritual alienation may see suicide as the only salvation. If this theme is emerging in the crisis story, you can follow the strategy of acknowledging and checking. You might say, "After all that's just happened, it sounds like you're wondering if there's any point to life right now. What would need to be happening for you to begin feeling better about going on with your life?" If the person names a change in the situation or behavior of someone else, you can ask the follow-up questions, "What difference would that make for you? How would you be changed by that?"

**Plan for Choosing Life.** In spite of the popularity of using a *"no-suicide" contract*, there is no evidence to support its effectiveness in preventing suicide (Weiss, 2001). Drye, Goulding, and Goulding (1973) were the first to propose this technique, which many mental health professionals have used with clients who pose a risk for suicide. However, in a retrospective review of inpatient psychiatric records, Drew (2001) found that no-suicide contracting did not prevent self-harm behaviors. More recently, 28% of a sample of suicide cases had actually signed a no-suicide contract shortly before killing themselves (Busch, Fawcett, & Jacobs, 2003).

It may be that the no-suicide contract has become widely used as a therapeutic procedure because it appears to offer practitioners some semblance of legal protection. Although the counselor or therapist may sleep better at night as the result of having someone sign such a contract, this technique is a woefully inadequate substitute for comprehensive treatment for a person who poses a serious risk for suicide. When a no-suicide contract is effective, it is probably because the survivor does not want to break a promise with someone in a relationship that's based on acceptance, genuineness, and empathy.

Instead of using a legalistic "contract" that might seem coercive, you can offer to help someone develop a *plan for choosing life*. As you can see in Figure 7–6, a survivor can use this form for jotting down important names and telephone numbers of people to contact in case of an emergency. The person can also write reminders about coping strategies that he or she has found successful. Finally, someone can list the items in his or her hope kit (Henriques, Beck, & Brown, 2003). The hope kit can be an actual container in which a survivor keeps possessions that offer reminders that life is worth living and that the future holds promise. These items may be photographs of loved ones, inspirational quotations, souvenirs, mementoes, and religious objects.

**Reducing Suicide Risk and Promoting Survival.** By engaging in a supportive relationship, coconstructing a survival story, managing emotions, and helping someone cope, you are both reducing the suicidal risk and *promoting survival*. There are some

**My Plan for Choosing Life**

I, _____, am choosing life by getting help for my problems, taking better care of myself, and using my hope kit. If I am having thoughts of harming myself or committing suicide, I will get help immediately by:

Talking to a life-affirming friend, such as

_____

Contacting emergency services at

_____

Making a counseling appointment by calling

_____

Making a psychiatric appointment by calling

_____

I will also take better care of myself by:

Thinking about_____

Handling my feelings by_____

Doing something positive, such as_____

My hope kit includes these reminders of what gives me a sense of hope about my life:

_____

_____

_____

**FIGURE 7–6**  Plan for choosing life.

additional specific and practical strategies that you can pursue. One is to encourage the person to arrange for the means of suicide to be removed. Another is to "establish a life-line" (Wainrib & Bloch, 1998, p. 138) by linking the person in crisis with others who are personally committed to keeping the person alive. A third strategy is to develop a plan for choosing life with the person. Finally, whenever you encounter someone who poses some degree of risk for suicide, you must work to connect the person with services, particularly mental health treatment, to address the precipitating concerns. A referral is essential.

If, in spite of your interventions, you find that someone continues to threaten suicide, then you need to carry out emergency procedures for voluntary hospitalization. If the person presents an imminent danger to self and refuses to be hospitalized, you should seek, as a last resort, involuntary commitment (Clark, 1998).

## Listening In on Crisis Intervention

Review the narrative at the beginning of the chapter to refresh your memory regarding the crisis that Jasmine is confronting. As we resume their session, notice how the intervener begins the process of checking for suicide risk within the context of a relationship.

MIMI, INTERVENER: (*She introduces herself with an air of concern and confidence.*) Hello, my name's Mimi. What can we talk about that would be most helpful to you?

JASMINE: Well, for starters, I was raped by four scumbags, I'm not allowed to see my best friend, and I'm forced to live in this little jerkwater town with my Grandpa and Grandma, whose idea of a big night out is a cone at the Dairy Queen after dinner. (*She sighs and pauses before going on.*) I can't sleep most nights . . . I don't know . . . why fight it . . . (*Her shoulders slump forward and her voice trails away.*) . . . I give up.

INTERVENER: Hearing your story about what you've been through takes my breath away. You've suffered so much . . . the rape, the loss of a friend, and as you see it, your freedom. I guess having to keep it all inside must also be extremely hard for you, too.

JASMINE: Yeah, well like my dad used to say, suck it up, you're a big girl.

INTERVENER: A minute ago you said something about giving up. Tell me what that means . . . I don't want to assume anything, Jasmine, but from the way you looked and the way your voice sounded, I'm wondering if you have been giving some thought to hurting yourself.

## Reflecting on This Segment

1. How did the intervener use the LUV Triangle in this segment?
2. How did the intervener begin to check on the risk for suicide?

## *USING THIS TOOL*

Divide into groups of three. One of you volunteers to role-play a person who poses some level of risk for suicide. Another volunteers to check for risk and explore for strengths. If you like, you can refer to Figure 7–5 as a guide. Finally, the third person serves as the recorder who observes the activity and leads the feedback discussion. Rotate the roles so that each of you has a chance to practice these skills.

## Doing Crisis Intervention

When intervening with someone in crisis, you are working to help that person achieve two fundamental goals: to make it through this hazardous time and to resolve the crisis positively. Effective crisis intervention integrates concepts and techniques that we have been describing throughout this book. The process involves four basic steps that parallel the crisis resolution process portrayed in Chapter 2. These steps are:

1. Linking with the person in crisis
2. Coconstructing a survival story
3. Helping to manage emotions
4. Facilitating coping

In this section, we offer guidelines and suggestions for what you might do and say at each of these steps. Figure 7–7 offers an overview of the process of crisis intervention with individuals.

## Linking

When you focus on *linking* with someone in crisis, you are relying heavily on the social support tools of intervention: offering the LUV Triangle, "being with" the person, asking reaching-out questions, and giving an encouragement interlude. Particularly at the beginning of your encounter with a survivor, you are also carrying out the tasks listed in the following segment. To successfully link may only take a few seconds, but do not underestimate its value as the foundation for a successful intervention.

- *Connect rapidly.* The very act of rapidly connecting with someone in crisis is, in and of itself, a powerful form of intervention. Your presence as a concerned and caring person is reassuring to someone who may feel frightened, affirming to someone who may feel all alone, and supportive to someone who may feel helpless. When you first connect with someone in crisis, your opening line can begin with introducing yourself and simply asking, "What can we do together that would be helpful to you?" Because people in crisis have a strong urge to talk about their experience, it is typical for them to respond immediately to your introduction by telling their crisis stories.
- *Introduce yourself and identify your role.* Because you may be offering crisis intervention to a stranger, you can quickly say who you are. When you meet someone in a crisis situation, you can bond quickly by making eye contact, giving your name, offering your hand (whenever appropriate), and describing your role. For example, in a hospital emergency room, you may walk up to someone in obvious distress, extend your hand, and simply say, "Hello, my name is _____. I'm a counselor here." In a disaster assistance center or with an outreach operation, you may find it easier to wear an identifying tag with your name and position.
- *Offer asylum.* Not only is your presence helpful, but the setting itself offers a sense of physical security and psychological refuge to someone who may feel threatened. Because they tend to be hypervigilant and easily distracted, people in crisis respond well to a safe and quiet setting. A haven can give the survivor an opportunity to focus on resolution instead of self-protection.

  As Ackerman (1997) has pointed out, such a sense of sanctuary is becoming increasingly rare. "In this world of earthquakes, heartaches, rivalries, drive-by shootings, how we treasure the idea of a safe place . . . a pool of mental and emotional shade. We seek asylum" (p. 130). Many crisis and disaster programs also provide emergency shelter to those whose homes have been damaged or whose physical safety has been threatened.

**Facilitate Coping**

- **Follow Up**
  "How are things going for you now?"
- **Offer Suggestions and Refer**
  "Who else can be of help to you now?"
- **Offer Scaling on Coping**
  "On a scale of 1 to 10, with 1 being . . ."
- **Help Form Goals**
  "Where do you want to go from here?"
- **Ask Moving-On and What-If Questions**
  "As you move on in dealing with this crisis . . ."

**Help Manage Emotions**

- **Stay in "the Zone"**
  "I can't imagine not feeling scared in that situation."
- **Ask Taking Heart Questions**
  "How did you come up with the courage to do that?"
- **Enhance Feelings of Resolve**
  "You must have been terrified at that point."
- **Lower Emotions of Distress**
  "You're now somewhere."

**Cocreate a Survival Story**

- **Transform Crisis Metaphors into Ones of Survival**
  "You talked about feeling trapped here."
- **Ask Getting-Through and Making-Meaning Questions**
  "Where did you get the idea to try that?"
- **Track Resolution**
  "You're now looking for a way to make it through this crisis."
- **Enter the Crisis Story**
  "Tell me about what you're dealing with right now."

**Link**

- **Give an Encouragement Interlude**
  "I was honored by your honesty and openness in sharing this with me . . ."
- **Ask Reaching-Out Questions**
  "Who are the people who've been there for you in the past?"
- **"Be with" the Person**
  "As I hear you talk about this . . ."
- **Offer the LUV Triangle**
  "It sounds like you've been through a terrifying experience."

**FIGURE 7–7**  Crisis intervention with individuals.

Of course, if a person telephones you from the scene of a sexual assault or some other violent trauma, then your immediate goal is to ensure the safety of the caller (Walker, 1994). Every person in crisis, however, needs to feel the psychological sense of asylum that you offer with the LUV Triangle—listening actively, communicating your understanding, and validating the person's perceptions with respect.

- *Convene others.* Crises can bring people together. In fact, cultures throughout the world have developed rituals in which family members and friends congregate to deal with developmental crises, such as births and deaths. An important role that you may play is helping someone convene relatives and friends who can offer emotional support and practical resources to address this crisis. For example, you may ask, "Who else should know about this situation?"
- *Offer the encouragement interlude.* Later in your crisis intervention session, you can return to focus on the relationship by sharing your experience of the survivor. As you learned in Chapter 2, an encouragement interlude is your opportunity to point out someone's strengths, highlight the changes you've already observed, identify resources, and affirm the resolution process. You are presenting people, who may feel demoralized and discouraged, with a more productive view of themselves and others.

While you have been listening to the survivor, you have been alert to the instances of resilience, ingenuity, and perseverance. You've made a mental note of them so that you can then offer them as part of an encouragement interlude. For example, one of your comments during this interlude might be, "Wow! I don't think that I could have come up with that idea in the middle of all that turmoil."

## Listening In on Crisis Intervention

At this point in the meeting, the intervener continues to focus on relationship building. Take note of how the intervener avoids playing the role of expert.

JASMINE: I stay in my room all the time. Sometimes I read, but mostly I sleep and watch TV. Sometimes at night I look out my window and I can see those dumb bugs—moths or whatever—crashing into the porch light over and over. I think that they are the lucky ones.

INTERVENER: That's very intriguing, but I'm not sure I understand how the moths are lucky.

JASMINE: OK, I'll spell it out for you. (*She sits up, leans forward, and begins talking with more volume and more energy.*) They keep crashing into that light night after night. I don't know if it feels good or not, but at least they aren't kept in a cage and held prisoner. I feel like I'd like to fly out of here and crash into something, too, but I can't. I just sit here day in, day out, and rot while those bastards who raped me and beat up Derrick are free as birds.

## Reflecting on This Segment

1. How would you respond to the metaphor Jasmine used?
2. What would you do when Jasmine returned to the crisis in her last response?

## Coconstructing a Survivor Story

In crisis intervention, your fundamental purpose is to help a victim become a survivor. Telling their stories is one of the ways that people begin the process of crisis resolution. Once you have linked with someone in crisis, you can expect the person to have a desperate need to tell the story—to bear witness to the enormity of this overwhelming experience.

- *Enter the crisis story.* When you invite people to tell their stories, avoid asking, "What happened to you?" Although this question is a general open-ended one that encourages someone to talk, it also suggests that the person is only a passive victim of circumstances. You are better off asking, "What have you been dealing with?" or "What have you been having to face before you decided to come here?" These questions are open-ended but also suggest that the person has been actively involved in surviving the crisis.
- *Track resolution.* You may notice something different about the eyes of people as they tell their crisis stories. Compared with clients in most counseling sessions, people in crisis are often less likely to make direct eye contact with you. As people in crisis tell their stories, their eyes often become unfocused or gaze off to the side, similar to Erickson's transderivational search described in Chapter 1. Erickson suggested that defocusing was one indication of dissociative trance work. In other words, the storyteller's focus is not on the here-and-now of the session with you, but on the there-and-then of the traumatic event. Therefore, he or she may ignore the visual input that provides information about the current surroundings and instead respond to the pull of the crisis.

  Your job at this point involves using the LUV Triangle to acknowledge the crisis events, while, at the same time, you are noticing how the storyteller portrays himself or herself in the crisis story.
- *Ask getting-through and making-meaning questions.* In addition to acknowledging the crisis themes in the person's narrative, you also will be looking for the survivor in the story. If you are conscientious and observant, you are likely to find those nuggets of strengths and resources among the crisis events and reactions.

  Take care not to be drawn into the crisis story. It can be tempting to find out details about the crisis, but your job is to ask questions that support the survivor's resilience and resolve. For example, you may want to ask, "How did you manage to escape?" Or you may wonder out loud, "How were you able to handle that?" Asking exploratory questions about ingenuity, such as, "Where did you get the idea to try that?", is also an effective way to draw out the survivor embedded in the crisis story.

  Whenever you find examples of resilience, determination, creativity, and courage, be sure to compliment the person. Remember, a person in crisis is one whose self-esteem and confidence have suffered, so this is someone who can use frequent reminders of strengths and abilities. So, for example, you should compliment the survivor for dealing with this distress by saying, "It sounds like you were really determined to get through this." You can also make a mental note of several of these examples to share all together when you offer an encouragement interlude.

## Listening In on Crisis Intervention

At this point in the meeting, the intervener is tracking the resolution and offering the LUV Triangle. Notice how the intervener looks for the survivor in the crisis story.

INTERVENER:  Of all the things you've told me, Jasmine, the thing that stands out for me most is how courageous you were to . . .

JASMINE:  (*She interrupts, rolls her eyes, and replies with sarcasm.*) Yeah, right, that's me all right.

INTERVENER:  (*She leans forward and her voice lowers and softens.*) Jasmine, hold on a second. I really do mean what I'm saying. I admire you too much to make something up just to make you feel better . . . OK?

JASMINE:  (*She looks at the intervener for the first time in several minutes. It's as if Jasmine is trying to figure out if she's telling the truth. Mimi seems to be genuine, but Jasmine's voice retains some skepticism.*) Well, maybe I don't know what you mean exactly by courageous.

INTERVENER:  Before you and I met for the first time, your granddad called me on the phone and told me that after the attack, you saved Derrick's life. The rescue workers told him that you realized that Derrick may have had a concussion and so you kept him awake, warm, and still until they arrived at the meadow.

JASMINE:  Grandpa told you that? Humph. How'd he know? He sure as hell doesn't like to call long distance—too expensive! (*She tries to sound disbelieving but she is obviously pleased by the news.*)

## Reflecting on This Segment

1. How did the intervener use the encouragement interlude?
2. In what ways did the intervener have to "read between the lines" to get the full meaning from Jasmine's statements?

## Managing Emotions

There is no doubt about it—people in crisis are in a powerful state of emotional turmoil. In their entire lives, they may never have felt such overwhelming feelings of agony, fear, grief, or rage. How they portray themselves handling this distress has important implications for how they resolve the crisis.

In times of crisis, people portray themselves and their emotions in ways that can either facilitate or undermine a successful resolution. They may depict the distress either as evidence of a permanent character flaw, or as a temporary response to a disturbing situation. For example, a person may say, "I'm a coward for being so afraid" or "That was the most terrifying experience I've ever had."

Another portrayal that can affect the possibility of a positive outcome is depicting oneself as either powerless or capable of dealing with intense emotions. Someone may comment, for instance, "I was so mad at my boss that there was nothing I could do but take it out on my girlfriend" or "I've decided to channel my rage into doing something positive to make sure this doesn't happen to anybody else."

A third possible portrayal is interpreting intense feelings during a crisis either as symptoms of pathology or as normal reactions. It is not unusual to hear a person in crisis say, for instance, "I must be going crazy to feel this way." On the other hand, other survivors see their distress as painful, but not symptomatic or abnormal, and may comment, "I was feeling upset and overwhelmed, just like everyone else there."

The fourth portrayal that you are likely to see is depicting emotional expression as either a sign of weakness or an indication of strength. Someone may describe apprehension about "giving in" to these feelings by confessing, "I'm afraid that if I start to cry, I'll never be able to stop." Or a person in crisis may see giving expression to emotions as an act of courage or creativity.

As you listen to the person talk about distress, pay attention not only to what emotions are expressed, but also to what this distress means to the person. People who successfully resolve crises come to portray themselves as competent, normal, and confident in their handling of powerful emotions.

- *Lower emotions of distress.* As we discussed in Chapter 1 and Chapter 5, catharsis itself is not a necessary component of the resolution process. Instead of encouraging people in crisis to have an emotional abreaction, you can help them focus on how they have been managing their distress. As they discuss their distress, you are looking for occasions in which they effectively used the distress and managed their emotions to cope with the challenges confronting them.

  You want to take care in how you portray someone when you invite the person to talk about distress. "How did that make you feel?" is another one of those counseling clichés that you should avoid for a couple of important reasons—first, because the words are so trite and stereotypical. Every counselor and therapist in the movies uses that line. Instead of reciting lines, challenge yourself to genuinely encounter this person in crisis. Your words may not sound as polished and slick, but they're not from a script, they're from the heart.

  The second problem with the "How did that make you feel?" question is that it implies people's emotions are under the complete control of outside forces. Instead, you may want to ask something like, "How have you been dealing with all the feelings you've been having?" Such an open-ended question not only offers people a valuable opportunity to add emotional themes to their survival stories, but also suggests that they have continued to be resilient, in spite of their distress.

- *Enhance feelings of resolve.* During this phase of crisis intervention, you are helping people identify the strategies that they have found successful, however briefly or slightly, in regulating their emotions. At times during this crisis, they have been able to redirect their attention, find some meaning in the experience, give expression to their emotions, use their distress to mobilize themselves, or reframe the events. You are sifting through their narratives to find the times that they managed their distress to overcome threats and obstacles. You can then explore these occasions in detail to uncover more concrete examples of resilience. At this point, you can respond, for example, "It sounds like you acted quickly on that fear to save yourself from getting killed."

- *Stay in the zone.* As we mentioned earlier, during times of crisis, people sometimes wonder if their intense reactions may suggest that they are abnormal or even crazy. Many crisis interveners have been trained to play the expert role in this situation by asserting reassuringly, "You're having a normal reaction to an abnormal situation." As crisis workers, we know this statement is probably true, but to say it to the person in crisis is not useful. We would discourage you from taking this one-up position with the survivor.

Instead, without actually stating the message, you can suggest the normality of the reaction by indicating your confidence that the person is able to deal with these powerful emotions. You can communicate this message throughout your encounter with the person in crisis by offering your respectful presence, refraining from "rescuing" him or her with quick reassurances, and by responding empathically.

In addition to these techniques, you can offer your own fantasized reaction by hypothetically placing yourself in those circumstances. For example, you may say, "I can't imagine not feeling scared stiff in that situation. How did you get yourself moving so you were able to get away from there?"

## Listening In on Crisis Intervention

At this point in the encounter, the intervener is looking for emotions of resolve, helping Jasmine in managing her emotional arousal, and reverting to the LUV Triangle whenever Jasmine returns to the crisis story.

INTERVENER: Most people I know would not have been able to think so quickly, especially after going through the ordeal that you went through. How on earth did you manage to pull yourself together enough to call for help and administer to Derrick?

JASMINE: I don't know, I haven't thought about that part much. Mostly I think about being held down and raped and hearing Derrick scream as they kicked the hell out of him.

INTERVENER: It's almost as if there's a part of you that won't give up, and it comes out fighting when there's a threat.

JASMINE: I don't know about that, he is, I mean was, my best friend and I knew that I was the only one who could do anything to help us. (*She pauses and begins to smile slightly.*) I've always been good in emergencies. One time when I was about 12 or 13, my dad accidently cut off the end of his finger with a chain saw and was running around the back yard bleeding like a stuck pig. I got him to sit down and squeeze his finger to stop the bleeding while I called 911. Then I put the part he cut off in a plastic bag full of ice and gave it to the rescue squad. They said I saved his finger. It looks a little weird, but he still can use it.

INTERVENER: Wow! That's amazing. That makes two people so far that you have saved with your quick thinking and bravery.

JASMINE: Yeah, it's too bad Wonder Woman can't save herself. I guess I have to quit worrying about what I could have done differently.

## Reflecting on This Segment

1. What could the intervener say after Jasmine's last statement?
2. How did the intervener get Jasmine to focus on her strengths?

## Facilitating Coping

Immediately after the point of impact, victims are already becoming survivors. They are creatively evading hazards, courageously coping with dangers, and making the most of their few opportunities to protect themselves and others. However, because their focus may have been on the crisis events, survivors usually are not aware of their own resilience. Your goal in this phase of the crisis intervention is to help people in crisis focus on their resilience, resources, and future.

- *Ask moving-on and what-if questions.* Although the actual crisis events may now be in the past, the survival story is still a work in progress—unfinished and unfolding. Therefore, you want to invite the survivor to envision changes and future possibilities by asking, "What do you want to be doing when you leave this meeting?" Or you may encourage someone to explore options by asking, "Where do you want to go from here?"

    At first, the person may not accept your invitation to envision the future and, instead, may begin to talk about the crisis experience again. If so, you can return to the LUV Triangle by actively listening, communicating that you understand, and validating the survivor's retelling of the crisis experience. Keep in mind that retelling a crisis story is both common and important for resolution. After this retelling, you can extend another invitation to turn someone's attention to the future.

- *Offer scaling on coping.* After someone has had an opportunity to tell the crisis story, you may want to use a scaling question. As you learned in Chapter 6, this question can be particularly valuable in crisis intervention, because it helps people recognize the progress they have already made toward resolution in a short period. By their nature, crises are times of rapid change, so scaling will often help people in crisis appreciate their own movement since the impact point of the trauma. Of course, the ultimate advantage of the scaling technique is that it encourages someone to envision a better future. For example, you might ask, "What number will you be getting to that will let you know that you are on top of this situation? How will you be different then?"

- *Offer suggestions and make a referral.* As you learned in Chapter 6, because people in crisis usually need to connect with a variety of community resources, making a good referral is an essential part of crisis intervention. A good referral is much more than passing along a name and telephone number. If you have taken the time to go through the simple steps of crisis intervention, then the person who needs help is more likely to follow through on getting it. Sometimes, just a few extra minutes can make a big difference. You can make the best referral when you have successfully linked, heard the person's story, addressed the person's emotional arousal, and facilitated coping. After engaging in that process, both you and the survivor now have a better sense of the person's situation, strengths, resources, and goals. Even if someone asks only for the name and number of a specific referral, it is still wise to invite the person to talk more with you. You usually can be of more help when you know the BASICS. Most often, at this stage of the intervention, all a person needs is an invitation to talk with you about the types of assistance available.

## Listening In on Crisis Intervention

As the intervener begins to sense that Jasmine is ready to focus on envisioning possibilities for the future and to connect with professional counseling, the process turns to coping.

INTERVENER:  In these last few minutes I think I've seen a change in you, Jasmine. You seem more alive, more vibrant, more hopeful. What do you think?

JASMINE:  Yeah, maybe . . .

INTERVENER:  Well, let's check it out. On a 1 to 10 scale, if a 1 represents those times when you felt the least hopeful and a 10 is when you felt the most hope, like you could do anything you wanted, what number would you give to the way you are feeling right now?

JASMINE:  (*She ponders a moment.*) Oh, I don't know . . . a 2, I guess. No, more like a 5. Yeah, a 5.

INTERVENER:  What would you be doing—how would your life be different—as you head toward a 6?

## Reflecting on This Segment

1. How seamless do you think the scaling was?
2. How would you improve it?

## *PRACTICING THIS TECHNIQUE*

Join with two of your colleagues to form a practice group. One of you plays the role of someone who is contemplating suicide. Another takes on the role of crisis intervener, whose task is checking for risk while promoting resilience. The third person serves as observer, who offers feedback to the intervener and leads the group discussion of the roleplay. Then switch roles until everyone has had the opportunity to practice intervening.

### RESOURCES FOR SUICIDE PREVENTION

The following are a number of excellent resources, including organizations, hotlines, and Web sites, for information and help in preventing suicide.

American Foundation for Suicide Prevention
http://www.afsp.org
Toll Free: 888-333-AFSP

The AFSP offers information on government involvement, professional projects, and research related to suicide and its prevention. A directory of support groups throughout the United States and Canada is listed on the Web site.

American Association of Suicidology
http://www.suicidology.org

This is a nonprofit organization dedicated to providing an understanding of suicide and its prevention. Helpful information located on the site includes lists of local support groups in the United States and in some parts of Canada, a bookstore, local crisis center information, a virtual library, and links to other helpful Web sites.

National Hopeline Network
1-800-SUICIDE

Callers to this hotline are connected to over 750 local crisis centers in the United States.

Covenant House Nineline
http://www.covenanthouse.org/nineline/kid.html
1-800-999-9999

This hotline is for youth who desire advice for their problems. The Web site provides a place to submit messages under "E-mail Nineline" that will be answered through e-mail.

## SUMMARY

In this chapter, you learned how to integrate specific techniques into a protocol for working with individuals in crisis. You became acquainted with the basic crisis intervention steps of linking, creating a survival story, managing emotions, and facilitating coping (see Figure 7–8). You also learned how to deal with someone who is considering suicide. In Chapter 8, you will learn how to apply resolution-focused techniques with couples and families in crisis.

### Segue to Chapter 8

To help you encounter the ideas and tools in the next chapter, look at a favorite photograph of your family. As you gaze at the figures, go beyond the superficial appearances. In what ways is this picture a portrait of survivors? What values, strengths, and connections lie below the surface?

---

**Essential Tools**

- Reduce suicide risk and promote resilience.
- Link with the person in crisis.
- Cocreate a survivor story.
- Help the survivor manage emotions.
- Facilitate coping.

---

**FIGURE 7–8**    Essential tools of Chapter 7.

# Crisis Intervention with Couples and Families: Resolving with Relatives

"Call it a clan, call it a network, call it a tribe, call it a family. Whatever you call it, whoever you are, you need one."
*Jane Howard*

## CHAPTER GOALS

After completing this chapter, you should be able to:

- Understand the dynamics of couple and family systems
- Appreciate the typical developmental crises that couples and families face
- Help couples and families to resolve crises

# OVERVIEW

Up to now, we have focused on individuals in crisis. In this chapter, we broaden our focus to include the most fundamental of all human relationships: couples and families. Of course, implicit throughout this book is the assumption that individual human beings are not islands unto themselves. You may have noticed that all the crisis stories in the previous chapters have put the crisis experience in a family context. For example, Marcos in Chapter 1 was dealing with the death of his daughter, Maria. In Chapter 2, the firefighter Trey planned to seek her husband's emotional support as she coped with a critical incident. And in Chapter 5, Nelda Ann's husband was the perpetrator of violence against her. Truly, no crisis takes place outside of a family context. Family members may experience the emotional fallout of an individual's crisis, offer nurturance to someone reeling from some catastrophic event, or even instigate a crisis.

As we turn our attention to couples and families, there are several important principles to keep in mind. First, you may be intervening with an individual person, but the family is always present psychologically. To play on an old saying, you can take the person out of the family, but you can't take the family out of the person. We carry our families in our hearts and minds; their values, expectations, voices, images, and histories are permanent fixtures of our inner world. As a crisis intervener, you need to appreciate this family context, even when you are working with only one person.

Another point is that humans are not constrained by the limits of biology when it comes to family relations. Many adopt strangers from foreign countries as their own sons and daughters. A person may not have a biological sibling, but he or she has forged a long and close relationship with someone who is *like* a brother or sister. People also respond with surprising emotional intensity to someone who represents a father or mother figure to them. And an individual may create an entire "family" if his or her own biological relatives are unavailable, distant, or rejecting. Fundamentally, we all need a psychological sense of family.

Third, couples and families are changing dramatically in U.S. society. In your crisis intervention work, you will encounter couples and families that do not conform to the stereotyped and traditional models of the past. Same-sex partners, stepfamilies, single parents, and other forms of families are becoming more common. The conventional family of a married man and woman living together with their own biological children is now, in fact, the minority. We will describe the changes in couples and families in more detail later, but we mention it in this chapter's overview to alert you early on that you need to avoid narrow assumptions when you read the words *couple* and *family*.

The fourth important principle is that a couple or family forms a dynamic system. If one member is in crisis, then the entire system is likely to be in turmoil. And, like individuals, family systems in crisis face both dangers and opportunities. If they fail to resolve a crisis, families may come away with a sense of alienation from one another, in a state of confusion and chaos, and on the verge of disintegration. However, if they cope successfully, families can emerge from crises feeling closer, having a greater sense of commitment to one another, and working more effectively as a system. With families, therefore, the stakes are even higher in crisis intervention.

Finally, keep in mind that, in many crisis circumstances, bringing together family members will be inappropriate for intervention. In crises involving partner abuse, sexual abuse, and other forms of family violence, you need to provide an asylum from such traumatic incidents. A fundamental condition for any effective intervention is for the survivor to feel safe and protected. Moreover, many persons in crisis need distance, not togetherness, to continue their individuation process and separation from, for example, an enmeshed relationship with an overinvolved parent. A family session could undermine this process.

In this chapter, you will learn about family developmental crises, family dynamics in troubled times, and how to promote systemic changes that can lead to a positive resolution of a family crisis.

## CRISIS STORY

Her family doctor had warned Meredith that not taking her medication could lead to a seizure. But she was 21, exams were over, her summer job would start on Monday, and it was time to celebrate. Because of her epilepsy, Meredith couldn't drink even a glass of light beer because the interaction between her seizure medication and alcohol could be deadly. So, to be safe, Meredith didn't take her pills on the occasional weekend that she would have a couple of drinks at a party. She calculated that the odds of her having a seizure were almost nonexistent, even if she missed a day or two. Since high school, she had suffered only one seizure—and that was because she had the flu one winter and hadn't taken her medication for almost a week.

On her first day of work at the summer day camp for inner-city kids, Meredith was excited about being back. This would be her third year and she had been promoted to be one of the senior counselors. It was great to be frolicking in the pool with her 8-year-old swimming buddy, Lakita, the smallest of a bunch of squealing day campers. Meredith and Lakita were wading in the shallowest end of the pool, an area that the other campers disdainfully referred to as the "baby pool." That was fun for a while, but then Lakita noticed that some of the bigger kids were swimming out to the rope that bordered the deep end of the pool and then swimming back to the shallow end.

Feeling embarrassed and left behind, Lakita asked Meredith if she would carry her out to the rope where, Meredith knew, the water was only about 4 feet deep. Lakita couldn't swim, but Meredith would be holding the little girl, who was a quiet, sweet, and well-behaved child. What could go wrong? Meredith, who knew what it was like to be the smallest kid, decided that a little adventure might be good for the camper's self-esteem.

Meredith was holding Lakita around her waist when the seizure struck. Suddenly, her face grimaced, her body convulsed, and her arms locked Lakita in a tight embrace as the two sank below the surface of the water. At first, Lakita thought that Meredith was playing "dunk 'em" or some other game—but she didn't like this game at all! She gulped for air but swallowed water instead and coughed spasmodically. She tried to wriggle free, but Meredith's arms trapped her like iron bands. Finally, Lakita managed a short, gasping scream for help just before they both went underwater again.

Meredith's mother, Ellen, had decided to leave work early that afternoon, but she wasn't looking forward to her cavernous and empty home. She was the only one living there, now that her youngest daughter had rented an apartment and her husband, Fred, had separated from her. She had set her telephone to the mute position, the house was quiet, and she was alone—just like every other evening since Fred had left. Ellen had already purged the house of most of his belongings and was occupying herself this particular evening by exorcizing his photos from the family album.

For some reason, something told Ellen to turn the phone on in case someone called. Perhaps it was one of those Jungian synchronicities or a mother's intuition. Immediately, the phone rang and Ellen grabbed the receiver with an unexplainable sense of urgency. The voice at the other end blurted out that he had some bad news for her: Meredith had been in a swimming accident. He had hardly finished delivering the message when Ellen grabbed her large canvas tote bag and jacket and headed for her car. The young man offered to drive her to the hospital, but Ellen clenched her teeth, thanked him for calling, and started toward the university, determined to go it alone.

A few minutes later, Ellen pulled into the hospital visitor's lot and, after jumping through a few bureaucratic hoops, she finally was taken to her daughter. Ellen gave an involuntary gasp as she saw the sallow and gaunt face of her youngest child in the cold, stark, and vaguely threatening emergency room. Her eyes filled with tears as she rushed to Meredith's bed, extending her arms in her impatience to comfort and console her "baby." The door opened again and Fred, almost as pale as his daughter, ran to them both.

### Reflecting on This Crisis Story

1. What thoughts and feelings did this story provoke in you?
2. With which family member did you most identify?
3. What could you offer this family to help promote a positive resolution to their crisis?

# IDEAS

## It's About Families

A man and a woman meet and fall deeply in love. They are both attractive, virgins, drug free, law abiding, mentally and physically healthy, and successful at their work. They marry with the approval of their intact families of origin and have two children who are obedient, respectful, do well in school, are free of handicaps, have straight teeth and clear complexions, behave as good citizens, go to college, and follow in the footsteps of their parents until they themselves meet someone of the opposite sex and marry. And the cycle begins again.

Where in the world do such families exist? Actually, nowhere. This myth of the family life cycle persists in our culture as the model of a successful family, but you can be sure that no family even approximates this image. In reality, successful and thriving families take on diverse forms, exist within different cultural value systems, and sometimes encounter crises. Like individuals, families face two types of crises: developmental and situational. Developmental family crises are predictable because they occur when members change over the life span. Situational family crises are those unexpected catastrophes and other painful events that wreak havoc and create turmoil in families.

To work effectively with families in crisis, you will need to understand something of family dynamics and their effect on the individual members within the family. Entire books, journals, graduate courses, and professional disciplines have been devoted to the understanding of, and effective intervention with, families. Because of the enormity of the topic, we can hope only to scratch the surface in this chapter. We urge you to read books and take courses to further your understanding of families and family therapy.

In this chapter, we will offer an overview of family crises and a few ideas for how you might be helpful in easing such troubled times. The comedian Woody Allen once bragged that he speed-read Tolstoy's gigantic novel *War and Peace*. "It's about Russia," he proudly concluded. As we attempt to capture for you the essence of the vast literature on this topic, we can only, in the spirit of Woody Allen, make a similar declaration: "It's about families."

## Family Development

You are no doubt familiar with many of the theories of human development that are applied to individuals, but perhaps you did not know that there are theories of family development as well. Families go through predictable developmental stages, and at each stage, the family faces a challenge that requires adjustment. In the spirit of Erik Erikson (1963), each of these stages can be regarded as a family crisis. Failure to make a successful transition from one stage to the other creates critical tensions and tends to thwart the family's growth, placing inordinate pressures on all members of the family and threatening dysfunction.

Becvar and Becvar (1988) developed a useful model for viewing family development, and Kanel (2003) recently provided an overview of the evolutional crises of typical families. We have revised these models to include greater diversity, but keep in mind that any family life-cycle perspective takes a broad view and offers generalities to which there are innumerable exceptions. Such models can only approximate the rich variety of configurations to which we refer to as a "family." For instance, single-parent families, stepfamilies, gay families, childless couples, and unmarried couples all face their own challenges and crises, but in general, they also progress through some of the developments of a family life cycle.

We begin with Erikson's young adult (1963), an individual who may be still dealing with the identity crisis, or who may be in the next phase of "intimacy versus isolation." In this stage, the person is struggling with how to preserve that hard-won sense of identity while learning how to develop an intimate relationship with another person. This individual is also struggling with differentiating from the family of origin—going from being someone's child to being an adult—and finding an identity in the workplace. Becvar and Becvar (1988) described this stage as the *unattached adult*.

Next comes the *newly partnered stage*, in which individuals become a couple. To successfully resolve this developmental crisis, the individuals must fully differentiate from the family of origin, readjust friendships to accommodate to the partnership, and begin to think of career as supporting the partnership. Even if they do not participate in a wedding or commitment ceremony, most newly partnered couples experience a "honeymoon period" in their relationship.

When couples move on to the *early partnership stage*, they face several major tasks, including "keeping romance . . . , balancing separateness and togetherness, renewing . . . commitment" (Becvar & Becvar, 1988, p. 117). At this stage, it is likely that much of the pretense that existed during the courtship and honeymoon period is beginning to fall away. When each of them was attempting to manage the other's impression, the partners were not completely genuine with each other. Gradually, they have given up trying to get the other to see them as a "great catch." Instead, they begin to reveal their true likes and dislikes, belch and pass gas in each other's presence, and sit around the house with "bad hair," munching on snacks and dropping crumbs into the creases of the couch. As couples begin to reveal their true selves to each other, they face a family developmental crisis. Each may feel as if he or she has been betrayed by the other and may say, "You are not the person to whom I committed my life!"

To complicate matters even further, it is during this early partnership period that many couples begin the *child-rearing phase* of their family life. Many adults seek to have children, either biologically or through adoption, to enrich their lives and fulfill their yearnings for nurturing new life. However, even if the couple has successfully recommitted themselves to one another, the addition of a new member to the system is certain to create a crisis, although usually a joyful one. Biologically, two adults create a child. However, it is also true that, psychologically, a child "creates" two parents, a couple whose new role is taking responsibility for the care of another human being. The challenges at this developmental stage include "adjusting [the] family to the needs of specific children, coping with energy drain and lack of privacy, [and] taking time out to be a couple" (Becvar & Becvar, 1988, p. 116).

It should come as no shock to you that children are demanding and time consuming. From the moment they are born, they require tremendous amounts of care and vigilance from their caregivers. However, perhaps the most surprising characteristic of children is how quickly they transform themselves from infants to toddlers, from children to adolescents, and from young adults to independent human beings.

Along the way, children's process of individuation challenges parents to be flexible, accommodating, and sensitive to their changing needs. One moment, parents are coping with diapers, colic, and sleepless nights. The next, they are dealing with sleep-overs, camp, and soccer practices. Then, at a breakneck pace, parents are moving on to dealing with their children's adventures with driving, mood swings, and mystifying music. Of course, all these difficulties are normal and expected, but that knowledge doesn't make it any easier. Parents must be sustained by the faith that once during the teenage years, their relationship with their child will improve. Mark Twain is reputed to have said that when he was 17, his father was an idiot, but later, when Twain was in his early 20s, he was amazed at how much his father had learned.

The next stage of family development is the *launching phase*. After all, one of the important functions of a family is to successfully launch children into the adult world. The parents hope that the child will be educated, mature, confident, and skilled enough to begin a life that is truly independent of the family. As Becvar and Becvar (1988) put it, the family is "releasing adult children into work, college, marriage [while] maintaining [a] supportive home base" (p. 116).

Marcia's (1983) investigations have discovered that children these days are taking much longer to resolve their identity concerns than Erikson had reported. Therefore, the family must be prepared to welcome the child back after an aborted launch. Because of this extended *moratorium period*, young adults are often uncertain of their ability to cope with the "real" world. Their struggles with the "Who am I?" question extend well into adulthood. Thus, there is a growing tendency for children to return home after college, after a failed marriage, or because of their lack of readiness to leave the nest and assume the responsibilities of a full-fledged adult. If the family has accommodated to the child being gone, but then needs to redefine itself as the child returns, its members may feel "jerked around." Furthermore, the returning child may feel that he or she is a failure for not being able to cope with the demands of adulthood. Everyone feels as if this young adult has not done his or her job.

Another crisis that sometimes occurs after all the children have been launched is the *empty nest phase*, which requires the couple to redefine their relationship once again. First, they were lovers, then they were a married couple, and then they became parents—if they followed the conventional sequence. If both parents see the launching period as the end of their work together, they may discover that the attraction that originally brought them together has been eclipsed by years of parenting. They now have an "identity crisis" when it comes to their relationship. Their question becomes "Who are we?" Their parental coalition must metamorphose into a couple coalition once again if they are to sustain their marriage.

Another crisis that seems to be occurring with increasing frequency in American culture is what has been termed the *sandwich generation*. This phenomenon exists in families in which the children have returned home, or are still heavily dependent on the parents after they have ostensibly been launched. At the same time, the parents' parents have become old enough to be unable to adequately manage their own affairs, or they have become ill or senile. The couple who are attempting to rekindle their former relationship are now faced with the task of continuing to parent their children, while, at the same time, "parenting" their parents. They are "sandwiched" between the younger and the older generations.

Eventually, the children will be launched, and they will likely begin their own journey as they marry, raise children, and face these developmental crises again—only now in a different role. Their parents will usually work out an accommodation in their relationship, handle the additional crises that come with retirement, come to accept the death of their own parents, savor the joys of becoming grandparents, and deal with their own deaths.

To be a family is to be in crisis. The family developmental life cycle is one of continual crisis points in which the members experience anxiety, sadness, and anger. However, families rarely seek crisis intervention for these developmental crises. Instead, they are

## EXPERIENCING THIS IDEA

Briefly describe your own family's developmental history from its beginning to the present. You may want to interview older relatives as you pull together this information.

1. How did your family manage the developmental crises that it has faced in the past?
2. At what stage of development is your family at the present time?
3. How have you and the other family members changed through these crises?
4. What important lessons about life did you learn from these experiences?

Keep your family's developmental history in mind as you continue reading the material in this chapter.

more likely to contact you regarding specific situational crises that confront them. Nevertheless, you will find it helpful to keep these broader developmental crises in mind as you work with families. These issues often form the backdrop to the precipitating event and provide the context for exploring possible resolutions that promote the family's growth and development.

## Reconfiguring Couples and Families

The idea of marriage and family is rapidly changing in the United States. Although you may find it helpful to recognize that families go through predictable crises, you must also realize that the entire notion of "marriage and family" is in crisis. One small sign of this enormous cultural shift is that many counselor training programs have changed the course title "Marriage and Family Counseling" to "Couples and Family Counseling." This is an acknowledgment that more and more men and women are cohabiting without marriage contracts; that same-sex couples are living together, being denied the benefit of legal sanction; and that single-parent families are becoming a major demographic. You can no longer approach a "family" in crisis simply expecting to meet a father, mother, and their biological children.

In the cover story of the October 20, 2003, issue of *Business Week* magazine entitled "Unmarried America," Michelle Conlin called for a new definition of family, stating that we must begin to "say goodbye to the traditional family" and that we are becoming "a nation of singletons" (p. 106). Recent U.S. Census figures reveal that the percentage of married-couple households has slipped from nearly 80% in the 1950s to 50.7% today.

Soon, single adults will represent the majority of Americans. Already, according to Conlin, 42% of the nation's workforce is unmarried, along with 40% of homebuyers, and 35% of voters. The traditional *Leave It to Beaver, Ozzie and Harriet, Father Knows Best* "Honey, I'm home" families of 1950s television probably never existed in the first place, but now, even families we think of as "conventional" are no longer the majority. Conlin stated that 33% of all children are born to single parents, many of whom are underemployed and uninsured. Although 85% of Americans will marry at least once (down from 95% in the 1950s), the divorce rate for these marriages now stands above 50%. Forty percent of all children will live for a time with their mother and her boyfriend before reaching the age of 16. Thinking back to the family life cycle and its developmental crises, you now must add all the possible complications that reconfigured couples and families can face.

## Making Sense of Families

When you attempt to work with families in crisis, you will often find their dynamics confusing. As a counselor, you have been taught to look first to individual personalities in order to understand how people work. It is true that a family is a collection of individual personalities, but you cannot hope to understand a family by merely summing up the personalities of its members.

You have, no doubt, heard the expression, "The whole is greater than the sum of the parts." A complex system composed of its parts will display characteristics that cannot be explained by reducing it to its components. Pick up any newspaper. If there is a photograph on the front page, hold it up close to your face and you will notice that it is composed of tiny dots. If you are viewing it closely enough that you are seeing a section of this array of dots, then you cannot see the picture. But begin to move the paper away from your face and—voila!—a picture emerges. It is at this "picture level" that you must look to understand families.

Families are wonderfully complex and unique in their organization. Therefore, you will need to have some way of applying a template to family interactions that can make their structures more comprehensible. People in crisis often exhibit behaviors that, although they may appear momentarily strange, are simply normal reactions to abnormal situations. This is true of families as well.

Family systems also have their own personalities. They have characteristic ways of behaving that will be either a benefit or a hindrance to them when they encounter major stressors. If you know something of the way families are put together, this should give you some background knowledge for predicting how affected any given family might be in a crisis.

## Open, Closed, and Random Families

A number of family theorists have attempted to develop conceptual systems for understanding family functioning and the implications of various family structures. One example of this is the family typology model of Kantor and Lehr (1975). These researchers classified families according to the ways in which they communicated within their own system and with others: open, closed, and random.

*Open* families are those that have boundaries that neither close family members in, nor keep outsiders out. This means that family members move freely in and out of the family, have external contacts and friends, and can have a life outside the family. Likewise, the family is open to contact from non-family individuals. Obviously, if you are doing crisis intervention with such a family, its members will likely be accessible and welcoming of your initiations and offers of help.

A *closed* family is less available to your attempts to connect with them. Such families have stronger boundaries that both demand certain behaviors of their members and restrict entry of nonmembers. Closed families have rules that more narrowly dictate behaviors for their members and serve to make clear distinctions as to what is appropriate and acceptable. In such families, "parents make sure that doors are locked, family reading material and television programs are screened, and children scrupulously report their comings and goings" (Goldenberg & Goldenberg, 1991, p. 267).

This type of family seeks privacy that may sometimes border on suspiciousness of all strangers, and it tends to place stringent rituals on its members. Wake-up time, mealtime, and bedtime are likely to be strictly adhered to, and the notions of tradition and stability are paramount in the way the family functions. This type of family will likely be more difficult for you to work with because of its more rigid boundaries. In the extreme, such a family will be very reluctant to respond to any gestures of help from outsiders. This is a "fortress family," keeping interlopers at bay.

If the family's value system dictates that they must be cordial to strangers despite wishing to keep them outside the boundaries, you may find yourself dealing with a "rubber fence." The family appears welcoming, offers you a chair and a glass of iced tea, and tolerates your intrusion for a while, only to suddenly usher you out the door before you have had a chance to really join with them. Although it seems that you have been allowed in, you have only entered into the family to the extent that the elastic boundary will stretch, and then—"boing!"—out you go!

A *random* family is one that is fragmented in its organization. Individual members "do their own thing" and may not feel very committed to the family or connected to its other members. Family rules are unclear or nonexistent, boundaries are porous and easily crossed, people come and go, outsiders enter into the family's space and may have quasi membership at times. People eat when they are hungry, sleep when they are tired, and congregate spontaneously with little sense of family ritual.

When you work with a family that has a random style of organization, you may find it difficult to get everyone together, either physically or psychologically. This family will appear to be an aggregation of semi-independent agents in which the traditional notions of parental authority and discipline are not as prevalent as in other family styles.

Finally, keep in mind that in times of crisis, families increase their typical ways of interacting. Closed families may hunker down. Random families may fall apart. Open families may reach out. You cannot assume that all families will uniformly respond to your offers of help.

## The Circumplex Model

Olson and his associates created the Circumplex Model for making sense of families (Olson, 1986; Olson, Russell, & Sprenkle, 1983). There are two main dimensions to family organization: adaptability and cohesion. Think of adaptability as a vertical line that intersects with the horizontal line of cohesion. Now envision these intersecting lines forming four quadrants that reflect different family styles. At the extremes of the "adaptability" dimension are the "chaotic" and "rigid" ends. The poles of the "cohesion" dimension are "enmeshed" and "disengaged."

A family that is considered to be dysfunctionally *enmeshed* is one in which the members are too closely connected. No one is allowed to be happy if one of the family members is sad. All members are profoundly affected by the moods of the other members. If a member begins to individuate—valuing different ideas or wishing to become more autonomous—the family views it as an act of disloyalty. Whether the extremely enmeshed family is seen as chaotic or rigid is simply a matter of the predictability of its behavior. A chaotic family will likely have porous boundaries, erratic behavior patterns, and intense blowups. A rigid family will usually have closed boundaries, punitive recriminations, and extreme possessiveness.

A family that is dysfunctionally *disengaged* has relationships that are more distant, membership that is more tentative or estranged, and "cut-offs"—members who are so emotionally distant that they are disconnected from the system. Chaotically disengaged families are those in which the parents have little control over the behavior of the children, because the parents are either neglectful or ineffective disciplinarians. Children in these families often come up against the law for delinquent acts or fail to do well in school because of lack of family support. A rigidly disengaged family is one with a severely restrictive environment but little emotional connection among its members. The atmosphere may be generally chilly in this family, the transactions formal, and expectations for conformity extreme.

---

## *EXPERIENCING THIS IDEA*

Think of your family of origin and draw where it might be placed on the Circumplex Model. Family styles that fall closer to the intersection of the adaptability and cohesion dimensions are considered to be "normal" and simply an expression of the family's "personality." However, no family is truly normal. (Did you hear the one about the time they held a conference for survivors of fully functional families and no one showed up?)

---

## Situational Family Crises and Coping

Besides the crises that can be expected in traditional families, along with the added crises that could be brought about by reconfigured families, there exist events that add stress to any family. These are frequent, but unpredicted, happenings, such as "accidental death, divorce, job loss, early pregnancy, incarceration, workplace upheavals, and victimization by crime" (Day, 2004, p. 350).

In addition, the family may experience events such as drug and alcohol abuse, child sexual abuse, family violence, neglect or abandonment by a caregiver, poverty, homelessness, suicide, and runaway children. Besides all this, the family may fall victim to natural disasters and other catastrophes. At bottom, it is impossible for anyone to provide a complete list of *situational crises* that can inflict themselves on a family. The important thing for you to understand is that families are systems and that when something happens within that system, or when the system is insulted from without, the entire membership of the family is affected.

Caplan (1964) offered a list of effective coping behaviors that a person would find useful in weathering a crisis. These can apply to a family as well. A family copes best when it actively explores reality issues and seeks information, freely expresses feelings and tolerates frustrations, seeks help from others, solves problems by breaking them down into workable bits, understands its own limits and paces itself while maintaining control, is flexible in the face of change, trusts in its members, and maintains an optimism regarding the outcome of the crisis.

Earlier in this chapter, we discussed how families develop certain personalities and how these styles of operating create their unique configurations. Add to this the truism that, under great stress, individuals and families tend to intensify their regular ways of operating. As Day (2004) put it, "What goes wrong in a family . . . usually comes down to inflexibility in the face of stress" (p. 351). This amounts to an attempt at what is called a *first order change*. A first order change takes place when everyone thinks that a logical solution to a problem is to do more of what they are already doing.

It is not unusual for a troubled family to elect an *identified client*—a member who is manifesting symptoms for the entire system. Often, the identified client is a child who is failing in school, looking depressed or angry, exhibiting an eating disorder, or engaging in delinquent behavior. If you are working in an agency, the family may wish to drop the child off at your office for counseling, while the rest of the family goes to the mall. They will return expecting that you have "fixed" the identified client, and therefore, solved the family's crisis.

Sometimes, the identified client is a parent who abuses alcohol, experiences a sexual dysfunction, exhibits fits of rage, or has some other problem. Because you probably have been trained to work mostly with individuals, you may be tempted to fall for the "identified client" definition of the family's crisis. However, it is best to maintain your view of the family as a system and to intervene in such a way that fits their style and can help them to cope with their crisis. Families whose normal style of operating exists close to the intersection of the lines on the Circumplex Model will be easiest. Those that are operating further out will be more challenging.

## Families as Complex Adaptive Systems

Imagine your family members standing in a circle, tied together by a rope. Each member has the rope tied around his or her waist and is connected to every other member. Everyone is leaning back, so that the rope is stretched tight. This dynamic tension of the rope represents the homeostasis of your family's usual pattern of interaction. Now, imagine that one member suddenly leaps forward. What will happen to the family's established pattern? Obviously, everyone's balance will be thrown off, and their behavior will need to quickly change to keep them from falling. The behavior of just one member has altered the behavior of all the other members, as well as the total configuration of the family. This is the metaphor for a family crisis.

Families are complex dynamic systems. You cannot change one part of the system without changing everything. Furthermore, families are unstable systems that hold themselves together while existing at the "edge of chaos" (Kauffman, 1991). All living systems are like this. They maintain themselves while they are in the process of constantly falling apart. In Chapter 2, we introduced you to the concepts of chaos and complexity. In this section, we will apply some of those intriguing ideas to working with families in crisis. The one thing you must keep in mind is that because families are complex adaptive systems, when they seem to be falling apart, they are really attempting to reorganize. Furthermore, it sometimes takes only a small perturbation to throw such a system into disorder. As you learned in Chapter 2, this small perturbation is known as the Butterfly Effect, and the emergence of a new adaptive pattern from disorder is what we usually think of as a crisis.

## Crisis as the Butterfly Effect

Family counselors have begun to apply the Butterfly Effect to families in crisis. Butz, Chamberlain, and McCown (1997) pondered the issue of the amount of perturbation a family system needs to achieve optimal change.

> Critical losses or changes certainly push families to reorganize. A death in the family, a bankruptcy, chronic illnesses, and other events impose a period of transition and adjustment. (p. 87)

When families are in chaos, their main desire is to return to a former pattern of stability, but they will never be the same. Instead, they will find a new level of organization.

## A Word (or Several) About Attractors

Scientists who study chaos and complexity have suggested that three main types of attractors exist in nature. Because everything in the universe is in movement, you could say that everything is headed somewhere, as if it had some sort of teleonomic direction. This does not mean that events are predestined, but rather that change processes are drawn or compelled by *attractors*.

In a way, attractors are like gravity. The sun is an attractor in our solar system. Some pieces of space dust are drawn toward the sun so compellingly that they crash into it. This type of attractor is sometimes called a fixed point. You can also see a *fixed point attractor* in action if you roll a marble around the rim of a bowl and watch it eventually come to rest at the bottom. This is *entropy*—the notion that everything eventually runs down and loses all its energy.

But planets in our solar system seem to be resisting the gravity of the sun, while at the same time, relying on it for their trajectories. As we ride our planet around the sun, as has been the case for Earth's inhabitants for a very long time, we can recognize the second type of attractor—the *limit cycle*. Our planet, although attempting to head in a straight line, is nevertheless held in orbit by the sun's gravity so that it cannot escape, and it goes round and round in the same elliptical pattern.

Sometimes, you will encounter families who look as if they are headed for entropy. They seem to be nearly out of energy and headed toward the death of their existence. Other times, you will observe families that are held in a limit cycle. They keep repeating the same destructive patterns over and over and do not seem to be able to reach escape velocity.

But there is a third type of attractor that has emerged out of the study of chaos and complexity. It is the *strange attractor*. If you are around people who smoke, did you ever notice that smoke from a cigarette, when exhaled, seeks a pattern? Or have you seen flooding water find a point of ebb and flow? Or have you ever watched as your bath water forms a tornado above the drain of the tub? Scientists state that these patterns emerge as a result of strange attractors that are nonlinear. "Patterns in strange attractors are never repeated exactly" (Chamberlain, 1998, p. 8).

The metaphor of the counselor as butterfly is a good one because, as chaos theorists say, though a butterfly flapping its wings can create a hurricane, the butterfly is also regarded by most of us as a gentle, calming, and beautiful creature. You know the feeling of encountering a butterfly in your garden on a warm summer's day and becoming captivated by its presence. As a counselor, when you come upon a family that seems to be stuck in a dysfunctional pattern, you must "flap your wings" to create a little turbulence.

When, however, the family is already in the eye of the storm, you must be a soothing and captivating presence. Most of the techniques we offer in this book are of the latter variety—calming and supportive. But thinking about the Butterfly Effect as creating temporary chaos in the family system is also useful because it will strengthen your faith in the resilience of families. As you saw in Chapter 5, if you can help a family to stay in the zone—not too stagnant and not too turbulent—you will have aided them as they pass through the phase state from chaos to order.

## Families as Dissipative Structures

A family is always in the process of changing. As you saw with the developmental life cycle of families, they all move through somewhat predictable crises. Families that adapt well to these changes are those that are able to reconstitute themselves while, at the same time, experiencing their structure as falling apart. For example, when children go off to school or leave home to lead their own lives as adults, the family must accommodate to these major milestones without dissipating. Most families accomplish such tasks without too much disruption of their structure.

The term *dissipation* means to break up, scatter, or vanish. Prigogine and Stengers (1984) identified the type of structure that is dynamic—always changing, always losing its structure, always falling apart—but which somehow maintains its general pattern in spite of such chaos. When we think of structures, we normally envision them as going out of existence if they fall apart. Once a building, a factory, or a corporation goes into decline, it will eventually cease to exist. However, a dissipative structure will continue to maintain itself in spite of such dissolution, so long as the energy that has supported it is present. A water fountain, so long as the water is turned on and the pressure is up, will continue its changing pattern.

So long as the energy that drives you is present, your body, your self, will be maintained—although with subtle changes. You are what chaos theorists call a *complex adaptive structure*. Rebuilding, while at the same time falling apart, is the essence of life.

Most of the time, families maintain themselves without any thought of how to do so. But when a major crisis takes place, one that overwhelms the family's rebuilding processes, the members will be thrown into chaos and experience themselves as falling apart. They may seem fragmented, and they "may have difficulty discerning the existence of choices or may feel incapable of selecting from existing, perceived choices. It is not uncommon for thoughts to be jumbled and confused" (Hudgens, 1998, p. 115).

We could say that families experience the catabolic processes of the crisis to be exceeding the anabolic processes of reorganization. They may feel that they are compelled by a fixed point attractor and are headed toward entropy, which would be total dissolution. Furthermore, families have histories. They may have suffered from former crises, so that they have not totally rebuilt themselves. Alcohol, incest, drugs, affairs, job or school failures, unwanted pregnancies, and ongoing disagreements and cut-offs may have left the family vulnerable. This is the "diathesis" part of the diathesis-stress model of breakdown.

The family has maintained itself as best it can by entering into a limit cycle attractor in which old wounds keep coming up and less than optimal communication takes place. They are in a dysfunctional orbit, but at least they are not out of energy. Furthermore, a new crisis has confronted the family, supplying still more energy. As Hudgens (1998) stated, this is "chaos as opportunity for change" (p. 121). The family has the opportunity to come through the crisis, arriving in a better place with a better structure. As the crisis intervener for the family, you become the "strange attractor" that helps them arrive at this new organization without having to dissipate or return to negative circular patterns.

As you can see in Figure 8–1, families are constantly evolving, always dynamic, and changing dramatically. In the next section, you will learn how to apply the skills you have been learning to working with families in crisis.

# TOOLS

## Intervening with Families

You will find it easier to help families in crisis if you understand the nature of the crisis at hand and possess a theory of change that you can keep in mind when things get confusing. Families face many developmental crises as they move through the family

---

**Key Ideas**

- All crises take place in the context of a family.

- Families are undergoing dramatic changes in the United States.

- Families are dynamic systems that face developmental crises.

- If one member is in crisis, then the entire family is in crisis.

---

**FIGURE 8–1**   Key ideas of Chapter 8.

life cycle. In addition, families are sometimes confronted with unexpected or sudden crises that catch them by surprise. How the family responds will be based on the family's general style of operating, as indicated by the Circumplex Model, and the intensity of the crisis.

When dealing with developmental crises, some families do quite well at some stages and not at others (Barker, 1992). For example, it is sometimes the case that a family will function smoothly until a child reaches adolescence, and then begin to manifest an inability to cope. On the other hand, when crises intrude from the outside, families who have interacted quite well may sometimes fall apart.

Although working with families involves more complex dynamics than with individuals, the overall process of crisis intervention remains basically the same. Like individuals, families are more likely to successfully resolve crises when they have reached out to one another for support, made meaning of the experience, taken heart by managing their emotions, and moved on as a system. Therefore, as you can see in Figure 8–2, the process of family crisis intervention involves:

- Linking family members in support
- Cocreating a family survival story
- Helping to manage emotional arousal
- Facilitating family coping

## Linking Family Members with One Another

As a crisis intervener, your first task is to "join" the family in crisis. This means that you must accommodate to the family's style so that you are viewed as fitting in rather than as an alien. Just like individuals, families "resist efforts to change them by people they feel don't understand and accept them" (Nichols & Schwartz, 1998, p. 257). To join the family, you can use the LUV Triangle as you hear their story and acknowledge their version of events. You must respond to all elements of the story with "positive connotation," no matter how you personally feel about the circumstance being described (Barker, 1992).

For example, if the crisis incident involved the parents mistreating the children, you will want to help the family change this set of behaviors. However, you must cling to the hope, until proven otherwise, that the parents do not regularly harm their children deliberately. Without your positive connotation of the family's attempts to cope with

**Facilitate Family Coping**

- **Follow Up with the Family**
"How have you been doing?"
- **Give Suggestions and Refer**
"Who else can be involved in helping?"
- **Offer Scaling on Family Coping**
"On a scale of 1 to 10, with 1 being . . ."
- **Help the Family Form Goals**
"What do you all hope to achieve now?"
- **Ask "Moving On" and "What If" Questions**
"What do you want to go from here?"

**Manage the Family's Emotions**

- **Review the Emotional Journey of Resolve**
"At first, you were overwhelmed with feelings of helplessness and now you're beginning to feel a sense of hope."
- **Ask "Taking Heart" Questions**
"How did you call up the courage to face that situation?"
- **Enhance the Family's Sense of Resolve**
"It sounds like you found a way to get yourself out of that mood."
- **Reduce the Family's Level of Distress**
"How have you been handling your feelings?"

**Cocreate a Family Survival Story**

- **Summarize the Family Survival Story**
"Together, you coped by taking quick action and working as a team."
- **Look for the Survivors in the Family Crisis Story**
"How in the world did you manage that?"
- **Track Individual and Family Resolution**
"And that is when you decided to call the others."
- **Enter the Family Crisis Story**
"Tell us about what you saw and did."

**Link Family with One Another**

- **Offer a Family Encouragement Interlude**
"This group really feels like a family that's looking out for everyone."
- **Help Family Members "Be With" One Another**
"It looks like you'd like to say something to Ellen."
- **Offer LUV Triangle to the Family**
"Hmmm . . . I see . . . yes."
- **Join by Introducing Self, Explaining Purpose, and Accommodating**
"We're meeting together so everybody can help each other through this."
- **Invite the Family to Connect with One Another**
"Let's all get together to talk about how everybody's handling this."

**FIGURE 8–2**  Family crisis intervention.

stress, you will be viewed as an unwanted critic or a threat to the family's established style. As Barker (1992) put it, "By attributing good intentions to whatever the family members have done, therefore, we can establish ourselves as being on the family's side" (p. 156). The last thing you or the family needs is for you to be perceived as an external enemy. If this were the case, you would be left ineffective and they would not receive your help.

Often, workers who attempt to deal with families in crisis assume that they know best what the family should do, or that they could be better parents to these children. This attitude tends to show through and cause the family to mobilize its defenses against the intruder. Remember that the family has enough problems already; they do not need the extra burden of having to defend against you.

In the case of developmental types of crisis, in which the difficulties lie within the family structure, you must proceed cautiously. If the parents feel that you are trying to alienate the affection of their children, they will close down. If the children feel that you are attempting to remove them from the family, they will be uncooperative. On the other hand, when the family is dealing with an unexpected crisis, such as a flood or fire, they are often open to your intervention. But either way, the family will self-protectively revert to, and intensify, its usual style, and it will be your job to understand what that style is and accommodate to it.

To join families in crisis, you typically are working "where the action is"—at the hospital emergency room, community free clinic, disaster assistance center, accident scene, neighborhood center, religious setting, or the family's home. Working under these conditions can be challenging if you are used to a more traditional counseling setting. However, many families, even if they are in crisis, are unwilling to seek help in a mental health setting.

**Invite the Family to Connect with One Another.** As you join with a family in crisis, you will also be connecting family members with one another to work in resolving the crisis. In all cultures, families traditionally convene as members deal with important milestones in life. The events may be joyful ones, such as a wedding or birth of a child, or they may be sorrowful ones, such as a funeral. In a time of crisis, people turn to their families for support. Therefore, instead of taking over this essential family function, you are facilitating the natural process of successful resolution by bringing relatives together.

Although you may be in a nontraditional setting, you want to ensure that the physical environment is conducive to crisis intervention. Find a private space that is large enough to comfortably accommodate all the members who are present. If possible, the seating should be in a circle so that people can easily see one another. If you are working with a cofacilitator, then you can sit separate from one another so that you can scan the entire family and observe the dynamics.

**Join by Introducing Yourself, Explaining Your Purpose, and Accommodating.** As you start your encounter with the family, you can tell the members who you are, what your role is, and how you'll be working with them. Keep in mind that how you relate to the family is just as important as what you say. You must "convey respect, not only for the individuals in the family, but also for their hierarchical structure and organization" (Nichols & Schwartz, 1998, p. 257). You should make eye contact and shake hands with each family member, young and old. Be sure to speak directly to everyone, and learn each individual's name and check its pronunciation if you're uncertain. Finally, show your deference for the authority of the parents by checking with them regarding practical matters, such as the seating arrangement. By your manner and tone of voice, you can communicate a concern for the family's well-being during this troubled time, as well as an underlying trust in the ability of this family to successfully resolve this crisis.

Given the circumstances, you may be feeling anxious to "get down to work," but you should not underestimate the importance of these introductory social rituals. This social ceremony helps you to join the family at both the individual and systemic levels. You have made physical contact with every member, have learned their names so that you can address them personally, and you have acknowledged the hierarchy of the family. Such a familiar and comforting ritual is particularly helpful because it reduces the family's level of distress.

You can then explain the purpose of this meeting by simply saying, for example, "This is a chance for your family to come together, support one another during this difficult time, and decide how you're going to help each other through this."

Instead of offering any formal rules for behaving during family crisis intervention, you can simply invite the members to openly and honestly engage with one another, be positive in your expectations, and model these behaviors by your own commitment to be supportive, empathic, and respectful. Never force or coerce families to talk about painful experiences and tragic events.

Unless you are writing referral information or a brief message to offer the family, avoid taking notes during crisis intervention with a family. Any behavior that smacks of formal therapy can make it difficult for you to join the family. You should also dress in a manner that's appropriate for the setting, but not in a way that places you in a distant, "expert" role.

**Offer the LUV Triangle to the Family.** In the beginning of your work with a family, take advantage of every opportunity to offer the LUV Triangle by listening actively, checking your understanding with people, and validating respectfully the family's experience. As valuable as this technique is with individuals, it is especially powerful in family intervention because every member is witnessing each of these LUVing encounters. Directly or indirectly, the entire family feels heard, understood, and respected.

**Help Family Members "Be With" One Another.** In family crisis intervention, the primary source of emotional support and bonding is not you—it is the family itself. Therefore, your job is to help the family "be with" each other by reaching out, engaging authentically, offering support, and bearing witness to one another's experience.

You can ask presumptive questions about how family members have "been there" for one another in the past when the family faced troubled times. Even dysfunctional families have somehow managed to make it through challenging circumstances more or less successfully. Sharing a family history and drawing on common roots, these members are the ideal sources of emotional support for one another. They can bear witness to someone's ordeal, offer a shoulder to cry on, provide practical assistance, give encouragement, and lend an understanding ear.

As you are meeting with the family, be on the lookout for when one family member is resonating with another's words. Take advantage of those moments of "being with" to call attention to them. Then you can invite the family member to talk about this experience of connecting by turning to the person and saying, for example, "When Meredith was talking about what she's going through, I noticed that you looked like you were really tuning into what she was saying. What would you like to say to her?"

**Offer a Family Encouragement Interlude.** At the start of the meeting, you joined with the family and reinforced their support of one another. As you come to the close of the session, you can strengthen these emotional bonds by offering an encouragement interlude. Invite the family to talk about their emotional bonds and the strengths that they see in one another and in their family as a whole. However, somewhere near the end of the session, a powerful technique is to invite the family members to reflect on their experiences of one another's resilience during this encounter.

You read about using this procedure with individuals in Chapters 3 and 7. With families, an encouragement interlude can take about 10 to 15 minutes. You first set the stage and acknowledge the crisis experience. Then you share the many examples of strengths, compassion, creativity, and resourcefulness that you have observed in this family. Using their metaphors and success experiences, you can offer speculations about how the family will be resolving this crisis. As you carry out the encouragement interlude, invite the family members to share their own reflections about this family's resilience.

Throughout the meeting, you have been helping family members to give and receive supportive comments. However, the encouragement interlude can serve as a powerful culmination by portraying the family as a resilient, dynamic, and resourceful system of survivors. Keep in mind that a family does not need to be perfect and intact for an encouragement interlude to succeed. For example, parents who are separated can still work together in supporting a child in crisis. And relatives may not get along well, but they often can set aside their differences for the sake of the family.

To start a family encouragement interlude, you might say something like the following:

- "If it's OK with you, I'd like to share some things that I've noticed about how this family has come together to deal with this crisis."
- "I've really been struck by how you've been able to take advantage of the different talents that each of you brings to this painful situation."

## Listening In on Crisis Intervention

Review the story at the start of the chapter to refresh your memory about the crisis that this family is confronting. In the emergency room at the hospital, a crisis intervener meets with Meredith and her parents. Meredith is in good condition and she expects to be released after an overnight stay, but Lakita is in critical condition.

ALISON, INTERVENER: Hi, my name is Alison and I'm a counselor with the hospital's crisis response team. I've been told about the accident you had, Meredith, and I've stopped by to chat for a few minutes and see how everyone is doing.

ELLEN: Oh, we're fine. The doctor said that our daughter can go home as soon as her vital signs are normal.

ALISON: The lab is running behind tonight so it may take a while. (*She pauses for a few seconds and looks at Meredith.*) It's good that your parents are able to be here with you after your terrible ordeal, Meredith. (*She smiles as she makes eye contact with Fred and Ellen.*) It's really important that the family is here to be with and support each other."

MEREDITH: (*She speaks in a barely audible voice.*) I wish I were the one that had to stay in the hospital and Lakita got to go home instead of me.

ELLEN: Meredith, don't even think of such a terrible thing!

MEREDITH: (*She raises her head, sits up straighter in her chair, and looks at her mother.*) I'm not even thinking about anything—all I can do is *feel* so bad about what I've done. (*She pauses and her voice begins to crack as she suppresses a sob.*)

FRED: Honey, it's not your fault! Hell, you didn't know you were going to have a seizure and I heard that the little girl's gonna be OK.

MEREDITH: Daddy, that little girl's name is Lakita, and, you see . . . it was my fault . . . I didn't take my medication . . . I wanted to drink a couple of beers and celebrate yesterday and now . . . Oh, God, I just want to go home. (*She begins to cry.*)

ELLEN: Meredith, your dad is right, you didn't mean to hurt the girl, and after we finish here, you and I will go home. Maybe we can . . .

FRED (*Interrupts*): What, Ellen, bake cookies? What we really need to do is to listen to Meredith and help her get her life back on track.

MEREDITH: Mom, I hate to burst your bubble, but I meant I wanted to go back to *my* home, to *my* apartment.

ELLEN: (*She sighs, her shoulders slump forward, and her eyes turn to Alison.*) I don't know what you can do for us since Fred and I are separated, and Meredith doesn't live at home. We're not much of a family anymore. What we really need is some legal advice—that poor little girl's family could sue us for everything we've got.

MEREDITH: Her name is Lakita, Mom, and they are not going to sue us. (*Fred glares at his wife and shakes his head in disbelief while Meredith slumps down into her chair and emits a loud groan.*)

ALISON: It must be really hard to think about ways of supporting each other when there are all these unresolved family issues and legal matters hanging over your heads, to say nothing about the individual heartache you each must feel. (*The room grows silent and after a few seconds Alison continues.*) Meredith, it sounds hard for you to feel anything but guilt after what happened, but as painful as it is, you sound willing to talk, in an open and courageous way, about your part in the accident.

## Reflecting on This Segment

1. In what ways did the intervener join with the family?
2. What developmental issues are confronting this family?
3. How might you respond to Meredith's last statement if you were the intervener?

## Cocreate a Family Survival Story

Any crisis poses dangers. One of the risks for a family is that one member's crisis can have a domino effect of cascading negative consequences onto other members until the entire system is overwhelmed. Therefore, another one of your important tasks as a crisis intervener is to cocreate with the members a family survival story.

As you will explore in more detail in Chapter 9, one of the advantages of bringing people together is that it provides a forum for individuals to contribute their personal stories to an interconnected and multifaceted narrative of the entire system. You can help members to cocreate a family survival story by encouraging them to participate in the process of tying together the bits and pieces of their individual experiences into a complex patchwork of shared meanings.

**Enter the Family Crisis Story.** Once you have successfully joined the family and have members linked with one another, you can invite members to share their personal experiences. Although in groups you may simply turn to the person on your right to begin this process, with families you should support the authority of the parents by giving them the honor of speaking first. Typically, people feel a need to put their crisis experiences into words; so as long as they feel safe, they are likely to speak without much encouragement. You can start by turning to the parents and saying, "Ayako and Chong, I'd like to invite you to start us off by describing what your family has been going through."

As you learned in Chapter 4, you can enter each person's story by, for example, bearing witness to the enormity of the experience, being a responsive audience, mirroring the narrator's emotions, and showing your gratitude and admiration. Although entering the crisis story is an effective tool with individuals, there are a couple of advantages to having other family members involved in this process. First, this meeting may be the family's first chance to hear the entire sequence of events from each member's perspective. As the narrative unfolds and another person is mentioned, you can turn to that person to check with his or her perceptions. You might, for example, ask, "So, Mary Lou, it sounds like you were the next person to make it to the hospital. Does Caleb's memory fit with your recollection? What do you remember happening after that?"

At times, one of the family members may remain quiet and hesitant to speak, even when you have made an invitation or two. When this happens, take care to "find the pony" and openly share your appreciation for the person's willingness to be a part of this meeting. You can comment positively when you notice the person showing any nonverbal signs of support and involvement.

**Track Individual and Family Resolution.** In addition to entering the family's crisis story, you also are tracking any examples of resolve that you notice a member or the entire family demonstrating. Like individuals in crisis, families are in danger of feeling demoralized because they are more aware of their failures, limitations, and vulnerabilities. You can help draw their attention to the ways that this family is reaching out, making meaning, taking heart, and moving on with resolve.

As family members tell their stories, take care to place their crisis experiences in the past and to speak of their coping in the present tense. For example, you might say, "It sounds like you all were in shock at first about Ashir's accident, and now you're trying to figure out how you can work together to handle this new situation."

**Look for the Survivors in the Family Crisis Story.** A family's reactions to a crisis can cover up their resilience and resourcefulness. As you recall from Figure 1–1, it's often much easier to see the victim than the survivor. Therefore, while you acknowledge the distressing events that this family is facing, you must be particularly curious about the family's rich history of survival. With a family, you have the wonderful opportunity to explore its past for examples of resolve. Ask such getting through questions as:

- "How in the world were you able to succeed here in America after arriving as 'boat people' with absolutely nothing?"
- "When Dad was injured, how did you all pull together to make it through that tough time?"

You can also ask "making meaning" questions that tap into the insights, values, and discoveries that this family has made. You might ask something like,

- "What has kept your family going through all this pain?"
- "What advice might you offer another family that was facing this crisis?"

Whenever you find examples of perseverance, resourcefulness, and creativity, be sure to point them out to the family. Like an artist designing a family crest, you are highlighting the values and qualities that have contributed to this family's roots of resilience.

**Summarize the Family Survival Story.** Once the family members have shared how they have been dealing with the crisis, you can involve them in the process of summarizing their survival story. Like participants in an old-fashioned quilting bee, you are working together to connect the patchwork pieces of material that everyone has contributed. What can emerge from this process is a complex and rich portrait of family survival.

# Managing the Family's Emotions

In families, emotions can be powerful catalysts—for better or worse. One expression of compassion can deepen the emotional bonds of an entire family. A single outcry of fear can panic the whole system. Therefore, helping individual family members to lower their distress and enhance their resolve can create a benign emotional cycle that promotes successful coping with a crisis.

**Reduce the Family's Level of Distress.** If the family is extremely upset, then you need to take quick action. Only when their level of distress is lower will they be able to cope effectively with the crisis. Speak in a soothing tone of voice, offer comfort, and give assurances that they are safe and secure. One reason that people express intense distress is that they haven't felt heard. Therefore, you should keep offering the LUV Triangle, reflecting their feelings of distress, and acknowledging that the family has been through a troubling ordeal. Most important, you want to communicate, by your respectful and supportive manner, that you have faith in the family's ability to cope with crisis.

**Enhance the Family's Sense of Resolve.** As you learned in Chapter 5, your role is not to give a family a sense of resolve. Instead, you help the family to notice the many acts of courage, compassion, and hope that they may have been ignoring. In times of tragedy and turmoil, be alert to the comforting gesture, the act of generosity, and the words of consolation that one family member offers another.

As you explore the family's previous successes in dealing with crises, ask presumptive questions about their feelings of resolve in those situations. For example, you might ask, "When you were giving so generously of your time and energy for the family's well-being back then, where did you find it in your heart to carry on day in and day out?"

Make a conscious effort to notice and reflect the emotions of resolve that a family demonstrates. Like many counselors, you may be more likely to reflect negative feelings, such as anger and sadness. Therefore, we encourage you to practice reflecting positive feelings by saying things like:

- "It sounds like you have a deep and profound sense of compassion for your partner as she deals with this cancer."
- "That must have been a gutsy thing for you to do as a couple!"

Ask taking-heart questions not only about individual members, but also about the family as a whole. Such questions invite people to become more in touch with their positive emotions—joy, a sense of humor, hope, love, and elevation. You can ask, for example,

- "How is this family able to laugh together in spite of these difficult and frightening times?"
- "In what ways do you show how much you really care for one another?"

**Help the Family Stay in the Zone.** As a crisis intervener, your job is not to provoke an emotional catharsis among family members. Instead, you are working with families to reduce their emotions of distress, enhance their feelings of resolve, and stay in the zone as they cope with a challenging situation. Families are similar to individuals in that they perform at their best when their emotional arousal is at an optimal level. When families have a sense of passion for one another and are determined to achieve their goals, then they are successful and thriving systems. But if they are plagued by intense feelings of threat or burdened by overwhelming feelings of desperation, then they are likely to be dysfunctional. Families can stay in the zone by comforting members in times of distress, energizing one another, and looking forward to a promising future.

**Review the Emotional Journey of Resolve.** Whenever you work with a family in crisis, you will witness a wide range of emotions. Families cry together, laugh together, seek solace in one another, and gain emotional strength from one another. You can add "music" to the words of the family survival story you have cocreated by inviting the family to review their emotional journey of resolve.

You can start this process by offering your observations of the emotions that family members have been experiencing. In particular, you want to describe with enthusiasm and awe the emerging emotions of resolve that you have seen. Then invite family members to contribute their own reflections.

## Listening In on Crisis Intervention

Later in the family meeting, when every member has had an opportunity to participate in sharing his or her experiences, the intervener invites everyone to talk about their feelings of resolve.

ELLEN: (*She offers an aside comment to the intervener.*) That's not her home, you know, it's an apartment.

FRED: Ellen, give it a rest, let her be on her own, she's a grown-up now.

ELLEN: Oh, now he's talking. After the kids were all gone, he never talked. (*She continues to look at Alison.*) Maybe Mr. Know-It-All can tell us what we should do next. Well, (*Her voice grows louder as she looks at Fred for the first time.*) say something!

MEREDITH: (*Her voice is very loud and shrill.*) Please quit bickering. I could have died in that pool! Lakita still might die! Don't you understand?! This is the worst family in the world. (*She looks straight at Alison.*) Don't you think?

ALISON: (*She pauses for a few seconds, leans forward, and tries to draw the three of them into her response with an inclusive gesture and a softened voice.*) In my 3 years at the hospital, I've seen a lot of people in pain and a lot of families who shared in that pain. Very, very few of them don't care or can't care about each other. Mostly, families just forget how to tell each other that they do care. I barely know you folks, but I can tell that even though you have your differences, I've heard a lot of love in what you've said today. If I'm not mistaken, it seems that both of you (*She looks directly at Fred and Ellen.*) have always put your children above all else and would do anything to get behind Meredith and help her through this crisis. Am I right about that?

(*A long pause ensues. Finally, Fred breaks the silence.*)

FRED: Yes, you're right. Ellen, here we are—you and I—in a tug-of-war over Meredith just after coming close to losing her. We need to get our act together. Do you remember when we used to sit out on the porch after all the kids were tucked in and have those long talks about everything? There wasn't a week that went by that we didn't have someone sick or some other kind of a problem, but we handled it all. What happened to us? I'd like for us to do that again—you, too, Meredith. Maybe we could figure out something to do for Lakita and her family. We used to be a pretty good team, maybe we can do it again.

## Reflecting on This Segment

1. What strategies did the intervener use to reduce the family distress?
2. How did the intervener enhance feelings of resolve?

## Facilitating Family Coping

Families are always changing and crises are times of dramatic change—for better or worse. At this point in your crisis intervention session, you are facilitating this change process by encouraging the family to envision and achieve a successful resolution of the crisis.

**Ask Moving-On and What-If Questions.** By now, you have helped the family to connect with one another, cocreate a family survival story, and stay in the zone. Therefore, you can now invite the family to consider future possibilities. One approach is to ask a moving-on question, such as "As you begin to move on with your lives, what's the next step that you're going to take?"

Another approach is to ask a what-if question. For example, you might say, "What if this family went home this evening, had a nice dinner together, went to bed, and sometime during the night, something happened so that you all, even your pet dog, were one step closer to living the kind of life you'd like to have. What would be the first thing that you would notice that would be different?"

Both types of questions are future oriented and invite family members to explore potential paths for resolution.

**Help the Family to Form Goals.** As a family in crisis turns its focus to the future, you can begin helping them to formulate a goal. You might say something like any of the following:

- "What do you want to do as a family to handle this situation?"
- "Where does this family want to go from here?"
- "If our work together turns out to be completely successful, in what ways will you be feeling different from how you felt when we started?"

As family members offer responses to your question, you can work with them to come up with a detailed, positive, and possible goal.

**Offer Scaling on Family Coping.** In Chapter 6, you learned how to practice this technique with individuals, but scaling can be particularly useful with families. You use the same procedure, but you can expect that members will have different opinions regarding the rating. This situation gives you an opportunity to facilitate an exchange of speculations and hunches about the future.

**Give Suggestions and Refer.** As the session nears its conclusion, you will want to offer suggestions and make an appropriate referral for ongoing counseling or other services.

## PRACTICING THIS TECHNIQUE

Arrange with a few colleagues to participate in a family crisis intervention practice. Each of you selects one of the following roles: intervener, at least three family members, and one observer. The family members develop a crisis scenario and brief the intervener regarding the family's background and current circumstances. During the practice, the observer takes notes on the family dynamics and intervention process. Following the exercise, the participants discuss the experience and offer feedback to one another.

## Following Up with the Family

Writing a follow-up letter to the family is a great way to reconnect with members, to remind them of their resilience, and to offer additional reflections regarding their efforts to seek resolution.

### Listening In on Crisis Intervention

Below is the follow-up letter that Alison sent to the family about a week after their meeting.

Dear Meredith, Ellen, and Fred,

I decided to write to you all because I thought of a couple of things that I didn't get a chance to say during our brief time together. Meredith, I mentioned how courageous I thought you were to talk about your part in the accident, and I realized later that your sharing what had happened with your medication seemed to encourage your folks to do some important self-examination.

Fred, you mentioned fondly how you and Ellen used to be a team when your children were growing up. It also sounds like you realize that Meredith is an adult now and that you would love to have her as a teammate. I think your idea about going to counseling as a family is an excellent one as it will give all of you a chance to work on your concerns together.

Meredith, I was very pleased to read in the paper about your decision to become an advocate and spokesperson for helping young people understand the dangers of mixing prescription medication and alcohol. I am sure that you will touch many lives and maybe save someone from having to endure what you did.

Sincerely,
Alison Parcell

## RESOURCES FOR COUPLES AND FAMILIES

The following is an excellent resource for couples and families in crisis.

All Family Resources
http://www.familymanagement.com

All Family Resources is a comprehensive Web site that provides information and services to enrich families. The topics include aging, child care, communication, parenting, and dealing with catastrophes.

## SUMMARY

In this chapter, you learned about the dynamics and developmental histories of couples and families. You also became acquainted with the application of chaos and complexity theories to families. Finally, as you can see in Figure 8–3, you learned about

---

**Essential Tools**

- Link the family with one another.

- Help the family cocreate a family survival story.

- Promote emotions of resolve.

- Facilitate the coping of the family.

---

**FIGURE 8–3**   Essential tools of Chapter 8.

the special challenges and opportunities when working with couples and families in crisis.

## Segue to Chapter 9

To help you encounter the ideas and tools in Chapter 9, think about a special group to which you belong. What is important about your membership in that group? Reflect on what you would miss if you were not a part of this group. How does membership in this group give you courage or help you clarify your beliefs?

# Crisis Intervention with Groups: Coming Together with Resolve

"We can survive anything you care to mention."
*Doris Lessing*

## CHAPTER GOALS

After completing this chapter, you should be able to understand the concepts and practice the skills related to crisis intervention with groups. Although the steps are similar to those with individuals, groups present unique challenges and opportunities.

The resolution-focused crisis techniques involve:

- Linking people in crisis
- Coconstructing a collective survival story
- Promoting emotions of resolve
- Facilitating the group's coping

## OVERVIEW

In Chapter 8, we offered some basic strategies you can use to intervene successfully with couples and families. However, because crises can also strike groups of people who are not relatives, this chapter describes some of the common dynamics of a group in crisis and presents techniques involved in group crisis intervention. You will learn some guiding concepts and practical skills for working with classmates, work colleagues, teammates, members of a religious group, and virtual strangers whose only commonality may be a shared crisis experience. Offering supportive intervention and connecting groups to other resources immediately after an incident can facilitate a successful collective resolution.

## CRISIS STORY

Everyone knew it was going to be a challenging season. With only one starter returning from last year's undefeated team, the local sportswriters predicted that the Maryville High School girls basketball team might have its first losing season in 9 years. Of course, the players had different ideas. They were confident that their enthusiasm, team spirit, and winning tradition would overcome their lack of experience, size, and speed.

In a manner of speaking, both the sportswriters and the players were proven correct. Midway through the season, the Wildcats' record was a respectable six wins and four losses—far better than predicted—but the wins had been hard fought and close this year, whereas those of last year's perfect season were rarely in doubt.

The one returning starter, Heather Wilson, was by far the most talented member of the team and the primary reason for its surprising performance so far this season. To say that Heather was a well-rounded student would be an understatement. She was a senior who had never failed to make the Honor Roll and was the first African American homecoming queen in the school's history. A petite girl with beautiful eyes, an engaging smile, and gentle manner, Heather was a valued friend and trusted confidante to many. Soft-spoken, thoughtful, and endearingly self-conscious in class, she was also a joy to teach.

On the basketball court, however, Heather became transformed. She grew intense, confident, aggressive, and even intimidating. She could drive to the basket, set a mean pick, pass off for an assist, dive for a loose ball, or pull up for a 3-point shot—her favorite play. The play was such a trademark for Heather that when her parents bought her a used car, they ordered for it a vanity license plate that read "3SHOOTER."

Four days before a game, Heather came down with the flu during school and missed practice. She continued to feel nauseated and unsteady on her feet, so she reluctantly missed another day of school. When she finally returned, Heather was a little weak, but she had completed all her assignments, participated actively in all her classes, and refused to take it easy in practice. She was determined that a little flu was not going to stop her from hitting the books and the court at full speed. By the day of the game, which was an away game in a neighboring county, Heather appeared slightly ashen, but she was so adamant about playing that the coach decided to start her, but to watch her closely for any signs of fatigue.

Just like every other time, Heather went through a transformation once she stepped on the basketball court. She suddenly had more energy and even had healthier color. The first half was a classic Heather performance. If anything, she was even more aggressive in her drives and opportunistic with her assists than usual. But with 2 minutes left in the third quarter, Heather grimaced, bent over, and called for a time-out. Clenching her teeth and choking back the tears, she told the coach that she felt sick and, for the first time in her basketball career, asked to be taken out of the game.

Mrs. Watkins, a registered nurse and parent of another player, served as the team's athletic trainer. Heather wanted at least to watch the game from the sidelines, but Mrs. Watkins firmly led her to the locker room. There, Heather lay on a bench and assured Mrs. Watkins that she would be fine, she just wasn't over the flu yet, and a little rest and some water were all she needed. Mrs. Watkins kept a close eye on her and, as she heard the buzzer ending the game, decided that Heather was in no shape for a shower and bus ride with her teammates. Instead, she helped Heather back into the warm-up suit, grabbed her daughter to help, and began to drive Heather directly home.

An hour later, the girls were still celebrating their win when their bus pulled into the school parking lot. There, the players noticed that several parents were waiting to meet them. One parent quickly approached the bus door and asked to speak to the coach alone. They conferred for several minutes in front of the bus, where they could not be heard, but their faces, spotlighted by the headlights, looked pale and troubled. The coach returned, gathered the players together, and told them that Mrs. Watkins had taken Heather to the emergency room, where her condition was unknown. The coach suggested that they join hands to pray for her. The younger players then went home with their parents, while the older ones, promising to telephone the other players, decided to drive directly to the hospital for an update on her condition. When they arrived, they were told that Heather had died.

## Reflecting on This Crisis Story

1. What were your own reactions to this story?
2. What strengths did you notice about this group?
3. How might the individuals in this group help one another to resolve this crisis?
4. What other groups may be affected by this death?

# IDEAS

## Groups in Crisis

Crises do not occur in a vacuum and no crisis affects only one person. Those who witness the event; those who are co-workers, friends, or relatives; and those who identify with the person in crisis are also affected. These vicarious survivors may feel overwhelmed, experience guilt or shame, be plagued by tension and fears, have eating and sleeping problems, and feel haunted by the scenes of the incident (Dixon, 1991). In other words, like the person who is directly affected, they may also be in crisis. In fact, you should keep in mind that whenever you are engaged in crisis intervention, you may also experience a vicarious impact (Karakashian, 1994).

## EXPERIENCING THIS IDEAS

To experience the ideas about crises in earlier chapters, you examined some of your own crises that you have resolved. Of course, it is rare that a crisis is truly an individual event that involves no one else. To encounter the ideas in this chapter, we would like you to pick a crisis that one of the groups in your life had to face and resolve. This group may have been a class, team, club, close friends, co-workers, or members of a faith group.

Once you have selected a particular crisis, go over the entire resolution process, including all the high and low points. Keep referring back to that experience as you reflect on the following questions:

1. How did the dynamics of the group change as a result of the crisis?
2. In what ways were individual members affected?
3. What helped your group to resolve this crisis?

As you continue to read this chapter, keep in mind your group's experience with crisis resolution.

## Efficiency and Efficacy of Groups

We humans are a gregarious species. However, the idea that group work is a powerful way of intervening with people was a realization that dawned very slowly during the 20th century (Gladding, 1999). At first, groups were used simply because it was not possible to work with each person individually. The prevailing thought was that a group format was a trade-off which, although perhaps not as effective in dealing with people's concerns, was at least an efficient way of seeing all who needed to be seen. The belief that groups were a less effective approach began to fade as positive results were increasingly noted.

For example, Pratt (1907) began treating tuberculosis patients in groups because of the overwhelming number of people at that time who were afflicted with the disease. Surprisingly, what started as an efficient way of dealing with patients turned out to be quite effective as well. Patients who attended weekly meetings remained in good spirits and 75% of them recovered, although many had been given no hope of recovery (Kline, 2003).

Likewise, Burrow (1928) found that working with psychiatric patients in groups proved to be effective. Burrow concluded that the effects of isolation and poor interpersonal relationships played a major part in the development of psychopathology. Having people work together in a group setting mitigated some aspects of their disorders.

Later, in response to the overwhelming needs of the military during World War II, groups were set up to handle the psychiatric problems of returning soldiers. "Although the group therapists during this time were relatively unsophisticated, they recognized that something powerful was taking place in their groups" (Kline, 2003, p. 9).

Throughout the 1950s and 1960s, the group movement continued to accelerate (Gladding, 1999). In 1973, the Association for Specialists in Group Work (ASGW) was established and several journals devoted to group work began to publish around that time. A number of outcome studies were conducted on the efficacy of group therapy and yielded encouraging conclusions. Yalom (1995) wrote that "the answer is very clear: there is considerable evidence that group therapy is at least as efficacious as individual therapy" (p. 218). Dies (1993) reached the same conclusion after conducting a meta-analysis of 40 years of group studies.

In many ways, working with people in groups offers advantages over one-to-one contact. People can experience feelings of belonging and affiliation with others who share their concerns. They have the opportunity to exchange ideas and personal stories and to actually experience firsthand the normality of their own reactions. Hearing a crisis intervener explain that certain responses are common may be informative, but actually seeing another survivor having this experience can be powerful, reassuring, and enlightening. As they share their stories in a group setting, survivors realize that they are not alone in having these experiences. In their encounters with others, survivors also observe other effective coping strategies, practice crisis resolution skills, and receive feedback. And members can share their meanings while producing a collective narrative of their individual stories.

Whether it is called a process of "therapy" or simply referred to as nourishment for the human spirit, people sharing their concerns with each other in groups has been found to be productive. We now know that working with people in groups is not only an efficient method, but it is effective as well.

In times of crisis, a group format can be a particularly powerful medium for intervention. Because survivors of crises are more open to turning to their peers for support (McCammon & Long, 1993), two important strategies would be to offer group crisis intervention and to encourage organizations, schools, and other community systems to offer ongoing social support to these affected groups. These strategies give survivors opportunities to develop collective survival stories, share information and ideas, and offer encouragement and support to one another.

As you will see later in this chapter, group crisis intervention is based on the belief that groups, like individuals, are resilient and quickly begin a process of resolution. The phases of group crisis intervention are also similar to those of individual crisis intervention: linking, creating a group survival story, managing emotions, and envisioning possibilities. Likewise, the goals of both interventions are to enable people to survive the crisis and to achieve a positive crisis resolution. Although the principles, process, and goals of group crisis intervention are similar to those with individuals, groups present different dynamics, challenges, and opportunities for the intervener. Your fundamental role as an intervener is neither to be the rescuer of victims nor the expert consultant of a group's crisis. Instead, you serve as the facilitator inviting a group to come together, explore its own resilience, and embark on its own resolution process.

## Traditional Debriefing

Currently, the most commonly used group intervention immediately following a shared traumatic experience is Critical Incident Stress Debriefing (CISD) (Everly & Mitchell, 1999; Mitchell & Everly, 2001). However, many practitioners and researchers have criticized this technique as posing serious problems (see, for example, Gist & Woodall, 1999). In fact, one recent major review of the CISD literature discouraged the use of this technique (McNally, Bryant, & Ehlers, 2003). In this section, we describe and critique the limitations and problems of the CISD model.

Traditional CISD brought together everyone who was in an incident involving serious threat, horrific circumstances, severe injury, or violent death. Debriefing sessions were "structured group meetings that emphasize ventilation of emotions and other reactions to a critical incident" (Mitchell & Bray, 1990, p. 143).

Although such debriefings have been routinely offered to a variety of groups, Jeffrey Mitchell originally developed CISD for firefighters and other emergency workers who encountered critical incidents (Mitchell, 1988). He contended that such individuals typically repress their natural psychological reactions and concentrate on the task of confronting the threat. According to Mitchell's argument, the repression of these emotions, although effective in dealing with the critical incident, can lead to PTSD and other disorders. The value of a debriefing, Mitchell asserted, is that it offers these action-oriented emergency workers an opportunity to talk to their "buddies" and vent their emotional distress in a safe and supportive environment.

**Process of Traditional CISD.** The "Mitchell Model" of CISD (Everly & Mitchell, 1999; Mitchell & Bray, 1990) involves seven phases, each of which focuses on a different issue. In the *introduction phase*, the leaders describe the CISD process, encourage participation and set the ground rules. During the *fact phase*, participants describe their roles and what happened during the incident. The *thought phase* involves discussing their initial and subsequent impressions. In the *reaction phase*, leaders encourage an emotional catharsis by asking, for example, "What was the worst part of the incident for you?" Ventilating feelings during this phase has been considered crucial to preventing stress-related disorders (Mitchell & Bray, 1990). During the *symptom phase*, members describe the traumatic "symptoms" they experienced both during and since the incident. The *education phase* involves teaching the members about the typical traumatic stress reactions and how to alleviate them. Finally, in the *reentry phase*, the leaders address any additional issues, summarize the debriefing session, make any needed referrals, and encourage ongoing support. The entire process generally takes about 2 hours.

Other practitioners have developed variations on the original CISD model (Carll, 1995). For example, Bohl (1995) inserted an additional phase, the unfinished business phase, to encourage participants to bring up previous crises that may be unresolved. Solomon (1995) designed an intensive follow-up program, the critical-incident peer support seminar. The intervention is a retreat that lasts 2 or 3 days and takes place several months after an incident. Dyregrov (1997) presented a type of psychological debriefing, developed and widely used in Europe, that emphasizes group process.

**Shortcomings of Traditional CISD.** Although debriefings have become popular, some authors have expressed concerns regarding the technique. First, some practitioners worry that overuse of the procedure and policies of requiring CISD attendance can create passive participation and even resentment (Miller, 1998).

Another concern is that the structure and format of the CISD fails to take full advantage of the resources that group participants bring to the session (Dyregrov, 1997). For example, instead of inviting *participants* to share how they are successfully handling the experience, CISD protocols encourage *debriefers* to dispense generic suggestions for alleviating symptoms. Such an approach reinforces a rescue mentality for interveners and may undermine survivors' already threatened sense of personal agency.

A third issue questions the underlying assumption of CISD: that ventilating pent-up feeling is essential to prevent the development of PTSD and other disorders. On the

---

**Key Ideas**

- No crisis affects only one person.
- Group crisis intervention can be both efficient *and* effective.
- Like individuals, groups are resilient and seek resolution.
- Groups present unique challenges and opportunities.

---

**FIGURE 9–1**   Key ideas of Chapter 9.

basis of this premise, group debriefers are instructed to encourage and support emotional catharsis during the reaction phase of the session. In Chapter 5, we discussed and critiqued the pervasive emphasis on catharsis in both crisis theory and practice. Provoking painful emotions in a debriefing can be counterproductive (Woodall, 1997).

A final, and most critical, concern is that, despite CISD's tremendous popularity, the evaluation studies of CISD generally have not supported its efficacy. Robinson and Mitchell (1993) reported that a majority of debriefing participants believed that the experience had been valuable. However, most controlled studies have not demonstrated CISD's effectiveness in reducing traumatic stress (cf. Gist & Woodall, 1999; Kenardy et al., 1996). Three recent meta-analyses of the research found no evidence that CISD is useful in promoting natural recovery from psychological trauma (Rose, Bisson, & Wessely, 2001, 2003; van Emmerik, Kamphuis, Hulsbosch, & Emmelkamp, 2002). Finally, in the most comprehensive and detailed review of the CISD literature, McNally et al. (2003) concluded that the technique is, at best, ineffectual in preventing PTSD and may even pose an emotional risk for some survivors. There is overwhelming evidence that traditional CISD techniques sabotage resilience by focusing on the trauma and undermine resolution by encouraging survivors to reexperience painful emotions.

In the following section, you will be learning group crisis intervention techniques that offer an alternative to those of traditional CISD. Before you turn your attention to these tools, take a moment to review the key ideas (see Figure 9–1) that you have encountered in the first part of this chapter. These ideas can serve as guides for your work with groups.

# TOOLS

## Promoting Resilience and Resolve in Groups

In this section, we offer a protocol for group crisis intervention that is based on the research, summarized in Chapters 1 through 6, that has identified conditions that promote resilience and resolution. As you can see in Figure 9–2, the process involves group members participating in the following four phases:

1. linking people in crisis
2. cocreating a collective survival story
3. managing emotions
4. facilitating the group's coping

$\bigcirc$ **Facilitate Group Coping** $\bigcirc$

- **Follow Up with the Group**
  "How have you been doing?"
- **Give Suggestions and Refer**
  "Who else can be involved in helping?"
- **Offer Scaling on Collective Coping**
  "On a scale of 1 to 10, with 1 being . . ."
- **Help the Group Form Collective Goals**
  "What do you all hope to achieve now?"
- **Ask "Moving-On" and "What-If" Questions**
  "Where do you want to go from here?"

$\bigcirc$ **Help the Group Manage Emotions** $\bigcirc$

- **Review the Emotional Journey of Resolve**
  "At first, you were overwhelmed with feelings of helplessness
  and now you're beginning to feel a sense of hope."
- **Ask Taking-Heart Questions**
  "How did you call up the courage to face that
  situation?"
- **Enhance the Group's Sense of Resolve**
  "It sounds like you found a way to get yourself out of that mood."
- **Reduce the Group's Level of Distress**
  "How have you been handling your feelings?"

$\bigcirc$ **Cocreate a Collective Survival Story** $\bigcirc$

- **Summarize the Collective Survival Story**
  "Together, you coped by taking quick action and working as a team."
- **Look for the Survivors in the Collective Crisis Story**
  "How in the world did you manage that?"
- **Track Individual and Group Resolution**
  "And that is when you decided to call the others."
- **Enter the Collective Crisis Story**
  "Tell us about what you saw and did."

$\bigcirc$ **Link with One Another** $\bigcirc$

- **Offer a Collective Encouragement Interlude**
  "This group really feels like a family that's looking out for everyone."
- **Help Members "Be With" One Another**
  "It looks like you'd like to say something to Ellen."
- **Introduce Self and Explain Purpose**
  "We're meeting together so everybody can help each other through this."
- **Invite the Group to Connect with One Another**
  "Let's all get together to talk about how everybody's handling this."

**FIGURE 9–2**  Group crisis intervention.

## Linking People in Crisis with One Another

Just as it does with individuals, the work of crisis intervention with groups begins long before the actual meeting. You will have completed a great deal of groundwork in order to have an effective, accessible, and responsive service for groups in crisis. Your crisis team should be involved in developing the crisis or disaster plan for your school, organization, or community. It is vital that you develop a plan that makes a positive statement acknowledging the resilience, resourcefulness, and resolve of people in general. The plan should articulate the strategies you will follow to facilitate the process of resolution and support the informal helping networks that friends, co-workers, relatives, fellow believers, and classmates forge in times of crisis. Finally, the plan should emphasize the crisis team's role as facilitators rather than as rescuers.

Once the plan is in place, you can help maintain it by offering in-service training and participating in emergency drills. If you're a school counselor, then you can also maintain a crisis plan by teaching guidance lessons and giving presentations to parents and school administrators. Engaging people in training and drills prepares them to become skilled at carrying out effective procedures for responding to crisis incidents. These experiences also help people to be psychologically prepared to cope with crises.

Laying this groundwork gives you an opportunity to clarify the nature and purpose of your crisis intervention services to the members of a system, particularly those involved in making policies. For example, if you are a member of a school system's crisis team, then taking the time before incidents occur to educate students, teachers, staff, and administrators can help create an organizational culture that promotes successful crisis resolution. As we discussed in Chapter 3, you also want to get your message out to the general public by, for example, providing community presentations, printing handout literature, offering information on the Web, and producing public service announcements for the local mass media.

Although you often are working without colleagues at your side when you intervene with an individual in crisis, you typically have at least one co-worker with you for a group intervention. In a traditional CISD, there has been a hierarchy among group leaders, with one person, who may be the only professional clinician, serving as the team leader, and one or more others, who may be peer support personnel, assisting the leader (Mitchell & Bray, 1990).

However, there are significant advantages to egalitarian models of coleading groups (Shapiro, Peltz, & Bernadett-Shapiro, 1998). Equal coleaders tend to demonstrate greater flexibility, complement one another more efficiently, model better communication styles, and provide better coverage of group members. Therefore, instead of selecting one team leader among yourselves, it may be more fruitful to decide how you want to collaborate with one another to take full advantage of what each of you may bring to the intervention. For example, one of you may elect to take primary responsibility for explaining the purpose and guidelines whereas another may volunteer to invite the group members to share their stories.

You also have some time immediately before a session to complete some important preparations. Counselors have long recognized that pregroup preparation is crucial to a successful group (see, for example, Shapiro et al., 1998). For a counseling group, this process of determining group logistics and screening potential members may take weeks. However, for a group intervention, you may only have a few hours or, at most, a couple of days to prepare an environment that enhances the experience. It is vital that you work quickly with your fellow interveners and your contact person to arrange the session.

The person who contacted you can be an invaluable resource for answering the basic questions of what, when, where, who, and how. The contact person can provide you with background information to help you understand what has happened, determine when is the best time for people to meet, decide where the location should be, and know who will be attending the meeting.

Everyone who was directly involved in the crisis event should be invited to this meeting. However, never require attendance from anyone who's reluctant to participate in a group experience. Some people may prefer to seek out their own network for support. Your contact person should make certain that people know they are welcome to participate, but they are not obligated to attend. Another vital task is to exclude any outsiders, especially gossipmongers, thrill-seeking voyeurs, and members of the local media. Such intruders can sabotage the success of a group session.

The size of the group can be any number from 3 to 30, but anything smaller obviously is not a group and anything larger becomes an audience in which members may be reluctant to participate. Armstrong, O'Callahan, and Marmar (1991) suggested a limit of 15 members, but the ideal size of a crisis group is perhaps similar to that of counseling groups—8 to 12 participants. Such a size is large enough to have the benefit of group dynamics, but small enough to provide each member with opportunities to participate actively in the process. If you know that numerous people will be participating in a group experience, then you can arrange for more sessions to accommodate everyone.

As a final part of your preparation, you can briefly explain to the contact person how the meeting will be facilitated. This individual can then relay the expectations and guidelines, while informing people of the meeting time and location.

**Invite the Group to Connect with One Another.** At this first stage of crisis intervention, you are connecting survivors with one another to promote a successful resolution. Generally, you will want the meeting to take place as soon as possible—within 2 to 3 days after the crisis event. As you learned in Chapter 1, a natural and immediate response after trauma is to connect with others. Convening people who share a crisis experience can, by itself, serve as a powerful catalyst for offering mutual support and facilitating the resolution process among members. Being with others affirms that the survivor is not alone in facing this ordeal. With your cofacilitators and the contact person, you can schedule the meeting to take place quickly, but also at a time that is both possible and convenient for everyone involved.

The setting for the meeting should be convenient, familiar to all group members, and perceived as a safe place. It may be a work site, school, neighborhood center, or religious setting. Most important, the facility should not suggest pathology or illness, such as a mental health facility or psychiatric hospital.

Before the meeting, you can arrange the physical environment to encourage a positive atmosphere and productive group interaction. The room should be large enough so that everyone attending the meeting can sit comfortably in a circle, be free of interruptions and distractions, and feel that their privacy is protected. If you are working with emergency personnel, you should be sure that coverage has been arranged for the time of the meeting and ask all participants to turn off pagers and cell phones during the session.

In the United States, sitting in a circle with the group leaders seated apart from one another is typical for not only meetings, but also most counseling or personal growth groups. The advantages of this arrangement are that the participants can easily see one another; there are no physical barriers, such as tables or desks, between members; and the design has an egalitarian feel. Sitting in different parts of the circle allows the cofacilitators to scan the entire group and monitor the reactions of all the members. Sometimes, you and the other cofacilitators may come to the circle and find that the only available chairs are adjacent to one another. In that case, instead of sitting together or asking people to move from the chairs they have selected, each of you can simply pick up a chair and thank members as they allow you to squeeze into another part of the circle.

Interestingly, in contrast to the American emphasis on the circle, most European debriefing sessions have a rectangular seating arrangement, have tables in front of the participants, and have the coleaders seated together at the head of the table. Dyregrov (1997) believed that this arrangement enabled the facilitators to interact with each other more easily and presented a clear demarcation of the leader role. This contrasting preference is only one example of the variety of possible cultural differences that you can encounter in doing crisis intervention with groups. Being sensitive to diversity issues and keeping a flexible attitude can help you to design environments that are appropriate to the specific group in crisis.

**Offer Introductions and Explain Purpose.** At this beginning stage, you can participate in brief introductions, describe the purpose of this meeting, and provide some structure to the session. Introducing yourselves serves several important functions. First, it signals the beginning of the actual group work. Second, it provides members with some basic information about you and your fellow group facilitators. Most important, the introduction gives you a chance to set the tone of the session. By leaning forward, making eye contact with each member, and speaking directly to every person, you can connect individually with the participants. By your concerned tone of voice and respectful manner, you can communicate both an acknowledgment of the trauma they have endured and a fundamental confidence in their abilities to achieve a positive resolution.

After you and your cofacilitators have introduced yourselves, you can then say something like, "Even though you probably know one another, it would help us if each of you could briefly tell us your name and the role that you play in this group." At that point, you can turn to the member on your right and invite that person to begin.

Asking members to introduce themselves is a good opening task for three reasons. First, the task enables you later to personalize your comments by using people's names when you invite them to speak, point out similarities, or offer encouragement. A second advantage of this round of introductions is that it is a brief, clear, and concrete task that all members can successfully complete, even if their level of distress is high. Finally, this task is your first opportunity to offer the LUV Triangle by actively listening, checking your understanding, and respectfully validating each person's experience. For example, instead of silently allowing everyone to quickly give a name and role, you can repeat the name, check on pronunciation, and briefly confirm your understanding of the person's role. During this time, you are leaning forward and making eye contact with each person. You can also use this introductory round to foster group cohesion by identifying commonalities and interdependence in their positions and roles.

The purpose of a crisis intervention group is to give people in crisis an opportunity to help one another along the resolution process. When you do crisis intervention with an individual, during that encounter, you are the primary source of support that is present. However, when you work with a group in crisis, the crucial sources of support are the fellow members. Your primary role is to facilitate the process of mutual support—not to serve as the provider of support to hapless, passive victims. You may, for example, tell the group, "This meeting is a chance for you to come together, support one another, and decide how you're going to help each other through this."

You also want to provide structure for the session by clarifying expectations and setting boundaries. A crisis intervention group is much more structured than a typical counseling or personal growth group for two important reasons. First, greater group structure tends to reduce anxiety (Shapiro et al., 1998). The participants in a crisis intervention group are typically already at or near the overaroused end of the Yerkes-Dodson curve that we described in Chapter 5. Therefore, the group structure can help to enhance performance by reducing people's emotional arousal enough to get them into the zone. The second major reason for greater structure is that the crisis intervention group typically is limited to one session. Facilitators do not have the luxury of being able to return to an issue at the next session. Consequently, following a structured format ensures that the intervention has involved members in all the major facets of the resolution process: support, meaning, resolve, and coping.

At this point, you can take a few minutes to go over procedural information about the session. The session may last up to 2 hours and, during that time, everyone will have many opportunities to contribute to the discussion. You can invite, but not coerce, members to talk openly and honestly about their recent crisis events, current circumstances, and possible future. The participants should understand that whatever is said in the meeting is respected as confidential.

Traditional CISD protocols recommend presenting the guidelines as if group leaders were itemizing "rules of conduct." As we discussed in Chapter 7, rather than instructing, ordering, or advising, you can be more effective using other approaches. You can powerfully communicate these guidelines for the intervention group by modeling these behaviors yourself, presenting positive expectations, and encouraging participants when they do engage in behaviors that promote positive resolution. Your actions speak louder than your words, so it is essential that you demonstrate the guidelines by your example. In addition to modeling, you can frame the guidelines as positive expectations rather than prohibitions.

Although you may, as a rule, take notes when you are engaging in counseling, this procedure is not appropriate at a crisis intervention meeting. Such an action suggests that this meeting is a formal therapeutic treatment session. Instead, your behavior should imply that this meeting is an informal opportunity for people to come together and help one another through a challenging time. Dressing casually, but appropriately, for the setting is another way to suggest the informal nature of this meeting.

**Help Members "Be With" One Another.** As you know from Chapter 2, social support is vitally important in promoting resolution. In times of crisis, no one is an island. Of course, you want to "be with" members by authentically engaging with each person, genuinely offering your support, respectfully listening to their stories, empathically accepting and acknowledging their anguish, and truly recognizing their resilience. However, as a facilitator, your job is to create a group atmosphere in which members can "be with" one another during this difficult time.

Be presumptive that these people have much to offer one another as they begin the process of resolution. As fellow members of the natural support system, the group participants are the ideal sources of emotional support. They can bear witness to someone's ordeal, offer a shoulder to cry on, provide practical assistance, give encouragement, and lend an understanding ear. Therefore, during the meeting, take care to notice when another member is listening empathically to someone's story. Then invite the other person to offer this support by saying, for example, "When Cheree was talking about her experience just now, it looked like you were really in tune with what she was saying. What words do you want to share with her?"

**Offer a Collective Encouragement Interlude.** Throughout the entire meeting, you are reinforcing the supportive bonds between the group members. However, somewhere near the end of the session, a powerful technique is to invite the group members to reflect on their experiences of one another during this encounter. In Chapters 3 and 7, you learned how to offer an encouragement interlude with an individual. As you recall, the procedure involves quickly setting the stage, acknowledging the crisis experience, being positive in your observations, offering your remarks tentatively, highlighting the survivor in the victim, using metaphors and wonderments, and inviting the person to process the experience.

In a group setting, the encouragement interlude typically lasts around 10 to 15 minutes. As a facilitator, you can begin the process by discussing with other facilitators the resilience and resolve that you have noticed during this meeting. Typically, at the start of the encouragement interlude, the group members are listening to your comments, so you can then invite them to share their reflections with one another.

Throughout the meeting, people have been offering occasional feedback and encouraging comments, but the encouragement interlude is longer, more comprehensive, and integrated. You can use this time to help the participants tie together common themes of strengths, resources, resilience, and resolution.

Here are a few examples of statements you might offer at the beginning of an encouragement interlude:

- "It sounds like this group's strong sense of teamwork really helped everyone to band together quickly."
- "From the experiences you have shared here, it strikes me that you've been extraordinarily creative in handling this crisis."
- "You've already found some practical ways of making a positive difference in this tough situation."

## Cocreate a Collective Survival Story

When people reconnect with one another following a crisis, they naturally begin to share their stories with one another. As a crisis intervener, you can facilitate the group developing its collective survival story. During this stage, the group members give their personal accounts of how they have been dealing with these circumstances. Keep in mind that their stories are neither separate nor isolated from those of the other members.

One of the most important values of a meeting is that it provides a forum in which a group in crisis can begin to coconstruct a collective survival story. Members create a group narrative by assembling the bits and pieces of their personal impressions into an elaborate collage of shared meanings. The dynamic process of revealing one's own story, recognizing one's personal thoughts and emotions in the accounts of others, building on one another's metaphors, elaborating on common themes, and contrasting perspectives can transform solitary narratives into an evolving group survival story. By helping them coconstruct this narrative, you can enhance the group's sense of cohesion and help members to form a common identity.

**Enter the Collective Crisis Story.** Once everyone is clear about the purpose and format of the group, you can begin this phase of the meeting by briefly telling what you know of the crisis event and presenting any updated information that may dispel any rumors.

When you have updated the group, you can invite members to talk about their personal experiences. The typical format involves members taking turns to briefly describe what they have been doing since the crisis event. People rarely need much encouragement to begin telling their stories. As we mentioned in Chapter 1, once they feel safe and secure, most individuals in crisis are highly motivated to talk about their experiences—even with strangers. You may want to begin by simply saying, "Now we'd like to invite each of you to take just a couple of minutes to share how you dealt with these events." At that point, you can turn to the member on your right and request that person to begin.

Occasionally, a group member may be reluctant to share much, if anything at all. With such a person, you can respectfully acknowledge, "It looks like it's hard for you to talk right now about what's been happening. I want you to know that I really appreciate that you've offered your support to the group by coming here. Whenever you feel like it, you're welcome to contribute more at this meeting or later with one of the others."

**Track Individual and Group Resolution.** As you acknowledge each person's crisis story, you rely on the LUV Triangle again to listen actively, communicate your understanding, and validate each member's story. For example, you may check with a member by saying, "And that is when you first heard about the incident," or "At that point, you called the hospital."

In addition to offering the LUV Triangle, you also are tracking the beginning process of resolution that each person is demonstrating. You describe the ways that each person is beginning to reach out, make meaning, take heart, and move on. Keep in mind that one clear act of resolution that you can always refer to is how someone was able to come and participate in this meeting in spite of all he or she has been through. At the end of each person's brief account, you can acknowledge the contribution and connect the narrator's metaphors, observations, and experiences with those of other members.

As participants tell their stories, you may notice that it is not only the storyteller whose eyes sometimes defocus or gaze off to the side. Defocusing, as we discussed in Chapter 7, is one indication of a natural dissociative experience of setting aside the here-and-now to focus on the there-and-then of the crisis event. This transderivational search is an important part of the resolution process. In a group setting of fellow survivors, it is not unusual to scan the group and see many of the other members also defocusing, gazing off, looking down, and obviously experiencing powerful emotions as they listen to the entrancing accounts of their fellow survivors.

A benefit of having coleaders is that while one facilitator focuses primarily on the storyteller, the others are free to scan group members for the cues that suggest commonalities and important themes (Dyregrov, 1997). For example, you may invite someone to share a transderivational search by saying, "I noticed that you looked like you were doing some important work just then."

The format of this phase of the crisis intervention session is remarkably similar to that of the classic Japanese film, *Rashomon*, but there are striking differences. Like a group, the movie's plot unfolds as each person involved in a violent incident offers an account of the experience. However, in contrast to a successful group crisis meeting, each narrator of *Rashomon* debunks the previous accounts as biased and self-serving, asserting that his or her own interpretation of the events is the only "truth." Although groups also involve sequential narratives, the results are diametrically opposite from the tragic *Rashomon* because the participants are committed to creating a collective narrative that integrates the contributions of everyone. Therefore, with each new telling during a group, the narrator often notes similarities with previous stories, incorporates earlier phrases and metaphors, and adds new facets of the crisis experience. Instead of separate "individual realities," which result in differences of opinion, the group can create a shared reality that fuses the members together. Successful groups, unlike *Rashomon*'s cautionary tale of alienation, can bring people together to participate in a collective experience, support one another, and acknowledge their common identity.

A ritual song that the African Mbuti traditionally sing during times of crisis captures the collaborative spirit of successful groups. Individual singers are responsible for specific notes, but no one carries the entire melody. As a result, only the entire tribe sings the song (Turnbull, 1990).

**Look for the Survivors in the Collective Crisis Story.** People's reactions to a crisis event can mask their personal strengths and resources. As you noticed when you read the crisis stories at the beginning of these chapters, the pain, anguish, and helplessness can grab your attention, whereas perseverance, creativity, and sensitivity may fade into the background. Therefore, although you acknowledge the distressing events in people's crisis stories, you must be particularly curious about how they were able to survive this ordeal.

As people share their crisis stories, you are listening for the survivor behind the victim. Just as with individual crisis intervention, you are looking for examples of the strengths and resources that people have already used in dealing with the crisis so far. You focus on these exceptions to victimization because they are clues for ways the group can continue to resolve the crisis. For example, you can ask getting-through questions such as, "How in the world did you manage to do that?" or "Where did you get that idea to try that approach?" or "In what ways have you surprised yourself in how you handled this crisis?"

As you discover instances of perseverance, resourcefulness, and collaboration, you can point these out to everyone involved. Like individuals, groups in crisis often feel demoralized and discouraged and can certainly benefit from hearing reminders of their strengths and abilities. Remember that the storyteller is not the only one hearing these words—all the other participants are also hearing them.

**Summarize the Collective Survival Story.** At the end of this stage of sharing stories, you can help the group summarize the sequence of events involved in the crisis experience and the strategies that group members have been using to confront them. As you tie together the common strands of the individual stories, connect the chain of events, and highlight the strengths, you are reflecting back the collective survival story that the group is beginning to coconstruct.

## Listening In on Crisis Intervention

Review the narrative at the beginning of the chapter to refresh your memory regarding the crisis that this group is confronting. Immediately after Heather's death, a school official arranges for two counselors to facilitate a group meeting in a conference room at the school with the players and coaches. The two counselors arrive early to arrange chairs in a circle and invite the participants to have a seat as they enter the room. As the facilitators set the stage for their session and begin to coconstruct a survival story with the members, notice how they collaborate with one another.

ELLIE SOPER, INTERVENER: (*Once the team members have taken their seats, she nods slightly to her cofacilitator and catches people's attention. Leaning forward, making eye contact with each member, and gesturing occasionally to emphasize certain points, she introduces herself and offers guidelines on the session.*) Hi, my name is Ellie Soper. I'm a school counselor at Parnell High School and a member of our school system's crisis response team. I've been told about the terrible event that you've faced and I really appreciate how you've made the commitment of coming together here. This meeting is your chance to talk with one another and to help each other through this sad time. Kim, would you like to introduce yourself?

KIM WANG, INTERVENER: (*Seated across from Ellie in the circle, Kim also takes care to make eye contact with each person as she introduces herself and offers more expectations.*) Hello, I'm Kim Wang and I work at the same school as Ellie. My guess is that your willingness to come here and stay together for this meeting is just one of the ways you'll be helping each other deal with this painful matter. I also trust that you'll respect everyone's privacy by keeping confidential what others say here. I'm not sure exactly when you may finish this meeting—it may be an hour or two—but we're committed to staying here until you're ready to leave.

ELLIE SOPER: Thanks, Kim. Well, as you know, Heather became very sick during the basketball game yesterday. About an hour later, she was pronounced dead at the Maryville Hospital Emergency Room. The doctors now believe that her spleen ruptured. Heather's parents are making arrangements for the funeral. That's all the information that Kim and I have. Now, I realize that you all know each other really well, but it would help Kim and me if each of you could briefly introduce yourself and tell a little about what you've been doing to deal with this situation. (*She turns and gestures invitingly to the player sitting on her right.*) How about if you get us started?

CAMERON: (*She looks into the eyes of the intervener, pauses to swallow, and takes a deep breath as if to brace herself for what she's about to say.*) Well, OK. My name's Cameron and this team is like my second family. Heather . . . (*She chokes as she says Heather's name.*) was like a sister. (*Cameron, who is now crying, accepts a box of tissues that the intervener offers her.*) We went to basketball camps every summer since we were 10 years old. I . . . just can't believe that she's gone . . . (*Sighing, she wipes her eyes with the tissue and blows her nose.*) I drove to the emergency room to see how she was doing. On the way there, I kept thinking that Heather would be really happy to see me. I even thought about stopping at the store to get a "Get Well" balloon for her, but I figured I'd better hurry up in case she might be leaving already. I came running into the emergency room and that's when they told me she was dead.

ELLIE SOPER: (*While Cameron has been speaking, the intervener has been leaning forward, with her elbows on her knees and her fingers interlaced. As the intervener begins to speak in a soothing voice, she takes her hands apart and gestures slowly to emphasize her points.*) Cameron, it sounds like you've felt really close to Heather for a long, long time. And when you heard she was in trouble, you immediately did what you could to reach out and support her. It must have been quite a shock to hear that Heather was dead, and I'm wondering how you've been reaching out to the others who are left behind now.

CAMERON: Well, I guess that I've been calling a whole bunch of people to let them know. We wind up talking and crying together, remembering silly things about our times together with Heather . . . It's just so weird. How could somebody like Heather be dead all of a sudden?

ELLIE SOPER: It just doesn't seem possible to you that she's really no longer alive. It strikes me that you've been thinking about some important questions about life and death. You've also been connecting with lots of other people as one way of dealing with this tragedy. Thanks, Cameron, for getting us started here. (*The intervener turns to the person sitting to Cameron's right.*) How about you? Tell us who you are and what you've been doing to handle this sad situation.

KATE: OK, I'm Kate and I'm a sophomore. I play sometimes just to give Heather a little rest. Last night, my parents picked me up at school and took me straight home, so I didn't hear anything about Heather until Ana called me really early this morning. At first, I thought that Ana was playing a sick joke on me. I guess that this is kinda dumb to say, but Heather has always been like a hero to me.

## Reflecting on This Segment

1. In what ways did the cofacilitators collaborate with each other?
2. How did they structure the meeting and begin the process?
3. How might you respond to Kate's statement if you were a cofacilitator of this crisis group meeting?

# Managing the Collective Emotions

Like individuals, groups in crisis are dealing with intense emotional turmoil. Unlike a traditional CISD, however, the purpose of this phase is not to encourage a group catharsis. Instead, as the members express their emotions, you can help them reduce their distress, enhance their feelings of resolve, and point out the commonalities of their reactions.

As the members bring up their negative emotions, you are looking for occasions in which they used the distress and handled their emotions to cope with the challenges confronting them. You can assume that at least some members of the group are experiencing personal reactions that they consider to be abnormal or out of proportion to the event. You can listen for indications of this concern and acknowledge with something like, "It sounds like you feel that you are overreacting."

**Reduce the Group's Level of Distress.** While the group has been developing a collective survival story, you can tune into the emotional themes that accompany their narratives. If you're noticing a high degree of emotional distress, then you can take particular care to address their basic needs. Make sure that the members feel safe and comfortable. Rely heavily on the LUV Triangle to assure people that they are being heard. When you reflect the feelings of distress, you can use the tracking resolution technique of putting the crisis in the past and the resilience in the present. Speak in a concerned but soothing tone of voice. Your manner should communicate both that you recognize the group has been through a painful experience *and* that you have faith in the group's ability to cope with it.

The format of a crisis group provides you with an additional strategy for normalizing reactions. As members share, you can point out the commonalities of emotions and acknowledge their feelings. You and your cofacilitators can also scan the other members' reactions as each person shares feelings. It is likely that you will notice another member responding to the affect that someone is expressing. After reflecting the feelings of the speaker, you can then turn to invite that person to offer his or her here-and-now emotions.

As participants share their feelings, you are offering comfort and assurances to soothe their distress. If some of the members are emotionally upset, you may need to remind the group that the purpose of this meeting is to offer support and encouragement—not to criticize one another. If the group has responsibilities for responding to critical incidents, then a procedural analysis of its effectiveness may be beneficial for developing new procedures, but such a meeting should come later. It is important to keep in mind that harsh criticism is rarely productive, but it can be downright destructive during a time of emotional distress.

**Enhance the Group's Sense of Resolve.** When groups face threats and deal with tragic events, you need not look far for examples of courage, compassion, and hope. Someone may mention an act of kindness, a thoughtful gesture, or an expression of trust in the future. When you find such clues of feelings of resolve, you will want to become curious about the details. Ask taking-heart questions to explore the nuances and facets of the feeling of resolve, such as "Where did you come up with the idea of writing this poem for her?"

**Help the Group Stay in the Zone.** Like individuals, groups are most effective in dealing with challenges when they are at an optimal level of emotional arousal. Groups need to be energized enough to work together with passion, a sense of a common mission, and determination. However, if they become too emotionally aroused, particularly by fear, rage, and sorrow, then groups will be impaired in their attempts to respond to a crisis. As the facilitator, you can help the group members stay in the zone by inspiring them to comfort one another in their distress, encourage fellow members in their resolve, and pursue their collective goals with confidence.

**Review the Emotional Journey of Resolve.** In your role of facilitator, you are noting the instances of resolve that members have demonstrated during your meeting together. Earlier, we described your task of piecing together individual narratives into a mosaic of a collective survival story. Being a part of something bigger than oneself can be a powerful source of inspiration, support, and encouragement. By reviewing the emotional journey of resolve, you are adding the "heart and soul" to this story of collective survival.

You can begin this review by sharing some of your impressions of the common feelings that members have been experiencing and the emotions of resolve that are emerging. Once you have described the themes that have struck you, you can invite the members to share their reflections on the emotional journey they have taken with one another.

## Facilitating Group Coping

After summarizing the collective survival story and reviewing their common emotions of resolve, you can encourage the members of a crisis group to begin considering their collective future.

**Ask Moving-On and What-If Questions.** You may introduce this stage by asking, "As you work together to move on with your lives, what's the next thing you're going to do?"

### Listening In on Crisis Intervention

Later in the group meeting, after every member has had an opportunity to participate in sharing his or her experiences, the facilitators invite the members to talk about their feelings of resolve.

ELLIE SOPER, INTERVENER: We've heard some very touching stories from the group. It's obvious that Heather was an amazing person and you all are going to miss her terribly. (*She looks at her cofacilitator Kim, inviting her to comment.*)

KIM WANG, INTERVENER: What strikes me is that you have lost a valued friend and teammate and somehow you are finding ways to go on without her.

ELLIE SOPER: I agree, Kim. I wonder if it would be possible for the group to talk more about some specific things you have done to keep yourselves going. I'm guessing that even though you probably think about Heather a lot and feel sad and heartsick, you find ways to get yourselves to smile through the tears. (*She notices several group members nodding and asks for a volunteer to start.*)

### Reflecting on This Segment

1. At what point did Ellie have a sense that the group was ready to talk about managing emotional arousal?
2. How did the cofacilitators work together in this segment?

Questions such as these presume personal agency and communicate the message that members have some control over their lives.

**Help the Group Form Collective Goals.** When you sense that a group is ready, you can invite members to formulate their goals. For example, you could simply ask, "Where does this group want to go from here?" or "What do you want to do as a group to deal with what has just happened?" As participants begin to explore how they would like to shape their futures, they gain confidence in themselves as individuals and as a group. As DeJong and Berg (2002) pointed out, "Clients in crisis improve by focusing on what they want to see different and drawing on their past successes and strengths" (p. 166).

Helping people create a vision of the future is particularly important for those in crisis. Just like individuals, groups in crisis dread what lies ahead for them. Little reminders may trigger flashbacks, and nightmares may bring horrifying visions with all their original intensity. Survivors often have detailed and explicit memories of the circumstances leading up to the crisis, as well as the unfolding consequences of the incident. To guide themselves toward resolution, survivors need to envision a positive future that is just as vivid as their crisis memories.

At this stage of the meeting, you are working to help the group conceive and develop a detailed, powerful, and clear vision of a future that is both possible and positive. Like a photographer developing a picture in a darkroom, you are encouraging participants to allow those vague and fleeting images of a goal to take form, become more distinct, and acquire texture and richness.

Other examples of how you can invite members to envision their goals include:

- "If our work together were to be completely successful, what will you be feeling that is different from the way you felt when we started?"
- "If you had my job and were helping people get through something like this, knowing what you know now, what advice would you give them?"

**Offer Scaling on Collective Coping.** In Chapter 6, you learned how valuable scaling can be in your work with individuals, but this technique can also offer some useful variations with groups. For example, you could invite the group to scale the general functioning of the entire group. You might say,

> On a scale of 1 to 10, with 1 being how this group was at its lowest point and 10 being how you'd like this group to be in the future, where is this group right now?

Because people have different perspectives, this question can stimulate a productive group discussion. You can explore how members decided on certain numbers. For example, you might ask, "What are you noticing that led you to give this group a 4 right now?" As you know from Chapter 6, because crises are times of rapid change, most participants will select a number greater than 1, which provides a concrete indication of progress since the point of impact, which is usually the lowest point of functioning.

More important, however, is your follow-up, because the primary benefit of the scaling question is setting the stage for a concrete and detailed discussion of possible coping strategies. For example, you can say, "OK, you generally agree that your group is now at a 2 or 3. What would it take to help you continue moving on to a 3 or 4?"

**Give Suggestions and Refer.** At this time, you may invite participants to discuss how they plan to deal with future events, encourage members to continue offering one another mutual support, and close the session with an ending ritual. Individuals and groups often use rituals to help promote a successful resolution (Imber-Black & Roberts, 1992). For example, people of all cultures perform memorial services that may differ in their specific procedures, but share fundamental commonalities: bringing the grieving together, giving expression to their pain, bidding farewell to the dead, and beginning the resolution process. Rituals of resolve can also take the form of pilgrimages to the incident site or other locations. There, survivors may reflect on the meaning of their suffering and perhaps leave a memento or symbol. These mementos may include flowers, teddy bears, poems, drawings, and personal messages.

At the close of the meeting, after having scanned the reactions of the members throughout the session, you can approach those who were visibly shaken, but who participated little in the group, to invite them to talk individually. You can also explore the possibility of arranging a referral to a support group or counselor. Finally, you may encourage the group to explore joining with other systems by asking, "Who else can be involved in this work?"

## Listening In on Crisis Intervention

After all the members have dealt with how they are managing their emotions, the facilitators then move on to invite them to envision possibilities for future resolution.

ELLIE SOPER, INTERVENER: (*She looks to Kim, tilts her head, and gestures expansively with both arms.*) You know, Kim, as I've been listening to everybody in this group, (*Ellie makes eye contact with each member before returning her gaze to her cofacilitator.*) I've been struck by a couple of things in particular. One is how much this group is like a family. In fact, that was one of the first things that Cameron said. (*She gestures to Cameron.*) And it's not just Cameron's opinion because some of the others said how tight-knit and caring this group is. One other comment that I'd like to make is that I'm amazed by how many creative ways these people are finding to help themselves and each other get through this."

KIM WANG, INTERVENER: (*She returns Ellie's gaze and responds to her comments.*) Yeah, Ellie, I agree. You know, I noticed a minute ago, when Kate (*Kim glances at Kate.*) talked about how she wished she could have told Heather how much she admired her, that all of the others (*Kim now looks around the group.*) seemed to agree.

ELLIE SOPER: Maybe, if it's OK with the group, we could all put our heads together to come up with some ideas about how the people in this group can express their admiration for Heather and figure out how they want to offer comfort to the family and honor her memory.

## Reflecting on This Segment

1. In what ways did the interveners facilitate the group in working together?
2. What would you have done, as the intervener, if the emotional distress of a group member increased dramatically?

## *PRACTICING THIS TECHNIQUE*

Arrange with a few colleagues to participate in a group crisis intervention practice. Each of you selects one of the following roles: two cofacilitators, at least three group members, and one observer. As the cofacilitators meet to plan their collaboration, the group members, along with the observer, develop a crisis scenario that involves a sequence of events and a specific role for each member.

The observer then meets with the cofacilitators to provide the background information and circumstances. During the practice, the observer pays close attention to the dynamics and takes notes on the process. At the conclusion of the exercise, the participants discuss the experience and offer feedback to one another.

## Following Up with the Group

Because group crisis interventions are not anonymous, you have an opportunity to write a follow-up letter to the participants. As with your crisis intervention with individuals, follow-up notes can be an important tool to support a group's discoveries, decisions, and coping.

### Listening In on Crisis Intervention

You may want to review the story and the previous portions because Ellie Soper and Kim Wang, the group cofacilitators, refer to these experiences in their follow-up letter to the group.

Dear Members of the Maryville Girls Basketball Team,

We've been thinking about our meeting that we had the other evening and we decided to share with you some of our thoughts. First, we want to thank you all for taking the time to come to this meeting. We're especially grateful for your willingness to share yourselves so openly with us, strangers you had never seen before. Whether or not you said much, your actions spoke loud and clear. You all were open in showing your pain and just how much you care for one another.

The first thing that struck us was the powerful sense of family among you guys. Over and over again, somebody in the group would mention how you all were like a family. We were also awed by all the strength that you showed in our meeting. It takes a truly strong person to cry, to openly shed tears, and to let everyone see these feelings.

The caring among you was obvious every single minute of our time together. Every time we glanced around the room, we saw you offering one another small gestures of support. Someone might be passing along tissues to another person. Somebody else would be giving a little pat on a person's shoulder. Or a person would be giving a fleeting look of encouragement to someone else. And as we were finishing, everywhere we looked, there were lots and lots of hugs. You all showed that life may be short, but love endures.

Many of you were still reeling from the shock of Heather's unexpected death. You were still searching for the words to adequately express all your powerful reactions to this tragic event. We're sure that you realized that it would not be easy to come to this meeting, but you came together anyway and shared your grief. Another quality we saw was the creativity you showed with the memorials you are planning to share with Heather's family. Your gifts are truly from the heart and will be a tremendous source of comfort to them.

As you continue sharing with one another, taking care of one another, and reaching out to one another, remember that there is always help available when you need it. Besides your teammates, friends, and coaches, there are plenty of people who can help—your parents, teachers, and school counselors.

As we've been working together to write this letter to you, we realized that we felt this pressure to find the perfect words at the end to tie everything together for you. But, as you know, there aren't any easy or simple slogans that we can say to take away your pain or to make your sorrow disappear. Instead, we've decided to finish with some final words of thanks. Thank you, everyone, for your presence, involvement, sadness, compassion, concern, humor, and love.

We wish you the best,
Ellie Soper and Kim Wang

### Reflecting on This Segment

1. As you read this letter, what were your own thoughts and reactions?
2. Using your own words, write a P.S. message to the group from yourself as an observer of this meeting.

## USING THIS TOOL

Throughout this book, you have regularly worked in a group setting to practice crisis intervention skills. Write a follow-up letter to your group. Share your experiences and observations with your fellow members. In particular, write about the strengths and talents that you noticed, the memories that you'll take from your time together, and suggestions for achieving their potential in the future.

### Using the Natural Helping Network

When survivors do seek out the emotional help they need, they usually turn to their relatives, neighbors, friends, teachers, physicians, or members of the clergy, who form a community's natural helping network that promotes the recovery process. As we discussed in Chapter 3, the research on social support has consistently found that the informal helping network is a powerful factor in facilitating successful crisis resolution (Stephens, 1997).

You need to recognize that you are not alone in offering assistance and support. A group crisis intervention meeting is only one of many experiences that can help survivors along the resolution process. Other perspectives emphasizing religious or spiritual interpretations of stress also can help to alleviate psychological distress (Eisenbruch, 1992).

### Crisis Support Groups

Certainly, social support can be an important buffer of traumatic stress (see, for example, Reif, Patton, & Gold, 1995). Many survivors prefer to participate in groups with others who are dealing with similar crisis experiences (Tedeschi & Calhoun, 1995). Support groups serve as an excellent complement to crisis intervention and brief counseling. They provide a setting for connecting with others who are at different stages of resolution. Beginning survivors, for example, may see for themselves how others are successfully coping.

The site of the support group meetings should not be a counseling agency or mental health center. Rather, it should be a school, church, neighborhood center, or even a private home. Not only are survivors more likely to attend the group, but the location also reinforces the normality of their concerns. The meetings may be on a weekly or monthly basis and the groups may continue to meet indefinitely.

## RESOURCES FOR DEALING WITH TRAGEDY

Parents, teachers, coaches, faith leaders, and friends are important sources of support for a young person dealing with a tragedy. As a crisis intervener, you can provide practical information, helpful consultation, and emotional encouragement to those people. The following is an excellent resource for you as you equip your tool kit for dealing with the tragedies that young people inevitably must face.

> American Counseling Association
> http://www.counseling.org

The American Counseling Association has developed an extensive Web site of resources for helping children and youth deal with tragedies. The site includes suggestions for parents, information regarding school counselors, and ideas for talking to children about death.

## SUMMARY

In this chapter, you learned how to deal with a group in crisis. You became familiar with the group crisis intervention steps of linking with one another, cocreating a collective survival story, managing emotions, and facilitating the group's coping (see Figure 9–3). In Chapter 10, you will look at community-wide traumas and the roles that you can play as a crisis counselor.

---

**Essential Tools**

- Link the group in crisis.
- Help the group coconstruct a collective survival story.
- Promote emotions of resolve.
- Facilitate the group's coping.

---

**FIGURE 9–3**   Essential tools of Chapter 9.

## Segue to Chapter 10

To help you gain a feel for the themes and issues in *Chapter 10,* draw a picture of the neighborhood from your childhood. Enact a disaster by setting a match to it, holding it under water, balling it up, or tearing it into pieces. Next, try to rescue it from destruction and then repair the damage. Were you able to return the picture to its original condition? Reflect on the steps you took and how you felt going through this exercise.

# Crisis Intervention with Communities: Disasters, Catastrophes, and Terrorism

"We know that where community exists it confers upon its members identity, a sense of belonging, and a measure of security. It is in communities that the attributes that distinguish humans as social creatures are nourished."

*John W. Gardner*

## CHAPTER GOALS

After completing this chapter, you should be able to:

- Understand how natural disasters, large-scale accidents, and violence can challenge an entire community
- Learn community-wide approaches to crisis intervention

## OVERVIEW

It is estimated that about 200 million people worldwide were involved in some form of natural disaster (earthquake, famine, wind, flood) during each year of the 1990s. During that time, close to 1 out of every 25 people in the world was directly affected by a disaster.

In this chapter, you will learn the important role that you can play in helping an entire community in crisis. Community-wide catastrophes, such as natural disasters, technological disasters, acts of terrorism, large-scale accidents, and war, may last only a few minutes, but their physical, economic, ecological, social, and psychological impact can be deep, long-lasting, and widespread. If you act individually and rely only on traditional counseling approaches in dealing with community-wide traumas, then you will be both inefficient and ineffective. Instead, you need to participate in a coordinated program implemented by a community-wide disaster response team. Long before a disaster strikes, you can take part in developing or refining a community disaster plan that offers disaster preparedness, crisis intervention, community education, outreach, consultation, support, and follow-up interventions. These are components of a successful plan designed to promote a collective resolution.

## CRISIS STORY

The town's warning siren began its low, moaning wail at 4:17 P.M. on Good Friday. A few residents of the small community of Willow Creek hoped that it was part of the religious ceremonies that were taking place throughout the day. After all, every church bell in town had been somberly tolling a death knell each hour, and local ministers had led a solemn reenactment of the carrying of the cross down Main Street. But as soon as folks looked out their windows, they knew that the siren was a tornado warning. The sky was glowing a sickening shade of yellow, charcoal-black clouds loomed in the west, and telephone lines already were convulsing spasmodically in the wind.

No one is sure how many tornadoes touched down around the town in the next few minutes. The National Weather Service later reported that there were at least three, but Elias Errington, a farmer just on the outskirts of town, spotted four funnels before he and his wife Lottie fled to their storm shelter. Below ground and on their knees, the Erringtons began to say the rosary in the same entrancing cadence that they had used every night of that season of Lent, but soon they had to raise their voices to hear themselves over the maelstrom. Lottie later recalled, with her characteristic understatement, that it was vexing how what sounded like locomotives barreling toward them distracted her from her prayers.

It was when the noise grew to a high-pitched shriek directly overhead that they clung to one another, the flickering oil lamp casting a single quivering shadow on the creaking shelves of vibrating canned goods that lined the shelter wall. When they finally emerged from the shelter 50 minutes later, they found their house in ruins, the barn gone, and no sign of the livestock. It was curiously quiet—the only sound was the hissing of gas escaping from the broken lines. The eerie scene was so stripped of any familiar landmarks that Lottie suddenly felt that they were lost, abandoned, and forsaken in an alien world. The farm had been so much more than just their home and source of income. It had been the anchor of their lives, a point of reference for their children and grandchildren, and the center of their universe. While Elias went for help, Lottie began rummaging through the rubble, looking for the family photo album and the recipe box her father had made for her when she married, and wondering how on earth they would ever be able to rebuild after losing everything.

The rescue efforts that Good Friday evening too frequently turned into the recovery of bodies. Cathy Ahrens had rushed to what was left of her grandmother's home, where some of the town's rescue squad volunteers were picking through the ruins. Randy Kelly, a high school senior who had just joined the squad, found Grandma Ahrens' body near the sewing machine that she had used to sew Cathy's First Communion dress. The volunteers quickly converged around the lifeless, tiny, and frail figure—its arms and legs twisted unnaturally—to disentangle it from the wreckage. Without a word, they gently lifted debris that covered her, brushed the dust from her clothes, and laid her body on the stretcher. Cathy rode in the ambulance with her grandmother, clutching the family Bible she had recovered, its cover ripped, but still containing the record of family members' births, weddings, and deaths.

Randy, who had never before seen a dead body, much less all this devastation, watched the ambulance snake its way through the scattered wreckage. "What am I doing here?" he thought to himself, "I don't really know if I can handle this." He recalled that he had been excited when he had heard the call. In fact, as he had hurried to the scene, Randy had imagined himself involved in some heroic adventure and then bragging about it to his brothers, Denny and Kevin. But he hadn't counted on all this pain and suffering. Joining the other volunteers who had resumed searching the area, Randy felt a mixture of grim determination to continue the job he had started and a fearful dread that he might find another body.

## Reflecting on This Crisis Story

1. What were your own reactions to this story?
2. What are the strengths of this community?
3. What are the ongoing stresses that this community faces?
4. How could others be of help with this community?

# IDEAS

## Community Crises

It is a rare news day when you do not see a story about a natural disaster that has struck a community somewhere. The United States has the highest rate of tornadoes in the world (Barnes-Svarney & Svarney, 1999) and also faces many other hazardous weather conditions. Even controlling for inflation, disaster losses recently have risen dramatically in the United States. In fact, 7 of the 10 most costly disasters in U.S. history have occurred since 1989. Ominously, although the recent past has been plagued with disasters, the future appears even more bleak. Global warming will likely produce more extreme meteorological events, increasing the number of natural disasters. More people are settling in areas with high climatic hazards and fragile ecosystems, escalating the potential human impact of disasters (Mileti, 1999).

Even on television, the violent force of these natural disasters is obvious when you see the dramatic scenes of destroyed homes, obscenely mangled objects, and ravaged landscapes. Plundering areas so completely that they resemble combat zones, natural disasters leave in their wake billions of dollars in damages. People lose their possessions, homes, communities, and loved ones.

Unfortunately, since September 11, 2001, we are now acutely aware that natural disasters are not the only community-wide traumas that we face in this society. Acts of terrorism, widescale technological accidents, violent crimes involving many victims, and highly publicized individual traumas are also far too common.

Not only have you seen the physical destruction of catastrophic events on television, you also have found yourself captivated by powerful scenes showing injured and distraught people reeling from the impact of these calamities. Such scenes typically make up the top stories of television news shows because producers follow the slogan, "If it bleeds, it leads." As a result, television, as well as other media, generally portrays disaster survivors as pathetic victims (Elliott, 1989). Occasionally, the media focus on the other extreme by featuring stories of inspiring heroes overcoming extraordinary obstacles (Gans, 1979). However, in contrast to the media portrayals, the vast majority of disaster survivors are neither helpless nor superhuman. Instead, they are regular people coping actively, being resilient, and doing their best to get by (Kaniasty & Norris, 1999).

Of course, television is not the only medium that shows you catastrophes. In movies, you may have noticed that there is an almost obsessive fascination with disasters and terrorism. Such movies as *Twister*, *Volcano*, *Titanic*, the *Die Hard* trilogy, and *The Day After Tomorrow* are technically masterful, with computer-generated special effects that realistically depict the physical devastation of disasters. In all these movies, however, the portraits of psychological and social reactions are stereotypical, superficial, and downright wrong (Fischer, 1994).

Even if you do not specialize in disaster intervention, it is likely that, at some point in your professional career, your community, or one nearby, will be confronted by a collective trauma. Contrary to what you have seen in movies, you will not encounter hordes of people running amok and pathetically incompetent in their collective response. Instead, you will find people who are not only vigorously involved in rescue, recovery, and rebuilding efforts, but also feeling traumatized, shaken, and desperate to talk to someone.

## Personal and Community Crises

There are several important similarities between personal crises and community-wide traumas. First, for individuals and communities alike, a crisis presents both a danger and an opportunity. Most communities respond to a disaster by pulling together and developing a sense of common identity. They typically rebuild their physical environment, enhance their infrastructure, improve their economic base, initiate major policy changes, and develop new services (Morrow & Peacock, 1997). For example, the Johnstown Flood of 1889 led to the development of the American Red Cross as a national disaster volunteer workforce (McCullough, 1968). In other communities, however, disasters "force open whatever fault lines once ran silently through the . . . community, dividing it into fragments" (Erikson, 1994, p. 236). Groups of citizens may become less cohesive, break out in conflicts over the distribution of scarce resources, and blame one another for their difficulties. In other words, disasters can either strengthen community ties or rip the social fabric.

A second similarity is that, at both the individual and community levels, there is a struggle to interpret the catastrophic event and understand its meaning (Kalayjian, 1999). Unlike individuals, however, the community's attempts to make sense of a crisis may involve heated debates and intense disputes (Tierney, 1989) because how the issues are framed will guide the actions that communities take. A disaster is like a Rorschach inkblot. Because of the chaos of the events and ambiguity regarding its meaning, people tend to interpret the situation according to their own fears and values. Some people, for example, may see a natural disaster purely as an economic problem and urge that environmental regulations be eliminated to promote redevelopment. Others see it as essentially an ecological crisis that requires stricter environmental laws. Still others may argue that the disaster is a spiritual crisis that reflects the sins of the people.

Finally, the resilience of communities, like that of individuals, is no more emphatically demonstrated than in times of crisis (Zinner & Williams, 1999). Communities have often used disasters as catalysts for social movements and other dramatic changes in policies, laws, customs, and even popular culture (Echterling & Wylie, 1999). For example, most American communities immediately announce an "Amber Alert" when a child has been kidnapped.

## *EXPERIENCING THESE IDEAS*

Entire communities have experienced traumas that have a powerful impact on every member. The community-wide trauma may be a natural disaster, an act of political terrorism, a large-scale accident, or a highly publicized trauma. To encounter the ideas in this chapter, think about a crisis that may have confronted your entire school, religious community, neighborhood, or city.

1. How did this community crisis affect you?
2. How did the community respond to this crisis?
3. What helped members along the resolution process?
4. In what ways are you a different individual as a result of this community crisis?

As you continue reading this chapter, keep in mind your own experiences and discoveries.

## Disasters, Catastrophes, and Acts of Terrorism

It is easy to see the physical impact of these catastrophic events, but what about the psychological impact? For many survivors, the disaster divides their life stories into two major segments: before and after the event (Raphael, 1986).

**Short term.** There is now a substantial body of literature documenting the immediate psychological effects of disasters and other community-wide traumas (Baum, 1987). During and shortly after an incident, nearly all of the direct victims experience overwhelming distress, grief, and anguish. After severe natural disasters, domestic violence escalates (Palinkas, Downs, Petterson, & Russell, 1993) and divorce rates spiral (Morrow,

1997). However, psychological distress often remains concealed because few disaster survivors seek formal counseling and the incidence of severe psychopathology after disasters does not increase. Because mental health programs still carry a stigma for many people, survivors tend to avoid such services, even though they may be in great psychological pain (Freedy, Kilpatrick, & Resnick, 1993).

**Long term.** Although the community trauma itself is terrifying and overwhelming for many members, it is just the beginning of a long series of problems. The survivors of a catastrophe have to cope with constant reminders, economic hardships, and losses that continue for years later. Dealing with the bureaucratic nightmare of disaster relief has been so maddeningly frustrating that many have labeled it "the second disaster" (Weaver, 1995, p. 73). In other words, community crises involve both acute and chronic stress and immediate and long-term challenges.

For example, 7 years after a flood, one man shared his long-term struggles with us. His account describes some of the financial stressors and emotional challenges that some survivors face:

> We couldn't sell our house, so we had to remain here. We want to move . . . I don't enjoy the river the way I used to. We weren't able to afford vacations . . . Thanksgiving time has never meant the same since the flood. We don't decorate like we used to. Holidays are painful times now. All of our Christmas decorations were destroyed.

The disaster itself may terrorize and horrify its victims for only a few moments, but if survivors do not achieve a positive resolution, they may feel disheartened and demoralized by its repercussions for years to come.

Although the direct victims of a community trauma suffer many painful consequences, they are not the only ones to experience ongoing difficulties. Friends, relatives, and other members of the community also endure survivor guilt, anxiety, fatigue, and other distress. For example, disaster workers (Hartsough & Myers, 1985) often face extreme hardships, work in dangerous situations, and suffer high levels of stress. The ordeal is particularly upsetting to volunteer workers (Dyregrov, Kristoffersen, & Gjestad, 1996).

Other members of a community's helping network, such as the clergy (Bradfield, Echterling, & Wylie, 1989), experience a great deal of stress as a result of their intensive disaster work. Some members of the clergy may fail to achieve a successful resolution and continue to endure long-term distress and suffering (Echterling & Wylie, 1999). For example, one minister said, "Around the anniversaries of the flood, I go into withdrawal. I pretend that it doesn't exist. To this day, I have less interest in Halloween because the rains started on Halloween." Another acknowledged, "I left my congregation one and a half years after the flood because I felt burnt out. I'm invited back there often, but . . . I feel uncomfortable going back. I avoid the memories of those times."

In their efforts to face and meet the needs of their traumatized community, those who respond to disasters are themselves affected. As a result, the distinction between helper and victim becomes blurred. In a very real sense, a disaster affects everyone in a community.

## Resilience of Disaster Survivors

In spite of the devastation that they endure and the challenges they face, most survivors of disaster successfully resolve the crisis without any formal intervention (Salzer & Bickman, 1999). One longitudinal study of 98 disaster survivors (Echterling & Wylie, 1999) revealed that, after 7 years of coping with the consequences of a flood, most survivors were able to describe positive changes in their fundamental beliefs about life, the world, and themselves. For example, most of the survivors acknowledged that their disaster experiences had led them to change their thinking about the value of life. Because the flood was the single most destructive event in their lives, it seemed reasonable to assume that the disaster would negatively affect survivors' opinions about the benevolence of life. However, surprisingly, a large majority—75%—of the subjects whose beliefs changed reported that these changes actually were for the better. As one woman said, "It made me stop and think of how fortunate I was." Another declared, "I don't take anything for granted . . . It put things into perspective."

For a significant number of the survivors, the flood experience led to positive changes in themselves. "I'm more compassionate and understanding of others," said one survivor. Another asserted, "I wonder how I did what I did. I found out I could do some amazing things that I never imagined I could do."

Finally, most of the survivors also formed more positive beliefs about the meaning of life. One man expressed it this way: "It made me think, why did this thing have to happen? I value life much more. I take it one day at a time and value each day."

## Promoting Collective Resolution

One of our acquaintances shared with us a joke that demonstrates the fundamental distinction between disaster intervention and traditional therapy. "What's the difference between the responses of a disaster intervener and a traditional therapist to a flood survivor covered in mud? The disaster intervener says, 'Let's get that mud off you.' The traditional therapist asks, 'How does that feel to have mud all over you?'" The point of the joke is that, when a disaster strikes, empathy calls for action. As Miller (1998) pointed out,

> In times of disaster physical care is psychological care, and initial postdisaster interventions must focus on establishing safety, providing nourishment and medical care, and affording protection from the elements. (p. 149)

Recently, some practitioners have conceptualized disasters as serious threats to the mental health of victims (see, for example, Myers, 1994; Weaver, 1995). Similarly, some mental health researchers have used the concept of posttraumatic stress disorder to focus on the psychopathological consequences of disaster (Joseph, Williams, & Yule, 1993).

There are, however, several problems with characterizing disasters as a mental health problem. The first difficulty is the medical model's emphasis on traditional mental health services, such as formal psychotherapy, and less formal psychotherapeutic techniques, such as outreach crisis counseling and Critical Incident Stress Debriefing. One misguided strategy based on the medical model has been to expand the availability of clinical services at local mental health centers, although the use of these services rarely increases following disasters (Salzer & Bickman, 1999). In fact, after Hurricane Andrew, even highly disturbed survivors considered seeing a mental health professional as humiliating (Sattler et al., 1995). You can keep the office open longer and encourage referrals, but nobody comes.

A second consequence of the medical model is that it limits service providers to only those who are mental health professionals. Therefore, one common difficulty for mental health disaster programs is to recruit enough psychotherapists who are willing to offer pro bono counseling to disaster victims (Carll, 1996). The *Disaster Services Regulations and Procedures* manual of the American Red Cross has staffing guidelines that allow only licensed mental health professionals to offer disaster mental health services (American Red Cross, 1991). Promoting an entire community's collective resolution cannot depend only upon mental health professionals, who are limited in number and who traditionally work with small caseloads.

A third problem with this model is the belief that all survivors of a catastrophe need formal or informal mental health interventions. Such a perspective can sabotage a community's sense of self-efficacy (Gist, Lubin, & Redburn, 1999). In fact, the vast majority of disaster victims develop into resolute survivors without receiving any therapeutic intervention. Fundamentally and ultimately, the resolution of a community crisis depends on its members going about the tasks of supporting one another and addressing people's needs as they rebuild their community. Instead of characterizing disaster intervention as dealing with the problem of individual psychopathology, you can promote collective resolution on the basis of resilience and social support.

Not relying solely on crisis intervention with individuals or groups, effective disaster programs emphasize a variety of community-wide and resolution-focused strategies, such as participating in coordinated outreach services for survivors, offering follow-up programs, organizing support group activities, and providing consultation and education. Whatever the strategy employed, disaster programs subscribe to the helping principles introduced in Chapters 1 and 2: survivors are resilient, they are having normal reactions to abnormal events, and they need to tell their stories (see Figure 10–1). In successful communities, a natural helping network evolves to promote the resolution process by offering practical assistance, sharing stories, giving emotional support, and performing rituals. Your job is to encourage that natural resolution process.

---

**Key Ideas**

- Disasters, large-scale accidents, and violence can challenge an entire community.

- In times of crisis, communities face both dangers and opportunities.

- Like individuals, communities are resilient.

---

**FIGURE 10–1**    Key ideas of Chapter 10.

**TOOLS**

## Crisis Intervention with Individuals and Groups

Over a quarter century ago, a few professionals began to offer outreach crisis intervention to victims of natural disasters and other large-scale traumas (Lystad, 1985; Zarle, Hartsough, & Ottinger, 1974). Naively, they came to these stricken communities not sure what to expect, but nevertheless confident that they could help. Since then, the use of crisis intervention with disaster survivors has gained acceptance. In fact, the Federal Emergency Management Agency and the American Red Cross now sponsor crisis counseling at all major disasters (Myers, 1994). Most communities and school systems in the United States have organized crisis teams that are prepared to respond quickly to catastrophic events.

Recently, several practitioners have criticized the widespread use of immediate crisis counseling as overzealous and possibly harmful (Satel, 1999). At one recent, highly publicized incident, mental health practitioners were so plentiful that they interfered with the actual rescue and recovery efforts (Gist et al., 1999). In spite of these concerns, immediate crisis counseling is the standard protocol for responding to community traumas. In recent years, disaster teams have started to offer group defusing and debriefing not only to direct victims, but also to rescue and relief workers, who often experience stress reactions (Gibbs, Drummond, & Lachenmeyer, 1993). The American Red Cross, for example, provides stress debriefings to all its volunteer disaster workers (Armstrong, O'Callahan, & Marmar, 1991).

### Listening In on Crisis Intervention

One such small intervention served as a source of inspiration for Carmine, a woman whose home had been struck by a flash flood. The waters rose so quickly that she was able to escape in her car with only a few legal documents. When she arrived at the local high school's gymnasium that served as the area's disaster assistance center, Carmine was reeling from all her possible losses—house, furniture, family heirlooms, and, most heartbreaking of all, the family photo album. As Carmine sat on a cot, ruminating on the irony that she had rescued her mortgage papers but might no longer have the house, a volunteer, a young man in his twenties, came up to her.

INTERVENER: (*Speaking with energy and smiling enthusiastically*) Is there anything that I can do to help?

CARMINE: (*At first, she is startled out of her painful reverie by the intervener's words, which seem jarring and naive. Then she is struck by the intervener's clean clothes, "can do" attitude, and enthusiastic manner—all in marked contrast to her own physical condition and state of mind. Finally, her words begin rushing out with an intensity that surprises both the intervener and herself.*) Listen, everything I own just got washed away, I'm sitting here covered in all this muck, and I have no idea what's going to happen to me now!

INTERVENER: (*Stammering now, holding his hands up with their palms facing the distraught woman*) I . . . I . . . I . . .

CARMINE: (*Using a harsh sarcastic tone that she had never used before*) If you really want to be helpful, you can get me something so I can at least get cleaned up a little.

INTERVENER: (*Turning quickly on his heels and calling back over his shoulder as he speeds away*) Yes, Ma'am!

CARMINE: (*Dismissively waving off the volunteer, Carmine sighs deeply and lowers her face into her cupped hands. Immediately regretting her outburst, she begins to cry and murmur to herself*) Oh, my God! That was an awful thing to do! (*As she reflects on the incident, she finally decides to find the young man, apologize to him, and ask for his forgiveness. Rising, Carmine turns and finds that the volunteer has returned.*)

INTERVENER: (*Handing over an armful of articles, he breathlessly itemizes the booty he has collected to meet Carmine's needs*) I found a bar of soap, some shampoo, a towel, a comb, toothpaste, and a toothbrush for you. And there's a girls' shower over there you can use. Just let me know if there's anything else I can do!

CARMINE: (*As she holds these articles, Carmine feels overwhelmed by the volunteer's quick response to her needs and patient acceptance of her angry outburst. This person's simple gesture gives her comfort and reassurance that she is not alone*) Oh, no. No, just thanks . . . (*She begins to cry.*) . . . and I'm sorry for taking it out on you. Thanks for everything. (*Follow-up note: Carmine went on to rebuild her home, carrying the memory of this encounter as a source of encouragement and inspiration. Today, Carmine is an active disaster recovery volunteer, returning the generosity and acceptance she had received.*)

## Reflecting on This Segment

1. In what ways has Carmine demonstrated her resilience?
2. How did the intervener's response differ from traditional counseling?

## Creating a Collective Survival Story

The three previous chapters described crisis intervention with individuals, families, and groups. Although we recommend that your disaster response team offers such resolution-focused strategies, you should not rely on them as your primary service to a community in crisis. Instead, you want to emphasize community-wide strategies to help create a collective survival story. These strategies include community education, consultation, support groups, and follow-up services.

In earlier chapters on crisis intervention, you read about collaborating with individuals and groups to help coconstruct survival stories from their crisis experiences. When an entire community is traumatized, creating a collective survival story is also vital for a community's successful resolution. Cocreating survival narratives helps a community to gather individual experiences together to construct a mosaic of shared meanings of the disaster.

Because sharing stories necessarily includes others who hear them, the process helps to reconnect survivors, who may feel alone and alienated, to one another as they form a common identity. Disaster survivors develop a standard repertoire of stories that portray the catastrophe, characterize themselves, and chart a course, for better or worse, for the future.

After any catastrophe, people quickly seek out others to reconnect with, exchange information, offer impressions, and share experiences. The setting may be any available public place: a temporary shelter, disaster assistance center, local bar, church, or school. The communication may take place over the telephone, in the newspaper, on the television or radio, or face-to-face. Wherever or however the information and stories are shared, members of the community are engaged in an elaborate and complex creation of a collective survival story. Such narratives take several typical forms, such as rumors, jokes, and personal accounts, but whatever their form, they can either facilitate or undermine a positive collective resolution.

**Rumors.** Immediately after a disaster strikes, at the very moment that people crave information the most, regular communication systems are often damaged (Weaver, 1995). Telephone service may be out, electricity is often cut off, and families have been separated from each other. Rumors based on speculation and hearsay fill this information vacuum. They reflect people's attempts to make meaning of the confusion and turmoil of a catastrophe, and to give expression to their hopes and fears.

Positive rumors are usually vague, hopeful reports of possible rescue efforts and additional recovery resources. Such optimistic hearsay is common early in disaster recovery and may serve to buoy people's spirits during times of extreme danger and vulnerability. Negative rumors, which typically become more numerous over time, are those that describe political conspiracies, secret causes of the disaster, other potential hazards, and concerns that reflect prejudices and personal fears. After any disaster, rumors inevitably appear about members of minority groups either looting homes or exploiting recovery assistance. In actuality, looting is rare and minorities receive much less assistance (Morrow, 1997). Negative rumors, in particular, are more likely to maintain their momentum and be passed along to others (Hobfoll, Briggs, & Wells, 1995).

In disaster recovery, one of your tasks is to deconstruct negative rumors. The most effective way to do this is by helping survivors gain access to timely, accurate, and useful information.

**Jokes.** Another common form of disaster narrative is the joking that is shared among survivors. "As long as natural and human-made disasters occur," Dundes (1987) pointed out, "jokes about these disasters are probably inevitable" (p. 80). The lore regarding humor is that generally it is a natural and effective coping strategy, but gallows humor is often seen as a sign of burnout (Weaver, 1995). However, even gallows humor and sick jokes can be creative and defiant portrayals that reframe the disaster by poking fun at the threat (Thorson, 1993). Gallows humor is coping by "spitting in the eye" of the disaster. In addition to being a method that survivors use to handle their personal distress, humor also offers a means to bond with one another.

**Personal Disaster Stories.** The personal narratives of disaster survivors are often variations along three fundamental themes: horror stories, war stories, and happy endings

(Fine, 1995). Each of these stories invites the audience to engage in "emotional hitch-hiking" (Klapp, 1991) by sharing the affective experience of the survivor. Survivors who find some positive meaning in the traumatic event (Thompson, 1985) or identify positive outcomes of the disaster experience (Tobin & Ollenburger, 1996) are able to cope better and have less postdisaster stress.

Although they may welcome the stories of others during the early days of disaster recovery, many survivors grow reluctant to serve as an audience to others' narratives (Kaniasty & Norris, 1999). Therefore, disaster intervention programs should not squander all their resources on only offering immediate, intensive services. Providing support later in the resolution process, when many of the other members of the community are experiencing "compassion fatigue," can be a valuable follow-up intervention.

The great majority of survivors cope well with a catastrophe and its consequences but sometimes reveal their distress years later. For example, one survivor shared some of his feelings with us about his experience:

> We are still finding mud lodged in the cracks in the walls and in the joints of the furniture. We still have mud stains in the pots, pans, and in the Tupperware. We've scrubbed and cleaned but the stains will not come out . . . A couple of years ago, we found that some of the air ducts still had mud caked in them . . . Even our birth certificates and the family documents have mud stains on them.

The vivid image of the dried mud, packed so hard and so deep into the cracks and crevices that it virtually became part of the house, is a striking metaphor for the disaster survivor. To the casual observer, the repaired house may look as good as new. But the flood has left its mark, and the survivor's challenge is to make positive meaning of that mark.

In a sense, the process of resolving any crisis can be seen as making positive meaning of the psychological mark of a trauma. Like the dried mud, the psychological mark is often packed hard and deep inside someone. It may be a painful memory embedded in some distant part of the mind, a secret apprehension in the pit of the stomach, or a sense of vulnerability in a corner of the heart. When disaster survivors begin rebuilding their homes and their personal lives, they also construct positive meaning that can help to transform these marks.

## Community Education

Your community disaster team can design and present comprehensive community education programs on disaster preparedness that take place regularly, long before a disaster strikes. Immediately following the catastrophe, your team can implement a comprehensive, community-wide campaign involving all of the public media, including local newspapers, television, and radio stations. The mass media are indispensable communication tools in dealing with disaster (Gist & Stolz, 1982). People rely on mass media before, during, and after disasters for warning information, updates on conditions, and announcements about resources (Mileti & O'Brien, 1992). In particular, the extensive television coverage of a disaster can help create a "virtual community" (Gladwin & Peacock, 1997, p. 57) of viewers who share the compelling experience of watching events unfold that have actual life-or-death relevance to them.

As a member of a disaster response team, you can follow several strategies to use the media as a tool to "both record and transform the event" (Wainrib & Bloch, 1998, p. 182).

---

**After the Disaster:**
**What Parents Can Do**

*After the disaster, does your child have . . .*

- a need to talk about it? Your boy or girl may want to tell what happened again and again. Even a generally quiet child may talk a lot about what he or she saw, felt, and did during the disaster.

- nightmares and trouble sleeping? Your child may be afraid to go to sleep or wake up frightened from bad dreams.

- fears of being alone? Some children are afraid of being left alone anywhere, even if it's only in another room at home. Your child may cling to you and may even want to sleep with you at night. He or she may be afraid of leaving home to go to school.

- worries and fears? Your child may pay close attention to the weather now. When he or she feels a gust of wind or sees a few raindrops, your child may become nervous. And if the weather turns bad, your child may immediately panic that another disaster is on the way.

- vivid memories of the disaster? Your child probably can picture in his or her mind detailed scenes from the disaster. And many different sights, sounds, or smells can easily trigger these memories in your child.

- trouble sitting still? Your child may now be more active, have problems paying attention, and be more impatient.

- upset feelings or no feelings at all? Your child may become upset or angry easily. Or your child may seem not to care about anything.

- physical problems? Your child may suffer from headaches, stomachaches, nausea, and fatigue.

These are just some of the common and usually temporary reactions your child can have to a disaster. Keep in mind that they are normal responses to an abnormal event. Fortunately, there are some simple steps you can take to help your child through these difficult times.

---

First, quickly establish a close relationship by contacting media representatives and serving as a reliable source of information. Offering yourself as a spokesperson can also protect survivors from media exploitation (Butcher & Dunn, 1989). Second, during any interview, actively frame the issues in ways that promote community resolution. In a misguided attempt to encourage public donations, some disaster interveners have collaborated with the media's portrayal of survivors as hapless victims. Although you can certainly acknowledge the enormity of the problem, you also emphasize the resilience of survivors and communicate their vision of a better future. For example, you may state,

> People have been dealing with this terrifying and catastrophic experience by rescuing those in danger, taking care of one another, recovering what is salvageable, and beginning to rebuild their homes and their lives. It's a tough job and they can use your understanding, support, and help.

Your manner in interviews should communicate a powerful belief that the people in this community are fully capable of working toward a positive collective resolution.

*You can help your child by . . .*

- letting your child talk about it. It may be painful, but the best thing you can do for your child is to listen to him or her talk about the disaster. If you have a younger child, he or she may be drawing pictures of the disaster or even acting it out in play. Talking, drawing, and play-acting are healthy and natural ways for a child to work through his or her reactions.

- comforting your child. Feel free to hold and comfort your child more during this time. Your child is reaching out to you for security right now, and a little extra love and affection will not spoil him or her. You can also reassure your child that he or she is now safe, and that bad weather, even when it's severe, rarely causes a disaster.

- not being overprotective. This may be the most difficult for you to do, but you must fight the temptation to overprotect your child. It may be very hard even to let him or her out of your sight, but it's important that your child returns to a regular routine as soon as possible.

- being a good example. Actions speak louder than words, and by your actions, you can set an example for your child of how to handle these reactions in a productive way.

- encouraging your child to help. Your child can and should help in the cleaning and rebuilding that needs to be done. If your family has been spared from severe losses, you may want to encourage your child to offer help or give a donation to others in need.

- preparing your child. If you start now, you can prevent the upsetting reactions that can occur when the weather may bring back memories of the disaster. You can tell your child what to expect and what to do to handle that situation.

- seeking help if your child is suffering severe problems. If your child has had a serious loss, such as the death of a loved one, or the destruction of a home or farm, he or she may need more help. Your child needs more help if he or she is having extreme reactions to the disaster, such as repeated nightmares, "flashbacks" of the disaster, crying spells, behavior problems, and panic reactions.

**FIGURE 10–2**    Disaster brochure for parents.

You can emphasize important points—only one or two in each interview—and offer information that survivors can use at that particular time in the resolution process. Repeating and highlighting these major points with examples that protect confidentiality can dramatize the issues without being maudlin. By being personable and communicating directly with the interviewer, you offer an authentic presence. Finally, after the interview, you can provide written material that supports the important points you made, gives more detailed facts regarding the resources available, and provides background information.

As part of your community education program, you can make presentations to neighborhood organizations, church groups, work groups, parent-teacher associations, and other community groups. You can design brochures that provide practical, helpful information on such topics as managing stress, handling the reactions of children (La Greca, Silverman, Vernberg, & Roberts, 2002), and preparing for possible disasters in the future. See Figures 10–2, 10–3, and 10–4.

### After the Disaster:
### A Guide to Handling Your Stress

During the disaster, you may have had to save your own life and the lives of others. Since then, you may have had to find emergency shelter and other basic necessities such as food and clothing. Now that you are rebuilding after the disaster, you're facing all sorts of new problems. As you deal with all these challenges, don't forget that you are going through one of the most stressful times in your life. You probably are having some of these common stress reactions.

*Since the disaster, you may have . . .*

- a need to talk about the disaster. You may want to tell what happened again and again. Even if someone is a perfect stranger, you may tell him or her all about what you went through during the disaster. You may have kept pictures of the disaster damage to show people.

- upset feelings or no feelings at all. Maybe you're having "yellow" reactions to the disaster—feeling nervous or scared. Maybe you're having "red" reactions—getting angry. Maybe you're having "black" reactions—feeling down or depressed. Then again, like most people, maybe you're having a rainbow of reactions. You may be jittery at first, then you may start crying over nothing, and then you may take out your frustrations on an easy target—a door or someone you love. Or, maybe you don't seem to care about anything at all right now. It's as if you are emotionally numb and feel nothing.

- trouble thinking clearly. You may be confused, dazed or forgetful and may not want to think about the problems you are facing. Maybe you pester yourself with thoughts of what you should have done differently. Maybe you keep asking yourself, "Why me?"

- vivid memories of the disaster. You probably can close your eyes right now and picture in your mind detailed scenes from the disaster. And even now, many different sights, sounds, or smells can trigger these memories and upset you.

- nightmares and trouble sleeping. Unfortunately, at a time when you need your sleep, you may have problems falling asleep and staying asleep.

- a need to rely on other people. Much more than usual, you may want and need to be around other people.

- worries and fears. You may be paying close attention to the weather now. When you feel a gust of wind or see a few raindrops, you may become nervous. And if the weather turns bad, you may feel panicked that another disaster is on the way.

- a need to take action. You may feel that something—anything!—has to be done right now. You may be pacing, or rocking, or fidgeting more now. Or, at times you may feel so discouraged that you do nothing.

- physical problems. You may have more physical problems now, such as headaches, stomachaches, nausea, and fatigue.

Throughout the community education campaign, you can emphasize the three important themes of crisis resolution:

1. Resilience
2. Resolution
3. Survival stories

These are just some of the common and usually temporary reactions a person may be having to a disaster. Keep in mind that they are normal responses to an abnormal situation. Fortunately, there are some simple steps you can take to help yourself through these difficult times.

*You can handle this stress by . . .*

- being with other people. You may feel reluctant to impose on others, but just having a caring person at your side can be a great source of comfort. There are many people willing and able to be with you in your time of need. All you need to do is ask. What have you got to lose?

- letting other people help. Don't let foolish pride stand in the way of receiving what you truly need from relatives, neighbors, friends, and concerned volunteers.

- talking about your feelings. Talking about your feelings is one of the best ways of working through your reactions to the disaster. Go ahead and talk about your fears, frustrations, and sadness—you're not "just feeling sorry for yourself." And although it's true that eventually you need to put the disaster "behind" you, you can't do that by ignoring your feelings or trying to erase those memories. That's impossible. You have to face and deal with these feelings—the sooner, the better.

- getting the information and advice you need. You probably are handling many of your problems on your own. But because you are caught up in the middle of this situation, you may not be seeing it objectively. You may need to ask someone for information, advice, or suggestions.

- reassuring yourself. You can remind yourself that you are now safe and that there is nothing wrong with you for having these reactions. You are not going crazy. These feelings are normal reactions to an abnormal situation.

- preparing for the future. If you prepare yourself and have a plan of action, you can handle, without getting so upset, future situations that bring back memories of the disaster.

- taking care of yourself. You have plenty of work to do, but you won't be able to do it if you're sick. Be sure to take good care of yourself by eating well, getting plenty of sleep, and taking some time off for yourself. And be careful with alcohol and other drugs. In tough times like these, it's easy to abuse them.

- getting professional help if you're having severe problems. If you have had a serious loss, such as the death of a loved one, or the destruction of your home or farm, you may need additional help. Even if you had no serious losses, you still need additional help if you're having extreme reactions, such as repeated nightmares, "flashbacks" of the disaster events, crying spells, behavior problems, and panic reactions.

**FIGURE 10–3**   Disaster brochure for self-care.

Although these community-wide efforts are on a broader scale, you are using the same basic skills that you developed in doing crisis intervention. You are providing a forum for community members to give voice to their experiences. You are acknowledging their stories and you are providing information that they can use to reconstruct their crisis experiences into survival stories.

### After the Disaster: What Educators Can Do

Children will react differently to the traumatic and chronic stress of a natural disaster. Some will seem to come through the experience unscathed. They may even be excited about this "adventure." Later, once the thrill has worn off, some may begin to have delayed reactions. Others will react strongly from the start, even though they may have suffered little loss or - injury. However, most children have normal and typical reactions to these abnormal circumstances.

*Common Reactions*

Some of the common reactions you can expect to see are:

- A need to talk about the disaster. Children will repeat the stories of their experiences many times. Even shy children will open up to strangers about what they saw, heard, felt, and did during the disaster. Many children who were spared will worry about what happened to others and will ask many questions.

- Sleep problems. For children under stress, the nighttime can seem especially threatening. Many children will be afraid to go to sleep and will be unable to sleep through the night. They will often have nightmares.

- Separation anxiety. Some children will be afraid of being left alone anywhere, even if it's only in another room at home. They may want to sleep with their parents at night. They may be afraid of leaving home to attend school. And they may constantly seek reassurance from their parents.

- Worries and fears. Most children will be much more vigilant about the weather and other conditions similar to the disaster. They may notice when it becomes cloudy or windy. When they feel some vibration or see a few raindrops, they may become apprehensive. And if the weather becomes severe, they may immediately believe that another disaster is on the way.

- Vivid memories of the disaster. Many children will picture in their minds detailed and powerful scenes from the disaster. It's almost as if they have their own internal videotape that replays their experiences whenever a "trigger" reminds them of the disaster. They may draw many pictures of these scenes or even act out these events in their play.

- Hyperactivity. Most adults will have a strong need to take some action after a disaster. If nothing else, they will pace the floor. Children will react similarly. They will become more active, will have difficulty paying attention, and will be more impulsive.

- Emotional sensitivity or numbness. Many children will become much more sensitive. They will become upset easily and become angry quickly. But other children will seem to become numb or unfeeling. They won't show any sadness or anger, but they won't show any joy either. It's as if they are closing themselves off from any future hurts.

- Physical complaints. Often children will complain more of headaches, stomachaches, nausea, and fatigue.

*What Can You Do To Help?*

As teachers, your goals are to help students to learn from their experiences, even those involving disasters, and to help them handle the stress that can interfere with them doing good schoolwork. Here are some suggestions to achieve those goals:

- Give your students time to deal with these experiences. Naturally, you will be feeling pressured to make up quickly the missed school days. But if you set aside times for students to describe their experiences and to discuss the disaster's aftermath, they will be better able to turn to the work at hand. Of course, talking is only one of the ways to work through these reactions. Other ways are writing about the events and, especially for young children, drawing pictures or using puppets or toys to act out their experiences.

- Be especially calm, show your concern, and emphasize the positive. By your manner, you will be setting a powerful example of how students can manage their reactions in a productive way.

- Remind them that these reactions are natural. Many children, like adults, will believe that something is wrong with themselves for feeling the way they do. They will need reassurance that their feelings are normal reactions to an abnormal situation. Finding out that their fellow students have had many of the same reactions also can be a great relief.

- Control rumors and correct any myths they may have. During disasters, there is an information vacuum. People often fill it by passing along rumors. You can help to control rumors and reduce overreactions by stopping "tall tales" and giving students the facts. Also, students may have some mistaken ideas about reactions to disasters. You may need to point out that people rarely panic or "go crazy" during disasters. The vast majority show initiative, courage, reluctance to take charity, and willingness to help others.

- Give them an opportunity to help in the disaster relief work. Many of our students, fortunately, have been spared from severe losses. You may encourage these students to offer help to their neighbors in need. We have heard much about the obvious needs of victims for food, clothing, and shelter. But our students are ideal resources to offer what young victims can use, such as toys, games, and the support and friendship of people their own age.

- Identify students who may be suffering severe posttraumatic or chronic stress. Students who have had serious losses, such as the death of a loved one, or the destruction of their homes or farms, may need more help. Students who also need more help are those having extreme reactions to the disaster, such as repeated nightmares, "flashbacks" of the disaster events, crying spells, behavior problems, and strong phobic reactions.

- Begin preparing students for future situations that may trigger anxieties. If you start now, you can prevent the typically high absentee rates and emotional reactions that can occur in the future when conditions may evoke memories of the disaster. You can give both students and parents information on what they can expect and what they can do to handle those situations productively.

**FIGURE 10–4** Training handout for educators.

## Outreach Services

Because disaster survivors do not come to interveners, you have to go to them. Providing outreach services to survivors is an essential part of an effective disaster program. Instead of passively waiting in your office, make your services easily available and accessible by going to the incident sites, emergency shelters, and assistance centers (Weaver, 1995). As in telephone intervention, outreach requires that we recognize the particular demands and unique dynamics of this approach. Some pointers to keep in mind are:

- Take greater care to ensure your own safety.
- Recognize that you may be on the client's turf.
- Take resources with you.
- Have a line of communication available to the outside world.

In addition to going to where the survivors are, you can frame your services as promoting resolution. Instead of offering "mental health services" or "psychotherapy," you are there to provide practical assistance, hear how people are doing, offer support in handling the distress, and encourage survivors in continuing to cope in creative and enterprising ways.

The sheer number of survivors of a community-wide trauma would easily overwhelm the community's professional therapists, whose traditional individual and group therapy approaches would be woefully inadequate. Instead, you can help organize disaster recovery programs that can select sensitive indigenous nonprofessionals and train them to become outreach workers (Myers, 1994).

In the wake of a disaster, outreach workers can make contact with all those affected to assess their needs, give support and information, and offer any necessary disaster intervention. By providing these outreach services, workers can also identify individuals and families who are experiencing a great deal of distress and who are in need of referral for formal counseling. Outreach services are not limited to making face-to-face contact with survivors. Instead, because many survivors are physically isolated, outreach also includes telephoning and corresponding with survivors.

As you listen to their stories with compassion, you communicate to survivors the reassurance that there is nothing wrong with them for having these reactions. The message that you communicate is that there is help available. The goal of outreach services is to facilitate the process of resolution by helping survivors handle traumatic and chronic stress in healthy, positive ways.

## Listening In on Crisis Intervention

A team of disaster workers is going door to door in one of the neighborhoods that was hit hard by the tornado. They bring along supplies, such as drinking water and snacks, and information on community resources that are available. The workers make their way down one of the hardest-hit streets and stop at the first house that is still standing. They make the visit during daylight hours because electricity has yet to be restored. They are wearing badges around their necks, clearly identifying them as disaster workers. Alfredo, the team leader, knocks on the door (which has the words, *The Marchals*, etched on a brass plate).

INTERVENER: Hi, Mr. Marchal. I'm Alfredo, and this is Bonnie and Hap. We're a community assistance team and we're making our way around your neighborhood today to see how we can be of help with anything. We're also passing out some emergency supplies. As you probably know, the one store left standing in town is sold out of just about everything.

HOMEOWNER: Well, I'd ask you three in, but there's no room to sit. The twister missed us, but it got the neighbors next door and behind us. They're all staying with us for a few days 'til they get back on their feet. I don't know what they need—everything I guess. We're all still kind of in shock.

INTERVENER: Well, sir, I do have a list of some community resources that might be of some help and I think most of their telephones are working again. They have turned the gym at the high school into an emergency shelter if it doesn't work out for everyone to stay here tonight.

NEIGHBOR: I've got to get my car out of that garage over there; we got to get the tree off of it first and nobody has a chain saw. (*One of the team members jots down the information. She then asks if anyone else needs anything. Another neighbor steps out on the porch and asks if the team could find out about the status of an older neighborhood on the other side of town where her parents live. While another team member puts in a call to ask the dispatcher about the neighborhood in question, an 8-year-old with tear-streaked cheeks pokes her head around the crowd of adults.*)

INTERVENER (*Kneeling down to get closer*): My name is Alfredo. What's yours?

CLARE: My name is Clare and my cat's name is Emma. Will you find her for me? I've called for her and looked everywhere I could think of for a long time, but my mommy won't let me look in any of the broken houses because it's too dangerous.

INTERVENER: Well, all the disaster workers are keeping an eye out for lost pets, because some volunteers are keeping care of them until the pet owners can take them back. Let me get your cat's description and we'll keep an eye out for her. I'll tell your mother about the pet shelter.

## Reflecting on This Segment

1. Do you think many of the survivors would accept the help the team offered?
2. In what ways did the team try to link with the survivors?
3. How did the team separate themselves from specious helpers who take advantage and end up charging for their services?

## Consultation

In addition to reaching out to help the direct victims, it is essential to work with the formal and informal helping resources in the community. Consequently, another important strategy of your disaster team is consulting with the area's emergency services, volunteer groups, schools, churches, and community agencies.

One common form of consultation is providing in-service training, equipping consultees with the knowledge they need to promote resolution. The training can involve describing the typical reactions and providing opportunities to practice crisis intervention techniques. Because the distinction between helpers and victims becomes blurred after a disaster, any training you offer should also address how helpers can take care of themselves.

**The Role of Faith Leaders.** Recognizing the importance of meaning for long-term coping, you want to collaborate closely with the faith leaders and others who help survivors give coherence to these experiences. Through such collaboration, you can encourage community networks to offer not only emotional and material support, but also opportunities to create meaning.

People often refer to a natural disaster as "an act of God," view the destruction as a form of supernatural punishment (Bushnell, 1969), attribute the event to the work of a supreme being (Pargament & Hahn, 1986), interpret it as a sign of a coming apocalypse, and perform religious ceremonies in response to a natural disaster (Ahler & Tamney, 1964). Consequently, the clergy and faith-based organizations can play an important and special role in disaster intervention (Bradfield et al., 1989; Smith, 1978). When a disaster strikes a community, many people turn to their faith leaders for practical assistance, emotional support, rituals, and meaning.

Today, most clergy members in Western societies emphasize the spiritual implications of a disaster but do not present a cataclysm as evidence of a wrathful God (Bradfield et al., 1989). Instead, they portray the catastrophe as a time of spiritual crisis that challenges survivors to reaffirm their fundamental values, demonstrate their religious commitment of caring for fellow human beings, and integrate this traumatic experience into the context of their theological beliefs.

Faith leaders are often involved in all facets of flood relief work: rescuing people at risk; helping in cleanup; providing food, clothing, and shelter; offering emotional support; organizing relief programs; and generating and dispensing donations. Nevertheless, even in the midst of the rubble, clergy also respond to a disaster by convening their congregations as soon as possible to lead them in prayer, song, and other religious rituals in order to foster a sense of unity in vision, inspire a feeling of hopefulness, and help survivors to begin finding meaning in their suffering (Echterling, Bradfield, & Wylie, 1992).

**The Role of Teachers.** Consulting with school officials can address not only how to meet the students' immediate emotional needs on their return to school, but also how to prevent the high absenteeism and poor academic performance that can occur after a community-wide crisis (Echterling, 1989). Your disaster response team can help schools develop programs that offer immediate support at school and at home, provide opportunities for students to gain a sense of cognitive mastery over the disaster event, and identify high-risk students.

## Listening In on Crisis Intervention

A school counselor is meeting with teachers and administrators to discuss what they will do when the students return to school. The scene is a school cafeteria 2 days after the tornado hit. According to the crisis team's plan, members used a telephone tree to contact everyone by Sunday afternoon. An 8:00 A.M. Monday meeting was called by the principal and after a brief welcome, she turned the meeting over to Ms. Pierce, one of the school counselors.

MS. PIERCE:  Thanks for coming today. I know you are all very busy with the aftermath of the tornado. I know Mr. Wilson, our art teacher, and his family lost their house, but fortunately they made it safely to the cellar before the tornado touched down. How many of you had friends or family who suffered losses from the tornado? (*Every single person in the cafeteria raises a hand.*)

Since we all were affected, it's no stretch to imagine that the children also have been affected. We have information from the central office that 16 children in five grades lost their homes and 4 children in one family lost their grandparents. We'll be sending around a list of those children as soon as we get an update later in the morning. It's important for us to . . .

DAVID MAST  (*A fifth-grade teacher, interrupts*): I heard that we won't be able to have school for weeks because the bus garage and all of the buses were destroyed! (*After that initial outburst, others chime in. Everyone seems to have a rumor to share. Finally, the counselor looks beseechingly at the principal, who quickly moves to the front of the room and tries to quiet the crowd.*)

PRINCIPAL:  All right everyone, please! I know that these past 2 days have been rough. I know that a lot of you have hardly rested since the tornado hit and you've been out there pitching in and doing what you can to help. We are very proud of our teachers and staff for all that you've done, but now we have to ask you for more of your help. I'm happy to report that, contrary to the rumor David has heard, there was only minimal damage to a couple of buses, so they will be ready for tomorrow. I hope that most of the children will be coming to school then. Let's let Sue continue and maybe we'll have time for more discussion after the meeting.

MS. PIERCE:  Thank you, Ms. Tobias. I didn't have the heart to call the meeting to order earlier. We're all just worn out and have so many things to think about . . . it hardly seems fair but . . .

RENEE:  (*A school nurse, Renee speaks up from the back.*) OK, Sue, we're sorry and we'll all behave! Won't we, David? (*Everyone has a good laugh, the tension is broken, and Sue continues.*)

MS. PIERCE:  As you probably remember, the school crisis team put together an emergency response handbook that was designed to help us get through times like this. I know that when the phone committee called you over the weekend you were asked to bring your handbook to the meeting. It has been a while since we talked about the specifics in the handbook, so let's get started with the first topic, (*She looks briefly toward David.*) "What to do about rumors."

## Reflecting on This Segment

1. What percentage of schools in your hometown would you estimate have written guidelines for dealing with disasters?
2. What strengths do you see in this faculty and staff?

# Follow-Up

Unfortunately, community-wide crisis intervention programs often have been limited to providing intensive, short-term, and immediate help. Although such early interventions are vital, they are only the first step. The catastrophe may be a time-limited event, but its physical, economic, ecological, social, and psychological consequences are long term. Although interveners have come to recognize the immediate stress of disasters, they may fail to appreciate the long-term stressors. Survivors facing the chronic stresses of a disaster can benefit from ongoing information and support.

**Recovery period.** Although immediate short-term intervention is not enough, it nevertheless is essential for effective follow-up services. A successful follow-up program must be built on a foundation of early intervention. Survivors are not as responsive to follow-up efforts if there is not already a relationship based on trust and acceptance. Following a disaster, many systems form a "trauma membrane" (Lindy & Grace, 1985), or boundary, that is at first easily permeable to potential helpers but is later sealed against outsiders. The early work immediately after a disaster allows you passage later through the trauma membrane.

During the recovery period after the trauma, your crisis team can contact survivors periodically to reassess their needs and respond accordingly. Again, follow-up services can take a variety of forms, including face-to-face contact, telephone calls, letters, brochures, and newsletters. The brochures and newsletters can offer survivors helpful information and suggestions for dealing with the economic, environmental, physical, and psychological consequences of the catastrophe.

**The Anniversary.** One important follow-up intervention is to help survivors cope with the "anniversary effect" (Myers, 1994). The anniversary of a disaster often evokes vivid memories of the incident and spurs reflections on its meaning and place in one's life (Echterling & Wylie, 1999). The anniversary prods survivors to assess again the incident's impact and prompts them to review the changes that have taken place during the past year.

Survivors report that, as the anniversary approaches, their memories become not only more frequent, but also more vivid and clear. "Now I can remember it like it just happened yesterday," said one survivor on the anniversary of a disaster. "I can close my eyes and see that water gushing through my window." The anniversary also spurs many to reflect on the disaster's meaning and place in their lives. "How can we ever forget the lives, homes, property, and businesses that were destroyed in the raging waters?" asked one minister on the anniversary. "One year later, we take time to pause, reflect, and remember."

The original feelings and reactions to the event often reemerge at this time. For some members of the community, the anniversary is accompanied by feelings of frustration, hopelessness, and disappointment, because they now must acknowledge that many of their problems may be long-lasting, or even permanent. Survivors have a strong need to take some action on the anniversary. Some take practical steps and many commemorate their disaster experience in some way.

You can encourage survivors not to fight against the tendency to recall events from a year ago. Instead, people can channel this natural inclination in a positive direction by focusing on the inspiring memories they have, the positive experiences and changes that have occurred, and the realistic challenges they continue to face.

In community education programs and public announcements in the media, you can remind members of the community that they do not have to carry their burdens alone. They can talk with others about their thoughts and feelings—whether painful or positive. You can urge friends and relatives of survivors to be especially supportive during this time. Finally, you can recommend that members of the community take some constructive and positive action, such as participating in a memorial, learning about disaster preparedness, and sharing with other survivors.

Stories about a disaster evolve and change over time. Although members of a community discard some stories, they may retell, revise, and refine others. Over the years, the personal narratives of survivors may become more reflective, dramatically reframing the disaster's issues and meaning. Many people pass along disaster narratives to younger generations. A few stories go on to become family legends.

## Listening In on Crisis Intervention

A disaster hotline service was started soon after the tornado. After several months, the frequency of calls began to decrease. However, as the anniversary date approaches, there has been a rise in calls.

INTERVENER: You have reached the community disaster hotline. My name is Nicki, how may I help you?

CALLER: I'm calling for information for . . . well . . . this is hard. I don't know where to start. Maybe I'll call back later. I know you're busy . . .

INTERVENER: Well, I have plenty of time so maybe you could start by telling me how you happened to decide to call us.

CALLER: (*Her words spill out in a torrent.*) My husband and I were flooded out last year and he has started to bring up things about the flood and then I saw one of the rescue squad guys in the store and we started out just having a normal conversation but before I knew it, I was babbling . . . and bawling. I was so embarrassed, I thought I'd die. We went outside and talked for a few minutes but he said he couldn't stay. He gave me a card and made me promise to call your hotline though, before he left. (*Her voice cracks and she is obviously upset.*) I thought we were past it and we could move on . . . I guess not. Last night it rained and I had a nightmare. It was so real; I swear I could hear the river coming in the window. Pretty nutty, ha-ha (*She gives an uneasy, fake laugh.*)—guess we'll have to get some therapy, huh?

INTERVENER: Just when you think the flood is a thing of the past, you and your husband are starting to revisit it again. I imagine that's pretty upsetting and baffling since you two thought it was behind you, or at least the sadness and the nightmares.

CALLER: Exactly! Until this week it had been at least a month since I thought about the flood. Now, it seems like I think about it all day.

*(Continued)*

INTERVENER: It must have taken a lot of effort on your part to get your lives back to normal after the flood. I'll bet the cleanup involved a lot of backbreaking work and probably took forever.

CALLER: Yes, it did. I got really tired of being filthy dirty . . . but it wasn't all bad. We met some nice people and we helped clean up each other's houses. We also joined a kind of support group and it really helped. (*She pauses for a few seconds.*) Do you know if it still meets?

INTERVENER: Was that the one that was led by the minister at the First Methodist Church?

CALLER: Yes! That's the one.

INTERVENER: I was just talking to her yesterday after church and she mentioned that the anniversary of the flood was approaching so the support group was going to begin meeting again because so many people are starting to have experiences and memories like you and your husband have been having . . . and starting . . . one second, let me check my notes . . . yes, here it is . . . starting next Wednesday.

## Reflecting on This Segment

1. Should the intervener have given the caller more information about the hotline before they started their session?
2. What if the intervener did not have personal knowledge of the group, what could she have done?

## Support Groups

The presence of others offering support can serve as a "buffer" against the stressors someone may be facing. People with a strong support system are less likely to have physical, emotional, and social problems as a result of stress. The support may take different forms, such as cognitive guidance, socializing, personal encouragement, tangible assistance, and emotional support.

Although disaster survivors initially try to rely on their own resources, they often need to turn to their support systems for help. However, a community disaster can not only kill or injure people and destroy property, it also can disrupt the existing support systems at the very time that members need them the most.

Developing support groups can address several important needs of disaster survivors. The goals of such groups are to give survivors opportunities to share practical information and disaster experiences, exchange useful ideas, and offer encouragement and emotional support to one another. The group format takes advantage of many of the therapeutic qualities of counseling groups by, for example, helping individuals to recognize the universality of their experiences, to learn by observation more effective coping strategies, and to practice interpersonal skills such as self-disclosure and assertion.

## *Using These Tools*

Review the newspapers over the past week and select an article that covers a particular community disaster in detail. It may be a natural disaster, such as a flood, tornado, or hurricane, or it could be an incident involving widespread violence or a horrible accident affecting many people. With three colleagues, form a disaster team and develop a specific intervention plan to fit the incident, population, and community described in the paper. Decide how you are going to divide up the tasks that need to be done. Each of you then writes a news release presenting your particular program to the public.

Afterward, reflect on your work together and discuss with one another how your collaboration efforts might eventually become a disaster response handbook for the community.

## RESOURCES FOR DISASTERS, CATASTROPHES, AND TERRORISM

The following are excellent resources to use for dealing with the victims of disasters, catastrophes, and terrorism.

American Psychological Association (APA)
http://helping.apa.org/daily/terrorism.html
1-800-964-2000

The APA Web site offers information on coping with terrorism, managing anthrax anxiety, and dealing with any catastrophic event. The toll-free hotline, which is not sponsored by the APA, is strictly for referral to a local psychologist and not for crisis assistance.

American Red Cross
http://www.redcross.org/pubs/dspubs/terrormat.html
202-639-3520

The American Red Cross has numerous publications available on its Web site. One practical article, "Terrorism—Preparing for the Unexpected," is offered in both English and Spanish and discusses preparations and steps to take before, during, and after a terrorist event.

Sesame Workshop
http://www.sesameworkshop.org/parents/advice/

*Sesame Street* offers a Web site of information, tips, and suggestions for parents. By searching for "Stress & Fears" under "Behavior & Development," you can find articles that provide advice on helping children cope with crises, disasters, and acts of terrorism.

## SUMMARY

Most victims of disasters develop into survivors without formal counseling. A natural helping network evolves to promote the resolution process by offering practical assistance, sharing stories, giving emotional support, and performing rituals. As a member of a community's disaster response team, you can help all survivors—both the victims and the helpers—to carry on the recovery process by providing outreach, consultation, support, and follow-up interventions (see Figure 10–5).

---

**Essential Tools**

- Crisis intervention with communities involves
  - ↳ Working with individuals and groups.
  - ↳ Creating a collective survival story.
  - ↳ Offering community education.
  - ↳ Providing outreach services.
  - ↳ Consulting with formal and informal helping resources.
  - ↳ Providing follow-up services.

---

**FIGURE 10–5**   Essential tools of Chapter 10.

## Segue to Your Own Next Chapter

In the Preface of this book, we asserted that whatever your background or circumstances, we could guarantee that you were a crisis survivor. Now that you have completed this book, we can make another guarantee. As a counselor or therapist, you will regularly deal with people in crisis. We hope that reading this book, reflecting on its ideas, and practicing its tools will help you as you face those challenges. You can play a vitally important role in the lives of others—not as a rescuer of victims, but as a collaborator with survivors. Finally, we wish you the best as you face the inevitable crises in your personal and professional life. May you go on to not only survive, but also to thrive!

# REFERENCES

**CHAPTER 1**

Aguilera, D. C. (1998). *Crisis intervention: Theory and methodology* (8th ed.). St. Louis, MO: Mosby.

American Psychiatric Association. (2000). *Diagnostic and statistical manual of mental disorders* (4th ed., text rev.) Washington, DC: Author.

Antonovsky, A. (1990). Pathways leading to successful coping and health. In M. Rosenbaum (Ed.), *Learned resourcefulness: On coping skills, self control, and adaptive behavior* (pp. 31–63). New York: Springer-Verlag.

Aspinwall, L. G., & Staudinger, U. M. (Eds.). (2003). *A psychology of human strengths: Fundamental questions and future directions for a positive psychology.* Washington, DC: American Psychological Association.

Bifulco, A., & Brown, G. W. (1996). Cognitive coping response to crises and onset of depression. *Social Psychiatry and Psychiatric Epidemiology, 31,* 163–172.

Bolger, N., Foster, M., Vinokur, A. D., & Ng, R. (1996). Close relationships and adjustments to a life crisis: The case of breast cancer. *Journal of Personality and Social Psychology, 70,* 283–294.

Bowman, M. (1997). *Individual differences in posttraumatic response: Problems with the adversity-distress connection.* Mahwah, NJ: Erlbaum.

Breslau, N., Davis, G. C., Andreski, P., & Peterson, E. (1991). Traumatic events and posttraumatic stress disorder in an urban population of young adults. *Archives of General Psychiatry, 48,* 216–222.

Campbell, J. (1970). *The hero with a thousand faces.* New York: World.

Caplan, G. (1964). *Principles of preventive psychiatry.* New York: Basic Books.

Carver, C. S. (1998). Resilience and thriving: Issues, models, and linkages. *Journal of Social Issues, 54,* 245–266.

Cross, W. E., Parham, T. A., & Helms, J. E. (1991). The stages of black identity development: Nigrescence models. In R. L. Jones (Ed.), *Black psychology* (3rd ed., pp. 319–338). Berkeley, CA: Cobb & Henry.

Dunkel-Schetter, C., Folkman, S., & Lazarus, R. S. (1987). Correlates of social support receipt. *Journal of Personality and Social Psychology, 52,* 71–80.

Egan, G. (1994). *The skilled helper.* (5th ed.). Monterey, CA: Brooks/Cole.

Eisenberg, N. (2002). Empathy-related emotional responses, altruism, and their socialization. In R. J. Davidson & A. Harrington (Eds.), *Visions of compassion: Western scientists and Tibetan Buddhists examine human nature.* New York: Oxford University Press.

Erikson, E. H. (1963). *Childhood and society.* New York: W. W. Norton.

Finke, R. A., & Bettle, J. (1996). *Chaotic cognition: Principles and applications.* Mahwah, NJ: Erlbaum.

Fraser, J. S. (1998). A process view of crisis and crisis intervention: Critique and reformulation. *Crisis Intervention and Time-Limited Treatment, 4,* 125–143.

Ganzevoort, R. R. (1998). Religious coping reconsidered, Part One: An integrated approach. *Journal of Psychology and Theology, 26,* 260–275.

Gilligan, C. (1983). *In a different voice: Psychological theory and women's development.* Cambridge: Harvard University Press.

Glantz, M. D., Johnson, J., & Huffman, L. (Eds.). (1999). *Resilience and development: Positive life adaptations.* New York: Plenum.

Hendricks, J. E., & McKean, J. B. (1995). *Crisis intervention: Contemporary issues for on-site interveners* (2nd ed.). Springfield, IL: Charles C Thomas.

Kalayjian, A. (1999). Coping through meaning: The community response to the earthquake in Armenia. In E. S. Zinner & M. B. Williams (Eds.), *When a community weeps: Case studies in group survivorship* (pp. 87–101). Levittown, PA: Brunner/Mazel.

Kaniasty, K., & Norris, F. (1999). The experience of disaster: Individuals and communities sharing trauma. In R. Gist & B. Lubin (Eds.), *Response to disaster: Psychosocial, ecological, and community approaches* (pp. 25–61). Washington, DC: Taylor & Francis.

Kessler, R. C., Davis, C. G., & Kendler, K. S. (1997). Childhood adversity and adult psychiatric disorder in the U.S. National Comorbidity Survey. *Psychological Medicine, 27,* 1101–1119.

Keyes, C. L. M., & Haidt, J. (2003). *Flourishing: Positive psychology and the life well-lived.* Washington, DC: American Psychological Association.

Larsen, J. T., Hemenover, S. H., Norris, C. J., & Cacioppo, J. T. (2003). Turning adversity to advantage: On the virtues of the coactivation of positive and negative emotions. In L. G. Aspinwall & U. M. Staudinger (Eds.), *A psychology of human strengths: Fundamental questions and future directions for a positive psychology.* Washington, DC: American Psychological Association.

Lazarus, A. A. (1981). *The practice of multimodal therapy.* New York: McGraw-Hill.

Lindemann, E. (1944). Symptomology and management of acute grief. *American Journal of Psychiatry, 101,* 141–148.

Masten, A. S., & Coatsworth, J. D. (1998). The development of competence in favorable and unfavorable environments: Lessons from research on successful children. *American Psychologist, 53,* 205–220.

Masten, A. S., & Reed, M. J. (2002). Resilience in development. In C. R. Snyder & S. J. Lopez (Eds.), *Handbook of positive psychology* (pp. 74–88). New York: Oxford University Press.

McAdams, D. P. (1988). *Power, intimacy, and the life story.* New York: Guilford.

McNally, R. J., Bryant, R. A., & Ehlers, A. (2003). Does early psychological intervention promote recovery from posttraumatic stress? *Psychological Science in the Public Interest, 4,* 45–79.

Myers, D. G. (1993). *The pursuit of happiness: Who is happy—and why.* New York: Avon.

Norris, F. (1992). Epidemiology of trauma: Frequency and impact of different potentially traumatic events on different demographic groups. *Journal of Consulting and Clinical Psychology, 60,* 409–418.

O'Brien, L. S. (1998). *Traumatic events and mental health.* New York: Cambridge University Press.

Park, C. L. (1998). Implications of posttraumatic growth for individuals. In R. G. Tedeschi, C. L. Park, & L. G. Calhoun (Eds.), *Posttraumatic growth: Positive changes in the aftermath of crisis* (pp. 153–178). Mahwah, NJ: Erlbaum.

Presbury, J., Echterling, L. G., & McKee, J. E. (2002). *Ideas and tools for brief counseling.* Upper Saddle River, NJ: Merrill/Prentice Hall.

Resnick, H. S., Kilpatrick, D. G., Dansky, B. S., Saunders, B. E., & Best, C. L. (1993). Prevalence of civilian trauma and posttraumatic stress disorder in a representative national sample of women. *Journal of Consulting and Clinical Psychology, 61,* 984–991.

Ruzek, J. I., Polusny, M. A., & Abueg, F. R. (1998). Assessment and treatment of concurrent posttraumatic stress disorder and substance abuse. In V. M. Follette, J. I. Ruzek, & F. R. Abueg (Eds.), *Cognitive-behavioral therapies for trauma* (pp. 226–255). New York: Guilford.

Ryan, W. (1971). *Blaming the victim.* New York: Pantheon Books.

Ryff, C. D., & Singer, B. (2003a). Ironies of the human condition: Well-being and health on the way to mortality. In L. G. Aspinwall & U. M. Staudinger (Eds.), *A psychology of human strengths: Fundamental questions and future directions for a positive psychology* (pp. 271–287). Washington, DC: American Psychological Association.

Ryff, C. D., & Singer, B. (2003b). Flourishing under fire: Resilience as a prototype of challenged thriving. In C. L. M. Keyes & J. Haidt (Eds.), *Flourishing: Positive psychology and the life well-lived* (pp. 15–36). Washington, DC: American Psychological Association.

Saleebey, D. (Ed.). (1997). *The strengths perspective in social work practice* (2nd ed.). New York: Longman.

Saleebey, D. (2001). *Human behavior and social environments: A biopsychosocial approach.* New York: Columbia University Press.

Saunders, G. R. (1995). The crisis of presence in Italian Pentecostal conversion. *American Ethnologist, 22,* 324–340.

Seligman, M. E. P. (1974). *Helplessness: On depression, development and death.* San Francisco: W. H. Freeman.

Seligman, M. E. P., & Csikszentmihalyi, M. (2000). Positive psychology: An introduction. *American Psychologist, 55,* 5–14.

Slaikeu, K. A. (1990). *Crisis intervention: A handbook for practice and research* (2nd ed.). Boston: Allyn & Bacon.

Snyder, C. R., & Lopez, S. J. (Eds.). (2002). *Handbook of positive psychology.* New York: Oxford University Press.

Taylor, S. E., Wood, J. V., & Lichtman, R. R. (1983). It could be worse: Selective evaluation as a response to victimization. *Journal of Social Issues, 39,* 19–40.

Tedeschi, R. G., & Calhoun, L. G. (1995). *Trauma and transformation: Growing in the aftermath of suffering.* Thousand Oaks, CA: Sage.

Tedeschi, R. G., Park, C. L., & Calhoun, L. G. (Eds.). (1998). *Posttraumatic growth: Positive changes in the aftermath of crisis.* Mahwah, NJ: Erlbaum.

Wagner, A. W., & Linehan, M. M. (1998). Dissociative behavior. In V. M. Follette, J. I. Ruzek, & F. R. Abueg (Eds.), *Cognitive-behavioral therapies for trauma* (pp. 191–225). New York: Guilford.

Wethington, E. (2003). Turning points as opportunities for psychological growth. In C. L. M. Keyes & J. Haidt (Eds.), *Flourishing: Positive psychology and the life well-lived* (pp. 37–53). Washington, DC: American Psychological Association.

Yates, S., Axsom, D., & Tiedeman, K. (1998). The help seeking process for distress after disasters. In R. Gist & B. Lubin (Eds.), *Response to disaster: Psychosocial, ecological, and community approaches.* Washington, DC: Taylor & Francis.

**CHAPTER 2**

Bak, P. (1996). *How nature works: The science of self-organized criticality.* New York: Springer-Verlag.

Benezra, E. E. (1996). Personality factors of individuals who survive traumatic experiences without professional help. *International Journal of Stress Management, 3,* 147–153.

Bowman, M. (1997). *Individual differences in posttraumatic response: Problems with the adversity-distress connection.* Mahwah, NJ: Erlbaum.

Caplan, G. (1964). *Principles of preventive psychiatry.* New York: Basic Books.

Casti, J. L. (1995). *Complexification: Explaining a paradoxical world through the science of surprise.* New York: HarperPerennial.

Chessick, R. D. (1999). *Emotional illness and creativity: A psychoanalytic and phenomenologic study.* Madison, CT: International Universities Press.

Damasio, A. (1994). *Descartes' error: Emotion, reason, and the human brain.* New York: G. P. Putnam.

Fairchild, T. N. (1986). *Crisis intervention strategies for school-based helpers.* Springfield, IL: Charles C Thomas.

Fichter, L. S., Baedke, S. J., & Frangos, W. (2002). *Evolutionary systems.* Harrisonburg, VA: James Madison University.

Fraser, J. S. (1995). Strategic intervention: Constructing the process of rapid change. In

J. H. Weakland & W. A. Ray (Eds.), *Propagations: Thirty years of influence from the Mental Research Institute* (pp. 141–153). New York: Haworth Press.

Fraser, J. S. (1998a). A process view of crisis and crisis intervention: Critique and reformulation. *Crisis Intervention and Time-Limited Treatment, 4,* 125–143.

Fraser, J. S. (1998b). A catalyst model: Guidelines for doing crisis intervention and brief therapy from a process view. *Crisis Intervention and Time-Limited Treatment, 4,* 159–177.

Frazier, P. A., & Burnett, J. W. (1994). Immediate coping strategies among rape victims. *Journal of Counseling and Development, 72,* 633–639.

Gleick, J. (1987). *Chaos: Making a new science.* New York: Viking Penguin.

Horowitz, M. J. (1986). *Stress-response syndromes* (2nd ed.). New York: Aronson.

Janoff-Bulman, R. (1992). *Shattered assumptions: Towards a new psychology of trauma.* New York: Free Press.

Joseph, S. A., Brewin, C. R., Yule, W., & Williams, R. (1993). Causal attributions and post-traumatic stress in adolescents. *Journal of Child Psychology and Psychiatry, 34,* 247–253.

Jung, C. G. (1965). *Memories, dreams, reflections.* New York: Vintage Books.

Kalayjian, A. (1999). Coping through meaning: The community response to the earthquake in Armenia. In E. S. Zinner & M. B. Williams (Eds.), *When a community weeps: Case studies in group survivorship* (pp. 87–101). Levittown, PA: Brunner/Mazel.

Kulber-Ross, E. (1997). *The wheel of life: A memoir of living and dying* (p. 285). New York: Scribner.

Landreth, G. L. (1991). *Play therapy: The art of the relationship.* Muncie, IN: Accelerated Development.

Lewin, R. (1999). *Complexity: Life at the edge of chaos* (2nd ed.). Chicago: University of Chicago Press.

Macklin, M. L., Metzger, L. J., Litz, B. T., & McNally, R. J. (1998). Lower precombat intelligence is a risk factor for posttraumatic stress disorder. *Journal of Consulting and Clinical Psychology, 66,* 323–326.

Masten, A. S., & Reed, M. J. (2002). Resilience in development. In C. R. Snyder & S. J. Lopez (Eds.), *Handbook of positive psychology* (pp. 74–88). New York: Oxford University Press.

McCarroll, J., Ursano, R., Wright, K., & Fullerton, C. (1993). Handling bodies after violent death: Strategies for coping. *American Journal of Orthopsychiatry, 63,* 209–214.

McIntosh, D. N., Cohen, R., & Wortman, C. B. (1993). Religion's role in adjustment to a negative life event: Coping with the loss of a child. *Journal of Personality and Social Psychology, 65,* 812–821.

McMillen, J. C., Smith, E. M., & Fisher, R. H. (1997). Perceived benefit and mental health after three types of disaster. *Journal of Consulting and Clinical Psychology, 65,* 733–739.

Presbury, J., Echterling, L. G., & McKee, J. E. (2002). *Ideas and tools for brief counseling.* Upper Saddle River, NJ: Merrill/Prentice Hall.

Sarason, B. R., Sarason, I. G., & Pierce, G. R. (Eds.). (1990). *Social support: An interactional view.* New York: John Wiley & Sons.

Schwartzberg, S. S., & Janoff-Bulman, R. (1991). Grief and the search for meaning: Exploring the assumptive worlds of bereaved college students. *Journal of Social and Clinical Psychology, 10,* 270–288.

Thompson, S. C. (1985). Finding positive meaning in a stressful event and coping. *Basic and Applied Social Psychology, 6,* 279–295.

Viney, L. L. (1976). The concept of crisis: A tool for clinical psychologists. *Bulletin of the British Psychological Society, 29,* 387–395.

Wagner, A. W., & Linehan, M. M. (1998). Dissociative behavior. In V. M. Follette, J. I. Ruzek, & F. R. Abueg (Eds.), *Cognitive-behavioral therapies for trauma* (pp. 191–225). New York: Guilford.

Wainrib, B. R., & Bloch, E. L. (1998). *Crisis intervention and trauma response: Theory and practice.* New York: Springer-Verlag.

Walker, L. E. A. (1994). *Abused women and survivor therapy: A practical guide for the psychotherapist.* Washington, DC: American Psychological Association.

Witztum, E., & Malkinson, R. (1999). Death of a leader: The social construction of bereavement. In E. S. Zinner & M. B. Williams (Eds.), *When a community weeps: Case studies in group survivorship* (pp. 119–137). Levittown, PA: Brunner/Mazel.

**CHAPTER 3**

Ackerman, D. (1997). *A slender thread: Rediscovering hope at the heart of crisis.* New York: Vintage Books.

Atkins, C. J., Kaplan, R. M., & Toshima, M. T. (1991). Close relationships in the epidemiology of cardiovascular disease. In W. H. Jones & D. Perlman (Eds.), *Advances in personal relationships* (Vol. 3, pp. 207–231). London: Jessica Kingsley.

Bateson, G. (1972). *Steps to an ecology of mind.* New York: Ballantine Books.

Berscheid, E. (2003). The human's greatest strength: Other humans. In L. G. Aspinwall & U. M. Staudinger (Eds.), *A psychology of human strengths: Fundamental questions and future directions for a positive psychology* (pp. 37–47). Washington, DC: American Psychological Association.

Bloom, J. W. (2001). Technology and web counseling. In H. Hackney (Ed.), *Practice issues for the beginning counselor* (pp. 183–202). Boston: Allyn & Bacon.

Bowlby, J. (1969/1982). *Attachment and loss: Vol. 1. Attachment.* New York: Basic Books.

Bowlby, J. (1973). *Attachment and loss: Vol. 2. Separation: Anxiety and anger.* New York: Basic Books.

Bowlby, J. (1977). The making and breaking of affectional bonds. *British Journal of Psychiatry, 130,* 201–210, 421–431.

Bowlby, J. (1980). *Attachment and loss: Vol. 3. Loss, sadness, and depression.* New York: Basic Books.

Buck, R., & Ginsburg, B. (1997). Communicative genes and the evolution of empathy. In W. lckes (Ed.), *Empathic accuracy* (pp. 17–43). New York: Guilford.

Carter, C. S. (1998). Neuroendocrine perspectives on social attachment and love. *Psychoneuroendocrinology, 23,* 779–818.

de Waal, F. (1996). *Good natured: The origins of right and wrong in humans and other animals.* Cambridge, MA: Harvard University Press.

Echterling, L. G., & Hartsough, D. M. (1989). Phases of helping in successful crisis telephone calls. *Journal of Community Psychology, 17,* 249–257.

Eisenberg, N., Murphy, B. C., & Shepard, S. (1997). The development of empathic accuracy. In W. lckes (Ed.), *Empathic accuracy* (pp. 73–115). New York: Guilford.

Feeny, M. (2001). Better than being there. *Psychotherapy Networker, March/April, 25,* 31–70.

Flavell, J. H. (1992). Perspectives on perspective taking. In H. Berlin & P. Pufall (Eds.), *Piaget's theory: Prospects and possibilities* (pp. 107–139). Hillsdale, NJ: Erlbaum.

Frank, J. D., & Frank, J. B. (1991). *Persuasion and healing: A comparative study of psychotherapy* (3rd ed.). Baltimore: Johns Hopkins University Press.

Friedman, S. (1997). *Time-effective psychotherapy: Maximizing outcomes in an era of minimized resources.* Boston: Allyn & Bacon.

Goleman, D. (1995). *Emotional intelligence.* New York: Bantam Books.

Holahan, C. J., Moos, R. H., Holahan, C. K., & Brennan, P. L. (1996). Social support, coping strategies, and psychosocial adjustment to cardiac illness: Implications for assessment and prevention. *Journal of Prevention and Intervention in the Community, 13,* 33–52.

Kleespies, P. M., & Blackburn, E. J. (1998). The emergency telephone call. In P. M. Kleespies (Ed.), *Emergencies in mental health practice* (pp. 174–195). New York: Guilford.

Murphy, L., & Mitchell, D. (1998). When writing helps to heal: E-mail as therapy. *British Journal of Guidance and Counselling, 26,* 21–32.

Niederhoffer, K. G., & Pennebaker, J. W. (2002). Sharing one's story: On the benefits of writing or talking about emotional experience. In C. R. Snyder & S. J. Lopez (Eds.), *Handbook of positive psychology* (pp. 573–583). New York: Oxford University Press.

Pennebaker, J. W., Francis, M. E., & Booth, R. J. (2001). *Linguistic Inquiry and Word Count (LIWC 2001): A computerized text analysis program.* Mahwah, NJ: Erlbaum.

Pennebaker, J. W., & Graybeal, A. (2001). Patterns of natural language use: Disclosure, personality, and social integration. *Current Directions in Psychological Science, 10,* 90–93.

Piaget, J. (1926). *The language and thought of the child.* New York: Harcourt.

Reis, H. T., Collins, W. A., & Berscheid, E. (2000). The relationship context of human behavior and development. *Psychological Bulletin, 126,* 844–872.

Rimé, B. (1995). Mental rumination, social sharing, and the recovery from emotional exposure. In J. W. Pennebaker (Ed.), *Emotion, disclosure, and health* (pp. 271–291). Washington, DC: American Psychological Association.

Roberts, A. R., & Comasso, M. J. (1994). Staff turnover at crisis intervention units and services: A national survey. *Crisis Intervention and Time-Limited Treatment, 1,* 1–9.

Walter, J. L., & Peller, J. E. (1992). *Becoming solution-focused in brief therapy.* New York: Brunner/Mazel.

Wampold, B. E. (2001). *The great psychotherapy debate: Models, methods, and findings.* Mahwah, NJ: Erlbaum.

Waters, J., & Finn, E. (1995). Handling client crises effectively on the telephone. In A. Roberts (Ed.), *Crisis intervention and time-limited cognitive treatment* (pp. 251–289). Thousand Oaks, CA: Sage.

West, M. L., & Sheldon-Keller, A. E. (1997). *Patterns of relating: An adult attachment perspective.* New York: Guilford.

White, M., & Epston, D. (1990). *Narrative means to therapeutic ends.* New York: W. W. Norton.

Witmer, J. M. (1986). *Pathways to personal growth.* Muncie, IN: Accelerated Development.

**CHAPTER 4**

Brown, R., & Kulik, J. (1977). Flashbulb memories. *Cognition, 5,* 73–99.

Bruner, J. S. (1987). Life as narrative. *Social Research, 54,* 11–32.

Camus, A. (1955). *The myth of Sisyphus and other essays.* New York: Alfred A. Knopf.

Christianson, S. A. (1989). Flashbulb memories: Special, but not so special. *Memory and Cognition, 17,* 435–443.

Davis, C. G. (2002). The tormented and the transformed: Understanding responses to loss and trauma. In R. A. Neimeyer (Ed.), *Meaning reconstruction and the experience of loss* (pp. 137–155). Washington, DC: American Psychological Association.

de Shazer, S. (1985). *Keys to solutions in brief therapy.* New York: W. W. Norton.

Echterling, L. G., & Wylie, M. L. (1999). In the public arena: Disaster as a socially constructed problem. In R. Gist & B. Lubin (Eds.), *Response to disaster: Psychosocial, ecological, and community approaches* (pp. 327–346). Washington, DC: Taylor & Francis.

Emmons, R. A. (1999). *The psychology of ultimate concerns: Motivation and spirituality in personality.* New York: Guilford.

Emmons, R. A. (2003). Personal goals, life meaning, and virtue: Wellsprings of a positive life. In C. L. M. Keyes & J. Haidt (Eds.), *Flourishing: Positive psychology and the life well-lived* (pp. 105–128). Washington, DC: American Psychological Association.

Ferrara, K. W. (1994). *Therapeutic ways with words.* New York: Oxford University Press.

Frankl, V. E. (1969). *The will to meaning: Foundations and applications of logotherapy.* New York: New American Library.

French, S., & Joseph, S. (1999). Religiosity and its association with happiness, purpose in life, and self-actualization. *Mental Health, Religion & Culture, 2,* 117–120.

Gergen, K. J. (1997). *Realities and relationships: Soundings in social construction.* Cambridge, MA: Harvard University Press.

Guerber, H. A. (1960). *The myths of Greece & Rome.* London: George G. Harrap. (Original work published 1907)

Herman, J. L. (1992). *Trauma and recovery.* New York: Basic Books.

Janoff-Bulman, R. (1992). *Shattered assumptions: Towards a new psychology of trauma.* New York: Free Press.

Kaufmann, W. A. (1975). *Existentialism from Dostoevsky to Sartre.* New York: New American Library.

Korzybski, A. (1933). *Science and sanity.* Lakeville, CT: International Non-Aristotelian Library.

Labov, W. (1982). Speech actions and reactions in personal narrative. In D. Tannen (Ed.), *Analyzing discourse: Text and talk* (pp. 219–247). Washington, DC: Georgetown University Press.

Lepore, S. J., & Smyth, J. M. (2002). *The writing cure: How expressive writing promotes health and emotional well-being.* Washington, DC: American Psychological Association.

Loftus, E. F., & Palmer, J. C. (1974). Reconstruction of automobile destruction: An example of the interaction between language and memory. *Journal of Learning and Verbal Behavior, 13,* 585–589.

Luborsky, L., & Crits-Christolph, P. (1990) *Understanding transference: The CCRT method.* New York: Basic Books.

McAdams, D. P. (1988). *Power, intimacy, and the life story.* New York: Guilford.

McAdams, D. P. (1996). Personality, modernity, and the storied self: A contemporary framework for studying persons. *Psychological Inquiry, 7,* 295–321.

McLeod, J. (1998). *An introduction to counselling* (2nd ed.). Buckingham, GB: Open University Press.

Milo, E. M. (2002). The death of a child with a developmental disability. In R. A. Neimeyer (Ed.), *Meaning reconstruction and the experience of loss* (pp. 137–155). Washington, DC: American Psychological Association.

Nakamura, J., & Csikszentmihalyi, M. (2003). The construction of meaning through vital engagement. In C. L. M. Keyes & J. Haidt (Eds.), *Flourishing: Positive psychology and the life well-lived* (pp. 83–104). Washington, DC: American Psychological Association.

Neimeyer, R. A. (2000). Searching for the meaning of meaning: Grief therapy and the process of reconstruction. *Death Studies, 24,* 541–558.

Neisser, U., Winograd, E., Bergman, E. T., Schreiber, C. A., Palmer, S. E., & Weldon, M. D. (1996). Remembering the earthquake: Direct experience vs. hearing the news. *Memory, 4,* 337–357.

Payne, M. (2000). *Narrative therapy: An introduction for counsellors.* London: Sage Publications.

Pennebaker, J. W. (2002). What our words can say about us: Toward a broader language psychology. *Psychological Science Agenda, 15*(1), 8–9.

Piaget, J. (1972). *The psychology of intelligence.* Totowa, NJ: Littlefield Adams.

Pillemer, D. B. (1998). *Momentous events, vivid memories.* Cambridge, MA: Harvard University Press.

Polkinghorne, D. E. (1988) *Narrative knowing and the human sciences.* Albany, NY: State University of New York Press.

Seligman, M. E. P. (1974). *Helplessness: On depression, development and death.* San Francisco: W. H. Freeman.

Smyth, J. M., & Pennebaker, J. W. (1999). Sharing one's story: Translating emotional experiences into words as a coping tool. In C. R. Snyder (Ed.), *Coping: The psychology of what works* (pp. 70–89). New York: Oxford University.

Wainrib, B. R., & Bloch, E. L. (1998). *Crisis intervention and trauma response.* New York: Springer.

Wethington, E. (2003). Turning points as opportunities for psychological growth. In C. L. M. Keyes & J. Haidt (Eds.), *Flourishing: Positive psychology and the life well-lived* (pp. 37–53). Washington, DC: American Psychological Association.

White, M., & Epston, D. (1990). *Narrative means to therapeutic ends.* New York: W. W. Norton.

Wong, P. T. P., & Fry, P. S. (Eds.). (1998). *Handbook of personal meaning: Theory, research, and application.* Mahwah, NJ: Erlbaum.

**CHAPTER 5**

Bifulco, A., & Brown, G. W. (1996). Cognitive coping response to crises and onset of depression. *Social Psychiatry and Psychiatric Epidemiology, 31,* 163–172.

Bowman, M. (1997). *Individual differences in posttraumatic response: Problems with the adversity-distress connection.* Mahwah, NJ: Erlbaum.

Breggin, P. R. (1997). Psychotherapy in emotional crises without resort to psychiatric medications. *Humanistic Psychologist, 25,* 2–14.

Bruner, J. (1986). *Actual minds, possible worlds.* Cambridge, MA: Harvard University Press.

Corey, G. (1991). Invited commentary on macrostrategies for delivery of mental health counseling services. *Journal of Mental Health Counseling, 13,* 51–57.

Damasio, A. (1994). *Descartes' error: Emotion, reason, and the human brain.* New York: G. P. Putnam.

Davidson, R. J. (1993). Parsing affective space: Perspectives from neuropsychology and psychophysiology. *Neuropsychology, 7,* 464–475.

Emmons, R. A., Colby, P. M., & Kaiser, H. A. (1998). When losses lead to gains: Personal goals and the recovery of meaning. In P. T. P. Wong & P. S. Fry (Eds.), *The human quest for meaning: A handbook of psychological research and clinical applications* (pp. 163–178). Mahwah, NJ: Erlbaum.

Fernandez-Ballesteros, R. (2003). Light and dark in the psychology of human strengths: The example of psychogerontology. In L. G. Aspinwall & U. M. Staudinger (Eds.), *A psychology of human strengths: Fundamental questions and future directions for a positive psychology* (pp. 131–147). Washington, DC: American Psychological Association.

Frankl, V. E. (1969). *The will to meaning: Foundations and applications of Logotherapy.* New York: Plume/New American.

Frederickson, B. L. (1998). What good are positive emotions? *Review of General Psychology, 3,* 300–319.

Frederickson, B. L. (2002). Positive emotions. In C. R. Snyder & S. J. Lopez (Eds.), *Handbook of positive psychology* (pp. 120–134). New York: Oxford University Press.

Folkman, S., & Moskowitz, J. T. (2000). Stress, positive emotion, and coping. *Current Directions in Psychological Science, 9,* 115–118.

Goleman, D. (1995). *Emotional intelligence.* New York: Bantam Books.

Gross, J. J. (1998). The emerging field of emotion regulation: An integrative review. *Review of General Psychology, 2,* 271–299.

Gross, J. L., & Munoz, R. F. (1995). Emotion regulation and mental health. *Clinical Psychology: Science and Practice, 2,* 151–164.

Haidt, J. (2003) Elevation and the positive psychology of morality. In C. L. M. Keyes & J. Haidt (Eds.), *Flourishing: Positive psychology and the life well-lived* (pp. 275–289). Washington, DC: American Psychological Association.

Hampden-Turner, C. (1981). *Maps of the mind.* New York: Collier Books.

Hothersall, D. (1990). *History of psychology* (2nd ed.). New York: McGraw-Hill.

Kalayjian, A. (1999). Coping through meaning: The community response to the earthquake in Armenia. In E. S. Zinner & M. B. Williams (Eds.), *When a community weeps: Case studies in group survivorship* (pp. 87–110). Levittown, PA: Brunner/Mazel.

Kanel, K. (2003). *A guide to crisis intervention* (2nd ed.). Pacific Grove, CA: Brooks/Cole.

Keltner, D., & Haidt, J. (2003). Approaching awe, a moral, spiritual, and aesthetic emotion. *Cognition and Emotion, 17,* 297–314.

Kosslyn, S. M., & Koenig, O. (1995). *Wet mind: The new cognitive neuroscience.* New York: Free Press.

Larsen, J. T., Hemenover, S. H., Norris, C. J., & Cacioppo, J. T. (2003). Turning adversity to advantage: On the virtues of the coactivation of positive and negative emotions. In L. G. Aspinwall & U. M. Staudinger (Eds.), *A psychology of human strengths: Fundamental questions and future directions for a positive psychology* (pp. 211–225). Washington, DC: American Psychological Association.

Lazarus, R. S. (1991). *Emotion and adaptation.* New York: Oxford University Press.

LeDoux, J. (1996). *The emotional brain: The mysterious underpinnings of emotional life.* New York: Simon & Schuster.

Levenson, R. W., Ekman, P., Heider, K., & Friesen, W. V. (1992). Emotion and autonomic nervous system activity in the Minangkabau of West Sumatra. *Journal of Personality and Social Psychology, 62,* 972–988.

Lindemann, E. (1944). Symptomatology and management of acute grief. *American Journal of Psychiatry, 101,* 141–148.

Martindale, C. (1981). *Cognition and consciousness.* Homewood, IL: The Dorsey Press.

McCullough, M. E., Kilpatrick, S. D., Emmons, R. A., & Larson, D. B. (2001). Is gratitude a moral affect? *Psychological Bulletin, 127,* 249–266.

Milo, E. M. (2001). The death of a child with a developmental disability. In R. A. Neimeyer (Ed.), *Meaning reconstruction and the experience of loss* (pp. 113–134). Washington, DC: American Psychological Association.

Novaco, R. W., & Chemtob, C. M. (1998). Anger and trauma: Conceptualization, assessment and treatment. In V. M. Follette, J. I. Ruzek, & F. R. Abueg (Eds.), *Cognitive-behavioral therapies for trauma* (pp. 162–190). New York: Guilford.

Niederhoffer, K. G., & Pennebaker, J. W. (2002). Sharing one's story: On the benefits of writing or talking about emotional experience. In C. R. Snyder & S. J. Lopez (Eds.), *Handbook of positive psychology* (pp. 573–583). New York: Oxford University Press.

Oatley, K., & Jenkins, J. M. (1996). *Understanding emotions.* Cambridge, MA: Blackwell.

O'Brien, L. S. (1998). *Traumatic events and mental health.* New York: Cambridge University Press.

Puryear, D. A. (1979). *Helping people in crisis.* San Francisco: Jossey-Bass.

Snyder, C. R. (2002). Hope theory: Rainbows of the mind. *Psychological Inquiry, 13,* 249–275.

Snyder, C. R., Michael, S. T., & Cheavens, J. S. (1999). Hope as a psychotherapeutic foundation of common factors, placebos, and expectancies. In M. A. Hubble, B. L. Duncan, & S. D. Miller (Eds.), *The heart and soul of change: What works in therapy* (pp. 179–200). Washington, DC: American Psychological Association.

Stein, N., Folkman, S., Trabasso, T., & Richards, T. A. (1997). Appraisal and goal processes as predictors of psychological well-being in bereaved caregivers. *Journal of Personality and Social Psychology, 72,* 872–884.

Vaughan, S. C. (1997). *The talking cure.* New York: Henry Holt & Company.

Watson, D. (2002). Positive affectivity: The disposition to experience pleasurable emotional states. In C. R. Snyder & S. J. Lopez (Eds.), *Handbook of positive psychology* (pp. 106–119). New York: Oxford University Press.

Williams, R., & Williams, V. (1998). *Anger kills: Seventeen strategies for controlling the hostility that can harm your health.* New York: Harper.

**CHAPTER 6**

Bateson, G. (1972). *Steps to an ecology of mind.* New York: Ballantine Books.

Berg, I. K. (1991). *Solution-focused approach to family-based services.* Milwaukee, WI: Brief Family Therapy Center.

De Jong, P., & Berg, I. K. (1998). *Interviewing for solutions.* Pacific Grove, CA: Brooks/Cole.

de Shazer, S. (1985). *Keys to solution in brief therapy.* New York: W. W. Norton.

Dolan, Y. M. (1985). *A path with a heart: Ericksonian utilization with resistant and chronic clients.* New York: Brunner/Mazel.

Emmons, R. A. (1999). *The psychology of ultimate concerns: Motivation and spirituality in personality.* New York: Guilford.

Erickson, M. H. (1954). Pseudo-orientation in time as a hypnotic procedure. *Journal of Clinical and Experimental Hypnosis, 2,* 261–283.

Erickson, M. H., & Rossi, E. L. (1979). *Hypnotherapy.* New York: Irvington.

Furman, B., & Ahola, T. (1992). *Solution talk: Hosting therapeutic conversations.* New York: W. W. Norton.

Lankton, S. R., & Lankton, C. H. (1986). *Enchantment and intervention in family therapy: Training in Ericksonian approaches.* New York: Brunner/Mazel.

Nyland, D. & Thomas, J. (1994). The economics of narrative. *The Family Therapy Networker,* Nov./Dec., 38–39.

O'Hanlon, B., & Beadle, S. (1994). *A field guide to possibility land: Possibility therapy methods.* Omaha, NE: Possibility Press.

Palmer, D. (1994). *Looking at philosophy: The unbearable heaviness of philosophy made lighter* (2nd ed.). Mountain View, CA: Mayfield Pub. Co.

Rychlak, J. F. (1980). Concepts of free will in modern psychological science. *The Journal of Mind and Behavior, 1,* 9–32.

Seligman, M. E. P. (1991). *Learned optimism.* New York: A. A. Knopf.

Sklare, G. B. (1997). *Brief counseling that works: A solution-focused approach for school counselors.* Thousand Oaks, CA: Corwin Press.

Walter, J. L., & Peller, J. E. (1992). *Becoming solution-focused in brief therapy.* New York: Brunner/Mazel.

**CHAPTER 7**

Ackerman, D. (1997). *A slender thread: Rediscovering hope at the heart of crisis.* New York: Vintage Books.

American Foundation for Suicide Prevention (2004, December 12). *United States Suicide Rates: 1900–1999.* Retrieved April 15, 2004, from http://www.afsp.org/statistics/USA.htm

Busch, K. A., Fawcett, J., & Jacobs, D. G. (2003). Clinical correlates of inpatient suicide. *Journal of Clinical Psychiatry, 64,* 14–19.

Card, J. J. (1974). Lethality of suicidal methods and suicide risk: Two distinct concepts. *Omega, 5,* 37–45.

Clark, D. C. (1998). The evaluation and management of the suicidal patient. In P. M. Kleespies (Ed.), *Emergencies in mental health practice* (pp. 75–94). New York: Guilford.

DeJong, P., & Berg, I. K. (2002). *Interviewing for solutions* (2nd ed.). Pacific Grove, CA: Brooks/Cole.

Drew, B. L. (2001). Self-harm behavior and no-suicide contracting in psychiatric inpatient settings. *Archives of Psychiatric Nursing, 15,* 99–106.

Drye, R. D., Goulding, R., & Goulding, M. (1973). The no-suicide decision: Patient monitoring of suicidal risk. *American Journal of Psychiatry, 130,* 171–174.

Fowler, R. C., Rich, C. L., & Young, D. (1986). San Diego suicide study: Substance abuse in young cases. *Archives of General Psychiatry, 43,* 962–965.

Hendin, H. (1995). *Suicide in America.* New York: W. W. Norton.

Henriques, G., Beck, A. T., & Brown, G. K. (2003). Cognitive therapy for adolescent and young adult suicide attempters. *American Behavioral Scientist, 46,* 1258–1268.

Jacobs, D. G., Brewer, M., & Klein-Benheim, M. (1999). Suicide assessment: An overview and recommended protocol. In D. G. Jacobs (Ed.), *The Harvard Medical School guide to suicide assessment and intervention* (pp. 3–39). San Francisco: Jossey-Bass.

Kaplan, M. S., Adamek, M. E., & Johnson, S. (1994). Trends in firearm suicide among older American males, 1979–1988. *Gerontologist, 34,* 59–65.

Maslow, A. H. (1966). *The psychology of science: A reconnaissance.* Chicago: Henry Regery.

McNally, R. J., Bryant, R. A., & Ehlers, A. (2003). Does early psychological intervention promote recovery from posttraumatic stress? *Psychological Science in the Public Interest, 4,* 45–79.

Menninger, K. (1973). *Sparks.* New York: Crowell.

Moscicki, E. K. (1999). Epidemiology of suicide. In D. G. Jacobs (Ed.), *The Harvard Medical School guide to suicide assessment and intervention* (pp. 40–51). San Francisco: Jossey-Bass.

National Institute of Mental Health (2004, April 9). *U.S. Suicide Rates by Age, Gender, and Racial Group.* Retrieved April 15, 2004, from http://www.nimh.nih.gov/SuicideResearch/Suichart.cfm

Paulson, B. L., & Worth, M. (2002). Counseling for suicide: Client perspectives. *Journal of Counseling and Development, 80,* 86–93.

Rich, C. L., Warstadt, G. M., Nemiroff, R. A., Fowler, R. C., & Young, D. (1991). Suicide, stressors and the life cycle. *American Journal of Psychiatry, 148,* 524–527.

Rogers, J. R., Lewis, M. M., & Subich, L. M. (2002). Validity of the Suicide Assessment Checklist in an emergency crisis center. *Journal of Counseling and Development, 80,* 493–502.

Shneidman, E. (1999). Perturbation and lethality: A psychological approach to assessment and intervention. In D. G. Jacobs (Ed.), *The Harvard Medical School guide to suicide assessment and intervention* (pp. 83–97). San Francisco: Jossey-Bass.

Tedeschi, R. G., Park, C. L., & Calhoun, L. G. (Eds.). (1998). *Posttraumatic growth: Positive changes in the aftermath of crisis.* Mahwah, NJ: Erlbaum.

Wainrib, B. R., & Bloch, E. L. (1998). *Crisis intervention and trauma response: Theory and practice.* New York: Springer.

Walker, L. E. A. (1994). *Abused women and survivor therapy: A practical guide for the psychotherapist.* Washington, DC: American Psychological Association.

Weiss, A. (2001). The no-suicide contract: Possibilities and pitfalls. *American Journal of Psychotherapy, 55,* 414–419.

**CHAPTER 8**

Barker, P. (1992). *Basic family therapy* (3rd ed.) New York: Oxford University Press.

Becvar, D. S., & Becvar, R. J. (1988). *Family therapy: A systematic integration.* Boston: Allyn & Bacon.

Butz, M. R., Chamberlain, L. L., & McCown, W. G. (1997). *Strange attractors: Chaos, complexity, and the art of family therapy.* New York: John Wiley & Sons.

Caplan, G. (1964). *Principles of preventive psychiatry.* New York: Basic Books.

Chamberlain, L. (1998). An introduction to chaos and nonlinear dynamics. In L. Chamberlain & M. R. Butz (Eds.), *Clinical chaos: A therapist's guide to nonlinear dynamics and therapeutic change* (pp. 3–14). Philadelphia: Brunner/Mazel.

Conlin, M. (2003). Unmarried America. *Business Week,* October 20.

Day, S. X. (2004). *Theory and design in counseling and psychotherapy.* Boston: Lahaska Press.

Erikson, E. H. (1963). *Childhood and society.* New York: W. W. Norton.

Goldenberg, I., & Goldenberg, H. (1991). *Family therapy: An overview* (3rd ed.). Monterey, CA: Brooks/Cole.

Hudgens, B. (1998). Dynamical family systems and therapeutic intervention. In L. Chamberlain & M. R. Butz (Eds.), *Clinical chaos: A therapist's guide to nonlinear dynamics and therapeutic change* (pp. 115–126). Philadelphia: Brunner/Mazel.

Kanel, K. (2003). *A guide to crisis intervention* (2nd ed.). Pacific Grove, CA: Brooks/Cole.

Kantor, D., & Lehr, W. (1975). *Inside the family: Toward a theory of family process.* San Francisco: Jossey-Bass.

Kauffman, S. A. (1991, August). Antichaos and adaptation. *Scientific American, 265*(2), 78–84.

Marcia, J. E. (1983). Some directions for the investigation of ego development in early adolescence. *Journal of Early Adolescence, 3,* 215–223.

Nichols, M. P., & Schwartz, R. C. (1998). *Family therapy: Concepts and methods.* Boston: Allyn & Bacon.

Olson, D. (1986). Circumplex Model VII: Validation studies and FACES III. *Family Process, 25,* 337–351.

Olson, D., Russell, C. S., & Sprenkle, D. H. (1983). Circumplex Model of marital and family systems: VI. Theoretical update. *Family Process, 22,* 69–83.

Prigogine, I., & Stengers, I. (1984). *Order out of chaos: Man's new dialogue with nature.* New York: Bantam Books.

Tageson, C. W. (1982). *Humanistic psychology: A synthesis.* Homewood, IL: Dorsey Press.

**CHAPTER 9**

Armstrong, K., O'Callahan, W., & Marmar, C. R. (1991). Debriefing Red Cross disaster personnel: The multiple stressor debriefing model. *Journal of Traumatic Stress, 4,* 581–593.

Bohl, N. (1995). Professionally administered critical incident debriefing for police officers. In M. I. Kunke

& E. M. Scrivner (Eds.), *Police psychology into the 21st century* (pp. 169–188). Hillsdale, NJ: Erlbaum.

Burrow, T. (1928). The basis of group analysis, or the analysis of the reactions of normal and neurotic individuals. *British Journal of Medical Psychology, 8,* 198–206.

Carll, E. K. (1995). Trauma psychology: Psychological interventions in the aftermath of disaster and crisis. In L. Vandecreek, S. Knapp, & T. L. Jackson (Eds.), *Innovations in clinical practice: A source book* (Vol. 14, pp. 5–12). Sarasota, FL: Professional Resource Press.

DeJong, P., & Berg, I. K. (2002). *Interviewing for solutions* (2nd ed.). Pacific Grove, CA: Brooks/Cole.

Dies, R. R. (1993). Research on group psychotherapy: Overview and clinical applications. In A. Alonso & H. I. Swiller (Eds.), *Group therapy in clinical practice* (pp. 473–518). Washington, DC: American Psychiatric Press.

Dixon, P. (1991). Vicarious victims of a maritime disaster. *British Journal of Guidance and Counseling, 19,* 8–12.

Dyregrov, A. (1997). The process in psychological debriefings. *Journal of Traumatic Stress, 10,* 589–605.

Eisenbruch, M. (1992). Toward a culturally sensitive DSM: Cultural bereavement in Cambodian refugees and the traditional healer as taxonomist. *Journal of Nervous and Mental Disease, 180,* 8–10.

Everly, G. S., Jr., & Mitchell, J. T. (1999). *Critical Incident Stress Management (CISM): A new era and standard of care in crisis intervention* (2nd ed.). Ellicott City, MD: Chevron.

Gist, R., & Woodall, S. J. (1999). There are no simple solutions to complex problems: The rise and fall of critical incident stress debriefing as a response to occupational stress in the fire service. In R. Gist & B. Lubin (Eds.), *Response to disaster: Psychosocial, ecological, and community approaches* (pp. 1–20). Washington, DC: Taylor & Francis.

Gladding, S. T. (1999). *Group work: A counseling specialty* (3rd ed.). Upper Saddle River, NJ: Merrill/Prentice Hall.

Imber-Black, E., & Roberts, J. (1992). *Rituals for our times.* New York: HarperCollins.

Karakashian, M. (1994). Countertransference issues in crisis work with natural disaster victims. *Psychotherapy, 31,* 334–341.

Kenardy, J. A., Webster, R. A., Lewin, T. J., Carr, V. J., Hazell, P. L., & Carter, G. L. (1996). Stress debriefing and patterns of recovery following a natural disaster. *Journal of Traumatic Stress, 9,* 37–49.

Kline, W. B. (2003). *Interactive group counseling and therapy.* Upper Saddle River, NJ: Merrill/Prentice Hall.

McCammon, S. L., & Long, T. E. (1993). A post-tornado support group: Survivors and professionals in concert [Special issue]. *Journal of Social Behavior and Personality, 8,* 131–148.

McNally, R. J., Bryant, R. A., & Ehlers, A. (2003). Does early psychological intervention promote recovery from posttraumatic stress? *Psychological Science in the Public Interest, 4,* 45–79.

Miller, L. (1998). *Shocks to the system: Psychotherapy of traumatic disability syndromes.* New York: W. W. Norton.

Mitchell, J. (1988). The history, status and future of critical incident stress debriefings. *Journal of the Emergency Medical Services, 13,* 47–52.

Mitchell, J., & Bray, G. (1990). *Emergency services stress: Guidelines for preserving the health and careers of emergency services personnel.* Upper Saddle River, NJ: Prentice Hall.

Mitchell, J., & Everly, G. S. (2001). *Critical incident stress debriefing: An operations manual for CISD, defusing and other group crisis intervention services* (3rd ed). Ellicott City, MD: Chevron.

Pratt, J. H. (1907). The class method of treating consumption in the homes of the poor. *Journal of the American Medical Association, 49,* 755–759.

Reif, L. V., Patton, M. J., & Gold, P. B. (1995). Bereavement, stress, and social support in members of a self-help group. *Journal of Community Psychology, 23,* 292–306.

Robinson, R. C., & Mitchell, J. T. (1993). Evaluation of psychological debriefings. *Journal of Traumatic Stress, 6,* 367–382.

Rose, S., Bisson, J., & Wessely, S. (2001). Psychological debriefing for preventing post traumatic stress disorder (PTSD) (Cochrane Library, Issue 3). Oxford: Update Software.

Rose, S., Bisson, J., & Wessely, S. (2003). A systematic review of single psychological interventions ('debriefing') following trauma. Updating the Cochrane review and implications for good practice. In R. Orner & U. Schnyder (Eds.), *Reconstructing early intervention after trauma: Innovations in the care of survivors* (pp. 24–39) Oxford: Oxford University Press.

Shapiro, J. L., Peltz, L. S., & Bernadett-Shapiro, S. (1998). *Brief group treatment: Practical training for*

therapists and counselors. Pacific Grove, CA: Brooks/Cole.

Solomon, R. M. (1995). Critical incident stress management in law enforcement. In G. S. Everly (Ed.), *Innovations in disaster and trauma psychology: Applications in emergency services and disaster response* (pp. 123–157). Baltimore: Chevron.

Stephens, C. (1997). Debriefing, social support and PTSD in the New Zealand police: Testing a multi-dimensional model of organizational traumatic stress. *The Australasian Journal of Disaster and Trauma Studies, 1.* Retrieved *April 5,* 2004, from http://www.massey.ac.nz/~trauma/issues/1997–1/cvs1.htm.

Tedeschi, R. G., & Calhoun, L. G. (1995). *Trauma and transformation: Growing in the aftermath of suffering.* Thousand Oaks, CA: Sage.

Turnbull, C. (1990). Luminality: A synthesis of subjective and objective experience. In R. Schechner & W. Appel (Eds.), *By means of performance.* New York: Cambridge University Press.

van Emmerik, A. A. P., Kamphuis, J. H., Hulsbosch, A. M., & Emmelkamp, P. M. G. (2002). Single session debriefing after psychological trauma: A meta-analysis. *Lancet, 360,* 766–771.

Woodall, S. J. (1997). Hearts on fire: An exploration of the emotional world of firefighters. *Clinical Sociology Review, 15,* 153–162.

Yalom, I. D. (1995). *The theory and practice of group psychotherapy* (4th ed.). New York: Basic Books.

## CHAPTER 10

Ahler, J. G., & Tamney, J. B. (1964). Some functions of religious ritual in a catastrophe. *Sociological Analysis, 25,* 212–230.

American Red Cross. (1991). *Disaster mental health services: Disaster services regulations and procedures* (ARC Document No. 3050M). Alexandria, VA: Author.

Armstrong, K., O'Callahan, W., & Marmar, C. R. (1991). Debriefing Red Cross disaster personnel: The multiple stressor debriefing model. *Journal of Traumatic Stress, 4,* 581–593.

Barnes-Svarney, P., & Svarney, T. E. (1999). *Skies of fury.* New York: Touchstone.

Baum, A. (1987). Toxins, technology, and natural disasters. In G. R. VandenBos & B. K. Bryant (Eds.), *Cataclysms, crises, and catastrophes: Psychology in action* (pp. 9–53). Washington, DC: American Psychological Association.

Bradfield, C., Echterling, L. G., & Wylie, M. L. (1989). After the flood: The response of ministers to a natural disaster. *Sociological Analysis, 49*(4), 397–407.

Bushnell, J. H. (1969). Hupa reaction to the Trinity River floods: Post-hoc recourse to aboriginal belief. *Anthropological Quarterly, 42,* 316–324.

Butcher, J. N., & Dunn, L. A. (1989). Human responses and treatment needs in airline disasters. In R. Gist & B. Lubin (Eds.), *Psychosocial aspects of disaster* (pp. 86–119). New York: John Wiley & Sons.

Carll, E. K. (1996). *Developing a comprehensive disaster and crisis response program for mental health: Guidelines and procedures.* Albany, NY: New York State Psychological Association.

Dundes, A. (1987). At ease, disease—AIDS jokes as sick humor. *American Behavioral Scientist, 30,* 72–81.

Dyregrov, A., Kristoffersen, J. I., & Gjestad, R. (1996). Voluntary and professional disaster-workers: Similarities and differences in reactions. *Journal of Traumatic Stress, 9,* 541–556.

Echterling, L. G. (1989). An ark of prevention: Preventing school absenteeism following a flood. *Journal of Primary Prevention, 9,* 177–184.

Echterling, L. G., Bradfield, C., & Wylie, M. L. (1992, August). *Six years after the flood: Clergy's long-term response to disaster.* Poster session presented at the annual meeting of the American Psychological Association, Washington, DC.

Echterling, L. G., & Wylie, M. L. (1999). In the public arena: Disaster as a socially constructed problem. In R. Gist & B. Lubin (Eds.), *Response to disaster: Psychosocial, ecological, and community approaches* (pp. 327–346). Washington, DC: Taylor & Francis.

Elliott, D. (1989). Tales from the darkside: Ethical implications of disaster coverage. In L. M. Walters, L. Wilkins, & T. Walters (Eds.), *Bad tidings: Communication and catastrophe* (pp. 161–170). Hillsdale, NJ: Erlbaum.

Erikson, K. T. (1994). *A new species of trouble: Explorations in disaster, trauma, and community.* New York: W. W. Norton.

Fine, G. A. (1995). Public narration and group culture: Discerning discourse in social movements. In H. Johnston & B. Klandermans (Eds.), *Social movements and culture.* Minneapolis, MN: University of Minnesota Press.

Fischer, H. W. (1994). *Response to disaster: Fact versus fiction and its perpetuation: The sociology of disaster.* Lanham, MD: University Press of America.

Freedy, J. R., Kilpatrick, D. G., & Resnick, H. S. (1993). Natural disasters and mental health: Theory, assessment, and intervention. In R. Allen (Ed.), Handbook of post-disaster interventions [Special issue]. *Journal of Social Behavior and Personality, 8,* 49–103.

Gans, H. J. (1979). *Deciding what's news.* New York: Random House.

Gibbs, M. S., Drummond, J., & Lachenmeyer, J. R. (1993). Effects of disasters on emergency workers: A review, with implications for training and post-disaster interventions [Special issue]. *Journal of Social Behavior and Personality, 8,* 189–212.

Gist, R., Lubin, B., & Redburn, B. G. (1999). Psychosocial, ecological, and community perspectives on disaster response. In R. Gist & B. Lubin (Eds.), *Response to disaster: Psychosocial, ecological, and community approaches* (pp.1–20). Washington, DC: Taylor & Francis.

Gist, R., & Stolz, S. B. (1982). Mental health promotion and the media: Community response to the Kansas City Hotel disasters. *American Psychologist, 37,* 1136–1139.

Gladwin, H., & Peacock, W. G. (1997). Warning and evacuation: A night for hard houses. In W. G. Peacock, B. H. Morrow, & H. Gladwin (Eds.), *Hurricane Andrew: Ethnicity, gender and the sociology of disasters* (pp. 52–74). New York: Routledge.

Hartsough, D. M., & Myers, D. G. (1985). *Disaster work and mental health: Prevention and control of stress among workers* (DHHS Publication No. ADM 85–1422). Washington, DC: U.S. Government Printing Office.

Hobfoll, S. E., Briggs, S., & Wells, J. (1995). Community stress and resources: Actions and reactions. In S. E. Hobfoll & M. W. de Vries (Eds.), *Extreme stress and communities: Impact and intervention.* Boston: Kluwer Academic Publishers.

Joseph, S., Williams, R., & Yule, W. (1993). Changes in outlook following disaster: The preliminary development of a measure to assess positive and negative responses. *Journal of Traumatic Stress, 6,* 271–279.

Kalayjian, A. (1999). Coping through meaning: The community response to the earthquake in Armenia. In E. S. Zinner & M. B. Williams (Eds.), *When a community weeps: Case studies in group survivorship* (pp. 87–102). Levittown, PA: Brunner/Mazel.

Kaniasty, K., & Norris, F. (1999). The experience of disaster: Individuals and communities sharing trauma. In R. Gist & B. Lubin (Eds.), *Response to disaster:*

*Psychosocial, ecological, and community approaches* (pp. 25–61). Washington, DC: Taylor & Francis.

Klapp, O. (1991). *Inflation of symbols.* New Brunswick, NJ: Transaction.

La Greca, A. M., Silverman, W. K., Vernberg, E. M., & Roberts, M. C. (Eds.). (2002). *Helping children cope with disasters and terrorism.* Washington, DC: American Psychological Association.

Lindy, J. D., & Grace, M. (1985). The recovery environment: Continuing stressor versus a healing psychosocial space. In B. J. Sowder (Ed.), *Disasters and mental health: Selected contemporary perspectives* (pp. 137–149) (DHHS Publication No. ADM 85–1421). Washington, DC: U.S. Government Printing Office.

Lystad, M. (1985). Mental health programs in disasters: 1974–84. In M. Lystad (Ed.), *Innovations in mental health services to disaster victims* (pp. 1–7) (DHHS Publication No. ADM 85-1390). Washington, DC: U.S. Government Printing Office.

McCullough, D. (1968). *The Johnstown Flood.* New York: Simon & Schuster.

Mileti, D. S. (1999). *Disasters by design: A reassessment of natural hazards in the United States.* Washington, DC: Joseph Henry Press.

Mileti, D. S., & O'Brien, P. W. (1992). Warnings during disaster: Normalizing communicated risk. *Social Problems, 39,* 40–57.

Miller, L. (1998). *Shocks to the system: Psychotherapy of traumatic disability syndromes.* New York: W. W. Norton.

Morrow, B. H. (1997). Stretching the bonds: The families of Andrew. In W. G. Peacock, B. H. Morrow, & H. Gladwin (Eds.), *Hurricane Andrew: Ethnicity, gender and the sociology of disasters* (pp. 141–170). New York: Routledge.

Morrow, B. H., & Peacock, B. H. (1997). Disasters and social change: Hurricane Andrew and the reshaping of Miami? In W. G. Peacock, B. H. Morrow, & H. Gladwin (Eds.), *Hurricane Andrew: Ethnicity, gender and the sociology of disasters* (pp. 226–242). New York: Routledge.

Myers, D. (1994). *Disaster response and recovery: A handbook for mental health professionals.* Washington, DC: U.S. Department of Health and Human Services.

Palinkas, L. A., Downs, M. A., Petterson, J. S., & Russell, J. (1993). Social, cultural, and psychological impacts of the Exxon Valdez oil spill. *Human Organization, 51,* 1–13.

Pargament, K. I., & Hahn, J. (1986). God and the just world: Causal and coping attributions to God in health situations. *Journal for the Scientific Study of Religion, 25,* 193–207.

Raphael, B. (1986). *When disaster strikes.* New York: Basic Books.

Salzer, M. S., & Bickman, L. (1999). The short- and long-term psychological impact of disasters: Implications for mental health interventions and policy. In R. Gist & B. Lubin (Eds.), *Response to disaster: Psychosocial, ecological, and community approaches.* Washington, DC: Taylor & Francis.

Satel, S. L. (1999, April 23). An overabundance of counseling? *New York Times,* p. 25.

Sattler, D. N., Sattler, J. M., Kaiser, C., Hamby, B. A., Adams, M. G., Love, L., Winkler, J., Abu-Ukkaz, C., Watt, B., & Beatty, A. (1995). Hurricane Andrew: Psychological distress among shelter victims. *International Journal of Stress Management, 2,* 133–143.

Smith, M. H. (1978). American religious organizations in disaster: A study of congregational response to disaster. *Mass Emergencies, 3,* 133–142.

Thompson, S. C. (1985). Finding positive meaning in a stressful event and coping. *Basic and Applied Social Psychology, 6,* 279–295.

Thorson, J. A. (1993). Did you ever see a hearse go by? Some thoughts on gallows humor. *Journal of American Culture, 16*(2), 17–24.

Tierney, K. J. (1989). The social and community contexts of disaster. In R. Gist & B. Lubin (Eds.), *Psychosocial aspects of disaster.* New York: John Wiley & Sons.

Tobin, G. A., & Ollenburger, J. C. (1996). Predicting levels of postdisaster stress in adults following the 1993 floods in the Upper Midwest. *Environment and Behavior, 28,* 340–357.

Wainrib, B. R., & Bloch, E. L. (1998). *Crisis intervention and trauma response: Theory and practice.* New York: Springer.

Weaver, J. D. (1995). *Disasters: Mental health interventions.* Sarasota, FL: Professional Resource Press.

Zarle, T., Hartsough, D., & Ottinger, D. (1974). Tornado recovery: The development of a professional-paraprofessional response to a disaster. *Journal of Community Psychology, 4,* 311–321.

Zinner, E. S., & Williams, M. B. (1999). *When a community weeps: Case studies in group survivorship.* Levittown, PA: Brunner/Mazel.

# INDEX